After the Crime
Victim Decision Making

Perspectives in

Law & Psychology

Sponsored by the American Psychology–Law Society/Division 41 of the American Psychological Association

Series Editor: **THOMAS GRISSO,** *University of Massachusetts Medical School, Worcester, Massachusetts*

Volume 1   **THE CRIMINAL JUSTICE SYSTEM**
Edited by Bruce Dennis Sales

Volume 2   **THE TRIAL PROCESS**
Edited by Bruce Dennis Sales

Volume 3   **JUVENILES' WAIVER OF RIGHTS**
Legal and Psychological Competence
Thomas Grisso

Volume 4   **MENTAL HEALTH LAW**
Major Issues
David B. Wexler

Volume 5   **HANDBOOK OF SCALES FOR RESEARCH**
IN CRIME AND DELINQUENCY
Stanley L. Brodsky and H. O'Neal Smitherman

Volume 6   **MENTALLY DISORDERED OFFENDERS**
Perspectives from Law and Social Science
Edited by John Monahan and Henry J. Steadman

Volume 7   **EVALUATING COMPETENCIES**
Forensic Assessments and Instruments
Thomas Grisso

Volume 8   **INSANITY ON TRIAL**
Norman J. Finkel

Volume 9   **AFTER THE CRIME**
Victim Decision Making
Martin S. Greenberg and R. Barry Ruback

After the Crime
Victim Decision Making

Martin S. Greenberg

University of Pittsburgh
Pittsburgh, Pennsylvania

and

R. Barry Ruback

Georgia State University
Atlanta, Georgia

Plenum Press • New York and London

Library of Congress Cataloging-in-Publication Data

Greenberg. Martin S.
     After the crime : victim decision making / Martin S. Greenberg and
R. Barry Ruback.
        p.   cm. -- (Perspectives in law & psychology ; v. 9)
     Includes bibliographical references and index.
     ISBN 0-306-44160-8
     1. Victims of crime--Psychology.   I. Ruback, R. Barry, 1950-
II. Title. III. Series.
     [DNLM: 1. Crime. 2. Decision Making.   W1 PE871AS v.9 / HV
6250.25 G798a]
HV6250.25G74 1992
362.88'01'9--dc20
DNLM/DLC
for Library of Congress   92-16942
                                                              CIP

ISBN 0-306-44160-8

© 1992 Plenum Press, New York
A Division of Plenum Publishing Corporation
233 Spring Street, New York, N.Y. 10013

Printed in the United States of America

To my wife, Janelle
—MSG

To my brothers, Stephen and Albert
—RBR

Preface

Much has been written in recent years about the aftermath of criminal victimization. This book describes the findings from 20 studies designed to explore decision making by crime victims in the immediate aftermath of the victimization, as well as the role played by emotions and social influences in this process.

Immediately following the crime, victims experience a wide array of feelings, such as shock, anger, fear, and sadness. Amidst such feelings, victims are confronted with the dilemma of deciding whether to notify the police. How this decisional dilemma is resolved has important implications for the criminal justice system, since research has shown that victims are the primary activators of the criminal justice process. Without victims' notification, most crimes would not come to the attention of the police. Given the emotional arousal that accompanies the victimization, victims tend to be receptive to information and advice from others. A major aim of the research, therefore, was to examine the dynamics of social influence and the role that it plays in victim decision making in the moments immediately following the crime.

The research described in this volume is distinctive in that multiple methods were employed to study decision making by multiple types of victims. The research involved experiments in a field laboratory, use of archival data, and collection of self-reports via interviews and questionnaires. The victim population included victims of rape, robbery, burglary, and theft. Moreover, individuals of diverse ethnic backgrounds were represented, including participants in the United States, India, Thailand, and Nigeria.

These studies of reactions to criminal victimization should be of interest to researchers, service providers, informal-aid givers, those concerned with issues of public policy, and criminal justice personnel.

The work represents a true collaboration between the two authors. The research could not have been completed without the assistance of many others, however. In particular, we are deeply indebted to Chauncey Wilson, David Westcott, and Deborah Ivie. Chauncey played a vital role in the planning and the actual conduct of the experimental studies. David made valuable contributions to many phases of the research: he helped conduct the experimental research, interviewed crime victims, analyzed data, and contributed to the development of the model of victim decision making. Deborah provided invaluable assistance by interviewing sexual assault victims and by coding, checking, and analyzing data.

We were able to overcome innumerable problems in conducting the field experiments described in Chapters 2 and 3 because of an extremely competent and dedicated staff. Special thanks go to Mary Wartella, Amy Robins, Elizabeth Mahoney, Wayne Albitz, Michael Mills, Ann DeMay, Sheree Thomas, and Charles Muchow. We wish to express our appreciation to the following "thieves" and "bystanders" for their fine acting: Donald Case, Lynn Eckert, Blaine Givner, William Heller, Denise Herbol, Jim Kutzer, Tim Newell, Jim Silver, Edward Turner, and Lawrence Williams. In developing the experimental paradigm, we profited greatly from advice given by our two consultants, Dr. Arthur Van Cara and Detective Stephen Tercsak. Both were there when we needed them.

We owe a debt of gratitude to numerous individuals who helped us collect data on normative expectations for notifying the police (Chapter 6). We are particularly indebted to Rachel Kelly and Ladi Anjorin for assisting in the data collection in Nigeria and for their insightful comments on the data. In collecting the normative data, we were fortunate to have the able assistance of Biodun Anjorin, Bisi Anjorin, Mary Iketuonie, Theeraporn Uwanno, Rajesh Patnaik, Deepak Gupta, and Neena Kohli.

The archival studies reported in Chapter 7 involved time-consuming efforts by Amy Robins, David Westcott, and Sandra Stone. We are grateful for their efforts in this regard. We also wish to thank Dick Holland, who assisted in the statistical analysis of the archival data.

Numerous individuals assisted in the interviews with crime victims reported in Chapter 8: George Boguslawski, Felicia Chmelovsky, Aaron Geller, Gary Geller, Susan Knechtel, Mercedes Mahsoob, Olga Salvatori, Fred Stevens, William Vrbin, Danyel Wendroff, and Scott Westcott. We are indebted to Scott Beach, Michael Cross, and Matthew Torres for their able assistance in the analysis of the data. We express our warm thanks to the individuals who facilitated our access to crime victims. They include chiefs of police Ronald Lees (Swissvale, Pennsylvania), James Lundie (McKeesport, Pennsylvania), George Napper (Atlanta), and David Varrelman (Mt. Lebanon, Pennsylvania). For their help in studying the reactions of rape victims, we are also grateful to Patty Hayes, Molly Knox, the late Ann Pride of Pittsburgh Action Against Rape, and Peg Ziegler and Sherry Emery of the Rape Crisis Center at Grady Memorial Hospital in Atlanta.

We express our warm thanks to Jasmin Riad for her assistance in compiling the references and to Marla Beller for her help with data entry.

We express our appreciation to the grant agencies that funded the research reported in this book: the National Institute of Mental Health (Violence and Traumatic Stress Research Branch), formerly known as the Center for Studies of Crime and Delinquency (Grant No. MH275260), the National Institute of Justice (Grant No. 85-IJ-CS-0064), the Council for International Exchange of Scholars (Fulbright Scholar Program), and the Indo-American Fellowship Program of the Indo–U.S. Subcommission on Education and Culture.

Finally, we are deeply indebted to Tom Grisso for his careful reading of the manuscript and his many thoughtful and constructive comments. The manuscript profited greatly from his skillful editorial hand.

Contents

CHAPTER 1. INTRODUCTION 1

Victimization as a Social Problem 2
   Extent of Criminal Victimization 2
   Impact of Crime 2
   The Victims' Movement 3
   Research on Victims of Crime 5
Decision Making by Victims 7
   Victims' Decision to Notify the Police 7
   Social Psychology and Victim Decision Making 8
A Program of Research on Victims' Decisions 11
Purposes of the Research Project 11
   Strategy of the Research 12
Goals and Outline of the Book 13

CHAPTER 2. AN EXPERIMENTAL APPROACH TO VICTIM DECISION MAKING 17

The Experimental Paradigm 18
   Crime Scene and Victims 18
   The Crime 19
   Participants' Response 20

Study 1: Theft Magnitude and Thief's Race and Proximity as
    Determinants of Crime Reporting 21
    Method 22
    Results 29
Summary and Conclusions 35

CHAPTER 3. EXPERIMENTAL STUDIES ON THE ROLE OF SOCIAL INFLUENCE IN
    VICTIM DECISION MAKING 37

Study 2: Social and Emotional Factors in Victim Decision Making ... 38
    Method 38
    Results 42
    Discussion and Conclusions 44
Study 3: Type of Bystander Advice and Supporting Arguments 45
    Method 46
    Results and Discussion 48
Study 4: Parameters of Bystander Influence: Proximity, Support,
    and Knowledge of the Theft 50
    Method 50
    Results and Discussion 51
Study 5: Parameters of Bystander Influence: Sex Similarity, Type of
    Supporting Argument, and Level of Surveillance 53
    Method 54
    Results and Discussion 55
Study 6: The Effect of Fate Similarity on Theft-Victim
    Decision Making 57
    Method 58
    Results and Discussion 60
Summary and Conclusions 63

CHAPTER 4. EYEWITNESS IDENTIFICATION BY THEFT VICTIMS 65

Study 7: Effect of a Prior Lineup Identification on a Subsequent
    Lineup Identification 66
    Method 67
    Results 67
    Discussion 68
Study 8: Effect of Type of Identification Task on Subsequent
    Lineup Identifications 69
    Method 69
    Results 70
    Discussion 73

Study 9: Same Race and Cross-Race Identifications 74
    Method 74
    Results 75
    Discussion 76
Results Using Data from All Participants 76
General Discussion 77

CHAPTER 5. ANALYSES ACROSS EXPERIMENTAL STUDIES 81

Validity of the Experimental Studies 82
    Internal Validity 82
    External Validity 84
Variables Related to Reporting 86
    Effect of Individual Characteristics on Reporting 86
    Relative Effects of Advice and Individual Characteristics
        on Reporting 88
Variables Related to Delay in Reporting 89
Relationship of Reporting Decision to Participants' Perceptions 90
Variables Related to Participants' Recall of the Theft 92
    Reasons for Participants' Reporting Decision 94
    Reasons for Not Reporting 95
    Reasons for Reporting 97
Summary and Conclusions 99

CHAPTER 6. NORMATIVE EXPECTATIONS FOR CALLING THE POLICE 101

Study of Normative Influence 101
Crime Seriousness 103
Study 10: Crime Seriousness and Norms for Reporting in
        Four Countries 104
    Method 105
    Results 108
    Discussion 115
Study 11: Appropriateness of Reporting: Effects of Type of
        Offender and Sex of Victim 116
    Method 117
    Results 118
    Discussion 119
Study 12: Norms for Reporting among Different Ethnic Groups in
        the United States 121
    Method 121

Results and Discussion 121
General Discussion 126

CHAPTER 7. ARCHIVAL ANALYSES 129

Study 13: Calls to the Atlanta Council on Battered Women 130
Study 14: Police Records on Reported Thefts and Burglaries 131
    Method 131
    Results 132
Study 15: Rape Crisis Center Archives 134
    Method 135
    Results 136
General Discussion of the Archival Research 148

CHAPTER 8. SELF-REPORTS: SURVEYING CRIME VICTIMS 151

Study 16: Self-Reports of Rape Victims 152
    Method 153
    Results 153
    Discussion 154
Study 17: Interviews with Victims of Burglary, Theft,
    and Robbery 155
    Method 155
    Results 156
    Discussion 158
Study 18: Survey of Reporter and Nonreporter Victims of Burglary
    and Theft 159
    Method 159
    Results and Discussion 160
Study 19: Telephone Interviews with Victims of Burglary
    and Theft 163
    Method 164
    Results 165
    Discussion 169
Study 20: A Longitudinal Study of Rape Victims 171
    Method 171
    Results 173
    Discussion 176
Summary and Conclusions 177

CHAPTER 9. A MODEL OF CRIME-VICTIM DECISION MAKING 181

Stage 1: Labeling the Event a Crime 185
Stage 2: Determining the Seriousness of the Crime 187
  Stress Resulting from Perception of Being Wronged 188
  Stress Resulting from Perceived Vulnerability 190
Stage 3: Deciding What to Do 194
  Victims' Options 196
Social Influence and Victim Decision Making 204
  Providing Information 205
  Receptivity to Information from Others 205
  Applying Normative Pressure 209
  Providing Socioemotional Support or Nonsupport 211
Summary 212

CHAPTER 10. SUMMARY AND IMPLICATIONS OF THE RESEARCH 215

Summary of the Research 215
  The Reporting Decision 216
  Recall and Recognition 221
Implications of the Research 222
  Multimethod Research 222
  Theory-Related Research 224
  Policy Implications 236
Summary 243

APPENDIX: A LAWSUIT AGAINST THE RESEARCHERS 245

Description of the Incident 246
The Lawsuit 248
  Causes of Action 248
  Damages 251
The Immediate Aftermath of the Filing 251
Pretrial Discovery 254
The Trial 255
  The Plaintiff's Case 256
  Motion for a Directed Verdict 257
  The Verdict 258
  Posttrial Activities 259
The Defendants' Case 259
  Reasonableness of the Procedures 260
  Sensitivity of the Participant 261

Consequences of the Lawsuit 261
Lessons to Be Learned 262
    Should the Study Have Been Conducted? 263
    Could This Research Be Conducted Today? 264

REFERENCES 265

TABLE OF CASES 283

INDEX 285

1

Introduction

This book is about victims of crime. It examines how they feel, think, and act in the moments immediately following the victimization. Although the intensity of victims' immediate reactions may vary, they commonly report experiencing anger, fear, shock, confusion, and depression. And in some instances, they blame themselves for the incident. A world that they once perceived as safe and predictable suddenly may appear dangerous and unpredictable. Trying to make sense out of the victimization, victims often ask themselves, "Why me?" Amid these emotional and cognitive reactions, victims grapple with the question of deciding what to do. Should the police be notified? Should the matter be dealt with in some other way? Faced with this confusing array of feelings and thoughts, victims often turn to others for assistance. This book describes the results of a series of studies designed to explore the decision process of crime victims in the immediate aftermath of the crime, the effect of emotional factors, and the role played by others in this process.

This chapter consists of three sections. In the first, we focus on criminal victimization as a social problem. In the second section, we examine victims' reactions and relevant research by social psychologists. In the final section, we outline the purposes and strategy for a program of research that we conducted in order to investigate victim decision making.

VICTIMIZATION AS A SOCIAL PROBLEM

EXTENT OF CRIMINAL VICTIMIZATION

National surveys conducted by the Bureau of Justice Statistics (1992) show that in 1990 there were almost 35 million criminal victimizations in the United States. This included 130,000 rapes, over one million robberies, 4.7 million assaults, and more than 5.1 million burglaries. Indeed, so extensive is crime in American life that one in four households was touched by a crime of violence or theft in 1989 (Bureau of Justice Statistics, 1990a). Few can escape the impact of crime.

People's stereotypical conception is that crime is perpetrated by strangers on residents of inner cities. Although this conception is generally correct, recent surveys show that crimes also occur in suburban settings (Bureau of Justice Statistics, 1990b; Rengert & Wasilchick, 1985) and are frequently committed by perpetrators known to the victim. Almost 40% of the violent crimes (i.e., rape, robbery, and assault) measured by the National Crime Survey in 1990, were committed by nonstrangers (Bureau of Justice Statistics, 1992).

But annual victimization rates alone do not adequately convey the risk of criminal victimization. National estimates suggest that during their lifetime five out of six people will be victims of attempted or completed violent crimes such as rape, robbery, or assault (Bureau of Justice Statistics, 1987a). Moreover, three out of four households will suffer a burglary sometime during a 20-year period, and one in four will experience two burglaries during that same period.

IMPACT OF CRIME

Crime exacts an enormous toll on its victims in terms of material and financial losses, as well as physical pain. In 1985 alone, losses from personal robbery, theft and burglary were estimated at over $13 billion (Zawitz, 1988). Victims also suffer several hidden costs, the extent of which is incalculable. As Forst and Hernon (1985) noted, "Victim harm is not just broken arms, black eyes, lost wallets, or medical bills; it is also fear and shame, frustration and anger, depression and despair" (p. 2). Criminal victimization shatters cherished assumptions about the world, especially one's invulnerability to harm, one's self-worth, and the perception of the world as meaningful (Janoff-Bulman, 1989; Janoff-Bulman & Frieze, 1983).

Particularly troublesome are violent crimes. As the President's Commission on Law Enforcement and the Administration of Justice (1967) stated, "Suddenly becoming the object of a stranger's violent hostility is as frightening as any class of experience" (p. 3). Unlike victims of accidents and disease, victims of crime, whether violent or not, are often faced with the realization that their suffering is the product of another person's intentionally singling them out for harm (Janoff-Bulman, 1985). As a result of this disquieting realization, victims come to distrust others and to view their world as more hostile and less safe. Recent data indicate that for a substantial number of victims, particularly victims of sexual assault, the recovery process is slow (Burgess & Holmstrom, 1975; Ellis, Atkeson, & Calhoun, 1981; Resick, 1990) and uneven (Sales, Baum, & Shore, 1984). Similarly, for a sizable minority of burglary victims, the psychological scars of the victimization are slow to heal (Maguire & Corbett, 1987).

Crime affects not only its victims, but also relatives, neighbors, friends, and society in general (Friedman, Bischoff, Davis, & Person, 1982; Riggs & Kilpatrick, 1990). Aside from financial and other costs that these groups shoulder in order to help victims, numerous surveys show that a major by-product of criminal victimization is fear, an emotion that exacts an enormous toll on the quality of life of victims and nonvictims alike (Moore & Trojanowicz, 1988). The fear of criminal victimization motivates people to change their routines, to avoid being out after dark, and to invest time and money in protecting their homes. Efforts to reduce fear include the purchase of expensive alarm systems, extra locks, weapons, and watchdogs, and the hiring of private guards. Spending for private security in the United States is estimated at over $20 billion (Moore & Trojanowicz, 1988).

The fear of crime affects the fabric of society in many other subtle, untold ways. When people remain at home behind locked doors, they underutilize facilities such as parks, theaters, and libraries that can enhance the quality of their lives. Moreover, by remaining at home, people may increase the vulnerability of others to street crimes. Potential criminals want to avoid detection, and the mere presence of others is often a sufficient deterrent to crime. By remaining at home, people make crime less risky for the criminals and more likely to occur, further reinforcing the public's fear of crime (Shotland & Goodstein, 1984).

THE VICTIMS' MOVEMENT

Public and professional concern for crime victims appeared to accelerate in the late 1960s and early 1970s in what some have called the *victims' movement* (Pointing & Maguire, 1988). Today, the interest in victims is international and involves a wide variety of participants: psychologists, mental health professionals, criminologists, psychiatrists, and feminists, as well as victims and their families (Block, 1984; Sessar & Kerner, 1991; Wikstrom, 1991). Pinpointing the precise origins of the movement in the United States is difficult. Among the factors that probably contributed to its development were (1) a zeitgeist in the 1960s and 1970s that focused concern on victims of injustice and inequality (e.g., racial minorities, the poor, and women); (2) a rising crime rate (which leveled off in the mid-1970s); and (3) a number of U.S. Supreme Court decisions that were perceived as benefiting the accused at the expense of the victim (e.g., *Miranda v. Arizona*, 1966).

Two converging lines of thought emerged from this period: (1) that victims of crime were not receiving the assistance they needed, both materially and psychologically, and (2) that the criminal justice system by itself could not win the "war on crime" without citizen support (President's Commission, 1967). In essence, there was a growing realization that society was more concerned with rehabilitating the offender than with rehabilitating the victim (Van Dijk, 1988). Many felt that the failure to meet the needs of victims was deterring victims from cooperating with a justice system that needed their support. The system's dependence on victims was demonstrated by newly emerging evidence from victimization surveys, which showed that citizen notification accounted for the vast majority of crimes investigated by the police and that victims chose to report less than half of these victimizations (Ennis, 1967).

The callous treatment of victims by the system was viewed as being counterproductive for both victims and the justice system. The feminist movement, in particular, called attention to the system's insensitivity and indifference to the victims of rape and domestic violence. A loose alliance was formed between those primarily concerned about increasing victims' willingness to cooperate with the criminal justice system and those concerned about improving the treatment of victims. This led to the creation of a plethora of victim assistance programs and, more recently, to a variety of legislative reforms.

Many programs were developed to encourage victim cooperation with the criminal justice process. They included, among others, the institution of a "911" number to notify the police of emergencies, improved community relations programs, neighborhood block watch programs, the offer of financial rewards for notifying the police, and a federal witness-protection program. The first government-financed compensation scheme for victims of violent crime was established in New Zealand in 1963, followed by one in England in 1964. In the United States, California was the first state to adopt such a program, in 1965. At present, 43 states and the District of Columbia offer compensation to victims and their survivors. Similar programs were created in European countries in the 1970s: Sweden (1971), Austria (1972), the Netherlands (1975), Denmark (1976), Norway (1976), West Germany (1976), and France (1977).

The number of organizations serving the needs of victims increased dramatically in the 1970s and 1980s. They included Mothers against Drunk Driving, Parents of Murdered Children, and Society's League against Molestation. In 1979 the National Organization for Victim Assistance (NOVA) was established in the United States. In that same year in England, the National Association of Victim Support Schemes was formed. France established a similar organization in 1986, the National Organization for Assistance to

Victims and for Mediation. During this period much attention was focused on the provision of services to victims of rape and sexual abuse. Rape crisis centers first appeared in the United States in 1973, and in England in 1976. Therefore, by the late 1980s, the United States and Europe had a vast array of victim service organizations; they numbered over 5,000 in the United States (Davis & Henley, 1990), 300 in England, 120 in France, and 50 in the Netherlands (Pointing & Maguire, 1988).

The President's Task Force on Victims of Crime (1982) provided a major impetus for the victims' movement in the United States. After traveling to six cities and hearing testimony from over 1,000 people, the task force presented its report, with 68 recommendations for improving the treatment of crime victims. Implementation of the recommendations was fostered by the passage of the Comprehensive Crime Control Act in 1984. One of its provisions, the Victims of Crime Act, made federal funds available to the states for their compensation programs. The act also authorized the disbursement of funds through the Office of Victim Assistance, an agency within the Department of Justice, to aid victim service agencies, which had previously relied heavily on volunteers (Office of Justice Programs, 1986). In 1989, the federal government provided $43 million to the states for victim services, an increase of $8 million over the 1988 figure (NOVA, 1990).

In response to these federal initiatives, many states passed legislation to improve the treatment of victims by the criminal justice system. These mandates took many forms: providing separate and secure waiting rooms in courthouses for victims and witnesses, requiring a victim impact statement at sentencing, ensuring prompt return of property, keeping victim counseling records confidential, requiring that victims be notified of crucial developments in their case, and providing restitution to victims as part of the sentence (Elias, 1990; Kelly, 1990; National Organization for Victim Assistance, 1990). According to a National Organization for Victim Assistance report (National Organization for Victim Assistance, 1985), since 1980 the individual states have adopted more than 1,000 pieces of legislation to protect the interests of victims. Unquestionably, much has been done in recent years to ease victims' pain and facilitate their recovery.

RESEARCH ON VICTIMS OF CRIME

The surge of interest in victims of crime is further reflected in research on the topic. Research on criminal victimization has accelerated in recent years as evidenced by the appearance of professional journals devoted to research on crime victims (e.g., *Victimology: An International Journal; Child Abuse and Neglect; Journal of Interpersonal Violence;* and *Violence and Victims*). International conferences and symposia occur regularly, and special task forces on victims of crime were commissioned in the 1980s by the American Psychological Association and the American Psychiatric Association. The increase of research on criminal victimization can be attributed in part to the availability of federal funding. Federal agencies active in funding such research have included the National Institute of Mental Health's Violence and Traumatic Stress Research Branch (formerly known as the Antisocial and Violent Behavior Branch), the National Science Foundation's Law and Social Sciences Program, and the National Institute of Justice.

Research on criminal victimization has dealt with a diverse set of issues and questions. Whereas early efforts to study criminal victimization focused on criminals (e.g., their physiology, social background, and motivation), beginning in the 1960s there was a distinct shift in focus from the perpetrator to the victim. Pioneers such as Benjamin Mendelsohn (1963), who coined the term *victimology*, viewed the study of victims as separate and distinct from criminology. The shift in emphasis pertained both to the causal role played by victims in their victimization and to the impact of the experience on their emotions, beliefs, and behavior. Victimization research has addressed a wide range of questions: Are certain people more vulnerable to victimization, and if so, to what extent do they contribute to their own victimization? What is the psychological impact of crime on its victims and on society? What are the causes and consequences of the fear of crime? How do victims attempt to cope with the effects of criminal victimization? What role does social support play in the recovery process? What are the determinants of victims' willingness to notify the police?

Research on criminal victimization was encouraged by advances in method and theory. One of the most noteworthy methodological developments was the victimization survey. Developed in the late 1960s (e.g., Ennis, 1967), it led eventually to the creation in 1972 of a continuing survey of criminal victimization, the National Crime Survey. By surveying the general population about their experiences as victims of crime rather than relying on police reports, researchers gained information from a previously inaccessible population of nonreporting crime victims.

Coinciding with methodological advances was the development of theoretical frameworks and concepts for interpreting the new data, including crisis theory (Rapoport, 1965), the diagnostic category of posttraumatic stress disorder (American Psychiatric Association, 1980), equity theory (Adams, 1963; Walster, Berscheid, & Walster, 1973), attribution theory (Kelley, 1967), the concept of learned helplessness (Seligman, 1975), and the just-world model (Lerner, Miller, & Holmes, 1976). Research on criminal victimization was further inspired by general theoretical concerns about reactions to traumatic events (Figley, 1985), such as accidents (e.g., Weinstein, 1989), natural disasters (e.g., Kunreuther, 1978), and disease (Wortman & Dunkel-Schetter, 1979).

The study of criminal victimization is a multidisciplinary endeavor involving contributions from criminology and sociology, psychology, social work, nursing, and psychiatry. Each discipline has its own preferred methodology and research agenda. For example, criminologists and sociologists have tended to rely most often on large-scale surveys administered to victims of a wide variety of crimes. In contrast, research by psychiatrists has typically involved interviews with a smaller sample of victims of violent crimes who have sought therapeutic intervention. Psychological research has been conducted primarily by clinical psychologists interested in the mental health sequelae of victimization. This research has typically involved the administration of a battery of standardized tests to victims of violent crimes (mostly female) who have sought assistance from a victim service agency.

Much has been learned about the short- and long-term psychological effects of criminal victimization, but much remains to be known about the decision-making process of victims in the immediate aftermath of the crime.

DECISION MAKING BY VICTIMS

VICTIMS' DECISION TO NOTIFY THE POLICE

One of the most important decisions for the victim is the decision to notify the police. Reporting the crime to the police may have important immediate and long-term mental health consequences for victims (Frieze, Hymer, & Greenberg, 1987). If the suspect is apprehended by the police, victims may be comforted by the knowledge that the suspect may be punished, that their property may be returned, and that the suspect and others may be deterred from committing similar acts in the future. On the other hand, involvement with the police may only exacerbate the situation, producing what Symonds (1980) called "the second injury." Confronted by unsympathetic justice officials and cross-examined by a hostile defense attorney, victims may experience added stress and discomfort as a result of reporting the crime.

The decision to report the crime has important consequences for the criminal justice system as well. Data collected by the Bureau of Justice Statistics show that without the cooperation of citizens, particularly victims, the system would rarely learn about crimes. According to these findings, 97% of crime investigations by the police result from citizen notification, most often (60%) by victims (Bureau of Justice Statistics, 1985). Clearly, then, victims are the gatekeepers of the criminal justice system (Hindelang & Gottfredson, 1976).

The extent to which victims exercise discretion in reporting can be seen in results of the National Crime Survey showing that between 1973 and 1990 the percentage of crimes reported to the police ranged from 32% to 38% (Bureau of Justice Statistics, 1992). As expected, the rate of reporting was found to vary with the type of crime. Thus, in 1990, the crime most likely to be reported was motor vehicle theft (75%), and the one least likely to be reported was personal larceny or theft (29%) (Bureau of Justice Statistics, 1992). The reporting rates for the remaining crimes covered by the National Crime Survey are close to 50%: robbery (50%), rape (54%), burglary (51%), and assault (47%). In other words, less serious crimes are least often reported. They are also the most common, however, so that more alleged perpetrators "escape" the criminal justice system *before* entering the system than after entry, such as when the case is dismissed by the prosecutor or when the jury votes for acquittal. Victim decision making is important for law enforcement in another way; actions taken by the victim are the major source of delay in the arrival of the police on the scene (Spelman & Brown, 1981; Van Kirk, 1978). Before reporting the crime, victims engage in a variety of time-consuming information-gathering activities, such as searching the scene and talking with others.

Efforts to understand the decision-making process of victims in the immediate aftermath of the crime have yielded a confusing array of findings (e.g., Bureau of Justice Statistics, 1989a; Ennis, 1967; Hawkins, 1973; Hindelang & Gottfredson, 1976; Schneider, Burcart, & Wilson, 1976; Smith & Maness, 1976; Sparks, Genn, & Dodd, 1977). Relying primarily on information gathered via self-reports, these studies suggest that the decision to report the crime is a complex function of a wide assortment of variables relating to characteristics of the suspect and the crime, but *not* to characteristics of the victim, such as the victim's age, race, sex, or socioeconomic status. Whether a crime will be reported is best predicted by the nature of the crime; the greater the perceived seriousness of the crime, the more likely it is to be reported (e.g., Fishman, 1979; Schneider *et al.*, 1976; Sparks *et al.*, 1977). Although the consistent findings give us confidence in their accuracy, the relatively scant literature on victim decision making suffers from two defects: (1) most of the data have been gathered only from self-reports, and (2) there is a conspicuous absence of conceptual frameworks that can help reconcile conflicting findings and guide future research. We believe that social psychology can provide such an integrative framework.

SOCIAL PSYCHOLOGY AND VICTIM DECISION MAKING

Social psychology examines how an individual's thoughts, feelings, and behavior are influenced by others, and how this influence is mediated by the individual's motivational and cognitive processes. It examines, therefore, the effects on behavior of the complex interplay among social, affective, and cognitive variables. This approach makes social psychology's methods and theories particularly useful for studying reactions of crime victims.

Social psychological research on victimization has focused primarily on the reactions of victims of disease and accidents rather than on the reactions of crime victims. Much of this work details the sources of victims' distress, their immediate and long-term reactions, and their modes of coping. Victim-izations are distressing for victims because the event shatters very basic assumptions that they hold about themselves and their world, namely, that they are invulnerable, that the world is meaningful, and that they are wor-thy, decent people (Janoff-Bulman, 1985, 1989; Perloff, 1983). Others have emphasized the sense of injustice or inequity caused by the victimization (Walster et al., 1973).

Social psychologists have investigated various ways in which victims attempt to cope with the event, such as blaming their own behavior for the incident (Janoff-Bulman, 1979). By so doing, victims can convince them-selves that because they will not repeat the mistake, they are less vulnerable to subsequent victimization. Victims can also cope by comparing themselves with less fortunate others or by imagining worse outcomes that could have occurred (Taylor, Wood, & Lichtman, 1983; Wills, 1981, 1987, 1991). Such thoughts allow victims to minimize the seriousness of the harm. Social psychologists have also called attention to the role played by mental simu-lations in helping people cope with stressful life events. According to Taylor and Schneider (1989), the simulation of past, future, and hypothetical events helps victims make sense of the victimization, plan for the future, and regulate their emotions.

In addition, social psychologists have studied the role played by social support in the immediate and long-term recovery of victims (e.g., Cohen & Wills, 1985; Gottlieb, 1983; Sarason, Sarason, & Pierce, 1990; Shumaker & Brownell, 1984; Wortman & Dunkel-Schetter, 1987). This research suggests that social support plays an important role in ameliorating victims' distress and in improving their mental health in both the short and the long runs. Researchers have distinguished between support that is perceived to be available and support that is actually received (Dunkel-Schetter & Bennett, 1990), and they have studied the benefits of both. In addition, researchers have identified different types of social support, such as the provision of advice, information, emotional support, and material or tangible support. Moreover, it has been shown that the different types of support are not equally effective in reducing distress (Wills, 1991). Across a wide range of stressors, emotional support appears to have the strongest impact on psy-chological well being (e.g., Billings & Moos, 1985).

Social psychologists have called attention to the fact that victims do not always receive the support they need, and that they sometimes perceive as unhelpful the support they do receive (Lehman, Ellard, & Wortman, 1986; Silver & Wortman, 1980). People may fail to provide victims with needed support because associating with victims makes them feel uneasy, remind-ing them of their own vulnerability to similar misfortunes. As a result, others may tend to blame victims for their fate (Lerner et al., 1976). Silver, Wortman, and Crofton (1990) called attention to particular behavior of vic-tims, such as displays of anger or depression, that increases the discomfort of others and reduces further the likelihood that the victims will receive support. Clearly, the interactions that victims have with others have important implications for victims' subsequent adjustment. However, social psychologists have not yet examined the consequences of these interactions with others on victims' decisions to notify the police.

Research by social psychologists on the reporting of crimes has largely ignored the victim and has focused instead on the decision making of bystanders. The origin of this focus on bystanders is a single event that occurred in 1964: the murder of Kitty Genovese before 38 nonintervening witnesses. Efforts at the time to account for the seeming passivity of the bystanders failed to provide useful insights. Stock explanations, such as alienation and anomie, offered at the time by social scientists, proved unconvincing. There was no relevant body of empirical research on which to draw in order to provide more satisfying explanations.

Subsequent research by two social psychologists, Latané and Darley (1970), demonstrated that the social dynamics of bystander intervention are lawful and can be studied experimentally. Their research showed that social influence factors are powerful determinants of bystander decision making, particularly the decision to intervene in emergencies (Latané & Nida, 1981). In particular, they demonstrated that the presence of other bystanders tends to diffuse responsibility for aiding the victim. The greater the number of bystanders to an emergency, the greater the diffusion of responsibility and the less the likelihood that any one of them will intervene to aid the victim. These provocative findings stimulated others to investigate the dynamics of bystander intervention, primarily in terms of reactions to noncriminal emergencies (e.g., accidents) rather than criminal acts.

The few social psychological studies that examined reactions to criminal events focused on the reactions of bystanders rather than on the reactions of victims (Bickman, 1976; Bickman & Rosenbaum, 1977; Moriarty, 1975). This research demonstrated that bystanders are more likely to assist the victim when they have been encouraged to do so by others (Bickman & Rosenbaum, 1977) and when they have previously agreed to protect the victim's property (Moriarty, 1975). We believe that the emphasis of social psychological research on bystander decision making is misplaced, because it is the *victim* who is the principal mobilizer of the criminal justice system (Bureau of Justice Statistics, 1985).

The consistently strong findings concerning the impact of others on bystander decision making suggest that the study of victim decision making would not be complete without an understanding of the social context in which victim decision making occurs. Social factors may be particularly important in the decisions of victims because of the high amount of stress and confusion that they experience in the aftermath of the crime. The high level of arousal and distress may add to their confusion and cause them to rely on others. Indeed, social psychological research shows that individuals are likely to turn to others when confused and upset (Asch, 1952; Festinger, 1954; Schachter, 1959).

Other research indicates that victims in particular are likely to seek out others in the immediate aftermath of the crime. Van Kirk (1978) interviewed 949 crime victims and witnesses in Kansas City, Missouri, who had reported crimes to the police. Of these, Van Kirk found that 58% (70% of whom were victims) delayed reporting because they talked with another person. A similar study of 4,000 crime victim and bystander reporters in four cities (Jacksonville, Florida; Peoria, Illinois; Rochester, New York; and San Diego, California) found that 26% talked with one or more other people before calling the police (Spelman & Brown, 1981). The results of these two studies indicate that crime victims frequently consult with others before calling the police.

In the following section, we outline our program of research on the role of social influence in victim decision making.

A PROGRAM OF RESEARCH ON VICTIMS' DECISIONS

This book describes the findings from a 13-year program of research on the role of social influence in victim decision making. The project had several specific purposes that are described below.

PURPOSES OF THE RESEARCH PROJECT

Initial Reactions to the Crime

We attempted to learn about victims' initial thoughts, feelings, and actions on discovering their victimization, and about whether these reactions varied with the nature of the crime. Of particular interest was identifying the factors that best predict the victim's decision to notify the police and the delay in such notification. We addressed several questions about the reporting decision. For example, to what extent is this decision affected by the seriousness of the crime and victims' attitudes toward the criminal justice system? Which factors better predict the decision to report the crime: the characteristics of the victim or the characteristics of the situation?

Social Influence

Another specific purpose was to determine the frequency with which victims seek out others immediately after the crime, and to determine with whom they interact most often and for what purposes. In addition, we attempted to discover how often victims receive advice about what to do, what the nature of the advice is, and what effect it has on their decision making. We wished also to learn which arguments for calling or not calling the police were most persuasive for victims. We sought also to investigate the nature of social norms concerning the reporting of crimes to the police. We wished to determine whether such norms exist, how widely these norms are shared, and how much they tend to vary as a function of the circumstances of the crime.

Long-Term Reactions

Another purpose of the project was to study the longer term effects of criminal victimization, especially the long-term implications of victimization on victims' feelings and beliefs. A related purpose was to study the accuracy of victims' memories of the crime several months after the event: To what extent are victims able to correctly identify the suspect from a photo array administered several months following the incident? Do victims and eyewitnesses who have seen a lineup containing the suspect identify the suspect in a subsequent photo array more accurately than those who have not seen the lineup? Finally, we attempted to identify the factors that sustain victims' willingness to cooperate with the criminal justice system in the prosecution of the suspected offender.

Development of a Model of Victim Decision Making

The final purpose of the project was to develop a comprehensive model of crime-victim decision making that would provide an integrative framework for interpreting our findings and suggesting directions for future research.

STRATEGY OF THE RESEARCH

Three methodological concerns guided our research strategy: (1) the choice of method(s); (2) the method of generating the hypotheses; and (3) the sequence of the studies.

With regard to the choice of methods, we assumed that a *multiplist* strategy (Cook, 1985) would best serve our interest in theoretical and practical issues. This strategy involves, among other things, the use of multiple methods, multiple interconnected studies, and multivariate causal models. We reasoned that any one method is likely to have inherent flaws that may bias the research. Only by using multiple methods with differing sources of bias can one be confident that a finding is explained by a causal factor, rather than arising as an artifact of one particular method (Campbell & Stanley, 1966; Webb, Campbell, Schwartz, Sechrest, & Grove, 1981). While the use of this strategy is not without problems, as in the case of non-convergent findings (Shotland & Mark, 1987), it can yield many useful insights (Greenberg, Ruback, & Westcott, 1983).

Second, our strategy for hypothesis generation allowed the findings from a particular study to dictate the questions to be addressed in the next study. Both within and between methodologies, our strategy was to produce a programmatic series of studies linked by a set of interrelated questions and concerns.

Finally, concerning the sequence of the studies, we first identified key elements of victim decision making under controlled laboratory conditions, then tested the generalizability of these findings in more naturalistic settings. This strategy was predicated on the assumption that, when studying a phenomenon as complex as victim decision making, one should first examine the phenomenon under controlled conditions. Only after gaining some understanding of the dynamics of the phenomenon should one study it in its natural complexity (Banaji & Crowder, 1989). Once having gained such an understanding and demonstrated its generalizability, our strategy called for the development of a theoretical model that could integrate the findings.

GOALS AND OUTLINE OF THE BOOK

The primary goal of this book is to present data from a series of studies regarding victims' decision to notify the police and the role played by social influence and emotional factors in that decision. A second goal is to provide a unifying theoretical framework that (1) specifies the role played by affective, cognitive, and social factors in the decision process and (2) is sufficiently broad to encompass reactions of diverse groups of crime victims. A third goal is to examine other aspects of the victimization experience, such as the accuracy of victims' recall, their decision to cooperate with the system by pressing charges, and the long-term impact of the incident on their feelings, beliefs, and behavior. Our final goal is to explore the public policy implications of the research, especially policies that might improve victims' psychological well-being and their willingness to cooperate with the criminal justice system.

Chapter 2 describes the development of an experimental paradigm that we used to study theft-victim decision making under controlled laboratory conditions, as well as the results of the first experiment that employed this paradigm. In Chapter 3 we describe the results of five studies in which we used this paradigm to explore the effects of social influence on theft-victim decision making. Chapter 4 examines an important role that victims play vis-à-vis the criminal justice system: providing eyewitness accounts of the crime. This chapter presents our data pertaining to the accuracy of victims' memories of the crime for a period of up to 15 months following the victimization. The data were obtained in the six experiments reported in the two previous chapters.

In order to better understand factors that affected and were affected by the reporting decision, we combined the data from the six experimental studies reported earlier. Chapter 5 reports these results and consists of three parts: (1) an examination of the internal and external validity of the experimental findings; (2) an analysis of factors related to and predictive of reporting; and (3) an examination of the relations between the reporting decision and victims' recall of the event as well as their subsequent reactions.

Chapter 6 presents three simulation studies in which we explored normative expectations for reporting crimes to the police. The studies investigated features of the crime that predict the degree to which people approve of notifying the police. We studied diverse subject populations in order to discover cultural and subcultural variations in normative expectations. They included participants from Thailand, Nigeria, India, and the United States. Within the U.S. sample, subcultural differences among blacks, Koreans, Hispanics, and whites were examined.

Chapters 7 and 8 investigate the generalizability of our experimental findings to populations outside the laboratory and to victims of crimes other than theft. Chapter 7 presents the results of three archival analyses. The first involved an analysis of calls received by the Atlanta Council on Battered Women. The second involved a study of police records in a suburban community concerning the reporting of burglaries and thefts. In the third study, we examined the records maintained by the Rape Crisis Center of Grady Memorial Hospital in Atlanta, Georgia.

In order to investigate further the generalizability of our experimental findings, we obtained self-reports from victims of rape, burglary, theft, and robbery. Chapter 8 contains the findings from five studies in which we used this technique. The first study involved telephone interviews with victims of rape who had reported their victimization to a rape crisis center in Pittsburgh, Pennsylvania (Pittsburgh Action Against Rape). Participants in the second study were victims of burglary, robbery, and theft who had reported their victimization to the police in one of four communities. They were interviewed in their homes. Participants in the third and fourth studies were college students who had identified themselves as victims of burglary and theft. Those in the third study completed a questionnaire, and participants in the fourth study were interviewed on the telephone. The fifth study was longitudinal, involving rape victims who had visited the Rape Crisis Center at Grady Memorial Hospital in Atlanta. They were interviewed by telephone on two occasions, approximately 2 months after visiting the center and again 8–11 months later.

In Chapter 9 we present a model of crime-victim decision making that integrates our findings with those of other investigators in this field. The model construes the decision process as consisting of three stages: (1) labeling the event; (2) determining its seriousness; and (3) deciding what to do. The model further details various forms of social influence and the manner in which this influence occurs at each stage of the decision process. Chapter 10 contains a summary of the consistent findings across studies and a discussion of the theoretical and policy implications of the research findings. In our attempt to clarify the relationship between our research and theoretical issues in social psychology, we call attention to the bidirectional nature of the relationship. Research and theory inform, and are informed by, each other. In the chapter's conclusion, we identify issues related to the conduct of policy-relevant research, and we suggest directions that this research might take.

In an appendix, we discuss legal issues raised by field-laboratory research on crime victims. One of the hazards of such research is the potential for lawsuits against the investigator. Our research took many precautions to ensure the welfare of the participants in our field-laboratory experiments. Nevertheless, we were the objects of a lawsuit filed by a participant and her husband. The appendix presents a detailed account of the incident, the testimony in court, and the lessons that we learned from the experience.

2

An Experimental Approach to Victim Decision Making

The discussion in Chapter 1 noted that research on crime-victim decision making has relied almost exclusively on self-reports. Reliance on a single methodology, however, is unwise. The study of a phenomenon as complex as victim decision making requires multiple methods, each with different strengths and weaknesses. For our initial study, we decided to use an experimental approach that allowed us to isolate and control key variables involved in victim decision making. This choice reflects our training as experimental social psychologists and the fact that experimental research has provided many fruitful insights into the decisions of bystanders in emergencies (Latané & Darley, 1970; Latané & Nida, 1981).

The experimental approach is ideally suited to testing causal hypotheses because it permits the manipulation and control of variables, the random assignment of subjects to conditions, and the direct observation and quantification of subjects' responses. This approach thus seeks an understanding of victim decision making through the systematic manipulation of variables presumed to affect the decision-making process. In this way, we sought to examine the conditions under which social influence has a maximal impact on victim decision making. In addition, because this approach allowed us to manipulate the criminal incident and to monitor subjects' responses, we would be able to study factors that influence the accuracy of victims' recall.

This chapter first describes the general paradigm that we used throughout the six studies in this project to simulate the conditions of a theft that placed our research participants in the role of victim. The chapter then describes the first of six studies that used this paradigm.

THE EXPERIMENTAL PARADIGM

Studying the reactions of victims in an experimental context presents formidable problems. For example, how does one create an experimental condition in which the participants actually believe that they are the victims of a crime? How is this done without jeopardizing their emotional well-being? How does one protect the "criminal suspect" from retaliatory attack by an irate victim?

CRIME SCENE AND VICTIMS

We began by creating in November 1976 a fictitious research organization entitled Industrial Research Associates of Pittsburgh. It was housed in a suite of rented offices on the second floor of an office building located in a middle-class retail section of the city (see Figure 2-1). The location was chosen because of its proximity to public transportation and the availability

Figure 2-1. Street where bogus organization was located.

of nearby parking facilities. In order to enhance the appearance of legitimacy of the enterprise, the organization's name was listed on the directories
outside the building and in the entrance hall. The organization's apparent
legitimacy was also increased by the other occupants of the building, who
included a physician, an attorney, and a justice of the peace. The organization's offices were furnished with props that included desks, file cabinets,
and work cubicles. Human props included trained confederates who played
the roles of secretary, supervisor, and research participants.

In order to recruit a diverse group of adult participants, we placed
advertisements in the local newspapers, which read as follows:

VOLUNTEERS—PAID
Adults needed for research on
work efficiency. $10 for 1½
hours clerical work. Call . . .

Respondents to the advertisement were told that the organization conducted studies for local businesses on work efficiency and office manage-
ment. They were further informed that in addition to being paid $10, they
would have an opportunity to earn more money. All respondents were
screened on the telephone for health problems such as high blood pressure
and cardiac disease. Those who were willing to participate and who were
free of such problems were given an appointment time.

In the course of the research project (1976–1980), the paradigm was
used in six studies involving 1,209 participants. Some of these were participants in the pilot phase of each study ($n = 252$), and others were eliminated
for various reasons, such as procedural errors and failure to follow instructions ($n = 113$) or suspiciousness about the manipulations ($n = 76$). The
number of valid participants, therefore, was 768.

This group represented a broad spectrum of the Pittsburgh community. Their
ages ranged from 16 to 66 (mean = 31); 66% were female, 34% male. The racial
composition of the sample was 83% white and 17% black. In terms of the highest
educational level attained, 4% had graduated from junior high school, 55% had
a high school degree, 6% had a degree from a two-year college, 28% had a college
degree, and 7% had a graduate degree. With regard to family income, 42% listed
it as less than $6,000; 27% between $6,001 and $12,000; 17% between $12,001
and $18,000; and 14% above $18,000. A broad spectrum of occupations was
represented, including blue-collar workers (26%), white-collar workers (30%),
homemakers (20%), students (18%), artists (4%), and retirees (1.5%). At the
time of their participation, 69% classified themselves as unemployed.

THE CRIME

The paradigm that we developed created victims of petty theft or
larceny. We chose to study victims of theft for two reasons. Theft is the most

frequently occurring crime (Bureau of Justice Statistics, 1990b; Law Enforcement Assistance Administration, 1977a), and in comparison to other crimes (e.g., assault), it was expected to be less stressful for participants. Sixty-four participants served as pilot subjects during the development and testing of the paradigm. We were assisted by two consultants: a detective in charge of the Burglary and Theft Squad of the Pittsburgh police, and a clinical psychologist experienced in treating stress-related disorders. The detective provided information that helped to make the crime more realistic, thus enhancing the ecological validity of the paradigm. The psychologist helped in the construction of the debriefing procedure.

How does one arrange for research participants to become victims of a minor theft? We considered having a confederate steal money from a participant's purse or wallet. We rejected this idea, however; it would have sufficient realism to elicit reactions of anger and distress, but we believed that it might create an unduly high level of emotional distress. Eventually we chose a procedure that would generate less stress than a theft of money from one's purse or wallet, but that would generate the perception of being the victim of a crime. This was done by paying participants the money promised them in the ad, and giving them an additional sum of money, which they subsequently lost as a result of a theft perpetrated by a confederate posing as another participant.

The next question with which we grappled was how to engineer the theft. We began improvising on a procedure initially developed by Wilson and Greenberg (1976). Participants were placed in competition with the confederate on a clerical task in which the "loser" would have to pay the "winner" from the additional sum of money that both were provided. During the clerical task, the confederate "thief" stole some of the participant's completed work. As a result of this "theft," participants lost the competition and had to turn over all of the additional funds that they had received. (They still had the $10 promised them in the ad.) The confederate thieves, all of whom were male, were trained intensively, and none was ever caught in the act. To protect the thief from harm in the unlikely situation of his being detected while stealing the participant's work, the thief and participants were in individual cubicles separated by glass partitions. The thief was able to accomplish the theft by reaching his hand through an opening in the glass when the participant's back was turned. Later, in the privacy of the secretary's office, participants were given information that helped them discover their victimization.

PARTICIPANTS' RESPONSE

In order to measure participants' willingness to call the police after discovering that they had been victimized, the secretary used a set of verbal prods designed to induce participants to use her telephone to call the police.

The telephone, of course, was not connected, and no call was ever made. Participants were thoroughly debriefed about all of the deceptions following their decisions to make or not to make the telephone call. The debriefing was monitored by the clinical psychologist, who observed the proceedings in the secretary's office through a one-way mirror. Participants then completed an anonymous evaluation of their experience in the experiment. Results obtained from the 64 participants who served as pilot subjects indicated that the paradigm was believable and that it was minimally stressful. Consequently, it was deemed ready for use.

The six experimental studies examined the impact of four classes of variables on victims' decisions to notify the police: (1) the characteristics of the victim; (2) the characteristics of the thief; (3) the characteristics of others on the scene (e.g., bystanders); and (4) the characteristics of the crime (e.g., theft magnitude). Over the course of the six studies, the paradigm underwent fine tuning. Insights gained from each study produced modifications designed to strengthen the paradigm. The remainder of this chapter describes the initial paradigm in more detail and the results of the first experiment.

STUDY 1: THEFT MAGNITUDE AND THIEF'S RACE AND PROXIMITY AS DETERMINANTS OF CRIME REPORTING

The first experiment (Greenberg, Wilson, & Mills, 1982) examined the impact of three variables on the decision to notify the police: (1) the magnitude of the theft; (2) the race of the thief; and (3) the proximity of the thief at the time of the report opportunity. The variable of theft magnitude (an indicator of seriousness) was chosen because surveys have shown it to be correlated with crime reporting (Ennis, 1967; Schneider et al., 1976). By including this variable, we hoped to provide a test of convergent validity as well as to study the interaction of this variable with the other two independent variables. We chose to examine the impact of the thief's race on the victim's reporting because the research on racial stereotypes (e.g., Karlins, Coffman, & Walters, 1969) and on decision making in the criminal justice system suggests that blacks are more likely to be arrested, convicted, and given harsher sentences than whites (Greenberg & Ruback, 1982). We were interested in learning whether victims, as the gatekeepers of the criminal justice system, take the suspect's race into account when deciding to report the crime.

The third variable, the proximity of the thief, was selected because survey results suggest that a major reason for the failure to report theft victimization is the belief that "Nothing can be done." Presumably, the presence of the thief would negate this excuse. We expected this variable to interact with the other two variables. More specifically, we anticipated that, when the magnitude of the theft was "high," motivation to report the incident would be strong, regardless of the thief's proximity. However, when the magnitude of the theft was low, the willingness to report would be greater when the thief was present (and thus easier to apprehend) than when he was absent. Although a thief's continued presence in the situation may facilitate his apprehension by the police, his presence may also heighten victims' fear. We were interested in learning which cues predominate when the thief remains on the premises: cues concerning the thief's capture by the police, or cues concerning possible aggression by the thief.

METHOD

Design and Participants

Participants were randomly assigned to one of eight conditions in a $2 \times 2 \times 2$ between-subjects factorial design. The independent variables consisted of the magnitude of the theft ($20 vs. $3), the race of the thief (black vs. white), and the proximity of the thief (present vs. absent).

During the telephone screening of 188 respondents to the newspaper advertisement, we eliminated 40 people because of health problems. Of the remaining 148 participants for whom appointments were made, an additional 28 were eliminated for the following reasons. Twelve were judged to be suspicious of the manipulations. During the experiment these participants voiced suspicion that "This was a setup." Afterward, when being debriefed, these participants persisted in verbally proclaiming their suspicion and frequently gave nonverbal displays of such suspicion. Nine participants were dropped because they failed to follow the instructions. Of these nine, three refused to compete with the confederate, and six, upon being told that they had lost the competition, refused to surrender the money or left the testing room early in order to question the supervisor. Four participants were dropped because they refused to sign the consent form, and two were dropped because of a procedural error by the experimenter. One participant was eliminated because it appeared that she was about to break into tears after learning that she had lost the competition. This person subsequently regained her composure during the debriefing and willingly signed the consent form. The remaining 120 participants consisted of 94 females and 26 males (99 whites and 21 blacks).

Procedure

Upon their arrival, participants were instructed to take a seat in the waiting room (see Figure 2-2), where shortly afterward, they were joined by a male confederate (in actuality, the "thief") posing as another participant. (Only one participant was run at a time. However, in order to avoid the

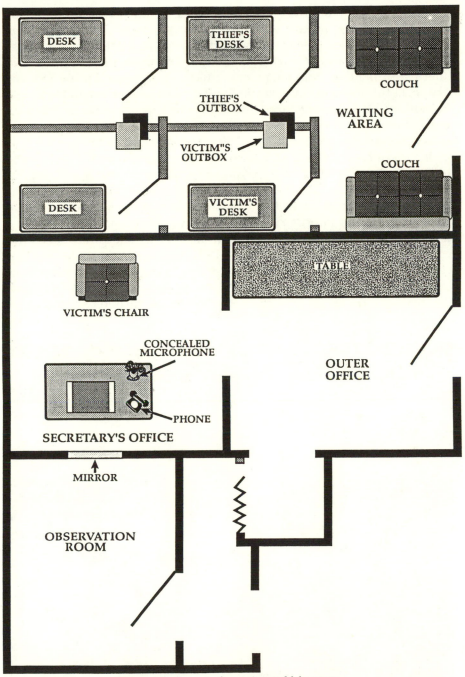

Figure 2-2. Layout of experimental laboratory.

awkward use of "him or her," we will use the plural, *participants*.) The role of thief was played by two white and two black males, all of college age. The supervisor then entered, introduced himself, and paid the participants the money promised in the ad. He questioned them about health problems, after reassuring them that the money could be kept regardless of how they answered the question. After seating participants in their separate cubicles, he explained that the organization was studying clerical efficiency in office settings and that they would be asked to complete some questionnaires before working on a clerical task. The questionnaires that they then completed asked for demographic information and assessed personality characteristics such as the need for approval and authoritarianism.

The clerical task was then described as involving several steps: transferring numbers from a card to a worksheet, adding the numbers, initialing the worksheet, and inserting the completed worksheet and card in an envelope (see Figure 2-3). Participants were instructed that immediately after completing each worksheet they should place the envelope containing their completed work in their respective outboxes, located directly behind them, and then return to their desks to repeat the procedure. As shown in Figure 2-4, the outboxes rested on a shelf attached to the partition separating the

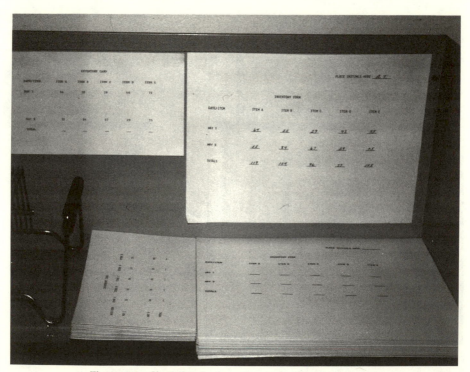

Figure 2-3. Clerical task of copying and adding up numbers.

Figure 2-4. Participant's cubicle and outbox.

participant from the confederate. This was accomplished by cutting away a portion of the glass partition. The opening in the glass gave the confederate access to the participant's outbox, which contained the completed worksheets.

Participants were then informed that, in order to simulate real-life work conditions, the supervisor would give them an opportunity to earn additional money. They were told that they would be placed in competition with the confederate and a monetary value (either $3 or 50 cents) would be put on each completed worksheet. At the end of the work period, their productivity would be compared, and the person who produced less would pay the other the appropriate amount from the funds provided her or him. The magnitude of the theft was manipulated by giving participants either $20 or $3, by having them sign a receipt for the money, and then by having them lose the money in the competition. In the $20-loss condition, each completed worksheet was worth $3, whereas in the $3-loss condition, the completed sheets were each worth 50 cents. Participants in either condition, therefore, could lose all of the additional money if the other person outproduced them by seven sheets (i.e., 7 × $3 per sheet = $21, or 7 × 50 cents = $3.50).

During the 10-minute work period, the thief stole approximately 30%

of the participants' completed worksheets from the outbox. In order to facilitate discovery of the theft, participants were told at the conclusion of the work period to check their work before it was scored by the secretary. The evidence of the theft consisted of several empty envelopes placed in participants' stack of completed work. In order to forestall participants' questioning why the empty envelopes had been left in their outbox, both the confederate and the participant were given highly visible color-coded envelopes, red for the participant and blue for the confederate. Participants were thus led to conclude that, by leaving the envelopes behind, the thief was trying to avoid being caught with obviously incriminating evidence. The subsequent debriefing of participants confirmed the effectiveness of this procedure. None thought it odd that the envelopes had been left behind.

After the allotted time for the task had expired, the secretary entered the room and collected the completed work from the participant and the confederate. Following a short interval, during which the worksheets were ostensibly being scored, the supervisor announced over the intercom system that the confederate had completed seven more sheets than the participant and, at $3 (50 cents) per sheet, that the participants had lost $20 ($3) to the confederate. The participant was then instructed to give the money to the confederate. The experimenter stated that before leaving, each person (i.e., the participant and the confederate) should individually stop by the secretary's office to sign some additional forms. The participant was either called in first to see the secretary or called in after the confederate had been seen. This procedure allowed us to manipulate the proximity of the thief. When the participant was called into the secretary's office first, the confederate was still on the premises (thief-present condition). When the participant was called in second, the confederate had already completed his meeting with the secretary and could be presumed to have left the premises (thief-absent condition).

The meeting in the secretary's office (see Figure 2-5) was the setting for measuring the dependent variable: participants' willingness to report the theft to the police. When entering the secretary's office, few participants were aware that they were the victims of a theft. Not having witnessed the theft themselves, most later reported that at the time they thought that they had mistakenly placed the empty envelopes in the outbox. It remained for the secretary to provide conclusive proof that a theft had occurred. After participants were seated, she casually inquired, "Well, how did things go?" In almost half of the instances (44%), this question was sufficient to elicit a statement about the empty envelopes. In response, the secretary appeared surprised and volunteered to check the worksheets, which were located in another room. If the participants failed to say anything about the empty envelopes, the secretary expressed surprise that they had lost all of their money because "Few participants ever do." She offered to check the worksheets and then left the room. Several minutes later, she returned with evidence that a theft had occurred. The evidence consisted of four of the

Figure 2-5. Secretary seated in front of one-way mirror.

participant's worksheets that had ostensibly been found in the confederate's work pile. The secretary showed participants where their initials had apparently been erased and the confederate's substituted. This evidence was sufficient to convince all but five participants that they were victims of a theft. The secretary, who gave the impression of being a new employee who had little authority, then explained that her supervisor had left the office and that she did not have the authority to give them their money back.

She then used a series of prearranged verbal prods of increasing intensity designed to induce the participant to use her phone to call the police (see Figure 2-6). The first prod was "The least I can do is get the police's number so you can file a complaint with them. They can be here in a few minutes." The second prod was "I think you ought to seriously consider calling the police." The third prod was "The police should definitely be notified. I'll dial and you can speak to them." These prods made it possible to quantify the participants' willingness to notify the police on a six-point response scale. A score of 6 was assigned if the participants spontaneously requested to call the police. A score of 5 was assigned if they agreed to call the police after the first prod; a score of 4 if they agreed to call after the second prod; a score of 3 after the third prod; a score of 2 if they resisted all

Figure 2-6. Participant taking phone from secretary.

prods; and a score of 1 if they failed to label the incident as a theft. The participants' responses were recorded on a special form by an assistant who observed the interaction through a one-way mirror and who listened to the conversation by way of a concealed microphone. The experiment was terminated immediately after participants agreed or failed to agree to phone the police. For those who agreed to call the police, no actual report was made as the phone was not connected.

The participants then received a lengthy debriefing by the supervisor, during which all of the deceptions and their rationale were revealed. The supervisor answered all questions that were raised and attempted to clear up any remaining misconceptions. Participants were then interviewed about their recall of the events in the experiment. In addition, they were asked to explain the basis for their decision to call or not to call the police. An additional part of the interview assessed their attitudes toward the criminal justice system. At the conclusion of the interview they were paid a bonus of $3 and were asked to sign a consent form and to complete anonymously a brief questionnaire that assessed their reactions to participating in the study. Approximately two months after their participation, they were sent a photo of a simulated police lineup and asked to identify the confederate-thief if they saw him in the photo. Finally, their recall of specific details of the theft was assessed again in a telephone interview. (See Chapter 4 for an analysis and discussion of the delayed recall and recognition data.)

Precautions Taken to Protect Participants' Welfare

Because of the many ethical questions raised by this paradigm, it might prove useful to review the precautions that were taken to protect the welfare of participants. First, all respondents to the ad were screened for health problems. Second, immediately upon their arrival, participants were paid the money promised them in the ad. Third, after receiving payment, participants were asked once again about any health problems that they might have and were told that they were free to leave with the money if there were any such problems. Fourth, the debriefing that participants received at the conclusion of the study was extensive and was conducted in a manner designed to increase their self-esteem. They were told about all of the deceptions, about the necessity for these deceptions, and about the importance of the research. Suggestions about improving the paradigm were solicited. If they appeared embarrassed by being taken in by the deception, it was explained to them that the procedure had been extensively pilot-tested and that almost all participants had been similarly taken in. In some cases, it seemed advisable to achieve a friendly reconciliation between the participant and the confederate-thief. Other participants were taken on a tour of the laboratory. All questions raised by participants were answered in a relaxed and unhurried manner. Almost all participants reacted to the revelations with good humor and a sense of relief that no real crime had actually taken place.

Fifth, after being informed about all of the deceptions and after being paid the bonus of $3, the participants were given an opportunity to withdraw their data by refusing to sign a consent form authorizing us to use their data. Only four participants (2%) refused to sign the consent form. Sixth, a clinical psychologist observed the pilot testing as well as the debriefing and participants' reactions to it. His suggestions were incorporated into the debriefing procedure. Further, he was available to consult with any participants who we felt were experiencing residual stress after leaving the laboratory. (We deemed this necessary in four cases.) Seventh, after the study was completed and the results were analyzed, all participants received a three-page feedback letter describing the findings.

RESULTS

Success of the Deception

Participants appeared to find the paradigm realistic and involving. Few were suspicious of the manipulations (just 8%), and most appeared to be highly involved in the task. This was suggested by their high level of productivity. They completed an average number of 14 worksheets during the 10-minute work period. A further indication of their involvement could be seen in participants' reactions to the evidence showing that they were victims of a theft. Many exhibited nonverbal signs of tension such as nervous laughter, running their fingers through their hair, lighting a cigarette, and pacing about the secretary's office. Further evidence of participants' involvement can be seen in their verbal responses to the secretary's prodding them to call the police. Consider, for example, the responses of a 35-year-old male participant:

PARTICIPANT: I'm just appalled that it took place. I don't care about the money.
SECRETARY: I think you ought to seriously consider calling the police.
PARTICIPANT: I'm just very much appalled by it. I thought I couldn't have grabbed two [envelopes] at a time, but I never suspected this.
SECRETARY: The police should definitely be notified. I'll dial and you can speak to them.
PARTICIPANT: No! I don't want to cause him any embarrassment. I think I'm more embarrassed than he is.

Tests of the Hypotheses

Across all conditions the percentage of participants notifying the police was 31%. Participants were judged to have reported if they had a report score of 3 or higher, that is, if they reached for the phone either spontaneously or in response to one of the secretary's prods. An analysis of variance performed on the report scores revealed no significant main effects for any of the three variables (i.e., magnitude of theft, race of thief, proximity of thief). The analysis yielded a significant interaction between proximity of thief and magnitude of theft, $F(1, 112) = 4.09$, $p < .05$, (see Table 2-1). *Post hoc* comparisons using Duncan's multiple-range test showed that when the thief had left the premises (thief-absent), victims of a $20 theft were more likely to call the police than were victims of a $3 theft. However, when the thief was still on the premises (thief-present), victims of a $3 and a

TABLE 2-1. MEAN REPORTING SCORES AS A FUNCTION OF THIEF PROXIMITY AND MAGNITUDE OF THEFT[a]

Proximity of thief	Magnitude of theft	
	$20	$3
Present	$2.40_{a,b}$	$2.50_{a,b}$
Absent	2.80_{a}	2.20_{b}

[a]Means with different subscripts differ at the .05 level of significance (Duncan's multiple-range test).

$20 theft were equally likely to report the theft. As predicted, when the theft was only $3 participants were more likely to report when the thief was still present than when he was absent, although the difference was not statistically significant.

Reporting as a Function of Victim's Sex and Race

We performed additional analyses in order to examine the effect that the victim's sex and race had on reporting. Since there were only 26 male participants in the study, inclusion of sex as a fourth variable in a four-way ANOVA would have yielded too few subjects per cell. Therefore, in order to test for sex effects, we performed three separate three-way ANOVAs, each involving sex of victim and two of the independent variables. These analyses yielded a significant interaction between proximity of thief and sex of victim, $F(1, 112) = 6.37$, $p < .02$. As shown in Table 2-2, females were more likely to report the theft when the thief was present than when he was absent, whereas the reverse was true for males. When the thief was still on the scene, males may have preferred confronting the thief to calling the police, whereas females showed less of a desire for direct confrontation and may have preferred instead to let the police settle the matter.

A similar procedure was used to examine the effect of the victim's race on reporting the theft. Results yielded no significant interaction effects, but they did yield a race-of-participant main effect: black participants were more likely than white participants to call the police, $F(1, 112) = 7.85$, $p < .01$. This difference could not be accounted for by differences in socioeconomic status or by differences on other demographic characteristics. The difference occurred even though the black participants expressed more negative attitudes than the whites on three of four questionnaire items measuring attitudes toward the police. Black participants believed that the local police provided poorer protection for people in their neighborhood, $t(114) = 4.61$, $p < .001$; were less prompt in answering calls, $t(111) = 5.02$, $p < .001$; and did a poorer job of enforcing the law, $t(113) = 2.05$, $p < .05$. The "crime," however, did not take place in their neighborhood, so they may have believed that the police would be more responsive to crimes occurring in the neighborhood where the laboratory was located.

TABLE 2-2. MEAN REPORTING SCORES AS A FUNCTION
OF THIEF PROXIMITY AND SEX OF VICTIM[a]

Proximity of thief	Sex of victim	
	Male	Female
Present	2.25_c	$2.51_{a,c}$
Absent	3.00_a	1.56_b

[a]Means with different subscripts differ at the .05 level of significance (Duncan's multiple-range test).

Reasons Offered by Participants for Not Calling Police

In addition to measuring the impact of the independent variables, we recorded the arguments offered by participants to the secretary for not wanting to call the police. The secretary always argued in favor of notifying the police, so her prodding stimulated participants to provide reasons for not wanting to call the police. In contrast, when they yielded to her prodding, participants rarely felt compelled to offer an explanation for their behavior. Typically, their consent was accompanied by a statement such as "OK, I guess I will." The procedure, therefore, was not informative about the reasons why participants chose to call the police.

An examination of the *first* reason offered only by those who resisted all of the secretary's prods (i.e., nonreporters, $n = 78$) showed that these reasons for not wanting to call the police were "Not important, not worth the time" (37%), "Not a police matter" (24%), "Police ineffectiveness" (20%), "Concern about the thief's welfare" (10%), "Fear of retaliation" (5%), and "Other" (3%).

Typical of responses classified as "Not important, not worth the time" was the following response of a 21-year-old female participant:

SECRETARY (PROD 1):   The least I can do is get the police's number so you can file a complaint with them. They can be here in a few minutes.

PARTICIPANT: Oh, it's not really important if he felt he had to do that to get it.

SECRETARY (PROD 2):   I think you ought to seriously consider calling the police.

PARTICIPANT: I don't think it's worth making a fuss over.

SECRETARY (PROD 3):   The police should definitely be notified. I'll dial and you can speak to them.

PARTICIPANT: I'm sure you have better things to do than worry about a few dollars.

Those who resisted the secretary's prods because they felt that it was not a police matter often preferred to settle the matter privately. Consider, for example, the responses of a 34-year-old female nonreporter. In response to the secretary's first prod, she asked, "Why don't you bring the other person in? You know my philosophy is to bring the two people together and work it out." Responding to the second prod, she added "I don't think it is a serious matter. I don't see the problem with bringing him in." Finally, in response to the third prod, she insisted, "I don't think it is a police matter. I would prefer to bring him in." When questioned afterward about her unwillingness to call the police, she explained, "I feel that when people are involved in something, you should talk to them first."

The following response of a 26-year-old male was typical of those who were unwilling to call because they believed that the police would be ineffective. In response to the secretary's first prod, he argued, "No, I work with the police. The money is too small. He must need the money really bad. If it were $30, I might." When prodded further by the secretary, he responded, "No, I work with the police. I know how they work. The money is too small." Afterward, when interviewed by the supervisor, he explained, "The police would probably have a big laugh over it. Even if they did find the guy, it would be tough to get him to give the money back."

Those who failed to report the incident because of their concern about the thief's welfare felt that if the police were involved, the thief would be punished excessively. This reluctance to harm the thief can be seen in the responses of a 26-year-old female participant. In response to the secretary's first prod, she stated, "I don't want to do that to him. I really don't. I figure it will get back to him somehow." Responding to the second prod, she said, "In this type of situation, I can't say it's a theft. It's cheating." When pressed further by the secretary (Prod 3), she exclaimed, "I just hate to put him through it. Not for $3. What are they going to do to the poor guy?"

The fear of retaliation deterred several participants from calling the police. Consider the reactions of a 25-year-old female participant to the secretary's prods: "That might bring a whole lot of trouble" (in response to the first prod). When prodded further by the secretary, she emphatically shook her head and muttered, "I'm just . . . He might . . . I don't know." She responded to the third prod by asking, "I have to give my name? He might be waiting. I'm scared."

There were significant differences in the reasons offered by nonreporters in the various conditions. Examination of all the reasons offered by the nonreporters (as opposed to just the first reason) indicated that 41% of those in the thief-absent condition referred to the ineffectiveness of the police as a reason for not wanting to report, as compared to 18% in the thief-present condition, $\chi^2(1) = 3.95$, $p < .05$. (This and all other 2 × 2 chi-square analyses in this book used Yates's correction.) Participants who failed to report a black thief more frequently cited fear of retaliation as a reason (26%) than did those who failed to report a white thief (2.5%), $\chi^2(1) = 7.26$, $p < .01$. Finally, there was a slight but nonsignificant tendency for nonreporters who had lost $3 to cite the triviality of the theft (62%) as a reason for not wanting to report the theft, compared to nonreporters who lost $20 (44%).

We cannot assume, of course, that the reasons offered to the secretary for not wishing to call the police reflect the "true" motives for participants' actions. These data are described simply to provide an understanding of the kinds of explanations offered by participants in this situation. These explanations might reflect participants' true motives for not wanting to notify the police, but they probably tell us more about the kind of arguments participants believed would be most convincing to the secretary.

Many participants expressed a strong sense of anger, not because they had lost money, but because they felt that the thief had taken advantage of them or played them for fools. Anger often coexisted with a state of uncertainty about what should be done. When confronted with this dilemma, many looked to the secretary for advice. Consider, for example, the responses of two participants to the secretary's final prod:

> You know, if you want to call them, it's up to you. What does he owe me? Seems like a strange way to try and steal money. Do you have his name? I hate to be played for a fool. The police are going to think I'm crazy. What do you think I ought to do? I wonder where the guy is now. OK, what the heck, go ahead and call them. (The participant agreed to call the police.)

> I don't want to get started with any trouble with him. What is the kid's address? I just don't want to start any trouble. The police might think it's ridiculous. I hate to let him think he got away with it. I don't want to get involved in a big thing and go to court, but I hate for him to think he can get away with it. I think I'll just forget it. I'll feel bad whatever I do. (The participant resisted calling the police.)

Participants' Reactions to the Experiment

How did participants feel about their participation in the experiment? Were they resentful of the deceptions? Was the debriefing procedure successful in eliminating stress, and did participants leave the situation any worse off than when they entered? Responses to an anonymous questionnaire administered after the debriefing show that reactions to the experiment were very positive.

In response to the question "In your opinion, how interesting was this experiment?" participants had a mean response of 4.62 on a five-point scale ranging from *Not interesting at all* (1) to *Very interesting* (5). When asked to describe their reactions to the study on another five-point response scale which ranged from *I am very sorry to have participated* (1) to *I am very glad to have participated* (5), the mean response was 4.80. Noteworthy is the fact that 85% of the respondents chose the highest response category. Another question asked them to indicate the extent to which they *disagreed* (1) or *agreed* (5) with the statement "More experiments of this kind should be carried out." The mean response was 4.31. When instructed to indicate the extent of their agreement with the statement, "I feel I have learned something of importance from this experiment," on a five-point scale ranging from *strongly disagree* (1) to *strongly agree* (5), the mean response was 4.21. Finally, when asked to indicate how strongly they would recommend to friends that they participate as subjects in this experiment on a scale which ranged from *I would very strongly recommend against participating* (1) to *I would very strongly recommend in favor of participating* (5), the mean response was 4.45.

Participants' responses to these questions clearly indicate that for the vast majority the experience was worthwhile. Many saw it as a valuable learning experience. As one participant wrote on the questionnaire, "I'm glad it happened to me, because now I know how I responded to being victimized. Up to now I had no idea of how I would feel if I was cheated." Another participant wrote, "It was also fun and will give me something to talk about. I think it will influence my decision if I am ever robbed. I will call the police."

In most instances, participants understood why we could not return the $11 that had been "stolen" from them. Of course, they would have liked to have had the extra money, but almost all agreed that the research would have been too expensive if each participant had been paid $24 instead of $13. We say "almost all" because there were a few who did not agree with us. Probably the most memorable of this group was a man in his late twenties who said he was "on the lam" from the police in Chicago and that he did not really care about the research. All he knew was that he wanted the $11 and he was going to beat up the experimenter (Ruback) if he did not get it. He got it.

SUMMARY AND CONCLUSIONS

In this chapter we described an experimental paradigm for investigating decision making by theft victims. Results from the first study using the paradigm showed that participants found it realistic, highly involving, and rewarding. Few participants were suspicious of the manipulations, and the procedures that were employed to ensure their welfare appeared to be successful. Among the more important results that emerged from the initial use of the paradigm is the finding that for thefts up to $20, an increase in the magnitude of the theft enhanced reporting only when the thief had already left the scene (see Table 2-1). When the thief was still on the scene, the amount of the theft did not influence the tendency to call the police. We did not find support for the prediction that the thief's proximity would affect the reporting of a $3 theft (i.e., greater reporting when the thief was present), but not of the $20 theft.

Contrary to expectations, the race of the thief was not related to reporting. However, somewhat different reasons were offered for not reporting as a function of the race of the thief. Those who failed to report a theft by a black suspect more often expressed fear of retaliation than did those who failed to report a white suspect. Unexpectedly, the race of the *victim* was related to reporting. Black victims were more likely to notify the police than were white victims regardless of the thief's race. This finding is difficult to explain given the finding that black participants expressed more negative attitudes toward the police and the criminal justice system. Other studies, however, have often found a tendency for attitudes to be imperfect predictors of specific behavior (Fishbein & Ajzen, 1975; Wicker, 1969).

Unexpectedly, we found an interaction effect for the victim's sex and the proximity of the thief (see Table 2-2). Females were more likely to report the theft when the thief was still in the building, whereas males were more likely to report when he had fled the scene. Females may have been particularly apprehensive about confronting the thief but felt less apprehensive when the confrontation would take place in the presence of a police officer. Males, on the other hand, may have preferred to confront the thief when he was still on the premises rather than to involve the police.

Most participants experienced some degree of conflict about what to do. As we observed them wrestling with this decision, it was readily apparent that many sought the secretary's advice and were indeed influenced by her prodding. The remaining five experiments, therefore, examined in greater detail the role of social influence factors in theft-victim decision making.

3

Experimental Studies on the Role of Social Influence in Victim Decision Making

Our observation of participants in the first study strongly suggested that social and emotional factors contributed to their decisions about whether or not to report the incident to the police. This chapter describes the results of five studies that examined the role of these factors in victim decision making. In the first of these studies (Study 2), we examined the joint effects of the victim's level of anger and the type of bystander advice on the victim's willingness to call the police. In the second study (Study 3), we compared the persuasiveness of different types of advice and supporting arguments used by bystanders when attempting to influence victims to notify or not notify the police. In the third study (Study 4), we investigated some of the potential moderators of bystander influence: the bystander's proximity to the victim after giving the advice, the bystander's willingness to support the victim in future dealings with the police, and the bystander's direct knowledge of the theft. The remaining two studies examined the effects of similarity between the influencing agent and the victim: Study 5 investigated similarity in terms of sex, and Study 6 examined similarity in terms of fate (i.e., covictim vs. bystander).

STUDY 2: SOCIAL AND EMOTIONAL
FACTORS IN VICTIM DECISION MAKING

In our initial study (Study 1), participants presented numerous signs of physical arousal upon discovering their victimization. Various emotional states were evident among participants. Some became angry, others expressed slight annoyance, some showed signs of fear, and many presented signs of diffuse arousal. We noted that those who reacted with anger were often likely to decide to call the police. These observations led us to consider seriously the mediating role of emotional arousal in victim reporting. Research by Schachter and Singer (1962) helped guide our thinking. Their research demonstrated that the experience of an emotional state involves two components: an arousal component and an appropriate label for that arousal. In a series of experiments, Schachter and Singer demonstrated that others in the situation can influence how people label their states of arousal. All that was required in our paradigm, therefore, was the presence of a bystander who would "help" participants label their state of arousal.

This experiment (Greenberg, Wilson, Ruback, & Mills, 1979) also examined a second function that bystanders often perform when interacting with a crime victim: advising the victim what to do. Many participants who decided to call the police in the first experiment claimed that they did so because of the secretary's influence. Bystanders may serve a similar function (Bickman & Green, 1977).

Mintz and Mills (1971) showed that the label one attaches to one's emotional state affects how much one will be influenced by a persuasive communication. Based on these findings, we predicted that there would be an interaction between the victim's level of anger and the type of advice offered by a bystander. More specifically, we predicted that the higher the victim's level of anger, the more persuasive would be the bystander's appeal to take some action concerning the theft. However, the victim's level of anger was not expected to influence the persuasiveness of the bystander's advice to do nothing about the theft. In the absence of any persuasive attempt by the bystander, we expected that the angrier the victim's reaction, the greater the likelihood that the victim would choose to notify the police.

METHOD

Design and Participants

The study used a 3 × 3 factorial design with 14 participants per cell. The two independent variables were (1) victim anger (high anger, low anger, no anger) and (2) bystander's advice (advised action, advised no action, no advice). As in the first study, participants were recruited by ads placed in local newspapers. Instead of being offered $10 for 1½ hours, they were offered $8 for 1¼ hours of participation. The telephone screening for health problems eliminated 46 respondents. Of the 145 respondents for whom appointments were made, 19 were eliminated for the following reasons: suspiciousness ($n = 8$), health problems ($n = 4$), inability to follow instructions or complete the task ($n = 3$), refusal to sign consent form ($n = 3$), and experimenter error ($n = 1$). The remaining 126 participants (90 females, 36 males; 109 whites, 17 blacks) were randomly assigned to the nine experimental conditions.

Procedure

The procedure was essentially similar to that used in the first experiment but with several important changes. Two confederates were used in each session, one posing as the thief and the other as the bystander. The thief was played by two black males in their early 20s who alternated in this role, and the bystander was played by a white female in her late 20s. As in the first experiment, the thief occupied the cubicle directly behind the participant's. The bystander worked in a cubicle diagonally opposite to the participant's (see Figure 2-2). Rather than competing with each other as they did in the first experiment, participants competed with the "norms" for their age group. This change was introduced because, in the first study, the element of competition with the other may have heightened participants' anger over losing to the thief, and this anger, in turn, may have affected their willingness to report the theft. Thus, in order to increase the generalizability of the paradigm, the situation was made noncompetitive. Further, in order to increase participants' sense of loss, we gave them an opportunity to "earn" the money which they subsequently lost. Rather than receiving the money gratis as in the first study, they "earned" $12 by doing an added alphabetizing task. After they were informed that the bystander had earned $13 and the thief $11, they were paid their earnings and were asked to sign a receipt.

The second task was identical to that used in the first study. It consisted of transferring numbers to a worksheet and then adding the numbers. As in the first study, participants were instructed to place their initials in the upper-right-hand corner of each completed worksheet. Unlike in the first study, the envelopes were not color-coded. In addition, none of the participant's work was stolen during the task; thus, there was no need of a check period during which they could discover the empty envelopes.

After the participants' work was collected and ostensibly scored, the supervisor announced the outcome over the intercom. Participants lost $11 of the $12 that they had earned on the first task because they had completed three sheets below the norm for their age group. It was also announced that the thief had earned an additional $11 and that the bystander had lost $5. Unlike in the first study, the transfer of the money took place in the secretary's office. Following the announcement of the results, all three were told that the study had been completed and that they should go to the secretary's office. After they were seated, the secretary proceeded with the transfer of money. The bystander was asked to return $5, and the participant was asked to give $11 to Mr. Collins (the thief) since Mr. Collins had earned $11 on the second task and the participant had lost $11.

The secretary then asked each of them to sign a receipt for the money. The thief completed his receipt first, handed it to the secretary, and left. After the thief's departure, the secretary asked the participant, "Oh, by the way, did you have some problem with the transfer task? I saw some empty envelopes in your pile." Generally, participants seemed perplexed by this remark, usually responding that they could not recall placing any empty envelopes in their outbox. The secretary said that she could be mistaken and that she would take just a few minutes to recheck the papers, which were located in another room. She returned shortly with the "evidence," which consisted of four of the participant's completed worksheets allegedly found in the thief's work pile. On their own, many participants discovered that their initials on the sheets had been erased and those of the thief substituted. However, the secretary "helped" other participants discover the evidence. In this way participants were led to believe that they had been victims of a theft of four sheets, that this theft had prevented them from meeting the norms for their age group, and that it had deprived them of at least $11. The secretary, appearing confused, left the office saying that she would try to find her supervisor.

Manipulation of Independent Variables. Just prior to entering the secretary's office, the bystander looked at a randomly drawn "condition card" that listed the condition to be run. Thus, until entering the secretary's office, the bystander was blind to the condition being run. During the secretary's absence, the bystander attempted to manipulate the level of the participant's anger. Based on Schacter and Singer's finding (1962) that the reactions of those present can influence how one labels a state of arousal, the bystander modeled one of three levels of anger about the theft:

1. *High anger.* "He erased your initials and put his own on your papers? I can't believe this! Boy, that really makes me angry. I'm really surprised that something like this happened." (Throughout, she appeared very agitated.)
2. *Low anger.* "You know, this really bothers me. It's annoying having something like this happen." (Throughout, she appeared somewhat agitated.)
3. *No anger.* During the secretary's absence, the bystander said nothing to the participant. She remained seated and responded only if the participant directed a question to her.

After displaying one of these three levels of anger, the bystander offered one of three forms of advice:

1. *Advised action.* "I wouldn't let him get away with this. I think you should do something about it."
2. *Advised no action.* "I wouldn't do anything. This probably isn't worth bothering about. He's already gone."
3. *No advice.* The bystander simply remained silent and offered no advice. After delivering her lines, the bystander looked at her watch, said she had to keep an appointment, wished the participant luck, and left the office.

While participants waited alone for the secretary to return, an assistant behind a one-way mirror observed their behavior. The assistant dictated his observations into a tape recorder. So that the assistant would be kept blind to the condition being observed, the assistant activated the concealed microphone in the secretary's office only after the bystander spoke her lines. The purpose of these observations was to provide a behavioral check on the effectiveness of the anger manipulation. Shortly after the departure of the bystander, the secretary returned, saying that she could not locate her supervisor. After explaining that she did not have the authority to compensate participants for their losses, she proceeded to use a series of preprogrammed prods to induce participants to phone the police.

Dependent Measures. Participants' willingness to call the police was measured by assessing which of the secretary's prods they yielded to, if any. The three prods used in the first study were retained, and a fourth was added. If a participant resisted the first three prods, the secretary said, "Well, if it's all right with you, I'd really like to call the police, and *you* can just tell them what happened." The secretary then began to dial and offered the phone to the participant. If the participant took the phone, that person was scored as yielding to this prod. A report score of 5 was assigned if the participant yielded to the first prod, a score of 4 if he or she yielded to the second prod, a score of 3 if the participant yielded to the third prod, a score of 2 if he or she yielded to the fourth prod, and a score of 1 if the participant resisted all the prods.

The procedure following assessment of the report score was similar to the one used in the first study. Participants' recall of the details of the event was measured, as well as their reasons for deciding to report or not to report. In addition, several forced-choice rating scales were employed to determine the success of the experimental manipulations. At the conclusion of the experiment, participants were given a $3 bonus and asked to complete anonymously a short questionnaire assessing their reactions to having participated in the experiment. Five weeks later (compared to two months in the first experiment) they were sent a questionnaire that measured their memory of the event. (The results of the delayed measures are discussed in Chapter 5.)

RESULTS

Across all conditions, 44% of the participants agreed to report the incident to the police. Reporters consisted of those who yielded to one of the first three prods (i.e., those with a report score of 3–5). Most of those who yielded to the last prod (i.e., Prod 4) later indicated that they felt that they had *not* agreed to report the incident. For this reason, they were included among the nonreporters.

Prior to testing for the significance of the independent variables, we analyzed the data to determine if any of the demographic variables were correlated with the reporting measure. Reporting was negatively correlated with participants' age ($r = -.20$, $p < .02$) and household earnings ($r = -.22$, $p < .01$). Therefore, both of these variables were employed as covariates in an analysis of covariance that was used to test the significance of the independent variables.

The analysis of covariance revealed a significant main effect of bystander advice, $F(2, 110) = 3.13$, $p < .05$, and no other significant effects. *Post hoc* comparisons among the adjusted means using the Duncan's multiple-range test showed that those advised to take no action ($M = 2.03$) were significantly less likely to report than were those in the no-advice (control) condition ($M = 2.72$, $p < .05$). However, participants who were advised to take action ($M = 2.57$) were no more likely to report the incident than were those who were advised to take no action or who were given no advice.

A subsequent manipulation check revealed that the level of *bystander* anger was perceived in line with the manipulations, $F(2, 117) = 14.69$, $p < .001$. The participant's perception of the bystander's anger was assessed by the question, "How angry did Ms. Robins appear before she left?" Responses were recorded on a seven-point bipolar scale ranging from *Very angry* (7) to *Not angry at all* (1). The means for the high-, low-, and no-anger conditions were, respectively, 5.02, 3.74, and 3.02. However, when the participants were asked to rate their *own* level of anger on the same scale, there was no significant difference among the high-, low-, and no-anger conditions. Thus, it would appear that the manipulation of the level of participant anger was unsuccessful. Participants may have been sufficiently aware of their subjective feelings of anger so that they did not need to rely on cues provided by the bystander to label their emotional state.

Therefore, in order to test for the relationship between victim anger and reporting, we reclassified participants according to their level of *self-reported* anger (high, moderate, and low). Participants were classified in the group with high self-reported anger ($n = 44$) if they had scores of 5, 6, or 7 on the anger scale, in the group with moderate self-reported anger ($n = 42$) for scores of 3 or 4, and in the group with low self-reported anger ($n = 39$) for scores of 1 or 2. One participant was omitted because she did not respond to the self-reported anger measure.

An analysis of covariance (using age and household earnings as the covariates) performed on the reconstructed self-reported anger × bystander advice matrix produced a significant main effect of self-reported anger, $F(2, 109) = 5.37$, $p < .01$; and a marginally significant advice main effect, $F(2, 109) = 2.70$, $p < .08$. Five participants were omitted from this analysis because they failed to provide information on one of the covariates (three failed to provide age information, and two failed to provide information about family earnings). The hypothesized interaction between level of anger and type of advice was not significant. The adjusted mean reporting scores for the conditions of high, moderate, and low self-reported anger were, respectively, 2.89, 2.41, and 1.89. The test for linear trend was significant, $F(1, 109) = 25.68$, $p < .001$, as was the difference between the conditions of high and low self-reported anger ($p < .01$). The data were consistent with the hypothesis that the greater the victims' level of anger, the greater their willingness to notify the police.

The marginally significant main effect of advice yielded exactly the same pattern of means as was obtained in the original analysis. When advised to take no action, participants were less likely to decide to call the police ($M = 2.03$) than were those given no advice ($M = 2.72$, $p < .05$). Participants who were advised to take action were no more likely to call the police ($M = 2.61$) than were those who were advised to do nothing or who were given no advice.

In addition to comparing conditions in terms of report scores, comparisons were made regarding percentages of participants who decided to notify the police. The analysis yielded a pattern identical to that achieved with the five-point reporting scale. The percentages of participants reporting in the conditions of high, moderate, and low self-reported anger were, respectively, 61%, 45%, and 34%. As in the covariance analysis, only the difference between the high- and low-anger conditions was significant, $\chi^2(1) = 4.03$, $p < .05$. With regard to the second independent variable (type of bystander advice), there was a marginally significant tendency for those who were advised to take no action to be less inclined to decide to call the police (31%) than were those who were given no advice (52%), $\chi^2(1) = 3.13$, $p < .10$, and those who were advised to take some action (51%), $\chi^2(1) = 3.10$, $p < .10$.

The data also yielded sex differences in reporting. When separate analyses of covariance were performed on the five-point reporting scores for females and males, there was a significant main effect of self-reported anger only for females, $F(2, 74) = 6.84$, $p < .002$. (Four females were omitted from this analysis because they failed to provide information regarding their age or family earnings.) The adjusted mean reporting scores for females in the conditions of high, moderate, and low self-reported anger were, respectively, 3.07, 2.48, and 1.73. The linear trend was significant, $F(1, 74) = 41.29$, $p < .001$. *Post hoc* comparisons using the Duncan's test showed that females in the conditions of high and moderate self-reported anger were significantly more willing to call the police than were females in the condition of low self-reported anger ($p < .05$).

DISCUSSION AND CONCLUSIONS

These data suggest that both the advice from a bystander and the victim's state of anger are important determinants of theft victims' decision to call the police. Victims' susceptibility to influence by a bystander appeared to depend on the direction of the advice. Victims were more inclined to follow the bystander's advice when advised to do nothing than when advised to take some action. The differential impact of the two forms of advice may be accounted for in terms of differences in the specificity of the advice. The advice to do nothing about the theft was concrete and specific. In contrast, the advice to "do something" was nonspecific and could imply other actions besides calling the police. For example, participants may have interpreted the advice to do something as meaning that they should complain to the secretary and ask her for reimbursement. Indeed, numerous participants pursued this mode of action. In so doing, they were following the bystander's advice to do "something." However, their actions did not involve notifying the police. A stronger test of the bystander's influence would have involved specific advice, such as, "I think that you should call the police."

The positive relationship obtained between the level of self-reported anger and the willingness to call the police is qualified by the fact that this finding emerged from self-reports rather than experimental manipulations. The self-reported anger scores may have reflected participants' *chronic* level of anger as well as anger specific to the victimization. This qualification notwithstanding, the data suggest that in the immediate aftermath of discovering a theft, the emotional state of victims plays an important role in their decision making. This conclusion may be more appropriate for female theft victims than for male theft victims, given the finding that the level of self-reported anger predicted the reporting decisions of female but not male victims. The failure to find an effect with males may, however, have derived simply from the fact that there were too few males in the study to provide a powerful enough test of this hypothesis. (There were just 36 males in the study, representing 29% of the sample.)

Reliance on self-reported anger rather than manipulated anger presents another interpretive problem. Since the self-reports of anger were obtained *after* participants had made their decision to report the theft, it can be argued that the causal relationship between anger and reporting is the reverse of what we have suggested. Self-perception theory (Bem, 1972), for example, would suggest that those who reported the theft may have reasoned that since they had agreed to call the police, they must have been quite angry. Likewise, those who had decided not to report the theft may have reasoned from their behavior that they were not very angry. In order to clarify the direction of influence, what is needed is a measure of anger or arousal obtained *prior* to the decision to report. Such a measure was obtained in this study.

As we described earlier, an assistant who was blind to the manipulations observed participants immediately after they had learned of the theft. The observer dictated his observations into a tape recorder. Two judges, blind to the condition being run, coded transcriptions of these tape recordings for overt signs of arousal. Participants' behavior was coded into two categories: high overt arousal (e.g., involuntary twitching of facial muscles, smoking, nail biting, pacing, and cursing to oneself) and low overt arousal (the absence of the above). Participants in the latter group tended to sit silently in their seats. The interjudge agreement was 92%. Differences between the judges were resolved through discussions. The percentage of participants showing signs of high overt arousal in the conditions of high, moderate, and low self-reported anger was, respectively, 74%, 59%, and 50%. Only the difference between the high and low conditions was significant, $\chi^2(1) = 3.86$, $p < .05$. These unobtrusive measures of arousal taken before the decision to report paralleled participants' self-reports and therefore lend support to the hypothesis that anger facilitated reporting decisions rather than the reverse.

In summary, this second study in the series of six experiments attested to the importance of victims' emotional state as a factor in their decision making. The data are less clear concerning the impact of the bystander's advice to report or not to report the theft. A third experiment was designed to examine this issue further.

STUDY 3: TYPE OF BYSTANDER
ADVICE AND SUPPORTING ARGUMENTS

There are several possible explanations for the relatively weak impact of the bystander's advice in the previous experiment. First, as already discussed, the bystander's advice to report may have been too diffuse. Second, the advice was not supported by any arguments that would have persuaded participants to report or not to report. Finally, the bystander's influence may have been weakened because, after having offered the advice, she left the scene. Her absence during the secretary's prodding may have diminished her influence. Together, these explanations suggest that the bystander's advice might have had a stronger impact if the bystander had been more explicit in her advice to report the theft, if she had provided supporting arguments, and if she had remained with the victim while he or she decided what to do. These ideas were tested in the third experiment.

Experiment 3 was designed to determine whether social influence in the form of specific advice from a bystander facilitates victim reporting and whether the persuasiveness of such advice is affected by the type of supporting argument. Three kinds of supporting arguments were employed. The first was based on the magnitude of the theft; the bystander argued that the amount lost was either trivial or significant. The second argument related to the probable effectiveness of the police in catching the thief (i.e., the police would be either effective or ineffective). The third argument focused on punishing the thief; the bystander argued in favor of or against punishing the thief.

METHOD

Design and Participants

The study consisted of a 2 × 4 factorial design. The two independent variables were (1) type of bystander advice (advised to report or advised not to report) and (2) type of supporting argument (theft magnitude, police effectiveness, punishment of the thief, or no supporting argument). In addition, we included a "baseline" (control) condition involving no advice and no supporting argument.

As in the previous study, participants were recruited with advertisements placed in local newspapers offering $8 for 1¼ hours of participation in a study of clerical efficiency. Of the 176 respondents who passed the initial telephone screening and for whom appointments were made, 38 were eliminated for the following reasons: suspiciousness ($n = 14$), inability to follow instructions or complete the tasks ($n = 15$), experimenter error ($n = 6$), refusal to sign consent form ($n = 2$), and emotional upset ($n = 1$). The remaining 138 participants consisted of 104 females and 34 males, of whom 108 were white and 30 were black.

Procedure

The thief was played by three college-age black males who alternated in the role. The bystander was played by a white female in her late 20s. With the exception of several methodological refinements to be described below, the paradigm was identical to that employed in the second experiment. One change involved the task on which participants "earned" the $12. Participants in the previous experiment indicated during the debriefing that $12 seemed to be an inordinate sum of money to receive for working on a single task (alphabetizing name cards). The change in procedure involved adding a second alphabetizing task, so that participants earned $5 on the first and $7 on the second task, and then having them sign a receipt for the money.

The remaining changes in procedure all took place in the secretary's office. Some participants in the second experiment had felt that the organization was in part responsible for allowing the thief to escape with the money. It may be recalled that in the first two experiments the secretary mentioned that she had seen some empty envelopes in the participant's work pile when the papers were ostensibly being scored. Several participants felt that if she had this information, she should not have allowed the thief to leave until the matter was cleared up. This problem was solved by the following change in procedure. Shortly after participants handed the $11 to the thief and while they were filling out a new receipt, one of the assistants asked to speak with the secretary. She excused herself and stepped outside the door, where she was told by the assistant (in a voice loud enough to be overheard by participants) that there were some problems with the worksheets. The secretary then stuck her head in the door and told everyone that there was a problem with the papers and that they should all remain seated while she went in the back room to check. Shortly after her departure, the thief disobeyed her instructions and walked out. She returned in a few minutes with the "evidence" and inquired where Mr. Turner (the thief) had gone. Typically, participants shrugged their shoulders in response. She then proceeded to lay out the evidence of the theft in the same manner as in the previous experiment. In this way we hoped to convince participants that the secretary had acquired information concerning the theft at about the same time that the thief was fleeing the office. This procedural change was designed to prevent participants from faulting the secretary for allowing the thief to get away.

Another change in procedure was designed to provide some rationale for the bystander's advising participants to call the police rather than merely advising them "to do something about it." The justification for mentioning the police came from the secretary. Shortly after she presented the evidence of the theft, she paused and stated, "I don't know what to do." And then, after another short reflective pause, she hesitantly remarked, "Well, uh, maybe the police should be called." She then exited, stating that she was going to look for her supervisor. The participant and the bystander were left alone in the secretary's office, and it was at this point that the bystander offered her advice about reporting or not reporting the incident to the police. She stated, "I think you should call the police," or "I don't think you should call the police."

The final change in procedure concerned the bystander's actions after offering the advice. Rather than leaving the office as she had in the previous study, she remained in the office with the participant. When the secretary returned and gave the first prod, the bystander immediately intervened and repeated her advice: "I think (don't think) you should call the police."

The advice to call the police was supported by one of three arguments: (1) *theft magnitude*—"Eleven dollars is $11. You can buy a lot with that"; (2) *police effectiveness*—"They can do something about this. I'm sure they could get your money back"; and (3) *thief punishment*—"I'd like to see him punished. I think it would teach him a lesson." The advice *not* to call the police was supported by one of three parallel arguments: (1) *theft magnitude*—"It's only $11. It's really not that much money"; (2) *police effectiveness*—"They can't do anything about this. I'm pretty sure they couldn't get your money back"; and (3) *thief punishment*—"I wouldn't like to see him punished. I don't think it would accomplish anything." In the no-supporting-argument conditions, the bystander offered no argument to support her advice to call or not to call the police. Finally, in the baseline or control condition (no advice–no supporting argument), the bystander silently remained seated during the secretary's absence and later during the secretary's prodding of participants.

The dependent variable (participants' willingness to report the theft) was measured in the same way as in the previous study. Four prods were employed by the secretary, and there was a five-point report scale. The earlier the yielding, the higher the report score.

RESULTS AND DISCUSSION

The success of the manipulations was assessed during the debriefing session. Participants were shown a list of eight statements and were asked to choose the statement that best resembled the one that they had heard from the bystander; 86% correctly identified the type of advice, and 63% correctly identified the bystander's supporting argument.

The reporting rate across all conditions was 25%. Since a preliminary analysis showed that the participant's age was negatively correlated with the report score ($r = -.20$, $p < .02$), an analysis of covariance was used to analyze the report scores, with age serving as the covariate. This analysis yielded a significant main effect for type of advice, $F(1, 116) = 36.86$, $p < .001$. Those advised to report the theft had a higher adjusted mean report score ($M = 2.54$) than did those advised not to report the theft ($M = 1.50$). There was no significant main effect for type of supporting argument, nor was there a significant interaction effect between the two independent variables.

In order to determine whether the bystander's advice increased or decreased victims' willingness to notify the police, a separate one-way analysis of covariance was used to compare the baseline condition with the two no-supporting-argument conditions. This analysis proved highly significant, $F(2, 38) = 7.61$, $p < .002$. Individual comparisons using the Duncan's multiple-range test showed that participants in the advised-to-report/ no-supporting-argument condition had a higher adjusted mean report score ($M = 2.95$) than did those in the baseline condition ($M = 1.76$, $p < .05$). In contrast, there was no significant difference between the advised-not-to-report/ no-supporting-argument condition ($M = 1.27$) and the baseline condition ($M = 1.76$).

That the bystander's advice to report the theft carried more weight than did her advice not to report the theft is consistent with self-report data obtained during the debriefing. When asked to evaluate the extent of the bystander's influence on their decision on a seven-point bipolar scale, those given the advice to report believed that they had been more influenced ($M = 2.39$) than did those advised not to report the theft ($M = 1.67$), $F(1, 120) = 5.88$, $p < .02$. The ineffectiveness of the advice not to report may have been the result of a "floor effect." The mean report score in the baseline condition was 1.76, suggesting that in the absence of any influence attempt, participants were disinclined to call the police. As there was little room for further movement in the direction of nonreporting, exposure to a bystander who advised against reporting may have served only to reinforce participants' resolve and not to change it.

In addition, participants may have been more susceptible to the advice to report the theft because of their emotional state at the time of the influence attempt. When asked to choose the one adjective that best described their emotional state following discovery of the theft from a list that included *fearful, calm, amused, angry, worried, hurt, confused, foolish,* and *indifferent*, the adjectives participants chose most frequently were *angry* (28%) and *confused* (25%). The state of anger and confusion may have predisposed participants to be more accepting of the advice to notify the police. This hypothesis is supported by self-report data showing that for those who were advised to report the theft, self-reported anger was correlated with the report score ($r = .26$, $p < .025$). In contrast, for those advised not to report the theft, the correlation between self-reported anger and the report score was essentially zero ($r = -.01$). We were able to gain some insight concerning the source of participants' anger by examining the reasons given by reporters for calling the police. The reason given most often (46%) was the "principle of the thing." Participants appeared angered by the fact that what the thief had done was "unfair" or "wrong."

The failure of the bystander's supporting argument to influence reporting may be accounted for by participants' failure to attend to and thus comprehend the message. In support of this reasoning, a manipulation check revealed that just 63% of participants correctly recognized the bystander's argument from a list of eight that was presented. Conceivably, participants were still sorting out details of the theft when the supporting argument was presented. Given this preoccupation, participants may have attended only to the first, and perhaps the clearest, of messages, namely, the bystander's advice to call or not to call the police (86% correctly recognized the bystander's advice). Moreover, the bystander's advice, because it preceded the supporting argument, may have added to participants' distraction, causing many to "tune out" during delivery of the supporting argument.

In summary, the data show that when a bystander offers unambiguous advice to call the police, this advice can be a strong facilitator of victim reporting. These data, however, leave unanswered the exact nature of this influence (i.e., how advice to call the police is likely to be interpreted). Situational factors may have contributed to this influence. Several of these factors were examined in Study 4.

STUDY 4: PARAMETERS OF BYSTANDER INFLUENCE: PROXIMITY, SUPPORT, AND KNOWLEDGE OF THE THEFT

The previous experiment demonstrated the ability of bystanders to influence victims' decision to call the police. Was it merely the bystander's advice that induced participants to call the police, or were other factors involved? The bystander's presence during the secretary's prodding may have led participants to infer that they could count on the bystander's continued support when dealing with the police. Moreover, because the bystander had been present when the theft occurred, participants may have believed that the bystander could provide the police with valuable information that would enhance the credibility of their case against the thief. These issues were explored in the fourth experiment.

METHOD

Design and Participants

Male and female participants were randomly assigned to conditions in a $2 \times 2 \times 2 \times 2$ factorial design. The variables were (1) proximity of the bystander (present vs. absent); (2) the bystander's willingness to support participants in their future dealings with the police and the criminal justice system (support vs. no support); (3) the bystander's direct knowledge of the theft (eyewitness vs. not an eyewitness); and (4) the participant's sex.

Participants were recruited in the same manner as in the earlier experiments with the exception that an attempt was made to include more males in the sample. Of the 160 subjects who participated, 40 were eliminated for the following reasons: suspiciousness ($n = 18$), procedural error ($n = 8$), recognition of confederate ($n = 7$), failure to complete the task ($n = 5$), and health problems ($n = 2$). The remaining 120 participants consisted of 73 females and 47 males, of whom 106 were white and 14 black.

Procedure

Unlike in the previous two studies, the role of thief was played alternately by two white males in their early 20s. In addition, the bystander *always* advised participants to report the theft. With the exception of the above changes, the procedure was the same as that employed in the previous experiment. Manipulation of the independent variables took place after the secretary presented evidence of the theft to the participant. In half the cases, the bystander (a white female) volunteered the information that she had seen Mr. Collins (the thief) take some of the participant's papers (eyewitness condition) but at the time did not label it as a theft. In the remaining cases she stated that she "didn't see anything" (not-an-eyewitness condition).

The bystander then advised participants to report the theft. In half the instances she indicated her willingness to support participants in their dealings with the police and the criminal justice system by stating, "I'll back you up. And if anything happens later on, you can call me at work." She then wrote her phone number on a slip of paper and handed it to the participant (support condition). In the remaining cases, after advising participants to call the police, the bystander indicated her unwillingness to support participants by stating, "But don't use my name. I don't want to get involved" (no-support condition). The bystander then either remained present during the secretary's prodding (present condition) or left the office after the secretary said that she could leave (absent condition). A change was made in the dependent variable: the fourth prod (dialing for the participant) was omitted, so that there was a four-point report score instead of the five-point score previously employed.

RESULTS AND DISCUSSION

The success of the manipulations was measured by responses to three questions posed during the debriefing. The first question assessed perception of the bystander's direct knowledge of the theft: "To what extent did Miss Johnson [the bystander] indicate that she was an eyewitness to the theft?" The seven-point response scale ranged from *Saw the papers taken* (7) to *Saw nothing* (1). Proximity of the bystander was measured by responses to the question, "Was Miss Johnson present or absent while the secretary was trying to convince you to call the police?" A two-point response scale was employed: *Present* (2) or *Absent* (1). Perception of the bystander's willingness to support the participant was measured by the question, "How much was Miss Johnson willing to help you?" Response alternatives ranged from *Very much* (7) to *Not al all* (1). Separate analyses of variance conducted on responses to each question showed that the three manipulations had been correctly perceived ($p < .001$ for all three tests).

Across all conditions the percentage of participants deciding to report the theft was 49%. This figure is higher than in any of the previous experiments, but it was not surprising, given that *all* participants were advised to report the crime. Since a preliminary analysis showed that age was negatively correlated with the reporting score ($r = -.30$, $p < .001$), the reporting data were analyzed by analysis of covariance, with age serving as the covariate. This analysis yielded two significant effects: a main effect for sex, $F(1, 103) = 8.86$, $p < .01$ (females were more willing to report than were males), and a Bystander Support × Bystander Proximity interaction, $F(1, 103) = 4.48$, $p < .05$. As shown in Table 3-1, the bystander's advice to report the theft facilitated reporting only when the bystander offered support *and* remained present. When one or both of these conditions were absent, participants were equally disinclined to call the police. That is, an offer of support that is not backed up by the continued presence of the bystander appears to weaken the impact of the bystander's influence. The finding that females were more susceptible to influence than were males may be due, in part, to the fact that the bystander was a female. Females may have been more willing to accept the bystander's advice because of the perceived similarity between themselves and the bystander. Males simply may have been reluctant to accept advice from a female.

The bystander's firsthand knowledge of the theft (eyewitness vs. no eyewitness) had no impact on reporting. It is likely that the evidence was already so strong that testimony from the bystander was not needed.

Participants' self-report data were largely consistent with the results of earlier studies. When asked to choose from a list of nine (see "Results and Discussion" for Study 2) the word that best described their feelings when learning of the theft, the words participants chose most often were *angry* (29%) and *confused* (25%). Given these reactions to the theft, the bystander's offer of support and her willingness to remain with the participants may have been particularly meaningful to them. The reason most often given by those who decided to report the theft was that "It was the principle of the thing—it wasn't right" (46%). Only 2% of participants who decided to report attributed their actions to the bystander's influence.

The remaining two experiments explored other factors that may con-

TABLE 3-1. ADJUSTED MEAN REPORTING SCORES AS
A FUNCTION OF BYSTANDER SUPPORT AND PROXIMITY[a]

	Proximity of bystander	
Type of bystander support	Present	Absent
Support	2.73[a]	1.80[b]
No support	1.80[b]	1.90[b]

[a]Higher numbers indicate earlier reporting of the crime. Means with different subscripts differ at the .01 level of significance (Duncan's multiple-range test).

tribute to victims' susceptibility to social influence. One of these factors is the degree of similarity between the victim and the influencing agent. As noted previously, the finding in the fourth study suggesting that females were more influenced by the bystander's advice may be attributed to their being of the same sex. In Study 5, therefore, we attempted to examine this issue by systematically varying the sex of the bystander and the victim. This study also explored two additional factors that may contribute to victims' susceptibility to social influence: (1) the type of supporting argument employed by the bystander and (2) the bystander's level of surveillance of the victim's response.

STUDY 5: PARAMETERS OF BYSTANDER INFLUENCE: SEX SIMILARITY, TYPE OF SUPPORTING ARGUMENT, AND LEVEL OF SURVEILLANCE

This study explored the effect of four variables on a bystander's ability to influence participants' decisions to notify the police. The first two variables concerned the sex of the participant and the sex of the bystander. Because of social psychological theorizing (Byrne, 1971; Festinger, 1954; Heider, 1958), we expected to find that social influence would be enhanced when the victim and the bystander were of the same sex. Research on persuasion and social influence (e.g., Eagly, 1983; Eagly & Carli, 1981), however, has suggested that men are slightly more influential than are women and that women are somewhat more susceptible to influence than men. Thus, we expected to obtain two main effects: one for sex of bystander (males being more influential than females) and one for sex of participant (females being more influenced than males).

Research by Eagly, Wood, and Fishbaugh (1981) suggests that females are more susceptible to influence than are males only when their responses are under surveillance by the group. In order to explore this possibility, we introduced a third variable: type of bystander surveillance. After advising the victim to notify the police, the bystander remained with the victim either to monitor compliance (intentional surveillance) or because the secretary insisted that he or she remain (unintentional surveillance). In a third condition the bystander left the scene (no surveillance).

The fourth variable concerned the type of supporting argument employed by the bystander. In the third study, this variable had had no apparent impact on participants' decision to report the theft. As previously noted, many participants in that study failed to attend to the bystander's supporting argument and thus failed to comprehend it. Therefore special efforts were made to increase the level of attention to, and comprehension of, the bystander's supporting arguments. Two types of supporting arguments were employed: one based on "principle" (i.e., "It's the right thing to do") and the other based on the probable effectiveness of the police in apprehending the suspect and returning the stolen money. We chose the argument based on principle because it was the reason most often given in the first four studies by participants who had agreed to report the theft. We selected the argument based on police effectiveness because victimization surveys have consistently shown that a major reason for victims' reluctance to report crimes to the police is their belief that "Nothing can be done" (Law Enforcement Assistance Administration, 1977a).

By including such arguments, we attempted to study possible interaction effects between participants' sex and type of supporting argument. Because of evidence showing that females are more likely than males to seek help from others in a variety of contexts (McMullen & Gross, 1983; Veroff, Douvan, & Kulka, 1981), we reasoned that female participants would be more responsive to arguments that emphasized the utility of such help seeking. In contrast, males being somewhat more reluctant to admit needing assistance because of self-esteem considerations (e.g., Nadler & Fisher, 1986), we reasoned that they would be more responsive to an appeal based on the moral principle that calling the police is the right thing to do.

METHOD

Design and Participants

Male and female participants were randomly assigned to conditions in a $2 \times 2 \times 2 \times 3$ factorial design. The variables were (1) sex of participant; (2) sex of bystander; (3) type of supporting argument (principle vs. police effectiveness); and (4) type of bystander surveillance (intentional, unintentional, or no surveillance). As in the previous four studies, participants were recruited by newspaper advertisements offering them $8 for 1¼ hours of light work. Extra efforts were made to include more males in the study. Of the 170 participants for whom appointments were made, 38 were eliminated for the following reasons: suspiciousness ($n = 15$), procedural error ($n = 5$), recognition of confederates ($n = 7$), failure to follow instructions ($n = 7$), emotional upset ($n = 3$), and health problems ($n = 1$). The remaining 132 participants consisted of 72 females and 60 males, of whom 113 were white and 19 black.

Procedure

The procedure was essentially the same as that employed in the previous study. The thief was played by a white male in his early 20s. The bystanders, who were played by two white males and two white females in their early 20s, always advised participants to report the theft.

Type of Supporting Argument. After the secretary left to look for her supervisor, the bystander advised participants to call the police and then offered one of two arguments to support this advice. In order to ensure that participants both attended to and comprehended the message, each argument consisted of four sentences rather than the two sentences employed in the third study. The argument based on *principle* was as follows: "You know, it's not the amount of money, it's the principle of the thing. He took something that didn't belong to him. What he did was wrong, and he shouldn't be allowed to get away with it. It's the right thing for you to call the police." The argument based on *police effectiveness* was as follows: "You know, the police will probably catch him. The secretary has the guy's address and phone number. And the police in Squirrel Hill [the local neighborhood] have a pretty good reputation with this sort of thing. It's the best thing for you to call the police."

Type of Bystander Surveillance. Upon returning from her unsuccessful search for her supervisor, the secretary proceeded to manipulate the bystander surveillance variable. In one third of the cases she asked the bystander to leave. The bystander replied, "No, I'm curious to see what he'll (she'll) do" (intentional surveillance). In another third of the cases the bystander asked if he (she) could leave. The secretary responded, "No, would you mind staying a little while longer?" (unintentional surveillance). In the remaining third of the instances the bystander asked if he or she could leave, and the secretary replied, "Yes, you're free to go" (no surveillance). As in the previous experiment, participants' willingness to report the theft was assessed by means of a four-point report score involving the use of three prods by the secretary.

RESULTS AND DISCUSSION

The success of the manipulations was assessed with questions posed to participants during the debriefing. In order to determine if participants correctly perceived the type of supporting argument employed by the bystander, participants were asked to identify the argument from a list of five shown to them; 98% correctly identified the argument used by the bystander. The success of the manipulation of type of bystander surveillance was measured by responses to an open-ended question which read, "What was the reason why Mr./Mrs. Johnson stayed in (left) the office?" An analysis of responses to this question revealed that 82% correctly recalled the reason for the bystander's presence or absence during the secretary's prodding of the participant.

This study produced the highest rate of reporting of the six experiments. Across all conditions the reporting rate was 60%. The impact of the independent variables on the report score was assessed by an analysis of covariance (with age as the covariate). This analysis yielded a single, marginally significant Sex of Participant × Type of Supporting Argument interaction, $F(1, 105) = 3.54$, $p < .07$. As predicted (see Table 3-2), the argument based on police effectiveness was more persuasive in inducing females to call the police, whereas the argument based on the moral principle that it was the "right thing to do" was more effective in inducing males to call the police. These data are consistent with the reasoning that females are more inclined than males to seek help from others and are responsive to appeals that emphasize the utility or effectiveness of such help. This interpretation is supported by findings from the first experiment (see Chapter 2), where it was shown that females (but not males) were more likely to call the police when the thief was still on the premises than when the thief had fled the scene. Presumably, females believed that with the thief still on the premises, the police would be more effective in helping them.

Interestingly, none of the other main or interaction effects proved to be significant. Sex similarity did not enhance the persuasiveness of the bystander's appeal. Male bystanders were no more influential than female bystanders, and female victims were no more susceptible to influence than male victims. The bystander's surveillance of the victim did not enhance the bystander's influence, and female victims were not more susceptible to influence when under surveillance by the bystander. Finally, the bystander's motives for maintaining surveillance had no significant impact on the victim's decision.

Participants' self-report data were consistent for the most part with the findings in the first four experiments. As in the previous studies, when asked to chose from a list of nine words the one that best described their reaction when first learning of the theft, the participants most often chose *angry* (21%) and *confused* (17%). Reporters, as opposed to nonreporters, perceived themselves as being more angered by the theft, $M = 4.58$ vs. 3.65, $t(130) = 2.70$, $p < .01$, and felt a greater moral obligation to call the police, $M = 4.36$ vs. 2.71, $t(130) = 4.66$, $p < .001$. The self-report data were particularly revealing about the dynamics of the perceived influence of the bystander. Reporters perceived that the bystander exerted greater influence over their decision to report the theft, $M = 5.19$ vs. 4.40, $t(130) = 4.72$, $p < .001$; believed that the bystander's argument had greater influence over

TABLE 3-2. ADJUSTED MEAN REPORTING SCORES AS A FUNCTION OF SEX OF PARTICIPANT AND TYPE OF SUPPORTING ARGUMENT[a]

Sex of participant	Type of supporting argument	
	Principle	Police effectiveness
Male	2.34	2.15
Female	2.08	2.78

[a]Higher numbers indicate earlier reporting of the crime.

their decision, $M = 3.88$ vs. 1.81, $t(130) = 6.27$, $p <.001$; and evaluated the bystander as being more persuasive, $M = 4.35$ vs. 3.12, $t(130) = 4.12$, $p <.001$. Reporters also perceived that the bystander's sex, $M = 2.38$ vs. 1.56, $t(130) = 2.17$, $p <.05$, and presence, $M = 3.21$ vs. 1.38, $t(130) = 5.54$, $p <.001$, exerted greater influence on their decision to notify the police. In order to learn more about the perceived qualities of bystanders that led to their influence, we asked participants who indicated that the bystander influenced their decision ($n = 76$) to select the most important reason for that influence from a list of 13. The reasons rated most frequently were "He/She seemed to be sincere" (33%), and "He/She seemed to understand my predicament" (21%).

This study shows that while males and females were marginally susceptible to different types of persuasive arguments, the similarity of sex between the bystander and the victim had no discernible impact on victims' reporting. Perhaps other dimensions of similarity are more important than sex, such as fate similarity. Victims may be more subject to influence by those who have shared a similar fate, such as a covictim. This similarity of fates may enhance covictims' credibility and thereby increase their influence over the victim. The sixth and final experiment was designed to study the effect of the influence agent's fate similarity on victims' decision to notify the police.

STUDY 6: THE EFFECT OF FATE
SIMILARITY ON THEFT-VICTIM DECISION MAKING

Social comparison theory (Festinger, 1954; Suls & Miller, 1977; Wood, 1989) provided the theoretical rationale for predicting an impact of fate similarity on victim decision making. Social comparison theory predicts that when people are uncertain about the accuracy of their opinions, they turn to others or compare their opinions with them, particularly those who are perceived as being similar on relevant dimensions. Social comparison theory predicts that when subjected to a social influence attempt by two others, a covictim and a bystander, theft victims will show a distinct preference for comparison with the individual who shared a similar fate, the covictim. This reasoning led us to predict that covictims, because they would be perceived as sharing the victim's perspective, would have greater credibility as communicators and would thus serve as more potent models for action (Berger, 1977). Similar reasoning suggested that victims would be interested in comparing themselves more to a victim who had suffered similar losses than to one whose losses were dissimilar. Thus, when confronted with three covictims, whose losses were less than, the same as, or greater than the victim's, victims would be most influenced by the covictim who had suffered the similar fate, that is, the covictim whose losses were the same as the victim's.

METHOD

Design and Participants

Male and female participants were randomly assigned to conditions in a 2 × 2 × 3 × 2 factorial design. The four independent variables were (1) covictim's decision to report (report vs. not report); (2) bystander's advice (report vs. not report); (3) magnitude of covictim's loss relative to participant's (greater, equal, less), and (4) sex of participant. As in the previous studies, participants were recruited by advertisements placed in local newspapers. Of the 159 participants for whom appointments were made, 27 were dropped for the following reasons: suspiciousness ($n = 9$), health problems ($n = 5$), recognition of one of the confederates ($n = 5$), failure to complete the task ($n = 5$), and procedural error ($n = 3$). The remaining 132 participants consisted of 72 females and 60 males, of whom 105 were white and 27 were black.

Procedure

As in the previous study, the role of thief was played by a white male in his 20s. The roles of covictim and bystander were played by two white females, also in their 20s, who alternated roles. All three confederates were present during each session. The procedure for creating the theft was basically the same as in the four previous experiments. In all conditions, participants learned that as a result of their failure to meet the norms for their age group on the transfer task, they had lost $11. The bystander in all conditions had exceeded the norms for her age group and had earned an additional $7. The amount lost by the covictim varied according to the condition. She lost more than the participant ($20), the same amount as the participant ($11), or less than the participant ($3). The thief's additional earnings were $30 when the covictim lost $20 and the participant lost $11, $21 when the covictim and the participant each lost $11, and $13 when the covictim lost $3 and the participant $11.

Several important procedural changes were introduced into the study. When the participant and the three confederates (bystander, covictim, and thief) were summoned to the "main office," they were met by the supervisor (one of two white males in their mid-20s who alternated in this role) rather than by the secretary. After everyone was seated, the supervisor instructed the participant and the covictim to surrender their losses to the thief. The supervisor then gave the bystander her winnings of $7. As in the previous studies, the proceedings were interrupted by an assistant who asked to speak with the supervisor in the next room. After a brief conversation, the supervisor returned and told everyone that there was a problem with the papers and that everyone should remain seated while he investigated. During his absence, the thief abruptly left the office. Upon returning, the supervisor asked where Mr. Collins (the thief) had gone. When informed of Mr. Collins's hasty departure, the supervisor proceeded to reveal the "evidence" that helped participants label the event as a theft. The procedure for accomplishing this labeling was identical to that employed in the first four experiments.

At this point, a major procedural change was introduced. Rather than prodding participants into calling the police, the supervisor merely addressed the two victims (i.e., the participant and the covictim) and asked if they wished to call the police. Before the participant could reply, the covictim and bystander both voiced their positions on reporting the theft. The order in which they spoke was counterbalanced so that we could control for order effects. (Subsequent analyses revealed no such effects.) In half the cases, the covictim stated that she would call the police, and in the remaining cases, she expressed her desire not to notify the police. Similarly, the bystander voluntarily offered the participant advice either to call or not to call the police. No supporting arguments were employed. Thus, in each instance, participants received an influence attempt from *both* the covictim and the bystander. In half the cases they agreed and in half they disagreed about whether or not the police should be notified.

Dependent Measure. A new measure of participants' willingness to call the police was introduced into this experiment to increase the generalizability of the findings. Rather than measuring the tendency to report in terms of which, if any, of the secretary's prods participants yielded to, a latency measure of reporting was constructed. An observer recorded the amount of time (in seconds) that it took participants to decide what to do after hearing the responses of the covictim and the bystander. This latency measure of reporting was based on the assumption that a decision to report the theft after a short latency represented more confidence in the decision to report than the same decision made after a longer latency. Similarly, a decision not to call the police made after a short latency represented greater confidence in the decision not to report than the same decision made after a longer latency. Employing this logic, we constructed a continuous "report score" in the following manner. First, +1 was assigned if the participant agreed to report, and a −1 if the participant failed to report. The report score was derived by multiplying this positive or negative sign by 201 (the longest obtained latency in seconds, plus 1) and subtracting from this the participant's latency score. This procedure yielded the following formula:

$$\text{Report Score} = +/-1 \times (201 - \text{latency score})$$

For example, a participant who agreed to call the police after a latency of 15 seconds would have a report score of 186 (+1 [201 − 15] = 186). If a participant took 50 seconds to decide to call the police, the report score would be

151 (+1 [201 – 50] = 151). The more positive the report score, the greater the willingness to report the theft. If the participant took 40 seconds to decide *not* to notify the police, the report score would be –161 (–1 [201 – 40] = – 161). In this case, the more negative the report score, the less the willingness to report the theft.

An additional question was asked of those who were unwilling to call the police: "Would you be willing to wait here until the police arrive?" Inclusion of this question made it possible to classify participants according to whether they were willing to call the police, whether they would at least wait until the police arrived, or whether they preferred to do neither.

RESULTS AND DISCUSSION

The success of the experimental manipulations was assessed by several questions posed to participants during the debriefing. Responses to these questions showed that 85% of the participants had correctly perceived the amount of the covictim's loss, and that 95% had correctly perceived that the bystander had not lost any money. With regard to the manipulation of the covictim's and bystander's positions on calling the police, 87% correctly identified the position taken by the covictim, but only 50% correctly identified the advice offered by the bystander.

For all conditions combined, the median response latency was 25.5 seconds. Across all conditions, 36% agreed to report the theft. Another 50% refused to report the theft but agreed to wait until the police arrived. The remaining 14% refused both options. An analysis of covariance was performed on the report scores, with participants' age once again serving as the covariate. This analysis yielded a significant covictim decision main effect, $F(1, 107) = 4.27$, $p < .05$. Victims' responses tended to mirror those of the covictim. That is, they were more willing to call the police when the covictim decided to call than when the covictim decided not to call. (This effect was significant even when the response latency-scores were normalized by means of a logarithmic transformation.) None of the other main or interaction effects was significant; neither the bystander's advice nor the amount of money lost by the covictim had a significant effect on victims' willingness to report the theft.

The bystander may have exerted less influence because the presence of the covictim distracted participants, causing them to pay less attention to the bystander's advice. As previously noted, in the postexperimental interview, just 50% correctly recognized the bystander's advice, whereas 87% correctly recognized the covictim's position on reporting the theft. This difference occurred despite the fact that the order in which the covictim and the bystander spoke was counterbalanced. The 50% correct recognition figure for the bystander's advice is decidedly less than the 86% figure achieved in Study 3, when only the bystander was present. The fact that the covictim shared the victim's fate may have aroused more intense social comparison concerns, causing victims to attend selectively to the actions of the covictim and to tune out the bystander.

On the basis of the postexperimental debriefing of participants, it appears that participants were aware of the greater influence exerted by the covictim. When asked to indicate whether the covictim and the bystander had each influenced their decision to report the theft, 55% said that they had been influenced by the covictim compared to just 24% who indicated that they had been influenced by the bystander, $\chi^2(1) = 26.8$, $p < .001$. The self-report data are particularly revealing of the dynamics of the influence exerted by the covictim and the bystander. Participants who said that they had been influenced by the covictim ($n = 73$) were asked to choose the reason, from a list of 15, that was most important in accounting for the influence. Three categories accounted for 67% of the responses: (1) social support (33%); (2) responsibility considerations (18%); and (3) normative influence (15%). The social support cluster included two items: "Her position was the same as mine, which gave me more confidence" (31%), and "I knew that I could count on her support in the future" (3%). Thus, having an ally in the situation served to *reinforce* rather than change the victim's position on reporting.

The responsibility cluster consisted of two items: "Since she wasn't going to call the police, I felt that I had to" (10%), and "Since she was going to call the police, I felt no need to do so myself" (8%). Interestingly, the two items composing this cluster produced a paradoxical or boomerang effect; participants responded in a manner opposite to the direction of intended influence. For these participants, the covictim's decision not to report the theft heightened their sense of responsibility to report, while the covictim's decision to call the police only served to diffuse such responsibility.

The third response category comprised items that reflected normative pressure to comply with or imitate the covictim's actions. It included items such as "Since she was going to call the police, I felt that I should do so too" (11%), "Since she wasn't going to call the police, I felt that I shouldn't either" (3%), and "She was watching me and I felt pressured to go along with her" (1%).

Similarly participants who said that they had been influenced by the bystander ($n = 32$) were asked to choose the reason, from a list of 14, that had influenced them the most. Consistent with data obtained in the earlier experiments, two reasons were cited most often: "She seemed to be sincere" (22%) and "She seemed to understand my predicament" (22%). Another 19% cited the bystander's dissimilarity as a reason for being influenced *not* to follow her advice. They endorsed the reason "Since she didn't lose any money, I didn't feel inclined to follow her advice."

Across all participants, reporting was correlated with a perceived moral obligation to report the crime ($r = .24$, $p < .01$) and a perceived influence by the covictim ($r = .16$, $p<.05$). Noteworthy are the variables that did *not* correlate with reporting, which included participants' self-reported anger and their attitudes towards the thief, the police, the covictim, and the bystander.

The results of Studies 5 and 6 suggest that fate similarity but not sex similarity increases the susceptibility of theft victims to social influence. Theft victims apparently responded to gross features of fate similarity, such as the other person's status as a covictim or a bystander, and not to finer features of similarity, such as the relative amount of the other's loss. An important confound in the design of the sixth experiment, however, raises an alternative interpretation of the data. Not only did the covictim and the bystander differ on the dimension of fate similarity, but they also differed with regard to the action that they took in the situation. The covictim acted as a model when she stated her intention to report (or not to report) the theft, while the bystander took a more passive stance, merely offering advice. Thus the covictim's greater influence, in part, may have been due to her willingness to take decisive action, calling to mind the aphorism "Actions speak louder than words." This reasoning is supported by a wealth of empirical studies testifying to the powerful impact of social modeling on behavior (e.g., Berger, 1977).

We were aware of the confound when we designed the study. We decided, nevertheless, to have the bystander and the covictim act in accordance with everyday expectations, in order to maintain the ecological validity of the experiment. That is, the bystander offered advice, and the covictim acted as a model for reporting or not reporting. We reasoned that participants would think it odd, and even suspicious, that a covictim would offer the victim advice but would not be willing herself to express an intention to report or not to report the theft. Similarly, we reasoned that participants would perceive as odd the behavior of a bystander who stated her intention to call (or not to call) the police, a decision more appropriately left to the victim in this situation.

We can conclude from this experiment that the expressed decision of a covictim to call or not to call the police has greater impact on theft victims' decision making than does advice from a bystander. Our results provide insight into how the covictims' actions enhanced their influence over the victim. The covictim's decision to report (or not to report) the theft (1) bolstered participants' initial resolve to call or not to call the police (social support function); (2) created normative pressure to conform with the covictim's action; and (3) served to enhance or diffuse feelings of responsibility to notify the police. Of the three forms of influence, the third produced a paradoxical effect, suggesting that when responsibility concerns are salient, victims are likely to act in a manner opposite that of the covictim.

SUMMARY AND CONCLUSIONS

Results from the six laboratory experiments suggest that theft victims' tendency to notify the police is a function of factors relating to the circumstances of the crime (e.g., the amount of money lost by the victim and the proximity of the thief), the victim's emotional state following discovery of the crime (e.g., the level of the victim's anger), and social influence factors. The experimental studies were particularly enlightening concerning the role of social influence in theft-victim decision making. They show quite clearly that under appropriate conditions, a relative stranger can influence victims of a small theft to notify the police. The actions of a covictim exert a particularly strong influence on theft-victim decision making, causing victims to all but ignore the advice of a bystander. In the absence of a covictim, however, victims are most likely to follow a bystander's advice when the advice is specific (e.g., "Call the police"), when the bystander remains at the victim's side while the victim is making his or her decision, and when the bystander offers to support the victim in his or her future dealings with the police and the criminal justice system.

While our experimental paradigm offers numerous advantages in studying victim decision making, such as the systematic manipulation and control of relevant variables, it does have liabilities. Foremost among these is the restriction placed on the external validity of the findings. Participants consisted solely of volunteers. They were unaware of the true nature of the research for which they had volunteered, but they were aware that they were participating in an experiment. This knowledge may have affected their behavior in unknown ways. Other liabilities derive from efforts to protect the welfare of participants. So that participants' distress would be minimized, the money stolen from them was not in their possession when they entered the laboratory; it was "earned" in the course of their participation. The impact of the independent variables might have been very different had the theft involved an equivalent amount of money from their wallets or purses.

Further efforts to protect participants' welfare by providing them with a full disclosure of the deceptions during the debriefing may have posed additional threats to the internal as well as the external validity of the data. Some participants may have shared the information with other would-be participants. There is evidence, in fact, that some participants had been told about the deceptions by former participants before they arrived and that they used this information to "victimize" the investigators. One instance of this type involved a female in her early 20s who showed up for her appointment dressed in a jogging outfit. While waiting for the experiment to begin, she mentioned to the confederate that a friend of hers had recently participated in the experiment. She was seen smiling while the instructions for the first task were being given. Upon learning that she had lost $12, she exclaimed, "Forfeit? You must be kidding!" Before anyone could react, she went out the door clutching the $12, left the building, and jogged up the street. After several fruitless efforts to reach her by phone, we finally made contact with a friend, who informed us that the participant had been in town only for the day and had left the city.

A more blatant example involved a male in his early 20s who did not wait to be informed of his loss of $11. After winning $12 on the first task, he simply put the money in his pocket and started to leave. When the by-stander asked where he was going, he just smiled. Efforts to reach him by telephone proved to be more successful than in the previous case. When contacted, he informed us that a friend of his had told him about the study and that he had planned beforehand to leave with the money. He was told that he could keep the $8 promised in the advertisement, but that he must return $11 of the $12. He agreed to do so. Several days passed without our hearing from him, and efforts to reach him by telephone were unsuccessful. The mood among the investigators and staff was one of frustration, anger, and resentment. We felt victimized and were determined not to let him get away with the "theft." It was not the amount of money that angered us, but the "principle of the thing." After a lengthy discussion among the investi-gators and the staff, a decision was reached to notify the police. The reac-tions of the two uniformed officers who arrived in response to our call was initially one of surprise and then amusement. When they informed us that there was a good chance that the incident would be written up in a local newspaper, we decided not to press charges. Like many theft victims, we decided that the incident was not worth reporting. Such incidents proved to be highly instructive, as they provided us with firsthand knowledge of how many of our participants must have felt when discovering that they had been victimized.

4

Eyewitness Identification
by Theft Victims

Since 1975, there has been much research on how eyewitnesses to a criminal event encode, retain, and retrieve information about what they have witnessed (see, e.g., Lloyd-Bostock & Clifford, 1983; Loftus, 1979; Yarmey, 1979). Although much useful information has been gained from this research, several investigators have questioned the generalizability of these results to naturally occurring situations (e.g., Malpass & Devine, 1980; Wells, 1978). For example, studies have questioned whether telling versus not telling eyewitnesses that a criminal event was staged affects the accuracy and confidence of their reports (Murray & Wells, 1982; Sanders & Warnick, 1981).

Other issues of generalizability concern the nature of the population of eyewitnesses (Brigham, Maass, Snyder, & Spaulding, 1982), the length of the retention interval involved, and the method of presenting the target person. Greater generalizability to the criminal justice system would probably occur if the eyewitnesses in research studies came from a heterogeneous population in terms of age, occupation, and other demographic characteristics than if all of the eyewitnesses were college students of roughly the same age and background. One would also expect greater generalizability if researchers used not only relatively short retention intervals of a few minutes but also relatively long retention intervals of several months (e.g., Egan, Pittner, & Goldstein, 1977; Malpass & Devine, 1980; Shepard, 1967). Moreover, one would expect to have greater external validity if the target person were presented initially in a live situation (e.g., Buckhout, Figueroa, & Hoff, 1975) than if the presentation were through photographs, slides, or videotapes, particularly if the situation were somewhat arousing (e.g., Johnson & Scott, 1976).

Another question of generalizability concerns the fact that in virtually all of the studies on eyewitness identification the subject-witness is a *bystander* rather than a *victim* (Wells, 1978). Bystanders are an important source of information about criminal events, but for many crimes it is the victim rather than a bystander who reports the crime to the police (Van Kirk, 1978). Moreover, for crimes like sexual assault, there are generally no bystander witnesses, only victims. It is important, therefore, to understand factors affecting both victims' and bystanders' abilities to identify criminal suspects.

The series of studies reported in this chapter was designed to extend the generalizability of findings on eyewitness identification from bystander-eyewitnesses to victim-eyewitnesses. The three studies dealt with four major issues: (1) the effect of making a lineup identification immediately after the crime on a subsequent identification two months later (Study 7—based on data from participants in experimental Study 5); (2) victims' ability to describe a criminal immediately after the crime and two months later (Study 8—based on data from participants in experimental Study 6); (3) the effect of the type of identification task after two months (i.e., photo identification or description) on a subsequent photo identification 15 months after the original viewing (Study 8—based on data from participants in experimental Study 6); and (4) the effect of victims' race on their ability to identify individuals of the same or a different race (Study 9—based on data from participants in experimental Studies 1, 2, 4, 5, and 6). We investigated additional questions by combining the data from the five field-experimental studies that explored questions about the accuracy of victim-witness identifications (i.e., Studies 1, 2, 4, 5, and 6).

STUDY 7: EFFECT OF A PRIOR LINEUP IDENTIFICATION ON A SUBSEQUENT LINEUP IDENTIFICATION

Research with bystander eyewitnesses suggests that persons who have previously seen a lineup containing the thief perform better in identifying that thief on a subsequent lineup task than do persons who have not previously performed a lineup task (Malpass & Devine, 1981). The purpose of the first experiment was to test this finding by using victim eyewitnesses rather than bystander eyewitnesses.

METHOD

The eyewitness identification studies reported here were continuations of the victimization experiments described in Chapters 2 and 3. That is, all participants in the eyewitness identification studies had just gone through the victimization experiment and had decided to call or not to call the police.

Participants

Participants were 132 individuals (60 males and 72 females) from the Pittsburgh metropolitan area who had been recruited through newspaper advertisements. There were 113 whites and 19 blacks in the study. They ranged in age from 17 to 59 ($M = 28.7$).

Procedure

Immediately after participants had made their reporting decision and had been debriefed, approximately half of them ($n = 58$) were asked to identify the thief from a photograph of a police lineup or to indicate that he was not present. This and all other lineup photographs used in these studies were black-and-white photographs that had been taken in the lineup room of the Pittsburgh Bureau of Police. The lineup photograph contained the thief and six distractors. The remaining participants ($n = 78$) were not shown the lineup photograph. Two months after the staged theft, all 132 participants were sent the same photograph that had been used in the first part of the study. Participants were paid \$2 for completing this questionnaire. On the questionnaire administered immediately after the reporting experiment and the one sent two months later, participants were also asked to rate their confidence in their choice on a nine-point scale ranging from *not at all confident* (1) to *very confident* (9).

RESULTS

Of the 132 participants who were sent a questionnaire after two months, 99 (75%) returned the questionnaire. Of this group, 43 had previously seen the lineup and 56 had not.

A chi-square analysis revealed that participants who had previously performed the lineup task were significantly more accurate after two months (98%) than were participants who had not performed the lineup task two months earlier (80%), $\chi^2(1) = 5.32$, $p < .05$. Although participants who had performed the lineup task previously were significantly more accurate, they were not significantly more confident in the correctness of their choice, $M = 8.33$, than were participants who had not performed the lineup task previously, $M = 7.76$, $t(96) = 1.48$, n.s. Participants who performed the lineup task twice achieved greater accuracy over time (78% vs. 98%), $\chi^2(1) = 4.17$, $p < .05$ (using McNemar's chi-square), and showed a significant increase in self-reported confidence, from a mean of 7.23 immediately after the theft to a mean of 8.33 two months later, $t(41) = 3.45$, $p < .05$.

A chi-square analysis was conducted to test whether the higher level of accuracy at two months might have resulted from differential attrition; inaccurate witnesses might have been more likely than accurate witnesses to drop out of the study. Although participants who dropped out tended to be less accurate (9 of 15 were correct on the initial identification) than those who had completed the identification at two months (36 of 43 were correct on the initial identification), a comparison of the two indicated no significant difference, $\chi^2(1) = 2.36$, $p = .12$. Similarly, witnesses with low confidence in the accuracy of their identification were no more likely to drop out of the study than were witnesses who were highly confident, $t < 1$. It must be noted that low statistical power to detect a true difference, rather than the absence of a real difference, may account for our failure to find differential attrition.

A comparison between those who had performed the lineup task immediately after the reporting experiment and those who performed it for the first time two months later found no significant difference in accuracy between the two groups, $\chi^2 < 1$. Moreover, there was no significant difference in confidence between those who had seen the lineup immediately afterward, $M = 7.24$, and those who saw it for the first time two months later, $M = 7.76$, $t(112) = 1.26$, n.s.

DISCUSSION

Results from this study are consistent with those using bystanders as eyewitnesses (Malpass & Devine, 1981). In our study, victims who had been shown a lineup containing the thief immediately after the reporting experiment performed better on the lineup identification task after two months than did a control group of victims who had not performed the earlier lineup-identification task. A possible reason for this effect was the participants' opportunity for rehearsal of the thief's characteristics and, presumably, deeper processing of this information (Craik & Lockhart, 1972). In their study, Malpass and Devine (1981) found that those subjects who had previously seen a lineup containing the vandal were significantly more accurate than were subjects who had previously seen a lineup not containing the vandal and subjects who had not previously seen a lineup. Apparently, the prior lineup must contain the criminal for eyewitness accuracy to be maintained. Because this condition was met in our study, it is not surprising that those participants who had performed the first lineup task were more accurate than were those who had not. The same reasoning could account for the increase in confidence over time. This increase may have resulted from the fact that participants were given an opportunity to rehearse their answer to a rather easy lineup task (79% of those viewing the lineup for the first time were accurate). Another possible explanation is that participants, most of whom had been correct initially, may simply have remembered whom they had chosen before, rather than who the thief actually was. This explanation cannot be discounted in our study. Surprisingly, six of seven participants who had been inaccurate on the initial identification were accurate on the identification at two months. One possible reason for this improvement is that witnesses made their identifications under more favorable conditions two months after the theft than immediately after the theft. Participants were probably less aroused and certainly under less time pressure during the second identification than during the first.

If we assume that participants who made a prior identification from a lineup containing the actual offender are more accurate on a subsequent identification from the same lineup containing the offender than are participants who did not make a prior identification, a question arises concerning the nature of the prior identification task (i.e., recognition vs. recall). Does the prior identification have to involve a lineup? Were we to ask participants instead merely to describe or recall the thief's characteristics, might this approach enhance accuracy on a subsequent lineup identification task as well as or better than a prior lineup identification? It could be argued that the greater effort needed to perform the recall task might facilitate retention better than the less effortful recognition task. The next study investigated this question.

STUDY 8: EFFECT OF TYPE OF IDENTIFICATION TASK ON SUBSEQUENT LINEUP IDENTIFICATIONS

Study 8 had two purposes. One purpose was to learn the effect of asking victims to describe the thief on their subsequent ability to identify him in a lineup. Second, we wanted to measure the accuracy of victim-eyewitness identifications of a "criminal" over a fairly long period of time (i.e., 15 months). In many studies the recall or recognition measure is taken on the same day, often within a few hours of presentation. Only a few studies have examined eyewitness recall of a criminal event over the longer period of a few months (e.g., Egan *et al.*, 1977; Malpass & Devine, 1981).

METHOD

Participants

Participants were 132 individuals, 60 males and 72 females. They ranged in age from 17 to 59 (*M* = 31.5); 105 were white and 27 were black.

All of these individuals had participated in the experimental studies of victim reporting.

Procedure

After participants decided to report or not to report the theft, they were debriefed, and then they answered questions related to the reporting study. In addition to these questions, all participants were asked to give a description of the thief, who was white. In particular, they were asked to recall the following information: the thief's hair color, the length of his hair, the color of his eyes, his height, his weight, any marks on his face, any facial hair, his age, and the clothes he was wearing. Participants were asked to give this information either in the above order or in the reverse order, so that we could test whether the order of initial questioning might affect subsequent recall and recognition.

Approximately two months after participating in the study, participants were sent a questionnaire. Half of them were asked once again to describe the thief. The remaining half of the participants were asked to identify the thief from a lineup photograph or to indicate that he was not present in the photograph. The lineup contained the thief and six distractors. Participants were paid $2 for completing this questionnaire.

Approximately 15 months after their participation in the reporting experiment, participants who had returned the questionnaire after 2 months were sent another questionnaire, which contained one of two lineup photographs. One lineup was identical to the one sent to half of them 13 months earlier. The other lineup photograph did not contain the thief; it contained only the six distractors. Thus, this lineup was a "blank" lineup, and any response other than that the thief was not present was incorrect. Participants were paid $3 for completing this questionnaire. On all the questionnaires involving lineups, participants were also asked to rate on a nine-point scale their confidence in their choice.

RESULTS

Rates of Participation

All 132 participants gave a description of the thief immediately after the reporting experiment ended. Two months later, 81 of the participants (61%) completed the questionnaire sent to them. They included 32 males and 49 females, of whom 73 were white and 8 were black. They ranged in age from 17 to 59 ($M = 33.6$). Of these 81 participants, 59 (73%) returned the questionnaire that had been sent after 15 months. These participants included 21 males and 38 females, of whom 57 were white and 2 were black. They ranged in age from 17 to 59 ($M = 35.2$).

Description of the Thief

All participants described the thief immediately after the reporting experiment ended, and 37 described him again two months later. For each of the nine items that participants were asked to recall (e.g., hair length and eye color), a range of responses was judged to be correct. For example, the reported height of the thief was judged to be correct if it was within two inches of the thief's actual height. Participants' descriptions of each of the nine items about the thief were coded as correct, incorrect, or no answer given. Results of this coding are presented in Table 4-1.

The range of correct responses varied depending on the particular category; therefore, only gross comparisons of the percentages of correct responses can be made across categories. In general, participants tended to be most accurate regarding hair color, hair length, and the presence or absence of facial hair, and least accurate regarding eye color, age, and the presence or absence of facial marks. Participants gave an answer for most items, even though it may have been incorrect. For three items (eye color, facial marks, and dress), however, the percentage of "no answers" was relatively high.

Generally, the percentage of correct responses *within* a category decreased only slightly over time, and there was little change in the percentage of "no answers." A 2 × 2 chi-square test was conducted for each of the nine descriptors, with time (immediate or two-month delay) as one dimension and score (correct or incorrect) as the other dimension. None of these tests was statistically significant.

In order to test whether or not the order of the questions affected recall, we created a composite score for each participant by adding the scores for each of the nine items described. For this measure, a three-point scale was used for each item: 3 if the item was correctly described, 2 if no information was given or the participant said he or she did not know the answer, and 1 if the participant gave incorrect information. Based on this

TABLE 4-1. CODING OF PARTICIPANTS' DESCRIPTIONS OF THE THIEF (PERCENTAGES)

	Immediate (*n* = 132)			Two months' delay (*n* = 37)		
	Correct	No answer	Incorrect	Correct	No answer	Incorrect
Hair color	86	5	9	84	3	13
Hair length	82	3	15	65	—	35
Facial hair	77	11	12	76	11	13
Height	67	—	33	59	3	38
Weight	58	—	42	43	—	57
Dress	46	35	19	30	43	27
Eye color	40	42	18	35	41	24
Age	31	—	69	16	8	76
Facial marks	25	70	5	38	51	11

composite measure, no effect for the order of the requested information was found, $t(130) = 1.09$, n.s.

Lineup Results

Of the 44 participants who performed the lineup identification at two months, 20 (45%) correctly identified the thief, 10 (23%) mistakenly said that the thief was not in the lineup, and 14 (32%) incorrectly identified someone other than the thief. The mean level of confidence was 7.23. The correlation of accuracy with confidence at two months was significant and negative, $r = -.28$, $p < .05$.

Of the 59 participants who returned the questionnaire after 15 months, 22 (37%) correctly identified the thief or correctly said that the thief was not present, 15 (25%) mistakenly said that the thief was not in the lineup, and 22 (37%) incorrectly identified someone other than the thief. Of the 22 mistaken identifications, 5 (23%) involved the identification of a person whom the participant had previously seen: the supervisor. A chi-square analysis performed on the responses of the 59 participants who completed the lineup task after 15 months revealed no significant difference in accuracy between those who had previously performed the lineup task at 2 months and those who had previously described the thief at 2 months ($\chi^2 < 1$). There was also no significant difference in the confidence of the two groups at 15 months, $t(57) = 1.64$, n.s.

A comparison of the accuracy of those participants who performed the lineup task for the first time at 2 months (45%) with those who performed it for the first time after 15 months (39%) yielded no significant difference between the two groups, $\chi^2 < 1$. However, those participants who performed the lineup task at 15 months for the first time were significantly less confident in their choice ($M = 5.00$) than were participants who performed the task for the first time after 2 months, $M = 7.23$, $t(64) = 3.19$, $p < .01$.

It should be noted again that the 59 participants who returned the questionnaire after 15 months had received one of two lineup photographs. Of the 59, 44 had received the same lineup photograph that had been used after 2 months. Examination of the responses of these 44 participants revealed that 16 (36%) correctly identified the thief, 15 (34%) mistakenly said that the thief was not in the lineup, and 13 (30%) made an incorrect identification. The remaining 15 participants who returned the questionnaire after 15 months had received a lineup that did not contain the thief (a "blank" lineup). Of this group, 6 (40%) correctly stated that the thief was not present, whereas 9 (60%) incorrectly identified someone in the lineup.

The mean level of confidence after 15 months, including that of participants who had and had not seen the earlier lineup, was 5.71, which represents a significant decline in confidence from the mean level at 2 months, $M = 7.23$, $t(100) = 3.10$, $p < .01$. When only those participants who had performed the lineup task on both occasions were included in the analysis (n = 44) and the 15 participants who had seen a blank lineup were excluded, mean confidence at 15 months (M = 6.14) was still significantly lower than at 2 months, M = 7.29, $t(34)$ = 2.69, $p < .02$.

For all participants (n = 59), the correlation of accuracy with confidence after 15 months was not significant, $r = -.11$, n.s. However, when only data from the 44 participants who had seen a lineup containing the thief were included in the analysis (i.e., when the 15 participants who saw a blank lineup were excluded), the correlation was significant and *negative, r = -.33,* $p < .05$. That is, the greater their confidence, the *less* accurate they tended to be. For those participants who had seen the lineup for the first time after 15 months, the correlation between accuracy and confidence was essentially zero, $r = .02$, n.s.

DISCUSSION

Results from Study 7 suggested that participant-victims who had made an identification immediately after the theft were more accurate on a lineup identification task 2 months later than were participant-victims who performed their only lineup identification task at 2 months. Study 8 found no difference in the accuracy of victims' identification of the thief 15 months after the crime as a function of the type of memory task (i.e., recall vs. recognition) given 2 months after the crime. This failure to find a significant difference between groups performing the two types of tasks may have been due to a number of factors. These include low statistical power to detect a difference, selective attrition of the sample, and the two-month interval after the crime.

It is also possible that it is not the type of task, but the fact of doing the eyewitness identification task, that is important in subsequent eyewitness-identification accuracy. This suggestion runs somewhat counter to a body of research showing no significant relationship between accuracy of recognition and accuracy of description (e.g., Chance & Goldstein, 1976; Pigott & Brigham, 1985). For a definitive conclusion to be drawn, however, a three-condition experiment would have to be conducted in which all victim-participants initially performed a recall task, a recognition task, or no identification task and then, at some later point, performed the same recognition task.

With regard to descriptions of the thief, it was clear that some information (e.g., hair color and hair length) was recalled quite well but that other information was recalled relatively poorly, either because of a high error rate (e.g., weight and age) or because of a high rate of "no answers" (e.g., eye color and facial marks). In one relevant study, Kuehn (1974) examined 100 police reports in which victims of violent crimes described up to nine physical characteristics of their unknown assailants. A rank order of the frequency with which characteristics of assailants were described revealed the following, from most to least frequent: sex, age, height, build, race, weight, complexion, hair color, and eye color. Just 7% of the victims failed to mention the assailant's sex, whereas 77% failed to give the assailant's eye color.

Consistent with Kuehn's archival study, over 40% of the participants in our study did not give a response regarding the color of the thief's eyes. This high rate of "no answers" for some characteristics, such as eye color and facial marks, suggests that these items may never have been encoded. Alternatively, the inner features of the face, like eye color and facial marks, may have been encoded with less strength than were external characteristics, such as hair length. Given the same rate of decay for the two types of memory traces, the memory traces of inner features would be lost faster than would memory traces of external characteristics (Walker-Smith, 1978).

The data pertaining to confidence in this study present two interesting findings. First, the significant decline in confidence from 2 months to 15 months is evidence that confidence can be affected merely by the passage of time as well as by other factors, such as a briefing before the identification (Wells, Ferguson, & Lindsay, 1981). It should be noted that the lineup in this study was more difficult than the one used in Study 7, as indicated by the fact that less than half of the participants were correct the first time they saw it (45% in Study 8 vs. 80% in Study 7). Moreover, the time interval between lineup presentations in this study (13 months) was much longer than the one used in Study 7 (2 months). The second interesting finding is that at both 2 and 15 months, the correlation between accuracy and confidence was *negative,* lending further support to the notion that the relationship between the two is not strongly positive (e.g., Wells, Lindsay, & Ferguson, 1979; see also Kassin, Ellsworth, & Smith, 1989).

STUDY 9: SAME RACE AND CROSS-RACE IDENTIFICATIONS

Previous research by others has generally indicated that observers are better able to identify persons of their own race than those of a different race (e.g., Anthony, Copper, & Mullen, 1991; Brigham & Barkowitz, 1978; Platz & Hosch, 1988) although there is some evidence that this generalization applies to whites but not to blacks (Cross, Cross, & Daly, 1971). The purpose of Study 9 was to test the generalizability of previous findings on cross-racial identification to the case of *victims* of a live theft.

METHOD

Participants and Procedure

Participants were 390 individuals (120 males and 270 females; 358 whites and 32 blacks), who ranged in age from 17 to 61 ($M = 31.9$). In the initial reporting experiment, approximately one third of the participants (32%) saw a white thief and about two thirds (68%) saw a black thief. Two months after participating in the reporting experiment, participants were sent a lineup photograph containing the actual thief. The lineup containing the white thief consisted of the thief and six distractors. The lineup containing the black thief consisted of the thief and five distractors. Participants were asked to identify the thief or to indicate that he was not present in the lineup, and to rate their confidence in their choice on a nine-point scale. Participants were paid $2 for completing the questionnaire. The 390 individuals who completed the questionnaire, which was sent to them two months after the reporting experiment, represented 69% of all individuals who had participated in Study 1.

RESULTS

Two months after the theft, white participants were significantly more accurate in identifying a white thief (71% correct) than in identifying a black thief (49% correct), $\chi^2(1) = 54.19$, $p < .01$. Black participants were not significantly different in the accuracy of their identification of black thieves or white thieves (87% and 77%, respectively; $\chi^2 < 1$). It should be emphasized, however, that the absence of a significant difference may have been due to the low power of the test, as there were only 32 black participants. Overall, blacks were slightly more accurate than were whites, but the difference was not significant, $\chi^2(1) = 3.05$, $p = .08$.

A 2×2 (Race of Thief $\times$ Race of Participant) analysis of variance performed on the confidence ratings of the 378 participants who completed the measure yielded a significant main effect for race of thief, $F(1, 374) = 72.58$, $p < .001$. Participants were more confident when the thief was white ($M = 6.66$) than when the thief was black ($M = 3.82$). Neither the main effect for race of participant nor the interaction between race of thief and race of participant attained significance (both F's < 1).

The correlations between confidence and accuracy for white participants paralleled these results. For white participants, confidence and accuracy were significantly related when the thief was white ($r = .12$, $p < .05$, $n = 243$) but not when the thief was black ($r = -.12$, n.s., $n = 105$). The pattern was less clear, however, for black participants. Confidence and accuracy were not significantly related when the thief was white ($r = .14$, n.s., $n = 16$) and were *negatively* related when the thief was black ($r = -.64$, $p < .01$, $n = 14$). For both black and white participants, therefore, when the identification was cross-racial, confidence and accuracy were not significantly related. For same-race identifications, however, the relationship between accuracy and confidence was positive for white participants and negative for black participants.

DISCUSSION

Many prior studies indicate that same-race identification is more accurate than cross-race identification. This study suggests that this generalization is true for white victims but not for black victims. Consistent with prior research, we found that white victims identified white thieves significantly better than they identified black thieves. However, we found that black victims identified white thieves as well as they did black thieves (consistent with Cross *et al.*, 1971). The sample size of black victims was small, however, and the conclusion must therefore remain tentative.

RESULTS USING DATA FROM ALL PARTICIPANTS

Data from all participants receiving the lineup photograph in Studies 7–9 were combined so that additional analyses could be conducted. These analyses revealed that two months after their victimization, participants' accuracy correlated negatively with age ($r = -.09$, $p < .05$), younger participants tending to be slightly more accurate. In general, accuracy at two months was significantly correlated with participants' confidence in their choice, although the correlation was relatively small ($r = .09$, $p < .05$). Participants who agreed to report the theft tended to be more accurate after two months than were those who decided not to report, $t(388) = 1.89$, $p < .06$; and they were more confident, $t(381) = 2.27$, $p < .05$. There was no significant sex difference in accuracy ($\chi^2 < 1$) or in confidence, $t(381) = 1.63$, n.s. A correlational analysis revealed that two months after the victimization experience, recalled anger was positively related to accuracy and confidence, such that participants who recalled themselves as feeling more angry at the time of the theft were more accurate ($r = .11$, $p < .05$) and more confident of the correctness of their choice ($r = .16$, $p < .005$) than were participants who reported feeling less angry.

In order to determine which variables were the best predictors of accuracy at two months, a discriminant function analysis was performed. This analysis uses a group of discriminating variables to predict a discrete variable. The following discriminating variables were used to predict eyewitness accuracy at two months: (1) participants' sex, race, age, income, confidence in their identification, and reporting decision (report/no report); the delay between the date of participation in the experiment and the date the questionnaire was sent (delay); and the race of the thief; (2) the three two-way interactions involving race of participant, race of thief, and confidence in identification; and (3) the three-way interaction of race of participant, race of thief, and confidence in identification. Thus we performed a within-level discriminant-function analysis with a hierarchical structure, so that the main effects were entered first, the two-way interactions were entered second, and the three-way interaction was entered last.

Results showed that the predictive importance of these variables, from most to least predictive, was the following: race of thief, delay, race of participant, sex of participant, age of participant, interaction of race of thief and confidence, interaction of race of participant and race of thief, and the three-way interaction of race of participant, race of thief, and confidence. The overall discriminant function was highly significant, $\chi^2(8) = 36.62$, $p < .001$. The canonical correlation of this function with accuracy was .31. The use of dichotomous discriminating variables violates the requirements of a multivariate normal distribution and equal group covariance matrices, so the reported statistics should be viewed with some caution. Nevertheless, the relatively large sample size allows some deviation from these requirements (Klecka, 1980).

Race of participant was the third best predictor of eyewitness accuracy in the discriminant function. This finding was surprising because blacks were only marginally more accurate than whites ($p = .08$). This result may have arisen because race of participant, although not a very good predictor in absolute terms, was a better predictor than most of the other variables.

GENERAL DISCUSSION

These studies make an important contribution to the literature on eyewitness identification, because they are among the few studies that have examined the accuracy of and confidence in identifications made by crime victims. There might be relative differences in accuracy between victims and bystanders (a question not tested here; see Hosch & Cooper, 1982; Hosch & Bothwell, 1990; Kassin, 1984; Ruback & Greenberg, 1985), but these studies suggest that victim eyewitnesses are subject to the same shortcomings and biases as are bystander eyewitnesses. For example, our results indicated (consistent with previous research on bystanders) that victims' recall and recognition accuracy decreases over a period of 15 months. In addition, our findings are consistent with other work showing that participants given a blank lineup often pick someone as the culprit rather than say that the person is not present, particularly if they have seen the innocent person before (Loftus, 1976).

Another unique feature of our research in comparison to earlier studies concerns the length of time that participants were exposed to the thief. Exposure times in earlier studies have often been only a few minutes, whereas in our studies victims were exposed to the thief for about 50 minutes. Despite this difference, however, the results of our research were generally consistent with earlier research findings. This consistency suggests that memory for a crime may be based more on the *level* of processing than on the mere duration of exposure (Wells & Murray, 1983).

There are two important differences between the situation that participants experienced in these studies and the situation some real crime victims experience. First, most victims in our studies probably did not realize they had been victims of a crime until after the thief had already left the scene. If they had learned of their victimization while the thief was still present, perhaps they would have paid closer attention to his characteristics and would have been more accurate in their identification.

This hypothesis is consistent with the results of a study by Leippe, Wells, and Ostrom (1978), who found that the knowledge that a stolen object was of great value rather than of low value improved the accuracy of identification when this knowledge was gained before the theft occurred, but not after its occurrence. As reported elsewhere (Greenberg, Wilson, & Mills, 1982), 120 participants in Study 9 were given an opportunity to discover the theft before the thief left the premises. Among this group, those who had lost $20 were more accurate in identifying the thief from the lineup photo two months later than were those who had lost just $3. These data extend Leippe *et al.*'s (1978) findings to include victim-eyewitnesses as well as bystander-eyewitnesses. As we stated earlier, however, most victims in the current research did not learn of their victimization until *after* the thief had left the scene.

A second difference between these studies and real criminal victimization situations concerns the witnesses' knowledge of the staged nature of the theft when they were asked to make the identification. In our studies, when participants' recall and recognition were assessed, participants already knew that the crime had been staged. They may therefore have differed from real crime victims in their motives for a correct identification (e.g., they did not have a desire to "get even"). Moreover, participants may have been more willing to guess when identifying the thief of the staged crime than they would have been had the crime been perceived as real when they made their identification (Malpass & Devine, 1980; Wells, 1978). Thus, the error rate may have been higher than that of real victims. It should be noted, however, that Sanders and Warnick (1981) found no difference in accuracy between those subjects who believed that their identification would have real consequences and those who believed that their identification would not have real consequences. Similarly, Murray and Wells (1982) found no simple effect on accuracy when participants knew that a criminal event had been staged.

An additional point about the generalizability of our studies is that participants who responded to the questionnaires approximately 2 months and 15 months after they had participated in the reporting experiment did so voluntarily. Thus, it may be that the reported rates of accuracy may have been affected, presumably toward increased accuracy, by the fact that the responders were self-selected. The individuals who were likely to return the questionnaire might also have been more accurate eyewitnesses. Internal analyses of our data suggest no significantly different dropout rate for accurate and inaccurate victims, but the question of self-selection may still be important.

In real criminal situations, eyewitnesses who are asked to identify criminals in a lineup are often volunteers in that they have reported the crime to the police. Our finding that after two months, reporters tended to be more accurate and more confident than nonreporters suggests that self-selection may indeed have an effect on eyewitness accuracy in the criminal justice system. This suggestion is related to Wells's point (1978) that most research on eyewitness identification may be biased toward showing that eyewitnesses are not very accurate, since *all* participants in these studies were asked to identify the criminal, whereas in the "real world" usually only those who volunteer that they saw the criminal are asked to make identifications.

In support of the notion that volunteers and nonvolunteers may differ in some other relevant way, Pigott and Brigham (1985) found that for experimental participants who chose someone from a lineup there was a significant positive correlation between decision accuracy and confidence, whereas for participants who did not make a lineup choice the correlation was not significantly different from zero (see also Fleet, Brigham, & Bothwell, 1987). Clearly, more work is needed on the relationship between self-selection and eyewitness accuracy.

The three studies reported in this chapter took advantage of our unique opportunity to investigate *victims'* recall and recognition abilities as eyewitnesses to crime. We found that victims who had performed an earlier lineup identification task were more accurate on a lineup identification task than were victims who had not performed the earlier task. We also found that victims were fairly accurate in describing some aspects of the thief (e.g., his hair color) and fairly inaccurate at describing other aspects (e.g., his age). There was no significant change over a two-month period in the accuracy of these descriptions. In the final study, we found that white victims were significantly more accurate in making same-race than in making cross-race identifications. Our sample of white participants was large enough to give us some confidence in this conclusion.

Because of the similarities among the different field-experimental studies, we felt justified in pooling eyewitness-identification data across experiments. In the next chapter, we also combine data across the studies in order to obtain a better understanding of what factors are related to reporting and to accurate recall of information.

5

Analyses across Experimental Studies

Chapters 2 through 4 have described in considerable detail the experimental studies we conducted to investigate factors related to victims' decisions to report or not to report a crime to the police and their abilities as eyewitnesses to recall information about the thief and to recognize him in a lineup. In this chapter, we combine data from across Studies 1–6 in order to better understand factors affecting and affected by the reporting decision.

This chapter consists of three parts. In the first part, we look more carefully at the success of the studies in terms of internal and external validity, that is, the extent to which we can believe that the findings are true of our sample and the extent to which we can generalize the findings to other types of victims. In the second part, we look across the studies at factors related to and predictive of reporting, focusing particularly on the role of individual factors versus situational factors in the reporting decision. In the third part, we examine how the reporting decision was related to victims' recall of the events in the experiment and of their actions and perceptions afterward.

VALIDITY OF THE EXPERIMENTAL STUDIES

Internal validity refers to the confidence with which we can say that the significant differences obtained in an experiment are due to the experimental manipulations. *External validity* refers to the extent to which the results are generalizable to situations outside the experiment (Campbell, 1957). In this section, we first address the question of internal validity by showing that almost all participants found the procedure believable and that they were engrossed in the experimental situation. We then address the question of external validity by examining the types of individuals who participated.

INTERNAL VALIDITY

Our assumption is that the internal validity of the studies was affected not only by our attempts to eliminate random and systematic errors but also by the degree to which participants believed and took seriously the experimental procedure. For each of the studies individually, we have described our methods for randomly assigning participants to conditions and for eliminating potentially confounding variables. Here we focus on the experimental realism of the studies (Aronson & Carlsmith, 1968), that is, the degree to which the manipulations had an impact on the participants.

The first measure of impact is whether or not participants were suspicious of the experimental procedure. For each participant, this judgment was made by three different individuals: the thief, the bystander, and the supervisor (i.e., the experimenter). After their experimental roles were completed, the thief and the bystander each used seven-point scales, ranging from *not at all* (1) to *very much* (7), to rate how suspicious the participants were during the experiment. The average rating by the bystander was 1.34, with 81% of the participants rated at 1, 93% rated at 2 or less, and 97% rated at 3 or less. The average rating by the thief was 1.49, with 62% of the participants rated at 1, 93% rated at 2 or less, and 97% rated at 3 or less.

Further, during the postexperimental debriefing, the experimenter interviewed each participant to determine if he or she was suspicious. Across Studies 1–6, a total of 75 participants were judged by the experimenter to be suspicious, and their data, therefore, were not included in the statistical analyses. This number was 8.9% of the number of usable and suspicious participants and was 8.3% of all participants, including those who were eliminated because they did not follow instructions or could not complete the tasks.

The experimenters' ratings of the unexcluded participants' suspicion level on the same seven-point scale used by the bystander and the thief were slightly higher than were the ratings by the bystander and the thief. The experimenter's average rating of participants' suspicion was 1.76, with 57% of the participants rated at 1, 80% rated at 2 or less, 91% at 3 or less, and

97% at 4 or less. These numbers may be somewhat inflated because, by the time the experimenter made his rating, participants had already been told in the debriefing that there was more involved in the study than had originally been disclosed to them.

Admittedly, the experimental staff may have been somewhat biased perceivers, in that they had a stake in the determination that participants were not suspicious. However, the experimenters asked several questions to determine exactly how much participants suspected about the procedure. Most participants were surprised when the deception was revealed, and even those who had been somewhat suspicious had had only vague, general feelings about the study rather than specific ideas about what was actually being tested. In sum, we are confident that participants found the study believable.

The believability of the experimental situation is only the first step in achieving internal validity. As a second step, participants have to be involved in the procedure. Our primary measure of participants' involvement in the experiment was the number of worksheets they completed during the eight minutes of the second task, which we called the *bookkeeping task*. The number of completed worksheets ranged from 5 to 23, with a mean of 10.85, a median of 11, and a mode of 11. Given the amount of effort required for participants to copy 10 two-digit numbers from the card to the worksheet, put their initials in the upper-right-hand corner, clip the card and worksheet together, put them in an envelope, and place the envelope in an outbox, the production of 11 completed worksheets in eight minutes suggests that participants worked hard to earn more money.

Assuming that participants found the experiment to be involving, the next question was whether they perceived the manipulations as we intended them to be perceived. There were three measures that indicated the degree to which the experimental procedures worked: the number of papers participants believed had been taken, the amount of money they believed they had lost, and the extent to which they believed they had earned the money they had lost. With regard to the number of papers participants believed were taken, the mean was 3.88, the median was 4, and the mode was 4. As the actual number of papers taken was 4, the manipulation appears to have been perceived as intended.

The second check of the manipulations was the amount of money participants believed they had lost. The actual amount was $11, which was the amount of money participants had to give to the thief during the final settling of accounts in the secretary's office. Although participants' responses to the question of how much money they had lost ranged from $0 to $40, the mean response of $11.79 ($SD$ = 4.64) was very close to the correct figure. Moreover, 57% of the responses were $11. Only 12% of the responses were under $10, and 13% were $17 or more.

The final manipulation check was the extent to which participants believed they had earned the money that the thief had taken. Participants made this judgment on a seven-point scale that ranged from *not at all* (1) to *very much* (7). Across participants, the average was 4.32 (Mdn = 4). The modal response, given by 29% of the participants, was 7.

In summary, participants showed a low rate of suspicion, appeared to be highly involved in the task, and perceived the experimental manipulations as intended. We can conclude, therefore, that the procedure had experimental realism. Further, because of our success in eliminating confounding and in randomly assigning participants to experimental condition, we can conclude that the studies were internally valid.

External Validity

In addition to having high experimental realism, the experimental studies also have some degree of external validity. External validity (the extent to which the results can be generalized to other populations and settings) is a function of the degree to which the 768 participants were representative of adults in general, as well as the similarity of the theft in the field-experimental paradigm to other kinds of thefts in the "real world." With regard to the first question (the issue of the representativeness of the participants in the study), our sample came from a relatively broad cross-section of the community. As noted in Chapter 2 and as shown in Table 5-1, the participants in the six experimental studies included both blacks and whites, who ranged in age from 16 to 66. They came from diverse religious backgrounds, family income levels, and occupations. Moreover, their educational backgrounds ranged from leaving school in junior high to earning graduate and professional degrees, most participants having obtained a high school diploma.

The experimental participants were fairly representative of the metropolitan Pittsburgh area at the time. According to 1980 census statistics (Bureau of the Census, 1982), blacks represented 25% of the population of the City of Pittsburgh and just 8% of the population of the greater Pittsburgh metropolitan area. With regard to other demographic characteristics, the Pittsburgh Standard Metropolitan Statistical Area was 52% female, the median age of residents was 33.5, and the median household income was $18,069. About 68% of the population 25 years and older were high school graduates.

Even though the subject sample was generally representative of the larger community, there was some overrepresentation of females, younger-age individuals, low-income individuals, homemakers, and the unemployed. This overrepresentation of housewives and the unemployed probably occurred because most of the experiments were conducted during the work week between 9:00 A.M. and 5:00 P.M. In other words, individuals who worked during standard work hours were less likely to be participants

TABLE 5-1. DESCRIPTION OF 768 PARTICIPANTS
IN THE SIX EXPERIMENTAL STUDIES (PERCENTAGES)[a]

Sex	263 males	34
	505 females	66
Race	128 blacks	17
	640 whites	83
Age	Range 16–66	
	Mean = 30.7	
	Median = 27	
Religion	134 Protestant	35
	134 Catholic	35
	44 Jewish	12
	16 other	4
	52 atheist or agnostic	14
	(388 did not answer)	
Family income	319 $0–$6,000	42
	201 $6,001–$12,000	27
	125 $12,001–$18,000	17
	49 $18,001–$24,000	6
	57 over $24,000	8
	(17 did not answer)	
Education	28 junior high only	4
	413 high school diploma or advanced job training	55
	48 associate degree	6
	209 college degree	28
	52 advanced degree	7
	(18 did not answer)	
Occupation	24 artisan	4
	134 homemaker	20
	170 blue-collar worker	26
	79 white-collar business	12
	116 white-collar professional	18
	9 retired	1
	8 other	1
	121 student	18
	(109 did not answer)	
Employment status	158 employed	31
	354 unemployed	69
	(256 did not answer)	

[a]Percentages are of those who responded, excluding missing data.

in our study, even though we conducted some of the experiments during the evenings and on Saturdays.

The second important criterion for generalizability is the degree to which the experimental procedure resembles actual thefts. Although we cannot claim that most thefts occur under conditions similar to our experimental situation, there are several ways in which this situation resembles actual thefts. First, even though the amount of money involved in the theft was relatively small, a large percentage of thefts also involve small amounts.

According to the National Crime Survey, 46% of completed personal larcenies without contact involve amounts less than $50 (Bureau of Justice Statistics, 1990b).

Second, in most cases the thief is not present when the theft is discovered, and there is generally little likelihood of getting back the stolen money (Spelman & Brown, 1981). Finally, because much petty theft involves cash or losses less than most deductibles, there is little chance of reimbursement from insurance companies.

There are many factors, therefore, suggesting that the experimental studies had some degree of external validity. Nevertheless, we must acknowledge that participants were volunteers for the study and that, even though they did not know exactly what the study involved, they did know that they were part of a research project. Moreover, the secretary's prodding participants to call the police (in Studies 1–5) made the situation unlike most of those involving real crimes. However, it must be noted that social influence proved to be an important variable even when, as in Study 6, participants were not prodded by the secretary.

VARIABLES RELATED TO REPORTING

In this section, we first summarize the individual characteristics that were related to the reporting decision and the variables that were related to participants' delay in reporting. Then we examine how the reporting decision was related to participants' perceptions of the situation and their emotional reactions and how reporting or not reporting was related to participants' ability to recall the details of the theft and their subsequent behavior.

EFFECT OF INDIVIDUAL CHARACTERISTICS ON REPORTING

In all six of the studies we collected demographic information from each of the participants. In addition, in several of the studies we had participants complete personality measures, so that we could determine the relationship of each of these variables to the reporting decision.

The relations between individual characteristics and the reporting decision are presented in Table 5-2. Victims' sex, race, and education were not related to their reporting decision. However, younger victims and victims with lower family incomes were more likely to decide to call the police. As younger individuals in our sample were also more likely to have lower incomes ($r = .22, p < .001$), these two variables have some degree of overlap. In terms of personality variables, authoritarianism (Adorno, Frenkel-Brunswik, Levinson, & Sanford, 1950) was not related to reporting. In contrast, need for social approval (Crowne & Marlow, 1964) was related to reporting, with individuals higher in this need surprisingly being less likely to report. It

TABLE 5-2. CROSS-STUDY ANALYSIS OF THE
EFFECT OF INDIVIDUAL CHARACTERISTICS ON REPORTING

	Reporters ($n = 313$)	Nonreporters ($n = 455$)	
Victim sex	0.67	0.65	$\chi^2 < 1$
0 = Male; 1 = Female[a]			
Victim age	27.85	32.58	$t(757) = 5.96$***
Victim race	0.82	0.85	$\chi^2(1) = 1.56$
0 = Black; 1 = White[a]			
Family income	1.89	2.24	$t(749) = 3.91$***
1 = $0–$6,000			
2 = $6,001–$12,000			
3 = $12,001–$18,000			
4 = $18,001–$24,000			
5 = Over $24,000			
Education	2.82	2.77	$t < 1$
1 = Jr. high only			
2 = High school			
3 = A.A. degree			
4 = Bachelor's degree			
5 = Advanced degree			
Need for social approval	10.26	13.05	$t(243) = 2.84$**
Authoritarianism	2.59	2.59	$t < 1$
Papers completed	10.93	10.82	$t < 1$
Placement of money "earned"	0.70	0.73	$\chi^2 < 1$
0 = Desk; 1 = Person[a]			

[a]Means of variables coded 0 or 1 can be interpreted as the proportion of individuals in the category with a value of 1.
*$p < .05$.
**$p < .01$.
***$p < .001$.

may be that such individuals were seeking approval not from the people immediately present (the secretary and the bystander) but from those persons whose reactions would be more important to them (e.g., their family and friends). It may be that participants thought this latter group of individuals would not consider it worthwhile to involve the police for such a small amount of money.

The final two individual-difference variables we examined related to participants' actions during the experiment. First, we looked at what participants did with the $12 they received after the alphabetizing task. We hypothesized that participants who took possession of the money by putting it in their wallet, purse, or pocket would feel a greater sense of ownership and therefore would be more likely to report the crime. That assumption was incorrect, in that placement of the money was unrelated to the reporting decision. Second, reporters and nonreporters did not differ in the number of papers they completed during the bookkeeping task, a finding suggesting that it was not their differential performance which caused some participants to report and others not to report.

Relative Effects of Advice and
Individual Characteristics on Reporting

The experimental results from each of the studies separately indicated that situational factors, especially the nature of the bystander's advice, significantly affected victims' decisions to report or not to report the crime. The bivariate analyses described above revealed that some individual-difference variables are also related to the reporting decision. What is not clear is whether the individual-level variables would still be significant after situational factors were held constant. Further, we wanted to know which group of variables—situational factors or individual factors—better explained the reporting decisions.

To answer those questions, we conducted multivariate analyses of the reporting decision. We first conducted a multiple linear-regression analysis of the reporting decision, because some statisticians argue that multiple linear regression is sufficiently robust to handle the problems presented by dichotomous dependent variables. For this analysis we used those variables for which there were as few missing variables as possible. Regarding individuals, these variables were age, race, sex, income, and education. The one situational variable included was the type of advice the bystander gave, which was coded as advice not to report, no advice, and advice to report. This analysis revealed that the bystander's advice accounted for a unique 4% of the variance in reporting, $F(1, 721) = 34.23$, $p < .001$; and that the five individual difference variables accounted for a unique 5% of the variance, $F(5, 721) = 8.76$, $p < .001$. Together, the six variables accounted for 10% of the variance in reporting (Adjusted $R^2 = .09$), $F(6, 721) = 13.53$, $p < .001$. The bystander's advice and the family income, age, and sex of the victim were individually significant predictors of the reporting decision.

It can be argued that multiple linear regression is not an appropriate procedure in this circumstance, because the assumption of constant variance of the error term across observations (homoscedasticity) is not met with dichotomous dependent variables. In light of this problem, we used logistical regression analysis with the variables listed above to determine what factors significantly affected the reporting decision. The coefficients of the logistic regression equation are presented in Table 5-3. These coefficients indicate that reporting was more likely if victims were advised to call the police, if they were younger, if they were female, and if their family income was lower. Education and race were not significantly related to the reporting decision. A separate analysis on those 237 participants who completed the Crowne-Marlowe social desirability scale indicated that this variable, which was significantly different for reporters and nonreporters, was not significantly related to the reporting decision when other factors were held constant.

All of the above linear and logistical regression analyses were also conducted with the inclusion of the race of the thief as a predictor variable,

TABLE 5-3. LOGISTIC REGRESSION
ANALYSIS ON REPORTING FOR STUDIES 1 THROUGH 6

Variable	Coefficient	t
Bystander's advice	.30	5.64*
Sex	.18	2.13*
Age	−.02	4.97*
Income	−.09	2.57*
Education	.03	.87
Race	−.05	.47

*$p < .05$.

because a bivariate analysis indicated that 65% of reporting victims had a white thief, whereas only 53% of nonreporting victims had a white thief, $\chi^2(1) = 9.33$, $p < .01$. When other factors were held constant, however, in none of the multivariate analyses was race of the thief a significant predictor. This failure to find a significant effect for race of thief may have been due to the fact that, across studies, the race of the thief was sometimes confounded with the type of advice the bystander gave the victim.

Finally, the four multiple-linear-regression and logistical-regression analyses described above were also conducted excluding the data from Study 6, because the addition of the covictim in that study sharply reduced the influence of the bystander. As would be expected, the resulting equations were more explanatory of the reporting decision, and the individual predictors were also more significant.

Whether or not theft victims would report the crime was the primary question we addressed in the experimental studies. However, we were also interested in a related question: how rapidly reporters called the police. We discuss this question next.

VARIABLES RELATED TO DELAY IN REPORTING

To better understand the role of the bystander's advice in terms of the delay in victims' decision to call the police, we used a multiple linear-regression analysis to examine participants' different response to various prods. In Study 6 we had used elapsed time as a measure of delay, but for the following analyses we used the prod after which participants reported as an indication of reporting delay.

We constructed a three-point scale to score delay before reporting. If participants decided to call the police before the secretary gave any prod, they were assigned a score of 3. If they decided to call the police after the first prod, they were assigned a score of 2. If they decided to call the police after the second prod, they were assigned a score of 1. As we were concerned with delay in reporting, we looked only at those participants who decided to report the theft to the police. Study 6 was not included in this overall regression analysis, because it did not use prods from the secretary.

As predictors in this analysis we used characteristics of the victim and characteristics of the situation. The victim characteristics were age, sex, race, education, and family income. The situational characteristic was the advice of the bystander, coded, as before, on a three-point scale, with advice not to report equal to 1, no advice equal to 2, and advice to report equal to 3. The five victim characteristics together accounted for a unique 2.8% of the variance in reporting delay, $F(5, 239) = 1.44$, $p > .20$. Most of this unique variance (1.9%) was due to the family income of the victims. The advice variable accounted for a unique 2.5% of the variance in reporting delay, $F(1, 239) = 6.23$, $p < .05$. All six variables accounted for 5.8% of the variance in delay (adjusted $R^2 = .035$), $F(6, 239) = 2.46$, $p < .05$. The final table of betas and t tests is presented in Table 5-4.

This multiple-regression analysis suggests that the single best predictor of reporting delay is the type of advice, if any, given to the victim. The next best predictor is the family income of the victim, which might be a surrogate for the seriousness of the crime. That is, the lower the family income, the more serious is the theft of $11 (Sparks *et al.*, 1977). Because of the overlap between age and family income (i.e., younger participants generally made less money), family income in this multiple-regression equation might be the same variable as age in the multivariate analysis of reporting.

RELATIONSHIP OF REPORTING DECISION TO PARTICIPANTS' PERCEPTIONS

One may ask whether reporters and nonreporters may have perceived the experimental situation differently when questioned during the postexperimental debriefing. As can be seen in Table 5-5, reporters and nonreporters did not differ significantly in their judgments about their personal responsibility for the crime, the organization's responsibility for the crime, or the significance of the money to them.

TABLE 5-4. MULTIPLE-REGRESSION ANALYSIS ON DELAY IN REPORTING FOR REPORTING VICTIMS IN STUDIES 1 THROUGH 5

Variable	Beta	t
Bystander advice	.16	2.50*
Family income	−.14	2.13*
Race	.10	1.54
Age	−.02	.23
Educational level	−.02	.27
Sex of victim	−.01	.14

*p < .05.

TABLE 5-5. CROSS-STUDY ANALYSIS OF THE EFFECT OF REPORTING ON
SUBSEQUENT PERCEPTIONS DURING THE DEBRIEFING: MEANS AND SIGNIFICANCE TESTS

	Reporters ($n = 313$)	Nonreporters ($n = 455$)	
Anger	4.62	3.63	$t(519) = 5.49$***
Number of papers taken	3.94	3.85	$t(742) = 1.31$
Bystander influence (asked in two different ways)			
a. "influenced"	2.66	1.52	$t(261) = 5.60$***
b. "affected"	5.05	4.27	$t(250) = 6.54$***
Secretary's influence	5.30	2.30	$t(512) = 17.31$***
Participant's responsibility	2.17	2.06	$t < 1$
Organization's responsibility	3.97	4.18	$t(644) = 1.05$
Degree felt earned money	4.78	3.93	$t(497) = 4.21$***
Thief's race affected decision	1.75	1.83	$t(240) = 1.38$
Perceived money lost	$12.35	$11.40	$t(740) = 2.76$**
Perceived bystander presence 0 = Absent; 1 = Present	.30	.31	$\chi^2 < 1$
Effect of bystander's presence or absence	2.89	1.27	$t(250) = 7.41$***
Bystander's willingness to help	4.39	3.81	$t(250) = 1.93$
Significance of money	4.39	4.11	$t < 1$
Moral obligation	4.61	3.47	$t(262) = 4.26$***
Desire to punish thief	3.75	2.69	$t(254) = 3.94$
Police effectiveness	3.44	3.62	$t < 1$
Police responsiveness	4.53	4.37	$t(379) = 1.00$

*$p < .05$.
**$p < .01$.
***$p < .001$.

Compared to nonreporters, reporters said they were significantly more angry, were more influenced by both the secretary and the bystander, felt more strongly that they had earned the money, and perceived that they had lost about a dollar more as a result of the theft. In addition, even though they did not perceive a difference in the presence of the bystander, they did say they were more affected by the presence of the bystander. Finally, there was a marginal effect suggesting that reporters were more likely to believe that the bystander was willing to help them.

Might the reporters and nonreporters have differed in how they viewed the criminal justice system and their place in it? National surveys indicate that victims' attitudes toward the criminal justice system are unrelated to whether or not they call the police (e.g., Ennis, 1967). Consistent with these surveys, reporters and nonreporters in our studies did not differ in their judgments of the responsiveness or the effectiveness of the police. They did differ in their desire to punish the thief and the degree to which they felt morally obligated to report the crime, reporters having significantly more desire to punish and a greater feeling of moral obligation.

VARIABLES RELATED TO PARTICIPANTS' RECALL OF THE THEFT

During the debriefing immediately after the experiment was concluded, the experimenter asked all participants to recall factors about the experiment and about their behavior. About two months later, they were sent a questionnaire; they were paid $3 if they returned it completed. In this questionnaire they were again asked to recall items about the experiment and about their own behavior and perceptions. Finally, in one study, participants were sent a questionnaire about 15 months after they had participated in the experiment. Again, they were asked to recall events that had occurred during the experiment and to recall their own behavior and perceptions. In some of the studies they were also sent a photograph of a police lineup and were asked to pick out the thief or simply to describe the thief (as discussed in Chapter 4).

The discussion here is limited to participants' accuracy and confidence regarding their recall of events. We took measures at more than one time, so we were able to look at the accuracy of recall over time, as well as variables that were related to accuracy and to the decline in accuracy. These factors include both the manipulated aspects of the study and differences among individual participants.

The comparisons of reporters' and nonreporters' recall accuracy and confidence are presented in Table 5-6. Approximately two months after the experiment (M = 57.2 days; Mdn = 51), 66% of the participants completed the questionnaire sent to them. Compared to nonreporters, reporters recalled that they were significantly more angry and were more

TABLE 5-6. CROSS-STUDY ANALYSIS OF THE EFFECT OF
REPORTING ON RECALL ACCURACY AND CONFIDENCE TWO MONTHS AFTER THE THEFT

	Reporters (n = 313)	Nonreporters (n = 455)	
Money lost	$12.09	$11.35	$t(505) = 1.35$
Number of papers taken	6.47	6.81	$t(762) = 1.83$
Anger	4.69	3.55	$t(442) = 6.25***$
Bystander influence	5.06	4.00	$t(275) = 7.67***$
Subject's responsibility	2.30	2.10	$t < 1$
Organization's responsibility	5.00	4.67	$t < 1$
Significance of money	3.92	3.19	$t(354) = 3.79***$
Recall bystander's name[a]	2.20	1.74	$t(71) = 2.03*$
Recall thief's age[a]	2.34	2.40	$t(251) = .76$
Recall thief's name[a]	2.04	1.80	$t(182) = 2.05*$
Moral obligation	4.18	3.02	$t(179) = 3.83***$
Confidence in thief's age	5.82	6.24	$t(163) = 1.27$
Confidence in number of papers	6.31	6.42	$t < 1$
Confidence in money lost	6.62	6.91	$t < 1$

$*p < .05.$
$***p < .001.$
[a]Coded as 1 = incorrect; 2 = no answer; 3 = correct.

influenced by the bystander. Reporters also rated the money lost as being more significant to them, and they experienced a greater sense of moral obligation to report.

Repeated-measures analyses of variance were conducted on the six questions that had been asked of participants during the debriefing and that were asked again in the questionnaire two months later. These six questions asked participants how much they had been influenced by the bystander, how much they felt responsible for the theft, how much the organization was responsible for the theft, how much money they had lost, how signifi- cant the money was to them, and how morally obligated they felt to report the crime. The two answers to each question (at the debriefing and at the two-month follow-up) were the repeated measure, and participants' deci- sion to report or not to report was the grouping variable.

Consistent with the t tests presented in Tables 5-5 and 5-6, there was a reporting decision effect for three variables: the influence of the bystander, $F(1, 181) = 48.22$, $p < .001$; the amount of money lost, $F(1, 492) = 4.34$, $p < .05$; and felt moral obligation, $F(1, 179) = 17.74$, $p < .001$. Compared to non- reporters, reporters said they were more influenced by the bystander to report (5.05 vs. 4.18), thought they had lost more money ($12.15 vs. $11.25), and said the money was more significant to them (4.04 vs. 3.62).

There were significant repeated-measures effects on three questions: judged responsibility of the organization, $F(1, 165) = 12.28$, $p < .001$; signifi- cance of the money, $F(1, 173) = 18.12$, $p < .001$; and felt moral obligation, $F(1, 179) = 10.87$, $p < .001$. Participants said the organization was more responsi- ble two months later ($M = 4.81$) than immediately after the experiment ($M = 4.08$). They also said the money was more significant to them im- mediately after the experiment ($M = 4.11$) than two months later ($M = 3.42$). Similarly, they said they felt more morally obligated to report immediately after the experiment ($M = 4.02$) than two months later ($M = 3.63$). None of the interactions between the reporting decision and the repeated measures was significant.

The fact that the rated significance of the money and the felt moral obligation were higher immediately after the experiment than two months later is consistent with an arousal explanation for reporting. In other words, upon learning about the theft, participants were more upset and felt more obligated to report than, when asked two months later, they re- membered being.

Some of the participants were asked to recall several facts about the incident, such as the amount of money lost, the number of papers taken from them, the bystander's name, the thief's name, and the thief's age. There were no significant differences between reporters and nonreporters in their recall of the amount of money lost, the thief's age, or the abso- lute number of papers taken. However, when the number of papers taken was recoded on a three-point scale with four to six papers coded as 3 (accurate), one or two papers and six or seven papers coded as 2 (somewhat accurate), and more than seven papers coded as 1 (inaccurate), reporters ($M = 2.81$) were significantly more accurate than were nonreporters ($M = 2.69$), $t(393) = 2.21$, $p < .05$.

On the two measures of the accuracy of their recall of the names of the thief and the bystander, reporters were significantly more accurate than were nonreporters. The fact that reporters were more accurate in recalling the names of the thief and the bystander and in recalling the number of papers taken suggests that reporters may indeed be more accurate as eyewitnesses for some kinds of information. This issue is important because one of the criticisms of much prior laboratory eyewitness research is that it has involved all types of participants, whereas with actual crimes, eyewitnesses are generally self-selected (Wells, 1978; see Chapter 4). It may be that individuals who volunteer to talk to the police (e.g., by reporting a crime) are more accurate witnesses.

Reporters and nonreporters did not differ in their confidence about their recall of the thief's age, the number of papers taken, or the amount of money lost. As with number of papers taken (see above), the other two variables were coded on three-point accuracy scales. Participants' estimates of the thief's age were coded as 3 (correct) if they were within two years plus or minus of the thief's actual age. Participants were given a score of 2 if they were within three to five years (plus or minus) of the thief's actual age. Finally, participants were given a score of 1 (incorrect) if their answers were more than five years from the thief's actual age. Participants' estimates of the amount of money they had lost were scored as 3 (correct) if they answered $10, $11, or $12. Answers were scored as 2 (partially correct) if the estimates were between $5 and $9 or between $13 and $17. Their answers were scored as 1 (incorrect) if the estimates were $0 to $4 or greater than $17.

There was a positive correlation between accuracy and confidence for amount of money lost, $r = .21$, $df = 250$, $p < .001$, but nonsignificant correlations between accuracy and confidence for number of papers taken, $r = .08$, $df = 232$, n.s.; and thief's age, $r = .08$, $df = 158$, n.s. The results suggest that confidence cannot be considered an indicator of accuracy for all types of variables.

REASONS FOR PARTICIPANTS' REPORTING DECISION

Participants' reasons for deciding to call or not to call the police were assessed at three different times. First, in the secretary's office when participants were deciding whether or not to call the police, a research assistant wrote down the reasons offered by nonreporters for not wanting to call the police. (For reasons discussed in Chapter 2, participants who decided to call the police tended not to verbalize their reasons in the secretary's office.)

Second, during the debriefing immediately after the experiment, the experimenter asked participants to indicate why they had decided to report or not to report the crime. Finally, in the questionnaire sent to participants approximately two months after they had participated in the study, we asked them once again to indicate the reasons why they had decided to call or not to call the police. As a consequence, we can examine the reasons nonreporters gave for not reporting at three different times (during the decision-making process, 20 minutes later, and two months later). In addition, we can look at the reasons reporters gave for reporting at two different times (during the debriefing 20 minutes after the decision and two months later). In this section, we present both the kinds of reasons given and the consistency of the reasons across time.

The information regarding consistency of reasons across time is important because it has implications for the reliability and validity of victimization surveys. Such surveys, which are administered weeks or months after the victimization, implicitly assume that victims can accurately recall the reasons for their decisions many months after the event. Research on memory suggests that recall is eroded by the passage of time and by postevent information (Hall, Loftus, & Tousignant, 1984; Hawkins & Hastie, 1990; Loftus, 1979). Thus, if victims give different reasons for their actions depending on when they are asked, then questions must be raised about the validity of the reasons offered by respondents in victimization surveys.

REASONS FOR NOT REPORTING

The reasons offered by participants at three different times for not reporting are presented in Table 5-7. During the time that victims were deciding whether or not to call the police (Time 1), the most frequently given first reason for not reporting the crime (20%) was that the police are not effective in dealing with small thefts. The second most frequent first reason given (17%) was that the loss of $11 was not worth the trouble of becoming involved with the criminal justice system. The third most common reason for not reporting dealt with the specific nature of the crime in the experimental situation we constructed; 14% of the participants thought the crime had been committed against the organization (Industrial Research Associates of Pittsburgh) and that it was therefore the organization's responsibility to call the police and to reimburse the participants.

These reasons are similar to those given by nonreporters in victimization surveys. For example, according to the Bureau of Justice Statistics (1988), for personal larceny without contact involving less than $50, the most frequently given reason for not reporting (stated by 36% of the nonreporters) was that the event was not important enough. This reason is similar to the one offered by our participants that "It wasn't worth the

TABLE 5-7. REASONS GIVEN AT THREE
DIFFERENT TIMES FOR NOT REPORTING (PERCENTAGE OF PARTICIPANTS)

| | Time 1 | | Time 2 | | Time 3 | |
| | During experiment[a] (n = 455) | | During debriefing[a] (n = 441) | | Two months later[a] (n = 296) | |
Reason	First reason	Ever given	First reason	Ever given	First reason	Ever given
Police ineffective	20	34	16	25	10	18
Not worth it	17	33	30	43	32	41
Organization's responsibility	14	31	16	20	16	19
Suspicious or not sure	6	21	8	12	11	18
Private matter	6	18	4	7	3	6
Concern for thief	5	11	8	16	4	9
Not my money	4	16	4	9	7	13
Fear of retaliation	1	3	2	5	1	2
Other	2	4	13[b]	15[b]	16[c]	18[c]
No reason given	26	—	—	—	—	—

[a]Column percentages for "First reason" may add up to more than 100 because of rounding. Column percentages for "Ever given" will add to more than 100 because multiple responses were possible.
[b]Includes 46 respondents (10%) who gave reasons for reporting even though they did not report.
[c]Includes 44 respondents (15%) who gave reasons for reporting even though they did not report.

trouble" to become involved with the criminal justice system. The second most common reason (21% of the nonreporters) was that they had reported the crime to someone else, a reason that closely resembles our participants' reason that it was the organization's responsibility to deal with the theft, not theirs.

During the debriefing (Time 2), participants were asked to indicate which of several listed reasons were the basis for their decision not to call the police. Two months later 65% of the participants responded to the same questionnaire item (Time 3). Whereas the reason most frequently mentioned first at Time 1 referred to police ineffectiveness, the first reason most frequently given at Times 2 and 3 was that calling the police for an $11 theft was not worth the trouble.

In order to study the consistency of each participant's reasons across time, we made a series of pairwise comparisons (i.e., Time 1 vs. Time 2, Time 1 vs. Time 3, Time 2 vs. Time 3). The level of consistency between responses was graded on a three-point scale. Participants received a score of 3 if the first reason they gave was the same at both times. They received a score of 2 if the first reason they gave at the prior time was listed second or third at the subsequent time. And they received a score of 1 if the first reason they gave at the prior time was not given at all at the subsequent time. Thus, the three-point scale amounted to coding participants' reasons as consistent, partially consistent, or inconsistent. As a measure of reliability, two judges independently coded the consistency of nonreporters' reasons for a subset of the data. The two judges agreed in over 90% of the cases. Disagreements were resolved through discussion.

On this three-point scale the mean consistency between reasons given during the experiment (Time 1) and reasons given during the debriefing (Time 2) was 2.12 ($n = 333$). The consistency between reasons given at Time 1 and reasons given on the questionnaire two months later (Time 3) was 1.97 ($n = 227$). Finally, the consistency between reasons given at Time 2 and reasons given at Time 3 was 2.12 ($n = 292$).

Paired t tests were conducted to test if nonreporters were more consistent at some times than at others. A comparison of the Time 1–Time 2 consistency and the Time 1–Time 3 consistency indicated that there was significantly more consistency across the first time period, $t(224) = 2.76$, $p < .001$. A comparison of Time 1–Time 2 consistency and the Time 2–Time 3 consistency indicated no difference between the two measures, as the means were identical (i.e., 2.12). Finally, a comparison of the Time 1–Time 3 consistency and the Time 2–Time 3 consistency found that there was significantly more consistency in the reasons offered at Times 2 and 3 than there was in the reasons offered at Times 1 and 3, $t(224) = 4.07$, $p < .001$.

In summary, there was less consistency in reasons offered immediately after the theft (Time 1) and reasons offered two months later (Time 3), than there was in the reasons offered immediately after the theft (Time 1) and the debriefing (Time 2), and in reasons offered during the debriefing (Time 2) and the reasons offered two months later (Time 3).

REASONS FOR REPORTING

Participants' reasons for reporting are presented in Table 5-8. The participants' most common reason for reporting given during the debriefing (Time 2) was simply that they had been the victims of a crime, second was the influence of the secretary, and third was the desire to get the money back.

There was only a slight overlap of these reasons and the reasons given for reporting by reporters in victimization surveys. According to these surveys (Bureau of Justice Statistics, 1990b), the most common reason for reporting personal larceny without contact (given by 30% of reporters) was a desire to recover the property. The second most common reason (17% of reporters) was "because it was a crime," and third (11% of reporters) was to collect insurance.

As with the nonreporters, approximately two months after the experiment, participants who decided to report were asked to indicate why they had decided to do so. The most common reason (given by about one third of the respondents) was that they had been victims; second was that they had been influenced by the secretary to call the police.

As with the nonreporters, consistency of reasons given was measured on the three-point scale of inconsistent (scored 1), partially consistent (scored

TABLE 5-8. REASONS GIVEN AT TWO
DIFFERENT TIMES FOR REPORTING (PERCENTAGE OF PARTICIPANTS)[a]

| | Time 2 | | Time 3 | |
| | During debriefing[a] (n = 313) | | Two months later[a] (n = 227) | |
Reason	First reason	Ever given	First reason	Ever given
I was a victim	39	45	31	34
Get money back	12	18	4	6
Prevent from happening again	3	4	2	4
Secretary's influence	20	22	22	25
Bystander's influence	1	1	4	4
Covictim's influence	2	2	2	3
Secretary and bystander influence	4	4	11	11
Help organization	2	2	3	3
Other	18[b]	25[b]	22[c]	30[c]

[a]Column percentages for "First reason" may add up to more than 100 because of rounding. Column percentages for "Ever given" will add to more than 100 because multiple responses were possible.
[b]Includes 49 respondents who gave reasons for not reporting even though they reported.
[c]Includes 42 respondents who gave reasons for not reporting even though they reported.

2), and consistent (scored 3). Coding by two independent judges of a subset of reasons given by reporters showed reliability to be 88%. Across studies, the mean consistency for reporters in reasons they gave during the debriefing (Time 2) and reasons they gave on the questionnaire two months later (Time 3) was 2.06.

A t test comparing the Time 2–Time 3 consistency of reasons for reporters ($M = 2.06$) and nonreporters ($M = 2.12$) was not significant, $t < 1$, $df = 517$. That is, reporters and nonreporters were not significantly different in the consistency of the reasons they gave at the two times. This was also true when those individuals who gave reasons inconsistent with their actions (e.g., reasons for reporting even though they did not report) were excluded, $t < 1$, $df = 413$.

Although reporters and nonreporters were equally consistent from Time 2 to Time 3 in the reasons they gave for their behavior, it should be noted that nonreporters had become less consistent from Time 1 to Time 3. It may be that reporters had also become less consistent; but we had no data for reporters from the experimental period (Time 1), so we could not test this hypothesis.

The lower level of consistency of reasons from Time 1 to Time 3 for nonreporters does raise a question, however, about whether a single interview with crime victims can adequately capture their rationale for their behavior. That is, the reasons offered by victims for not reporting a theft appear to vary with the timing of the query. The relatively low consistency in reasons offered may reflect the inconsequentiality of the crime. Possibly, the decision not to report a crime of greater perceived seriousness may cause victims to use a deeper level of information processing, which may produce better recall and thus enhance consistency over time.

The relatively high consistency found in the reasons offered during the debriefing (Time 2) and the reasons offered two months later (Time 3) for both reporters and nonreporters suggests that what theft victims were recalling two months later was an updated version of the reasons that they had constructed shortly after the crime (during the debriefing). Our data do not permit us to determine the point following the victimization at which victims have the most insight about the reasons for their actions. While a short latency between the crime and the questioning may facilitate recall, the stress of the victimization may impair this process (Easterbrook, 1959). Alternatively, while a longer interval between the crime and the questioning may allow the stress to dissipate, the passage of time is likely to produce greater memory decay and to allow the intrusion of new information that may interfere with accurate recall (Hawkins & Hastie, 1990; Loftus, 1979).

SUMMARY AND CONCLUSIONS

In this chapter we reviewed data concerning the internal and external validity of the experimental studies. Although there was a higher rate of suspicion than we would have liked, participants generally found the procedure to be believable and involving. In terms of generalizability, our participants came from a wide variety of backgrounds and, with some few exceptions, mirrored the population of the community in most respects.

The multivariate analyses of the reporting decision and of the delay in reporting suggested that both situational and individual-level variables were significant predictors. The bystander's advice was the most important single predictor for both dependent measures. In general, reporters and nonreporters were equally accurate in remembering facts about the crime and were equally consistent in the reasons they gave for their actions. Finally, our data suggest that two months after the theft, participants were offering somewhat different reasons for their decision not to report the crime than they had originally expressed when making the decision.

We began this chapter with a discussion of internal and external validity, and we believe the experimental studies met these criteria. But clearly this belief must be conditional, in that our findings that social influence had strong effects on the decision making of crime victims may be due to the method we chose (field-laboratory experiments). Other methods with different sources of error may yield different results. Moreover, the significance of the findings is difficult to assess because they are not clearly embedded in a theoretical framework.

In the remainder of the book, we use the experimental studies as a starting point for extensions of the work in terms of both theory and generalizability. In terms of theory, the finding that social influence can strongly affect victims' decisions is not particularly important unless the direction of this influence can be predicted, that is, whether victims will be advised to call or not to call the police. For our subsequent research, we assumed that the direction of this influence is determined primarily by the normative environment in which the victim and the advice-giver are located. In particular, we investigated variables affecting normative beliefs about the reporting of crimes and the stability of these norms across locations and across groups within any one location. We suspected that the judged seriousness of a crime affects normative beliefs about the appropriateness of calling the police. Seriousness is a variable that we did not, and really could not, study in the field experiments. In Chapter 6, we extend our work on victim decision making by examining normative standards in different countries and within different ethnic groups in the United States.

A second way we wanted to extend our experimental research was to determine how often social influence occurs in natural settings, who these influence agents are, and how much influence they have. These questions meant that we had to obtain information about and from real crime victims. As part of our multimethod approach to the general question of crime-victim decision making, we analyzed existing data archives containing information about crime victims (e.g., police files; see Chapter 7), and we interviewed and administered questionnaires to crime victims (see Chapter 8).

6

Normative Expectations
for Calling the Police

The experimental findings indicated that victims are likely to be affected by social influence. However, knowing that social influence is important is only the starting point, because this influence occurs in a larger social context. The kind of information, advice, and support or nonsupport that victims receive depends on how crimes are defined and what responses are deemed appropriate.

These questions of definition and appropriateness relate more generally to the concept of *norm*, "a patterned or commonly held behavior expectation" (Bates, 1956, p. 314). There is some question about the utility of norms in predicting behavior (e.g., Darley & Latané, 1970; but see Cialdini, Reno, & Kallgren, 1990), but our primary goal is more descriptive in nature. Our focus is on people's general beliefs about the appropriateness of reporting crimes to the police.

STUDY OF NORMATIVE INFLUENCE

In all groups, individuals have expectations about how members of the group should behave. These expectations, or normative standards, may be explicit or implicit. At one extreme is the military, where the rules about appropriate dress and behavior are quite explicit. In other cases, the normative expectations are only implicit. For example, at a social gathering there are no written rules about what are appropriate topics of conversation. However, it is generally the case that some topics are considered unsuitable in such situations.

Regardless of whether the expectations are explicit or implicit, they are used by members to judge if a violation has occurred. Punishments follow a violation and range from a loss of status within the group to rejection by the group (Forsyth, 1983).

We assume that groups also have norms for defining crimes, how seriously they are viewed, and how the victim and others should respond, both affectively and behaviorally (Sparks *et al.*, 1977). Normative influence can be exerted on a victim in one of two ways. First, others can apply pressure directly on the victim by telling him or her what they think is appropriate behavior and that the victim's failure to comply will result in their imposition of sanctions.

The second way that others can apply normative pressure is to remind the victim of the norms of a group important to the victim, so that violating the group's norms will lead the victim to anticipate rejection by the group. For example, others may remind a victim of the group norms for defining a crime. If a gang member is beaten up in a fight with a fellow gang member, the group would probably impose severe sanctions if the loser labeled himself a victim of a crime and decided to call the police.

There has been very little empirical research on the role of normative influence on victim decision making. In one of the few studies on the topic, Feldman-Summers and Ashworth (1981) found that normative factors played an important role in the decision of rape victims to call the police. In particular, normative expectations (i.e., approval-disapproval from important others) were better predictors of intentions to report the crime than were other perceived outcomes. Feldman-Summers and Ashworth concluded that rather than making the outcomes of reporting more attractive through such programs as medical care and psychological counseling, "It is more important to convince rape victims that a decision to report is supported by family, friends, and especially by close males, such as [a] husband, boyfriend, or lover" (p. 67).

Because normative factors appear to be potentially important influences on the reporting decision, our first goal in this research was to identify normative expectations for reporting crimes to the police and for dealing with the matter privately. There has been virtually no cross-cultural research on the topic, so it was worth examining how these normative expectations might vary in different countries. In addition, normative expectations might differ between groups within a community in the United States. Such cross-cultural comparisons between and within countries can give researchers an idea of the possible range of responses and can provide the empirical basis for theoretical integrations (Archer & Gartner, 1984).

CRIME SERIOUSNESS

We believed that normative expectations regarding victims' behavior are primarily determined by the seriousness of the crime, in that less serious crimes should rarely involve notifying the police whereas more serious crimes should almost always involve notification of legal authorities. To understand normative expectations, therefore, we thought it was necessary to investigate perceptions of crime seriousness.

The most complete study of crime seriousness was conducted by Wolfgang, Figlio, Tracy, and Singer (1985) in the National Survey of Crime Severity (NSCS). The NSCS was a survey of 60,000 individuals who were participating in the National Crime Survey during a six-month period in 1977. Each of the individuals rated the seriousness of 25 crimes from 1 of 12 different forms, for a total of 204 crimes in the study. Respondents were 18 years of age or older and were representative of the population of the entire country as a result of stratified random sampling.

The ratings from all 60,000 respondents were combined and then scaled as ratios to the theft of one dollar. Thus, the most serious crime, planting a bomb that killed 20 people in a public building, was rated 72.1, or slightly more than 72 times as serious as stealing one dollar. The least serious crime, playing hooky from school, was rated 0.2, or only one fifth as serious as stealing one dollar.

Across all 204 crimes that were used in the study, Wolfgang *et al.* found that violent crimes were rated more serious than were property offenses. Within violent crimes, the type of victim affected the rating of severity. A husband's stabbing and killing his wife was rated more serious (39.2) than a wife's fatally stabbing her husband (27.9). Although there were no significant differences in how men and women rated the crimes, blacks and other racial groups tended to rate offenses as less serious than did whites. There was also evidence that prior victims gave higher seriousness ratings than did nonvictims. The NSCS scale suggests that respondents placed more weight on the harm done than on the intent and culpability of the offender, in contrast to the sentencing and parole guidelines used by decision makers (Hoffman & Hardyman, 1986).

In another study of crime seriousness, Rossi, Waite, Bose, and Berk (1974) found that crimes against police officers were judged more serious than were the same crimes against other persons. Rossi *et al.* also found that crimes against individuals known to the offender were regarded as less serious than were the same crimes against strangers.

Cross-cultural comparisons of rated crime seriousness have generally shown varying degrees of similarities across countries as diverse as Canada (Akman & Normandeau, 1967), Kuwait (Evans & Scott, 1984b), Puerto Rico (Velez-Diaz & Megargee, 1970), and Taiwan (Hsu, 1973). In general, there is a fairly high degree of consistency in seriousness ratings across countries.

However, there are several problems with seriousness ratings. First, the term is not clearly defined; respondents may base their judgments on the harm to the victim or on the offender's culpability (Hoffman & Hardyman, 1986). Research suggests that there is no simple relationship between the two factors and perceived seriousness, in that, depending on the type of crime, harm or culpability may be the primary determinant of seriousness (Warr, 1989). Second, only criminal acts are included in the list of items that are typically rated. Travis, Cullen, Link, and Wozniak (1986) suggested that there might be different effects if a wider range of acts were included. Third, respondents may give socially desirable answers rather than their true perceptions. Travis *et al.* suggested that future studies might ask participants both for their own perceptions and for other peoples' perceptions of each of the criminal acts. In spite of these problems, the consistency of results across studies and across countries suggests that the methods used are reasonably successful in capturing perceived seriousness.

In only one cross-cultural study has the researcher examined norms for reporting crimes. Newman (1976) asked individuals from six different countries (India, Indonesia, Iran, Italy, the United States, and Yugoslavia) about nine different potentially criminal acts. He was interested primarily in whether respondents believed the acts should be prohibited, how serious they believed the acts to be, and to whom, if anyone, they would report the act. Of the nine acts, only three were actual criminal acts, and only one, robbery, is relevant to this discussion, as it was also included in the Wolfgang *et al.* (1985) study.

Across the six countries, most people said that the robbery, defined as taking $50 and injuring the victim so as to require hospitalization, should be prohibited. As can be seen in Table 6-1, the percentage ranged from 97 (India) to 100 (Italy and the United States). In terms of seriousness, again across countries, most people thought the crime was quite serious. The range on an 11-point scale was from 8.10 (India) to 9.95 (Iran).

The fact that the United States had the highest percentage who said they would report the robbery to the police but had only the fourth highest seriousness rating suggests that reporting may be based on factors in addition to seriousness.

STUDY 10: CRIME SERIOUSNESS AND NORMS FOR REPORTING IN FOUR COUNTRIES

Students in four countries (the United States, Thailand, India, and Nigeria) were asked to rate how approving they were of calling the police for

TABLE 6-1. CROSS-CULTURAL DATA ON ROBBERY[a]

Country	Percent believing robbery should be prohibited	Mean seriousness ratings	Percent saying they would report robbery to police
India	97	8.10	84
Indonesia	99	9.62	70
Iran	98	9.95	81
Italy (Sardinia)	100	9.62	50
United States	100	9.28	95
Yugoslavia	98	8.95	92

[a]Based on G. R. Newman (1976). *Comparative Deviance: Perception and Law in Six Cultures.* New York: Elsevier.

a variety of crimes. It could be argued that samples of students are not representative of the larger society. In general, however, at least with regard to judgments of seriousness, respondents' demographic characteristics seem to have little effect (e.g., Travis *et al.*, 1986). Moreover, among their sample of Baltimore residents, Rossi *et al.* (1974) found that individuals with more education and individuals who were younger had higher levels of agreement with the average ratings of their entire sample than did individuals with less education and individuals who were older. Rossi *et al.* suggested that these individuals were most likely to be aware of the larger societal norms. To extend the point, students are probably as aware of norms regarding approval of reporting as they are of norms regarding seriousness.

Based on reported crime, the United States has a much higher known annual crime rate per 100,000 (4,890.8) than do India (187.9) and Nigeria (144.4) (Kurian, 1984). Because these figures represent reported crime, however, they may be somewhat misleading. For example, Nigeria may have a much higher rate of victimization than the above figure would indicate. In a survey of 484 relatively affluent university staff members in Nigeria, Odenkunle (1979) found that in the preceding year, 33% had been victims of attempted burglary and 21% had been victims of successful burglary. Rates of victimization were even higher (over 50%) in poorer residential areas (Joseph, 1977; Olowu, 1978).

METHOD

Participants

The sample from the United States consisted of 157 undergraduate psychology students at the University of Pittsburgh who ranged in age from 18 to 41 ($M = 19.4$; Mdn = 19). There were 78 males and 76 females;[1] 133 whites, 17 blacks, and 4 Asians.[2] The sample of students from the University

---

[1] Three participants failed to provide this information.
[2] Three participants failed to provide this information.

of Pittsburgh tended to be middle class. Almost half (47%) came from homes where the principal wage earner was a white-collar professional or businessperson. An additional 39% came from blue-collar families. Slightly over half of the students (51%) came from a large city with a population of over 250,000 or a suburb of such a city. About 29% came from areas with less than 50,000, and 20% came from areas with between 50,000 and 250,000.

In Thailand, respondents were 109 master's level students in education at Chulalongkorn University in Bangkok. There were 29 males and 79 females, who ranged in age from 21 to 40 ($M = 28.5$; Mdn = 28).[3] Almost all of the students (95%) were Buddhist; the remainder (5%) were Christian. Most were ethnic Thai (92%); the remaining 8% were ethnic Chinese. The fathers of most of the Thai students were businesspeople (39%), government workers (35%), or farmers (17%). Many of the students (42%) came from a large city of over 250,000 or a suburb of such a city. About 27% came from areas with a population less than 50,000, and about 32% came from areas with a population between 50,000 and 250,000.

The Indian respondents were 131 master's level students at Andhra University, Waltair, Andhra Pradesh. There were 53 males and 73 females ranging in age from 17 to 29 ($M = 21.2$; Mdn = 21).[4] Most of the students (89%) were Hindu; the remainder were either Christian (7%) or from some other religious group (4%). The fathers of most of the Indian students were white-collar professionals or businesspeople (55%), government workers (26%), or farmers (14%). About 33% came from a large city with a population over 250,000 or a suburb of such a city. About 47% came from areas with a population between 50,000 and 250,000, and about 20% came from areas with a population less than 50,000.

In Nigeria, the judgments regarding the propriety of calling the police were made by 76 secondary-school students in Lagos. They ranged in age from 14 to 23 ($M = 17.4$; Mdn = 17). There were 33 males and 41 females.[5] The seriousness judgments were made by a different sample of 37 high school students, whose age ranged from 14 to 21 ($M = 17.1$). There were 16 males and 19 females in this group.[6] The fathers of most of the Nigerian students (65%) were businesspeople or white-collar professionals, another 32% worked for the government, and 3% were farmers. Most of the students (74%) came from a large city with a population of over 250,000 or a suburb of such a city. About 15% came from areas with a population of less than 50,000, and about 11% came from areas with a population between 50,000 and 250,000.

---

[3] One participant failed to provide this information.
[4] One participant failed to provide this information.
[5] Two participants failed to provide this information.
[6] Two participants failed to provide this information.

Instruments and Procedure

Participants were presented with brief descriptions of 49 offenses and asked to rate each on a 10-point scale ranging from *Very strongly approve of calling the police* (10) to *Very strongly approve of dealing with the matter privately* (1). The rating scale was preceded by a brief introduction, which read as follows:

> Victims of crime often have difficulty deciding what they should do first after the event. In some situations people strongly approve of first notifying the police while in others they strongly approve of first dealing with the matter privately. Private solutions may include finding the culprit and retaliating, talking to him or his family and demanding return of the stolen property or payment for damages, or writing the crime off and trying to protect oneself against future victimization. Please consider the list of criminal events below and indicate the degree to which you would approve of the victim's first calling the police or first dealing with the matter privately.

The 49 different offenses were taken from the list of 204 used by Wolfgang *et al.* (1985) in the NSCS. From the 204 items we chose 49 as being broadly representative of crimes of different types and of different levels of severity. The crimes we chose ranged in seriousness from 30.0 for the forcible rape of a woman with injuries requiring hospitalization to 0.6 for trespassing in the backyard of a private home. We presented the 49 items in one of two orders, so as to control for possible effects of item order (Evans & Scott, 1984a). As there were no significant order effects, results were pooled across the two orders.

The questionnaires administered to the students in Thailand, Nigeria, and India were identical to the one given the American students, with the exception of the amounts of money involved in the robberies, burglaries, and thefts that described financial losses. For the Nigerian students, the amounts of money ($10, $100, and $1,000) were stated in Nigerian currency (naira) rather than in dollars.

For the students in India and Thailand, rather than simply convert the amounts of money in dollars to their own currency, we decided to use approximately equal amounts in terms of buying power. The exchange rate between the Indian rupee and the American dollar at the time of the study was about 11 to 1. However, in terms of purchasing power, the rate was between 1 and 2 rupees to the dollar. Thus, for India we used amounts of 10, 100, and 1,000 rupees to correspond to the dollar amounts. Based on a similar procedure, we used the amounts of 50, 500, and 5,000 baht for the study in Thailand.

Because of the differences in the values of the money used, it would not have been correct to compare across countries those 21 items that had monetary information. Instead, items involving money were compared only within each country. Those 28 items that did not include monetary information were compared across country.[7] Two items on the questionnaire used

---

[7] The 28 items are the items numbered 1, 2, 3, 5, 6, 9, 10, 11, 12, 20, 21, 23, 24, 25, 26, 29, 30, 32, 33, 34, 37, 38, 41, 42, 45, 47, 48, and 49 in Table 6-2.

in Thailand contained errors in the amount of money involved in a robbery and in the presence of a gun. These two items were not used in subsequent analyses.

In order to estimate the effect that crime seriousness had on the action participants thought would be appropriate, we needed some measure of seriousness. For the United States sample, we used the seriousness score obtained by Wolfgang *et al.* (1985). To get comparable measures of seriousness for the other three countries, we asked participants to use seven-point scales to rate the seriousness of each of the 49 crimes. Although it has been suggested that using the word *crime* confuses participants and biases their judgments (Miethe, 1984), other research indicates that it makes no difference whether the actions are referred to as *crimes, deviant behaviors,* or *behaviors* (Travis *et al.,* 1986).

Though this seriousness information is interesting in its own right, our primary purpose in collecting it was to use severity as a covariate to determine if the decision to report depends on factors other than the seriousness of the offense (Hembroff, 1987).

RESULTS

For each country, means and standard deviations for all 49 items pertaining to ratings of approval of calling the police are presented in Table 6-2. The results are discussed for each country separately and then across countries.

For the United States, across all 49 items the mean approval-of-reporting score was 7.78. The correlation between the mean approval-of-reporting score and the seriousness rating from the NSCS for the 49 items was $r = .67$, $p < .001$. For the 28 nonmonetary items common to all four countries, the mean approval-of-reporting score was 7.64. The correlation of the approval-of-reporting rating for the 28 common items with attitude toward the police was $r = .30, p < .001$.

For Thailand, across all 49 items the mean reporting score was 6.90. The correlation of mean approval-of-reporting scores and mean seriousness ratings for the 49 items was $r = .89, p < .001$. The mean reporting score for the 28 items common to all four countries was 7.24. The correlation of the approval-of-reporting rating for the 28 common items with attitude toward the police was $r = .09$, n.s.

For India, across all 49 items the mean reporting score was 5.79. The correlation of mean reporting scores and mean seriousness ratings for the 49 items was $r = .68, p < .001$. The mean reporting score for the 28 items common to all four countries was 5.56. The correlation of the reporting score for the 28 common items with attitude toward the police was $r = .21, p < .05$.

For Nigeria, across all 49 items the mean reporting score was 6.25. The correlation of mean reporting scores and mean seriousness ratings for the 49 items was $r = .73, p < .001$. The mean reporting score for the 28 items com-

TABLE 6-2. MEAN APPROVAL OF CALLING THE
POLICE FOR 49 SELECTED OFFENSES ACROSS FOUR COUNTRIES[a]

Offense	U.S. (n = 157)	Thailand (n = 109)	India (n = 131)	Nigeria (n = 76)	F value
1. A man forcibly rapes a woman. Her physical injuries require hospitalization.	9.78$_c$ (.092)	9.01$_b$ (1.64)	7.83$_a$ (3.02)	8.41$_{a,b}$ (2.34)	22.48***
2. A person intentionally shoots a victim with a gun. The victim requires treatment by a doctor but not hospitalization.	9.76$_c$ (0.62)	8.75$_b$ (1.63)	7.69$_a$ (2.44)	7.97$_a$ (2.34)	35.74***
3. A man forcibly rapes a woman. No other physical injury occurs.	9.59$_b$ (1.30)	7.78$_a$ (2.34)	7.39$_a$ (3.30)	7.12$_a$ (2.81)	27.07***
4. A person breaks into a home and steals $1,000.	9.56 (1.03)	7.50 (2.31)	8.22 (2.27)	8.49 (2.19)	
5. A person intentionally shoots a victim with a gun. The victim is wounded slightly and does not require medical treatment.	9.51$_c$ (1.06)	8.34$_b$ (1.82)	7.09$_a$ (2.72)	7.33$_a$ (2.58)	38.34***
6. A high school boy beats an elderly woman with his fists. She requires hospitalization.	9.46$_d$ (1.06)	7.61$_c$ (1.96)	4.62$_a$ (2.68)	6.56$_b$ (2.83)	127.39***
7. A person, using force, robs a victim of $1,000. The victim is hurt and requires treatment by a doctor but not hospitalization.	9.45 (1.11)	8.06 (1.62)	7.09 (2.77)	7.97 (2.46)	
8. A person, armed with a lead pipe, robs a victim of $1,000. The victim is injured and requires treatment by a doctor but not hospitalization.	9.34 (1.20)	8.37 (1.40)	7.69 (2.35)	7.80 (2.43)	
9. A person intentionally hits a victim with a lead pipe. The victim requires hospitalization.	9.27$_c$ (1.67)	8.61$_b$ (1.64)	6.75$_a$ (2.75)	6.80$_a$ (2.78)	43.75***
10. A person attempts to kill a victim with a gun. The gun misfires and the victim escapes unharmed.	9.23$_c$ (1.67)	8.42$_b$ (1.83)	7.28$_a$ (2.55)	7.09$_a$ (3.07)	24.96***
11. A person stabs a victim with a knife. The victim requires treatment by a doctor, but not hospitalization.	9.18$_c$ (1.46)	7.96$_b$ (1.65)	7.27$_a$ (2.48)	7.30$_a$ (2.50)	26.75***
12. A high school boy beats a middle-aged woman with his fists. She requires hospitalization.	9.14$_d$ (1.21)	7.67$_c$ (1.89)	4.94$_a$ (2.86)	6.86$_b$ (2.47)	94.63***
13. A person, armed with a lead pipe, robs a victim of $10. The victim is injured and requires hospitalization.	9.13 (1.38)		6.42 (2.60)	7.72 (2.36)	
14. A person, using force, robs a victim of $1,000. No physical harm occurs.	9.08 (1.57)	7.15 (1.79)	7.35 (2.52)	7.05 (2.87)	

Continued

TABLE 6-2. (CONTINUED)

Offense	U.S. ($n = 157$)	Thailand ($n = 109$)	India ($n = 131$)	Nigeria ($n = 76$)	F value
15. A person robs a victim of $10 at gunpoint. The victim is wounded and requires treatment by a doctor, but not hospitalization.	8.99 (1.46)		5.67 (2.37)	6.37 (2.66)	
16. A person, armed with a lead pipe, robs a victim of $1,000. No physical harm occurs.	8.94 (1.71)	7.17 (2.06)	7.63 (2.41)	6.80 (2.80)	
17. A person breaks into a home and steals $100.	8.65 (1.80)	6.48 (2.50)	6.71 (2.61)	7.67 (2.44)	
18. A person threatens to harm a victim unless the victim gives him money. The victim gives him $1,000 and is not harmed.	8.64 (1.98)	7.04 (2.10)	7.19 (2.62)	7.27 (2.43)	
19. A person, using force, robs a victim of $10. The victim is hurt and requires hospitalization.	8.59 (1.78)	7.69 (1.91)	5.78 (2.54)	7.29 (2.55)	
20. A person stabs a victim with a knife. No medical treatment is required.	8.50$_c$ (2.11)	7.42$_b$ (1.98)	6.86$_a$ (2.71)	6.38$_a$ (2.85)	17.85***
21. A man beats a stranger with his fists. He requires hospitalization.	8.37$_c$ (2.27)	7.44$_b$ (2.11)	5.94$_a$ (2.50)	6.63$_a$ (2.88)	25.97***
22. A person robs a victim of $10 at gunpoint. No physical harm occurs.	8.37 (2.23)	5.76 (2.45)	5.35 (2.79)	6.37 (2.84)	
23. A man beats his wife with his fists. She requires hospitalization.	8.34$_c$ (2.17)	5.92$_b$ (2.87)	3.95$_a$ (2.84)	4.55$_a$ (2.76)	75.65***
24. A person beats a victim with his fists. The victim requires hospitalization.	8.29$_d$ (2.03)	7.50$_c$ (2.02)	5.11$_a$ (2.58)	6.37$_b$ (2.76)	48.66***
25. A man drags a woman into an alley, tears her clothes, but flees before she is physically harmed or sexually attacked.	8.22$_b$ (2.10)	7.93$_b$ (2.26)	6.68$_a$ (3.19)	7.48$_b$ (2.80)	9.01***
26. A person intentionally hits a victim with a lead pipe. The victim requires treatment by a doctor but not hospitalization.	8.18$_b$ (2.07)	7.74$_b$ (1.76)	5.95$_a$ (2.62)	6.47$_a$ (2.53)	27.92***
27. A person, armed with a lead pipe, robs a victim of $10. The victim is injured and requires treatment by a doctor but not hospitalization.	8.17 (2.07)	7.32 (1.98)	5.64 (2.43)	6.59 (2.78)	
28. A person, using force, robs a victim of $10. The victim is hurt and requires treatment by a doctor but not hospitalization.	8.07 (2.01)	7.08 (1.87)	5.63 (2.43)	6.90 (2.46)	
29. A person robs a victim. The victim is injured but not hospitalized.	8.02$_c$ (1.97)	6.90$_b$ (1.87)	5.19$_a$ (2.62)	5.58$_a$ (2.74)	42.41***

TABLE 6-2. (*CONTINUED*)

Offense	U.S. ($n = 157$)	Thailand ($n = 109$)	India ($n = 131$)	Nigeria ($n = 76$)	F value
30. Ten high school boys beat a male classmate with their fists. He requires hospitalization.	7.86$_d$ (2.59)	7.10$_c$ (2.20)	4.95$_a$ (2.71)	5.93$_b$ (2.78)	31.53***
31. A person picks a victim's pocket of $100.	7.68 (2.43)	5.31 (2.63)	6.84 (2.69)	6.96 (2.98)	
32. A teenage boy beats his mother with his fists. The mother requires hospitalization.	7.48$_c$ (2.73)	6.93$_c$ (2.96)	4.35$_a$ (3.08)	5.59$_b$ (3.07)	30.40***
33. Three high school boys beat a male classmate with their fists. He requires hospitalization.	7.38$_c$ (2.53)	6.34$_b$ (2.51)	4.05$_a$ (2.86)	5.63$_b$ (2.38)	41.53***
34. A person beats a victim with his fists. The victim requires treatment by a doctor, but not hospitalization.	7.15$_c$ (2.50)	6.72$_c$ (1.93)	4.43$_a$ (2.40)	5.74$_b$ (2.32)	35.87***
35. A person, using force, robs a victim of $10. No physical harm occurs.	7.13 (2.42)	5.41 (2.42)	4.88 (2.46)	5.81 (2.83)	
36. A person threatens a victim with a weapon unless the victim gives him money. The victim gives him $10 and is not harmed.	7.05 (2.57)	6.10 (2.48)	4.83 (2.42)	5.86 (2.82)	
37. A person intentionally injures a victim. The victim is treated by a doctor but is not hospitalized.	7.03$_{b,c}$ (2.48)	7.33$_c$ (1.84)	4.99$_a$ (2.39)	6.45$_b$ (2.66)	24.66***
38. A person intentionally hits a victim with a lead pipe. No medical treatment is required.	7.00$_b$ (2.55)	6.95$_b$ (2.25)	5.25$_a$ (2.61)	5.36$_a$ (2.49)	17.90***
39. A person, armed with a lead pipe, robs a person of $10. No physical harm occurs.	6.88 (2.59)	5.97 (2.25)	4.89 (2.48)	5.62 (2.78)	
40. A person snatches a handbag containing $10 from a victim on the street.	6.79 (2.75)	5.07 (2.55)	4.82 (2.70)	6.38 (2.69)	
41. A teenage boy beats his father with his fists. The father requires hospitalization.	6.60$_c$ (2.84)	6.88$_c$ (2.97)	4.47$_a$ (3.16)	5.75$_b$ (3.05)	16.68***
42. A person beats a victim with his fists. The victim is hurt but does not require medical treatment.	6.10$_c$ (2.59)	5.99$_c$ (2.23)	4.16$_a$ (2.23)	5.01$_b$ (2.51)	18.81***
43. A person threatens to harm a victim unless the victim gives him money. The victim gives him $10 and is not harmed.	5.98 (2.72)	5.26 (2.32)	4.92 (2.40)	6.00 (2.57)	
44. A person does not have a weapon. He threatens to harm a victim unless the victim gives him money. The victim gives him $10 and is not harmed.	5.67 (2.77)	5.10 (2.37)	4.73 (2.59)	5.78 (2.94)	

Continued

TABLE 6-2. (CONTINUED)

Offense	U.S. ($n = 157$)	Thailand ($n = 109$)	India ($n = 131$)	Nigeria ($n = 76$)	F value
45. A man runs his hands over the body of a female victim, then runs away.	5.42 (2.81)	5.51 (2.73)	5.29 (2.96)	4.67 (3.24)	
46. A person picks a victim's pocket of $10.	5.41 (2.82)	3.95 (2.49)	4.41 (2.72)	5.25 (2.76)	
47. A person threatens to seriously injure a victim.	5.22$_a$ (2.78)	7.83$_c$ (2.21)	5.62$_a$ (3.01)	6.42$_b$ (2.83)	21.73***
48. A person intentionally shoves or pushes a victim. No medical treatment is required.	2.26$_a$ (1.65)	4.46$_c$ (2.34)	3.62$_b$ (2.33)	4.07$_{b,c}$ (2.69)	25.06***
49. A person trespasses in the backyard of a private home.	2.03$_a$ (1.68)	5.58$_d$ (2.64)	3.60$_b$ (2.37)	4.82$_c$ (2.93)	55.38***
Across all 28 common items	7.93$_d$	7.03$_c$	5.94$_a$	6.58$_b$	66.66***

^{a}Within a row, means with different subscripts are significantly different according to a Newman-Keuls test ($p < .05$). Numbers in parentheses are standard deviations.
*$p < .05$.
**$p < .01$.
***$p < .001$.

mon to all four countries was 6.24. The correlation of the reporting score for the 28 common items with attitude toward the police was $r = -.04$, n.s.

In order to identify the sources of participants' ratings of seriousness and approval of reporting, we coded the characteristics of the 49 crimes in terms of 12 factors relating to the nature of the crime, the type of victim, the type of offender, and the amount of harm done. These factors were coded as 0 if the condition did not exist and 1 if it did. The 12 factors consisted of the following:

1. Battery—any harmful touching.
2. Threat—either explicitly stated as a threat or implicit, as when the offender was said to be armed with a gun, the victim gave the offender money, and the victim was not harmed.
3. Gun—explicit mention of a gun.
4. Other weapon—explicit mention of a weapon such as a knife or lead pipe.
5. Sex crime—rape, attempted rape, or fondling.
6. Invasion of home property—burglary or trespass.
7. Female victim—explicit mention of the victim's sex as female.
8. Male victim—explicit mention of the victim's sex as male.
9. Male offender—explicit mention of the offender's sex as male.
10. Relative—the offender and victim are related (e.g., spouse or son).
11. Degree of injury—a four-point scale consisting of no mention of injury, some injury, injury requiring the attention of a doctor, and injury requiring hospitalization.

12. Amount of money—a four-point logarithmic scale consisting of no money taken (0), a small amount of money (1), 10 times that amount (2), and 100 times that amount (3).

These 12 factors were used as predictors of mean rated seriousness and mean approval for calling the police. Two raters coded the 49 crimes on each of the 12 factors; they agreed on 98% of the codings. The disagreements were resolved through discussion. Results from the multiple-regression analyses are presented in Tables 6-3 (seriousness) and 6-4 (approval of reporting). The standardized coefficients can be interpreted as an indication of how the participants as a group reacted to the characteristics of the crimes. Within each country we have presented the standardized regression coefficients, the percentage of unique variance each variable accounts for, the F value for the overall regression equation, and the adjusted amount of variance the equation explains.

For the Thai, Indian, and Nigerian samples, mean seriousness scores came from participants' ratings of the crimes. For the U.S. sample, scores came from the ratings of the National Survey of Crime Severity (Wolfgang et al., 1985). As can be seen in Table 6-3, across all four countries, seriousness seemed to be determined by the offender's possession of a gun and the degree of physical injury to the victim. Crimes involving sexual assault were significantly related to seriousness in three countries: Thailand, India, and Nigeria. The presence of some other weapon was significant in Thailand

TABLE 6-3. MULTIPLE-REGRESSION ANALYSES
OF SERIOUSNESS WITHIN EACH OF FOUR COUNTRIES[a]

	U.S.		Thailand		India		Nigeria	
	Beta	Unique r^2	Beta	Unique r^2	Beta	Unique r^2	Beta	Unique r^2
Battery	−.02	.000	.34	.027	.14	.004	.01	.000
Threat	.07	.001	.22	.015	−.01	.000	.17	.009
Gun	.43***	.139	.41***	.123	.40***	.119	.28*	.057
Other weapon	.12	.010	.23*	.036	.34**	.073	.07	.003
Sex crime	.29	.027	.38*	.046	.53**	.093	.56**	.102
Home property	−.06	.002	.15	.014	.08	.004	.26	.040
Female victim	.50**	.061	.11	.003	.22	.012	−.01	.000
Male victim	.01	.000	.06	.002	.07	.003	.14	.012
Male offender	−.05	.001	−.11	.005	.04	.000	−.18	.010
Relative	−.09	.005	.15	.013	.12	.009	−.03	.001
Degree of injury	.55**	.104	.62**	.133	.39*	.052	.83***	.237
Amount of money	.21#	.031	.14	.013	.37**	.098	.26#	.047
F (12, 36)	7.13***		7.70***		6.50***		4.04***	
Adjusted R^2	.61		.64		.58		.43	

[a]Numbers are standardized regression coefficients.
#$p < .06$.
*$p < .05$.
**$p < .01$.
***$p < .001$.

TABLE 6-4. MULTIPLE-REGRESSION ANALYSES OF APPROVAL
FOR CALLING THE POLICE WITHIN EACH OF FOUR COUNTRIES[a]

	U.S.		Thailand		India		Nigeria	
	Beta	Unique r^2	Beta	Unique r^2	Beta	Unique r^2	Beta	Unique r^2
Seriousness	.57	.094	1.15***	.356	1.00***	.317	.73***	.227
Battery	−.03	.000	−.10	.002	−.23***	.012	−.26*	.017
Threat	−.23	.015	−.06	.001	−.13*	.005	−.18	.010
Gun	.25#	.030	−.05	.001	−.03	.001	.09	.005
Other weapon	.22#	.030	−.03	.001	−.08	.003	.01	.000
Sex crime	−.06	.001	−.03	.000	.09	.002	.11	.003
Home property	−.04	.001	.05	.002	−.04	.001	−.09	.004
Female victim	.00	.000	−.14*	.005	−.39**	.035	−.06	.001
Male victim	−.04	.001	−.16***	.015	−.18***	.020	−.21*	.025
Male offender	.14	.007	.01	.000	−.11	.004	−.01	.001
Relative	−.12	.009	−.31***	.053	−.20***	.023	−.22*	.028
Degree of injury	.22	.013	.01	.000	−.06	.001	.16	.006
Amount of money	.49***	.151	.07*	.003	.23***	.028	.39***	.096
F (13, 35)	7.25***		101.18***		72.68***		16.78***	
Adjusted R^2	.63		.97		.95		.81	

[a]Numbers are standardized regression coefficients.
#$p < .06$.
*$p < .05$.
**$p < .01$.
***$p < .001$.

and India. The amount of money taken was significant in India and marginally significant in Nigeria and the United States. Finally, crimes involving female victims were judged more serious only in the United States.

For each country, these same 12 factors and mean rated seriousness scores were used to predict mean approval for calling the police. As shown in Table 6-4, across all four countries, the best single predictor of approval for reporting was the seriousness of the offense. The only other predictor that was significant across all four countries was the amount of money involved in the crime. Both of these variables were positively related to approval for calling the police.

In Thailand, India, and Nigeria, there was lower approval for reporting if the victim was a relative and was explicitly identified as a male. If the victim was a female, reporting the crime was less likely to be approved in Thailand and India. Reporting batteries was less likely to be approved in Nigeria and India, and reporting threats was less likely to be approved in India. In the United States, the presence of a gun and the presence of another weapon were both marginally likely to increase approval of reporting to the police.

A multiple-regression analysis of approval for reporting was also conducted on the same 12 factors, but excluding seriousness. As would be expected, given the regression equation in Table 6-3, when seriousness was excluded the presence of a gun and the degree of injury became significant in all four countries. A sex crime became significant in Thailand, India, and Nigeria, and the presence of a weapon other than a gun became significant in India and the United States. With seriousness excluded, battery, threat, female victim, male victim, and relative were not significant predictors in any country.

DISCUSSION

This study indicates that the perception of crime seriousness was determined, across countries, by the presence of a gun and the degree of injury to the victim. The amount of money was a significant or near-significant predictor in three countries (all but Thailand). A sex crime was a significant predictor in all countries but the United States. In the United States, however, crimes involving a female victim were judged to be more serious than were crimes that did not involve female victims.

The best single predictor of the propriety of calling the police was the perceived seriousness of the crime. Across countries, however, crimes with approximately equal seriousness ratings had different approval-of-reporting scores, and conversely, crimes with different seriousness ratings had approximately equal approval-of-reporting scores. As an example of this point, compare item 21 ("A man beats a stranger with his fists. He requires hospitalization"), item 24 ("A person beats a victim with his fists. The victim requires hospitalization"), and item 23 ("A man beats his wife with his fists. She requires hospitalization"). In the United States, in spite of differences in ratings of seriousness, the three items were rated approximately equal in terms of approval of reporting to the police. In the other countries, in spite of approximately equal seriousness ratings, participants were less approving of reporting a crime of spouse abuse to the police (item 23) than they were of attacks on strangers.

In summary, the results of this study indicate that there are commonalities as well as differences among the four countries regarding the approval of reporting crimes to the police. Across countries, respondents thought it would be more appropriate to report crimes that are greater in seriousness and that involve a greater loss of money. Given the fact that the seriousness data were collected with different methods in the different countries, the relationship between perceived seriousness and approval of reporting appears to be quite robust. That is, in Thailand and India, all participants rated both seriousness and reporting, whereas in Nigeria there were two separate samples who rated seriousness and reporting. In the United States, we used the seriousness ratings from Wolfgang et al. (1985). The consistency of the results in light of these methodological differences increases our confidence in the findings.

But there were notable differences among countries as well. Variables that predicted approval of reporting in one country were not significant predictors in other countries. For example, domestic violence was judged less worthy of being reported in Thailand, India, and Nigeria, but not in the United States. Other cross-country differences emerged with regard to over-all approval of reporting. Consistent with the findings of Newman (1976), across all 49 crimes U.S. participants were most approving of notifying the police (M = 7.64). Indian participants were least approving (M = 5.56). Additional cross-country differences were found regarding the range of responses to the 49 offenses. The widest range of mean responses was displayed by the U.S. participants (2.03–9.78), whereas the Nigerians had the most constricted range (4.08–8.41).

These data suggest that while there is considerable agreement about the appropriateness of reporting certain crimes to legal authorities, there are numerous differences across countries that require further study.

STUDY 11: APPROPRIATENESS OF REPORTING: EFFECTS OF TYPE OF OFFENDER AND SEX OF VICTIM

In the prior study, Indian participants indicated that they did not favor reporting instances of wife abuse. Of the 49 crimes, only intentionally shoving a stranger and trespassing in the backyard of a person's home received lower ratings of approval of reporting. One reason for this negative attitude toward reporting wife abuse is that they may believe that crimes against relatives ought not to be reported to the police. This notion may be especially true in collectivist cultures like India's, where individuals subordinate their individual goals to those of a stable ingroup like their family (Triandis, 1989). This reasoning is consistent with the findings from the regression analysis in the previous study, which showed that the Indian sample was negatively disposed to reporting crimes involving relatives.

An alternative reason why many Indian participants did not think wife abuse should be reported relates to the sex of the victim. Students may have believed that crimes against women are less deserving of police attention than are crimes against men, possibly because women have lower status in a traditional Indian household (Sinha, 1988; Straus & Winkelmann, 1969). Again, the results from the regression analysis are consistent with this hypothesis.

These two hypotheses regarding less approval of reporting crimes committed by relatives than by strangers and less approval of reporting crimes involving female victims than of reporting those involving male victims are clearly tentative. First, they were based on a very small number of the 49 different crimes in Study 10. Second, even if there were a larger number, these hypotheses were derived post-hoc, and we therefore must not place too much confidence in them. What is needed is an experimental study with a larger number of crimes in which these two factors are manipulated.

In Study 11 we (Ruback, Gupta, & Kohli, in press) used a different group of Indian students to test two hypotheses: (1) Crimes involving relatives as an offender are less likely to be reported than are crimes where the offender is a stranger, and (2) crimes involving female victims are less likely to be reported than are crimes involving male victims. We used a methodology similar to that employed in the prior study. For some of the crimes for which participants made judgments, we systematically varied the sex of the victim and the type of offender (relative or stranger). In addition, for purposes of comparison with the Indian sample in the prior study, we included several items that were identical or very similar to those used in the earlier study. Finally, we included some crimes (e.g., dowry burning) that are unique to India and that pose an immediate social problem.

METHOD

Participants and Instrument

Participants were 103 postgraduate students from six programs of the Faculty of Arts and Faculty of Sciences at the University of Allahabad, located in the north Indian state of Uttar Pradesh. There were 55 males and 48 females, who ranged in age from 20 to 24 ($M = 21.8$; Mdn = 22.0).

The questionnaire contained brief descriptions of 48 crimes. Of these 48, 32 were part of the experimental manipulation. For these 32, there were 8 different crimes (man beats a person, attempt to kill a person, injury with a weapon, intentional shooting, teenage boy beats a person, threat to injure, sexual molestation, and a man beats a child). For each of these eight crimes, all four combinations of male or female victim and the offender being a stranger to or related to the victim were used. Thus, for example, there were items where a man beat a female stranger, a man beat a male stranger, a man beat his wife, and a man beat his brother.

In addition to these 32 crimes, there was 1 crime of burglary and 6 crimes of robbery in which the sex of the victim was varied (3 male and 3 female). Also included but not discussed here were 9 crimes against women or involving dowry, which were included to give an idea of participants' beliefs about these crimes.

Of the total 48 crimes, 13 were exactly or essentially the same as those presented to Indian participants in Study 10 (students at Andhra University in South India). The purpose of this overlap was to give some idea of the generalizability in India of normative beliefs regarding approval for calling the police.

Participants were first asked to rate the seriousness of all 48 crimes on a 10-point scale ranging from *Very serious* (10) to *Not at all serious* (1). Next, they rated the crimes on whether or not someone should be told on a 10-point scale ranging from *Very strongly believe the victim should tell someone* (10) to

Very strongly believe the victim should not tell anyone (1). Finally, they rated the crimes on whether or not they should be reported to the police. Participants used a 10-point scale ranging from *Very strongly approve of calling the police* (10) to *Very strongly approve of dealing with the matter privately* (1).

The 48 crimes were randomly ordered. The same order was used for all three scales, as Study 10 had indicated no effects for the order in which items or scales were presented.

One of two experimenters read instructions to the participants, who were in groups of about 15. The basic nature of the study was described, and all participants were told that their participation was voluntary. The questionnaire took 20–30 minutes to complete.

RESULTS

Across all 48 items the mean rating of seriousness was 6.24, the mean rating of telling someone was 6.45, and the mean rating of approval of reporting was 5.99. All three variables were significantly correlated with each other: (a) seriousness—telling someone, $r = .71$, $p < .001$; (b) seriousness—approval of reporting, $r = .61$, $p < .001$; (c) telling someone—approval of reporting, $r = .71$, $p < .001$.

Experimental Manipulations

Within each of the four cells of the 2×2 design of the study (Type of offender [stranger or relative] × Sex of the victim), we combined the eight crimes to form a composite score for seriousness, telling someone, and approval of reporting the crime to the police. These composite scores for the 32 crimes involved in the experimental manipulation, reported in Table 6-5, were analyzed by the two within-subject variables (type of offender and sex of victim) and one between-subject variable (sex of subject). Females rated the crimes as more serious ($M = 6.83$) than did males ($M = 5.58$), $F(1, 101) = 26.31$, $p < .001$. Crimes against women were judged more serious ($M = 6.46$) than were crimes against men ($M = 5.86$), $F(1, 101) = 101.47$, $p < .001$, regardless of whether the offender was a stranger or a relative. Finally, there was an interaction of sex of subject and sex of victim, $F(1, 101) = 6.42$, $p < .05$, so that female participants rated crimes against female victims ($M = 7.21$) as more serious

TABLE 6-5. MEAN RATINGS OF 32 CRIMES AS A
FUNCTION OF TYPE OF OFFENDER AND SEX OF VICTIM

Dependent measure	Stranger offender		Relative offender	
	Male victim	Female victim	Male victim	Female victim
Seriousness	5.83	6.45	5.88	6.48
Telling someone	6.29	6.78	5.97	6.37
Reporting the crime	5.99	6.57	5.23	5.45

than crimes against male victims (M = 6.45), whereas male participants showed less distinction between female victims (M = 5.81) and male victims (M = 5.34).

Beliefs about the appropriateness of telling someone about the crime were a function of the sex of the participant, the relation of the offender to the victim, and the sex of the victim. Females believed it more appropriate to tell (M = 6.95) than did males (M = 5.84), $F(1, 101)$ = 17.29, $p < .001$. Participants believed it more appropriate to tell someone about the crime if the offender was a stranger (M = 6.54) than if the offender was a relative (M = 6.17), $F(1, 101)$ = 23.36, $p < .001$, and if the victim was a female (M = 6.58) than if the victim was a male (M = 6.13), $F(1, 101)$ = 30.00, $p < .001$.

Beliefs about the appropriateness of reporting the crime to the police varied as a function of the sex of the participant, the relationship between the offender and the victim, and the sex of the victim. Females believed it was more appropriate to report the crime (M = 6.28) than did males (M = 5.41), $F(1, 101)$ = 12.45, $p < .001$. Participants were more approving of reporting crimes committed by strangers (M = 6.28) than crimes committed by relatives (M = 5.34), $F(1, 101)$ = 58.64, $p < .001$. And consistent with the results on rated seriousness and the appropriateness of telling someone, participants believed it was more appropriate to report crimes involving female victims (M = 6.01) than those involving male victims (M = 5.61), $F(1, 101)$ = 24.06, $p < .001$.

In addition to these effects, the sex of the participant interacted with the sex of the victim, $F(1, 101)$ = 7.62, $p < .01$. Consistent with the results on rated seriousness, female participants believed it more appropriate to report crimes against female victims (M = 6.60) than crimes against male victims (M = 5.96). In contrast, male participants showed less distinction between female victims (M = 5.50) and male victims (M = 5.31).

Finally, the sex of the victim interacted with the type of offender, $F(1, 101)$ = 12.24, $p < .001$. When the offender was a relative, the appropriateness of reporting did not differ for male (M = 5.23) and female victims (M = 5.45). However, when the offender was a stranger, participants considered it more appropriate to report crimes against women (M = 6.57) than crimes against men (M = 5.99).

For example, consider the crime of a man beating a child seriously enough to require treatment by a doctor. When the child was the man's daughter (M = 3.26) or son (M = 3.46), the approval of reporting scores were quite low; in fact, they were the lowest of all 48 crimes. However, when the child was unrelated to the offender, approval of reporting was higher if the child was a girl (M = 6.21) than if the child was a boy (M = 5.52).

DISCUSSION

In terms of the experimental manipulations, we found support for the idea that Indians believe it is more appropriate to report crimes committed by strangers than to report crimes where the offender and the victim are relatives. The fact that this result from North India was consistent with the correlational finding from South India in Study 10 gives us some reason to believe that it is probably true, in that the two parts of the country differ greatly in language, culture, and geography. Moreover, the fact that this finding is consistent with results from the United States suggests that this norm may be cross-cultural.

A larger problem, however, is the fact that in this study respondents thought that it was more appropriate to report crimes against women than crimes against men, a result exactly opposite to the finding in the prior study and also counter to a stereotype that in North India there is likely to be more damage to a woman's reputation if her victimization becomes public than would be true in South India. It is possible that this stereotype is simply incorrect, but Studies 10 and 11 are still inconsistent, and our Indian colleagues were unable to help us resolve the inconsistency.

One possible reason for the inconsistency looks not at regional differences but at the time difference between the two studies (1986 for Study 10 and 1988 for Study 11). In September 1987 an 18-year-old widow committed *sati* (throwing herself on her husband's funeral pyre), an event that was widely reported in the national press. It triggered protests and counterprotests and spurred wide discussion in Parliament and the media (e.g., Das, 1988) about the role of women in India (see Dalal, Singh, Sinha, & Sah, 1988). As part of this national discussion, there was particular concern about crimes against women. Indeed, on the Allahabad University campus, where the study was conducted, several women's groups had been formed during 1987 and 1988. It may be that this heightened awareness of women's issues in 1988, particularly among women (note the fairly consistent sex differences in Study 11), accounts for what might otherwise be considered a difference between North and South India.

In spite of the inconsistency between the South and the North regarding approval of reporting crimes involving female victims, the overall mean ratings of approval of calling the police in this study, although slightly lower than those obtained in Study 10 in South India, were not very different. Indeed, there were significant differences between the two regions on only 5 of 13 t tests; in 4 of them, the mean from the South was significantly greater than the mean from the North, and 1 showed the opposite pattern. Further, ratings of seriousness in the two parts of India were significantly correlated, $r = .76$, $p < .001$, as were ratings of the appropriateness of reporting, $r = .90$, $p < .001$. More importantly, the means from North India in Study 11 were closer to those from South India than to those from any of the other three countries examined in Study 10. This relatively smaller within-country difference suggests that Indians have more in common with each other, in terms of how they perceive the seriousness of crimes and the value of reporting, than they do with people in other countries. We had found even more within-country similarity in the approval of reporting when we compared ratings from students at Georgia State University ($r = .98$). More generally, it may be that, although there are likely to be some regional or ethnic variations within a country, countries are likely to have norms about the appropriateness of reporting crimes.

STUDY 12: NORMS FOR REPORTING AMONG DIFFERENT ETHNIC GROUPS IN THE UNITED STATES

We conducted our studies in Thailand, India, and Nigeria because we were interested in the extent to which normative beliefs about the appropriateness of reporting crimes exist across cultures. More relevant to the functioning of the criminal justice system in the United States is the degree of consistency in normative beliefs among demographic groups within the country. To investigate this question of whether normative standards vary among different ethnic groups, we conducted a study of four such groups in the Atlanta area.

METHOD

Participants and Instrument

Participants were 204 individuals in the Atlanta metropolitan area (81 males, 122 females),[8] who ranged in age from 11 to 83 ($M = 37.6$; Mdn = 35.0). There were 50 Latinos, who completed the form through the Latin American Association, and 71 Koreans, who completed the form through the Korean Community Service Center. There were also 47 blacks and 36 whites, who were recruited through crime prevention workshops.

Participants completed a consent form and then used 10-point scales to rate the same 49 different crimes used in Study 10. The scale ranged from *Very strongly approve of calling the police* (10) to *Very strongly approve of dealing with the matter privately* (1).

RESULTS AND DISCUSSION

The means for each of the 49 crimes are reported for each ethnic group in Table 6-6. There was at least one significant difference among the groups on 28 of the 49 items (57%). In general, the Latinos and the Koreans were less approving of calling the police than were blacks and whites. This effect also appeared in an analysis across all 49 crimes, $F(3, 203) = 3.81$, $p < .05$ (see Table 6-6).

---

[8] One participant failed to provide this information.

TABLE 6-6. MEAN APPROVAL OF CALLING THE
POLICE FOR 49 SELECTED OFFENSES ACROSS FOUR ETHNIC GROUPS[a]

Victims of crime often have difficulty deciding what they should do first after the event. In some situations people strongly approve of first notifying the police, while in others they strongly approve of first dealing with the matter privately. Private solutions may include finding the culprit and retaliating, talking to him or his family and demanding return of stolen property or payment for damages, or accepting the loss and trying to protect oneself against future victimization. Please consider the list of criminal events below and indicate the degree to which you would approve of the victim's first calling the police or first dealing with the matter privately. Use the following scale to make your judgment:

| Very strongly approve of calling the police | 10 9 8 7 6 5 4 3 2 1 | Very strongly approve of dealing with the matter privately |

Offense	Blacks ($n = 47$)	Koreans ($n = 71$)	Latinos ($n = 50$)	Whites ($n = 36$)	F value
1. A man forcibly rapes a woman. Her physical injuries require hospitalization.	9.57	9.70	9.14	9.92	1.89
2. A person intentionally shoots a victim with a gun. The victim requires treatment by a doctor but not hospitalization.	9.60$_b$	9.39$_b$	8.80$_a$	10.00$_b$	4.75**
3. A man forcibly rapes a woman. No other physical injury occurs.	9.51	9.39	9.44	10.00	1.30
4. A person breaks into a home and steals $1,000.	9.77$_b$	9.72$_b$	9.04$_a$	9.83$_b$	4.70**
5. A person intentionally shoots a victim with a gun. The victim is wounded slightly and does not require medical treatment.	9.72$_b$	9.54$_b$	8.78$_a$	9.50$_b$	3.43*
6. A high school boy beats an elderly woman with his fists. She requires hospitalization.	9.72	9.15	8.98	9.94	3.15*
7. A person, using force, robs a victim of $1,000. The victim is hurt and requires treatment by a doctor but not hospitalization.	9.64$_b$	9.20$_{a,b}$	8.76$_a$	9.83$_b$	3.79*
8. A person, armed with a lead pipe, robs a victim of $1,000. The victim is injured and requires treatment by a doctor but not hospitalization.	9.57$_{a,b}$	9.41$_{a,b}$	8.90$_a$	9.92$_b$	3.20*
9. A person intentionally hits a victim with a lead pipe. The victim requires hospitalization.	9.72$_b$	9.70$_b$	8.50$_a$	9.50$_b$	6.70***
10. A person attempts to kill a victim with a gun. The gun misfires and the victim escapes unharmed.	9.49	9.43	8.84	9.83	2.51

TABLE 6-6. (*CONTINUED*)

Offense	Blacks ($n = 47$)	Koreans ($n = 71$)	Latinos ($n = 50$)	Whites ($n = 36$)	F value
11. A person stabs a victim with a knife. The victim requires treatment by a doctor but not hospitalization.	$9.43_{a,b}$	9.01_a	8.63_a	9.92_b	3.87*
12. A high school boy beats a middle-aged woman with his fists. She requires hospitalization.	9.64	9.00	9.00	9.42	1.53
13. A person, armed with a lead pipe, robs a victim of $10. The victim is injured and requires hospitalization.	9.49_b	9.39_b	8.66_a	9.64_b	2.91*
14. A person, using force, robs a victim of $1,000. No physical harm occurs.	9.02	9.11	8.48	9.50	2.27
15. A person robs a victim of $10 at gunpoint. The victim is wounded and requires treatment by a doctor, but not hospitalization.	9.15_b	7.97_b	$8.12_{a,b}$	$8.97_{a,b}$	3.34*
16. A person, armed with a lead pipe, robs a victim of $1,000. No physical harm occurs.	9.36	9.20	8.84	9.75	2.12
17. A person breaks into a home and steals $100.	9.68_b	9.00_a	9.04_a	9.75_b	3.82*
18. A person threatens to harm a victim unless the victim gives him money. The victim gives him $1,000 and is not harmed.	9.40	9.27	8.92	9.83	2.58
19. A person, using force, robs a victim of $10. The victim is hurt and requires hospitalization.	9.30	9.15	8.70	9.56	1.63
20. A person stabs a victim with a knife. No medical treatment is required.	9.26	9.20	8.34	9.14	2.38
21. A man beats a stranger with his fists. He requires hospitalization.	9.49_b	$9.04_{a,b}$	$8.45_{a,b}$	8.13_a	3.16*
22. A person robs a victim of $10 at gunpoint. No physical harm occurs.	$8.96_{a,b}$	8.34_a	8.20_a	9.83_b	3.94**
23. A man beats his wife with his fists. She requires hospitalization.	9.22	8.85	8.78	8.94	.35
24. A person beats a victim with his fists. The victim requires hospitalization.	9.23_b	9.27_b	8.20_a	9.17_b	3.97**
25. A man drags a woman into an alley, tears her clothes, but flees before she is physically harmed or sexually attacked.	9.19	9.10	8.62	9.31	1.00

Continued

TABLE 6-6. (CONTINUED)

Offense	Blacks ($n = 47$)	Koreans ($n = 71$)	Latinos ($n = 50$)	Whites ($n = 36$)	F value
26. A person intentionally hits a victim with a lead pipe. The victim requires treatment by a doctor but not hospitalization.	9.79$_b$	9.25$_{a,b}$	8.60$_a$	9.25$_{a,b}$	4.03**
27. A person, armed with a lead pipe, robs a victim of $10. The victim is injured and requires treatment by a doctor but not hospitalization.	8.94	8.33	8.26	9.36	2.43
28. A person, using force, robs a victim of $10. The victim is hurt and requires treatment by a doctor but not hospitalization.	9.00	8.18	8.94	9.08	2.52
29. A person robs a victim. The victim is injured but not hospitalized.	9.26	8.35	8.68	9.08	2.25
30. Ten high school boys beat a male classmate with their fists. He requires hospitalization.	9.70$_b$	8.33$_a$	8.60$_a$	8.97$_{a,b}$	3.76*
31. A person picks a victim's pocket of $100.	8.40	7.41	8.24	8.17	1.77
32. A teenage boy beats his mother with his fists. The mother requires hospitalization.	9.45$_b$	8.37$_{a,b}$	8.64$_{a,b}$	7.92$_a$	2.88*
33. Three high school boys beat a male classmate with their fists. He requires hospitalization.	9.04$_b$	8.45$_b$	7.52$_a$	7.17$_a$	5.36**
34. A person beats a victim with his fists. The victim requires treatment by a doctor but not hospitalization.	8.87$_b$	8.34$_{a,b}$	7.58$_a$	8.67$_{a,b}$	2.79*
35. A person, using force, robs a victim of $10. No physical harm occurs.	8.77$_b$	7.44$_a$	7.14$_a$	7.92$_{a,b}$	2.94*
36. A person threatens a victim with a weapon unless the victim gives him money. The victim gives him $10 and is not harmed.	8.55	8.45	8.48	8.75	.13
37. A person intentionally injures a victim. The victim is treated by a doctor but is not hospitalized.	9.00	8.30	8.38	8.44	1.00
38. A person intentionally hits a victim with a lead pipe. No medical treatment is required.	9.34$_b$	8.49$_a$	7.98$_a$	8.17$_a$	3.57*
39. A person, armed with a lead pipe, robs a person of $10. No physical harm occurs.	8.68	7.69	7.90	8.61	2.00
40. A person snatches a handbag containing $10 from a victim on the street.	8.55$_b$	4.93$_a$	7.38$_b$	7.78$_b$	17.99***

TABLE 6-6. (*CONTINUED*)

Offense	Blacks ($n = 47$)	Koreans ($n = 71$)	Latinos ($n = 50$)	Whites ($n = 36$)	F value
41. A teenage boy beats his father with his fists. The father requires hospitalization.	8.60	8.04	8.06	7.86	.54
42. A person beats a victim with his fists. The victim is hurt but does not require medical treatment.	8.79$_b$	6.69$_a$	6.88$_a$	7.36$_a$	5.29**
43. A person threatens to harm a victim unless the victim gives him money. The victim gives him $10 and is not harmed.	8.91$_b$	7.44$_a$	7.52$_a$	8.06$_{a,b}$	3.22*
44. A person does not have a weapon. He threatens to harm a victim unless the victim gives him money. The victim gives him $10 and is not harmed.	8.15	7.94	7.14	8.19	1.38
45. A man runs his hands over the body of a female victim, then runs away.	7.60$_b$	6.32$_a$	8.00$_b$	8.11$_b$	4.71**
46. A person picks a victim's pocket of $10.	7.60$_b$	4.68$_a$	6.90$_b$	7.25$_b$	11.27***
47. A person threatens to seriously injure a victim.	8.28$_b$	8.90$_b$	7.10$_a$	6.14$_a$	11.05***
48. A person intentionally shoves or pushes a victim. No medical treatment is required.	7.30$_b$	6.87$_b$	5.46$_b$	4.31$_a$	7.95***
49. A person trespasses in the backyard of a private home.	7.09$_c$	2.69$_a$	5.82$_b$	2.08$_a$	33.76***
Overall 49 items	9.06$_b$	8.35$_a$	8.23$_a$	8.69$_{a,b}$	3.81*

[a]Within a row, means with different subscripts are significantly different according to a Newman-Keuls test ($p < .05$).
*$p < .05$.
**$p < .01$.
***$p < .001$.

Despite some differences, there was remarkable similarity among the four ethnic groups in the results of multiple linear-regression analyses that were conducted to determine what factors were most predictive of each group's approval of calling the police. The same 12 factors used in the cross-cultural analysis of the approval judgment (seriousness was not included in this study) were used within each ethnic group: battery, threat, use of a gun, use of another weapon, sex crime, invasion of home property, female victim, male victim, male offender, relative, degree of injury, and amount of money. As can be seen in Table 6-7, two factors were predictive of all four groups' mean approval of calling the police: the presence of a gun and the amount of money involved in the crime. A third factor, the degree

TABLE 6-7. MULTIPLE-REGRESSION ANALYSES OF APPROVAL
FOR CALLING THE POLICE WITHIN EACH OF FOUR ETHNIC GROUPS[a]

	Blacks		Koreans		Latinos		Whites	
	Beta	Unique r^2	Beta	Unique r^2	Beta	Unique r^2	Beta	Unique r^2
Battery	.21	.010	.48	.055	−.07	.001	−.02	.000
Threat	.00	.000	.38	.044	−.05	.001	−.10	.003
Gun	.39**	.112	.32*	.074	.36**	.096	.43**	.136
Other weapon	.23	.055	.21	.029	.29	.052	.31*	.062
Sex crime	−.12	.004	.10	.003	.21	.014	.17	.009
Home property	.14	.011	.09	.005	.02	.000	−.18	.019
Female victim	.29	.021	.12	.003	.36	.032	.19	.008
Male victim	.01	.000	−.03	.001	.00	.000	−.08	.003
Male offender	.17	.010	.07	.002	.05	.001	.19	.012
Relative	−.19	.022	−.07	.003	−.05	.001	−.14	.011
Degree of injury	.46*	.073	.39	.052	.53**	.096	.40*	.056
Amount of money	.41**	.119	.38*	.102	.54***	.203	.61***	.258
F (12, 36)	2.87**		2.47*		3.46**		3.69**	
Total R^2	.49		.45		.54		.55	
Adjusted R^2	.32		.27		.38		.40	

[a]Numbers are standardized regression coefficients.
*$p < .05$.
**$p < .01$.
***$p < .001$.

of injury to the victim, was a significant predictor for three of the groups and marginally significant ($p < .08$) for a fourth.

Although the same three factors were important across ethnic groups, there were differences in the amount of variance accounted for. In general, the 12 factors were better predictors of how whites and Latinos made their decisions than of how Koreans made their judgments.

GENERAL DISCUSSION

The three studies described in this chapter suggest that there are normative standards about what kinds of crime should be reported to the police. Obviously, because these studies involved responses to hypothetical situations, we do not know if respondents' ratings truly reflected the types of judgments they would make when confronting situations involving real crime victims. The evidence suggests, nevertheless, that norms regarding the appropriateness of calling the police vary with the characteristics of the crime and with the population studied.

Across diverse populations, characteristics of the crime associated with greater approval of reporting included the presence of a gun and the extent of the victim's injury and financial loss. When the rating of seriousness was entered in the regression equation in Study 10, it proved to be the single best predictor of approval of notifying the police. However, as a result of its inclusion, the presence of a gun and the extent of the victim's injuries dropped out as significant predictors of approval. This finding suggests that these two variables affected approval of reporting indirectly via their impact on perceived seriousness.

Another aspect of the crime that tended to influence approval across countries (except the United States) was the relationship between the offender and the victim. Participants expressed less approval of reporting crimes when the offender and victim were relatives than when they were strangers.

How can we interpret the findings regarding the impact of characteristics of the crime on approval of reporting? What was it about the presence of a gun, the victim's suffering greater injury and loss of money, and victimization by a stranger that prompted greater approval of reporting? As a tentative answer to this question, we offer the following explanation.

We propose that people view reporting to the police more positively when an incident is clearly defined as a crime and when it arouses the perceiver either because it strongly violates a moral precept or is perceived as dangerous or threatening. According to this reasoning, participants may have been less approving of notifying the authorities in incidents involving relatives because such incidents may not easily be defined as criminal. Because such incidents are viewed as private "disputes," participants may have been somewhat less sympathetic to a settlement that involved the police. In addition, hostile encounters between members of a family may be more difficult to label as a crime because of the ongoing nature of the relationship. In such instances, it is often easier to assign blame to the victim (e.g., "She provoked him"), so that perceivers may label the incident as just a "husband-and-wife thing."

Once labeled as a crime, incidents that involve use of a gun or that involve injury to the victim are likely to be more arousing or disturbing to perceivers. The potential danger or threat posed to the victim and to the community by such crimes may elicit more favorable attitudes toward intervention by legal authorities.

Crimes may also be arousing or disturbing because they violate basic moral precepts shared by the community and are therefore perceived as constituting greater "wrongs." Crimes likely to generate such feelings include thefts or robbery of large (but not small) sums of money and crimes resulting in severe (but not minor) injury to the victim. Participants may have felt that such gross violations of community standards justify intervention by community-appointed agents, namely, the police. Moreover, participants may have believed that the police would be equally disturbed by such crimes and therefore would be particularly responsive to requests for assistance. In Chapter 9 we discuss in greater detail a model of crime-victim decision making that incorporates feelings of vulnerability (or threat) and the sense of being wronged as important mediators of the decision to notify the police.

While there were commonalities across countries and across ethnic groups within a single country with regard to ratings of approval of reporting, there were differences as well. Group differences in normative beliefs about reporting were found not only for ratings of individual crimes, but also for composite measures of approval across all crimes. We suspect that such group differences are attributable, in part, to differences in social, religious, and economic values, and to differences in beliefs about the efficacy of the police in dealing with the situation. Much more needs to be known about how norms for reporting are acquired and about their linkages to important value and belief systems.

In summary, the direction of the social influence to which victims are exposed is almost certainly dependent on the norms of important groups to which victims belong. We suspect that these norms, communicated to victims via their relatives, friends, and sometimes strangers, and subsequently internalized, determine whether victims believe a crime should be reported because "It is the right thing to do" or should not be reported because "It is not a police matter."

The purpose of the studies reported in this chapter was to extend the results of our field-laboratory experiments by investigating the normative climate in which victim decision making takes place. Another way of extending our findings from the field-laboratory studies is to determine whether or not the results from Studies 1–6 are generalizable to real victims. We approach this question first by turning to existing archives of data about crime victims (Chapter 7) and then to interviews with actual crime victims (Chapter 8).

7

Archival Analyses

A reasonable way to begin testing the generalizability of our experimental findings about crime victims is to use a nonreactive method to describe what actual victims do. Such a method allows data collection without affecting the behavior of the victims (Webb *et al.*, 1981). The most useful nonreactive method for studying victim decision making is to examine records kept by agencies that deal with victims. These agencies include the police and crisis centers for specific types of victims, such as spouse abuse victims and rape victims.

Archival analyses can provide useful information, but there are problems with placing too much reliance on them. First, researchers are limited to the information in the archive. This generally means that there will be research questions that the researchers will be unable to answer because the appropriate information was not collected. Thus, for example, when looking at police records, we have no idea of how many individuals the victim might have talked to, what advice was received about reporting the crime, and whether the victim followed the advice. Second, records in an archive are likely to be a self-selected sample. Thus, unless the archive contains records of almost everyone (e.g., birth records), the records that are included are likely to exist for some reason (e.g., because the person reported the crime) that may be correlated with some other variable of interest (e.g., the severity of the crime). Therefore, generalizing beyond the sample should be done cautiously.

STUDY 13: CALLS TO
THE ATLANTA COUNCIL ON BATTERED WOMEN

To get an idea of the extent of reporting to the police, we analyzed the 543 calls received by the Atlanta Council on Battered Women from January 1 to April 20, 1983 (Ruback, Lutz, & Smith, 1983). Of this total, 65 (12%) were calls by someone other than a battered woman. In most cases, these third-party calls were requests for information made by individuals who wanted the information for someone else (e.g., a relative). An additional 65 (12%) of the calls did not involve battering. In most instances, these women were phoning about other events, such as being put out of their house. Excluding these 130 calls left 413 calls.

The 413 women who called the Council ranged in age from 16 to 72, with a mean age of 30.2 and a median age of 28.1. The majority of the women were black (53%); the remainder were white (44%) or from another ethnic group (3%). Most of the women (60%) were not employed outside the home.

In 297 cases (73%), the batterer was the victim's husband. In the remainder of the cases, the batterer was a boyfriend (20%), an ex-husband (3%), a common-law husband (2%), or someone else (3%). In the 164 cases for which information was available, 125 (76%) of the batterers were employed either full-time or part-time. Information about batterers' substance abuse was available in only 51 cases, but 50 of these cases involved substance abuse (see Abel & Suh, 1987).

In 127 (72%) of the cases for which there was information available, the battering relationship had been going on for longer than a year. In only 16 cases (4%) was the present incident the first occurrence of battering. The most frequent type of abuse reported was physical abuse (91%), followed by psychological abuse (21%), sexual abuse (7%), threats on the woman's life (7%), and threats to her children (6%). The percentages total more than 100% because it was possible for a case to involve more than one type of abuse.

In 101 cases (24%) the police had been contacted about the present battering incident. The victim was the caller in 77% of the cases. The most frequent responses by the police were the following: arresting the batterer (23%), issuing warrant information (22%), and doing nothing (16%). Of the 60 women for whom it was noted whether or not the police had been called before, 52 (87%) reported that the police had been called before.

The most frequently cited referral to the Council was from other agencies (25%). Some women knew about the shelter and called without prompting from others (20%), whereas others had been referred by the police (18%), friends (15%), the media (12%), a relative (5%), and medical personnel (4%). The main reason for calling the shelter was just to talk to someone (81%). Other reasons given for calling the Council were for counseling (39%), emergency housing (31%), and legal information (25%).

When asked if they could obtain help from others, most said they could. Slightly over half (55%) said they could get support from their families, and 66% said they could get support from their friends.

The results obtained in this study were generally consistent with what other researchers have found. First, we found that calling the police was relatively infrequent (see, e.g., Bowker, 1982; Carlson, 1977). Second, we found that even when the police were called, they generally did not arrest the batterer (Gondolf & McFerron, 1989). Third, we found that most of the women had sought help from others (Omer, Leanard, & Taylor, 1985), in that a majority of them had called someone before they called the Atlanta Council on Battered Women.

This descriptive study suggests that seeking advice and support from others is common, at least for battered women. Many of the women had made several calls: to the Council, the police, and someone else. This study also illustrates one of the major weaknesses of archival research: the frequent absence of data that would enable the investigator to answer questions of interest. For example, we had no way of knowing about the seriousness of the incident or the amount of time victims had delayed before contacting the Council. Moreover, domestic violence has several unique aspects (Friedman & Schulman, 1990) that limit the generalizability of the findings. In the next study, we used a data base that contained more information than the Council's records and that dealt with less unique crimes.

STUDY 14: POLICE RECORDS ON REPORTED THEFTS AND BURGLARIES

The records kept by police agencies contain information about criminal victimizations, who reported these victimizations, and how long these reporters had delayed before notifying the police. Like many types of records, police files vary in how much information they contain about the crime and the person who reported it. For the most part, however, these files include enough information about the victim (e.g., age, race, and sex), the individual who reported the crime to the police (the victim, a friend or relative of the victim, or a third-party bystander), and the crime itself (e.g., the type of property taken and the estimated value of the property) so that reasonable inferences can be made about why there was a delay in calling the police and, to a limited degree, why the crime was reported.

METHOD

Description of the Sample

To answer these questions, we sampled 989 reports of larceny-theft ($n = 597$; 60%) and burglary ($n = 392$; 40%) made to the Mount Lebanon,

Pennsylvania, Police Department during the years 1976–1978 (Ruback, Green-berg, & Westcott, 1981). Mount Lebanon is an upper-middle-class, largely white suburb of Pittsburgh.

RESULTS

Who Reported

As in other studies (e.g., Conklin & Bittner, 1973; Spelman & Brown, 1981; Van Kirk, 1978), the persons who reported the crimes were for the most part the victims themselves (85%). Smaller numbers were reported by relatives (8%), bystanders (4%), and friends (3%). Most of the reporters were male (59%) and almost all (99%) were white. The reporters ranged in age from 7 to 91 ($M = 39$).

There was a difference in who reported by type of crime. The reporter was more likely to be the victim when the crime was theft (89%) than when the crime was burglary (79%), $\chi^2(1) = 18.89$, $p < .001$. Two possible reasons may explain this difference. The first concerns the ease with which non-victims can label the event a crime. In most thefts it may be that only victims are likely to know that property has been taken, whereas because burglary involves unlawful entry, it is easier for nonvictims to know that a crime has occurred. A second possibility is that burglary victims are more likely than theft victims to tell others about the crime, and that these others are more likely to call police, either on their own initiative or at the request of the victim.

Female victims were more likely to report the crime themselves (89%) than were male victims (83%), $\chi^2(1) = 6.41$, $p < .05$. The existence or nonex-istence of a suspect had no effect on who reported the crime ($\chi^2 < 1$). When a nonvictim reported the crime, the sex of the reporter was not significantly related to the presence or absence of a suspect ($\chi^2 < 1$). However, the exis-tence or nonexistence of a suspect did interact with the sex of the victim; when there was a suspect, female victims were more likely to report the crime themselves (23%) than were males (17%), $\chi^2(1) = 3.95$, $p < .05$. This finding is consistent with our finding in the first field experiment (see Study 1) that women were more likely to report when the thief was present, whereas men were more likely to report when the thief was absent. Neither the victim's age nor the value of the property taken was related to whether a victim or a nonvictim reported the incident to the police (both t's < 1).

Delay in Reporting

In addition to knowing who had reported, we wanted to learn what factors might explain the delay between the time the crime was discovered and the time it was reported to the police. Data on these times were missing from 270 of the 989 cases, so analyses were conducted on only the remaining 719 cases. This subgroup did not appear to differ from the total sample in any of its defining characteristics: who reported the crime (86% by the victim); the sex of the reporter (59% were male); the race of the reporter (99% were white); the age of the reporter ($M = 38.5$); the type of crime (59% theft, 41% burglary); whether there was a suspect (20% yes); or the value of the stolen property ($M = \$488.23$; Mdn = \$84.60).

Most crimes were reported quickly; after discovering the crime, 36% of the callers reported within 30 minutes, and 84% reported within 24 hours, very close to what similar studies have found (Conklin & Bittner, 1973). The median reporting delay was 1 hour and 42 minutes. The delay was zero in 99 cases (14%), in that the crime was reported as soon as it was discovered. The longest delay was 115 days. Because the distribution of delay scores had a strong positive skew, the data were subjected to a common transformation for reaction time scores (Kirk, 1968, p. 66): adding 1 to each score and then taking the reciprocal.

Bivariate analyses of these transformed data scores indicated that there was significantly greater delay in burglaries than in thefts, $t(717) = 5.28$, $p < .001$, and in cases that did not have a suspect than in those that did have one, $t(685) = 3.69$, $p < .001$. The transformed delay score was positively correlated with age, $r = .13$, $p < .001$, and with time of day, $r = .15$, $p < .001$. Longer delays were associated with younger reporters and crimes committed earlier in the day.

In order to determine the factors that best predicted delay in reporting, we conducted a hierarchical multiple-regression analysis using as predictors crime characteristics, reporter characteristics, and the interaction of these factors. Entered first were factors about the crime: (1) type of crime (burglary or theft); (2) time it was discovered; and (3) whether or not there was a suspect. Entered second were factors about the reporter: (1) who the reporter was (victim or nonvictim) and (2) the sex of the reporter. The age of the reporter and the value of the property taken were not included in this analysis, because a large number of cases did not contain this information. None of the two-, three-, four-, or five-way interactions was significant after earlier terms had been entered. Therefore, these terms were dropped from the regression equation and included in the error term.

Three factors about the crime were significant predictors of delay in reporting: (1) type of crime, $F(1, 685) = 23.81$, $p < .01$; (2) the time of day when the crime was discovered, $F(1, 684) = 9.82$, $p < .01$; and (3) whether or not there was a suspect in the case, $F(1, 683) = 12.26$, $p < .01$. Longer delays were associated with burglaries, discovery of the crime earlier in the day, and the absence of a suspect. All three factors together accounted for 7% of the variance in the transformed delay scores, $F(3, 683) = 17.18$, $p < .01$. The subsequent addition of factors about the victim accounted for no significant amount of variance. Even when entered into the regression equation first, victim-related factors were not significant predictors of delay. The total amount of variance explained was low, as has been found in other studies (e.g., Van Kirk, 1978).

A second hierarchical multiple-regression analysis was conducted with the predictors from the prior analysis and also the age of the reporter and the value of the property taken in the crime. These two variables were not included in the prior analysis because of the large number of missing cases involving these data. As in the prior analysis, crime-related factors (type, time, value, and suspect) were entered first, and reporter-related factors (who reported, sex, and age) were entered second. Of the variance in reporting delay, 4% was accounted for by factors about the crime, $F(4, 371) = 3.81$, $p < .05$. Adding factors about the victim to the equation accounted for no significant amount of variance, and as in the prior analysis, this was true even when reporter-related factors were entered into the regression equation first.

In addition to providing information about who reports and how long it takes reporters to call the police, the data provide clues regarding factors that were probably not motivating reporters to call the police. In about 65% of the cases with complete data, victims would not have qualified for insurance compensation, either because the loss was less than $100 (55%), a conservative estimate of the typical deductible on most insurance policies, or because the loss was cash (21%), which is not covered by most policies.

In other words, if one assumes that victims were aware of the limitations of their insurance policies, it seems reasonable to conclude that, consistent with findings from other studies of burglary victims (e.g., Smith & Maness, 1976; Waller & Okihiro, 1978), reimbursement from their insurance company was not their primary motivation for reporting the crime. This conclusion is reinforced by the fact that the reporters were middle- and upper-middle-class suburbanites for whom a loss of less than $100 would not be the misfortune that it would be for individuals with lower incomes.

STUDY 15: RAPE CRISIS CENTER ARCHIVES

In order to examine in greater depth the factors affecting the reporting decision, we made use of another data archive, which was maintained by the Rape Crisis Center (RCC) of Grady Memorial Hospital in Atlanta, Georgia. The RCC was established in 1974 and since that time has helped thousands of sexual assault victims. Our sample consisted of the records for each of the 2,526 female sexual assault victims, 14 (the age of consent in Georgia) and older, who had visited the RCC from January 1, 1982, through December 31, 1984 (Ruback & Ivie, 1987b, in press).

METHOD

Each record contained information that had been recounted by the victim to one of the volunteers who served at the RCC. Each of these approximately 150 volunteers had received 20 hours of formal training, including training on how to record the information related by the victims. Volunteers recorded the information on the six-page standardized forms in use at the RCC since 1974.

Procedure

From each case, 41 items of information were coded by one of two coders. Intercoder reliability was assessed by having one of the two original coders recode 75 cases. These 75 cases were stratified by year and by coder, so that there were 25 from each of the three years and the coder recoded 25 of her own cases and 50 of the other coder's cases. Across all items, mean reliability was greater than 97%, with a range of 93% to 100%.

The 41 items of information covered four general topics: the victim, the rapist, the circumstances of the rape, and the victim's actions after the rape. The victim-related items were age, race, marital status, and history of prior sexual assaults. The rapist-related items were race; prior relationship, if any, with the victim; and the number of rapists (single or multiple). The circumstances of the rape included a number of items: the location of the attack (coded as indoors or outdoors); the time of day of the attack (coded as 6 A.M. to noon, noon to 6 P.M., 6 P.M. to midnight, and midnight to 6 A.M.); the length of time the woman was held by the attacker (coded as under 1 hour, 1–3 hours, 3–6 hours, 6–12 hours, 12–24 hours, and over 24 hours); the nature of the sexual acts suffered (vaginal penetration, oral penetration, anal penetration, and other types of sexual acts); whether or not the victim employed any verbal strategies, such as talking, screaming, or crying; the amount of physical resistance offered by the victim (coded as none, slight, or substantial); any verbal abuse or degrading acts the victim suffered, such as being urinated on, having beer poured on her, or being called a whore (coded as present or absent); whether or not the rapist used a weapon; whether or not the rapist threatened the victim; and the degree of physical injury the victim suffered (coded as no additional, minor, and major).

The final group of items described the victims' behavior and reactions after the rape. These reactions included the emotions victims said they felt immediately after the rape (coded as the presence or absence of guilt, fear, and anger) and the first action they took after the assailant left. There were three items about reporting: whether or not the police were called; who called the police (the victim or someone else); and the delay before the police were called (coded as less than 30 minutes, 30–60 minutes, 1–3 hours, and over 3 hours). Two other items concerned the number of people the victim planned to tell about the rape and whether or not the victim had left a phone number with the RCC.

Description of the Sample

About equal numbers of the 2,526 women in the sample came from each of the three years: 891 from 1982, 804 from 1983, and 831 from 1984. The women ranged in age from 14 to 98 ($M = 26.1$; Mdn = 23). The sample was 67% black, 32% white, and 1% other. For all remaining analyses, the "other" group was combined with "white." Most of the women were single (64%). The remainder were married and living with their husbands (11%), separated (10%), divorced (12%), or widowed (3%).

About 50% of the attacks were by strangers, about 47% were by friends or acquaintances, and just over 3% were by relatives. About 80% of the sexual assaults were intraracial: 66% were black victims of black rapists, and 14% were white victims of white rapists. Less than 19% were white victims of black rapists, and 2% were black victims of white rapists (percentages do not equal 100 because of rounding).

Virtually all of the women suffered completed sexual assaults. Based on self-reports, only 2% said the crime was an attempt. Other ways to define whether the attacks were attempted or completed are to dichotomize the sample on the basis of whether or not there was vaginal penetration and whether or not there was any phallic activity. When these definitions are used, the percentages of attempts were 8% and 4%. Because the number of attempts was small, regardless of how they are defined, the following analyses include all of the attacks.

RESULTS

Analyses of the data set focused on several different questions. First, we examined how the women had reacted emotionally to the crime and what behaviors they had performed immediately after the crime was over. Next, we investigated whether or not the crime had been reported to the police, and, if so, who had reported it and how long the reporter had delayed before notifying the police. Finally, we analyzed data from which we made inferences about victims' subsequent behavior.

Emotional Reactions

We investigated the emotional reactions of sexual assault victims because our experimental data (see Chapters 2, 3, and 5) suggested that theft victims' behavior is related to their level of arousal and the type of emotion they experience. In particular, we were concerned with the emotions of fear and anger.

All of the victims had described how they felt immediately after the rape was over. These descriptions were later coded for the presence or absence of fear, anger, and guilt. Most of the women (67%) said they were afraid, whereas only 26% said they were angry, and only 6% said they felt guilty. Compared to women who did not say they were afraid, women who said they felt afraid were more likely to have been held longer during the rape (1.54 vs. 1.44), $t(1501) = 1.98$, $p < .05$; to have been forced to perform a greater number of sexual acts (1.44 vs. 1.23), $t(2511) = 7.01$, $p < .001$; to have suffered greater injury (1.56 vs. 1.48), $t(2444) = 3.16$, $p < .01$; and to have offered greater physical resistance (2.17 vs. 1.98), $t(2379) = 5.47$, $p < .001$.

A composite measure of the amount of force used on victims (Coercion) was created by summing the number of weapons, threats, and assaults used against each victim. Women who reported being afraid had faced more Coercion than had women who did not say they were afraid (2.04 vs. 1.48), $t(2511) = 16.35$, $p < .001$.

The relationship between several nominal-level variables and fear are presented in Table 7-1. As can be seen, fear was greater if the victim had used verbal strategies, if she had suffered degrading acts, if she did not know the rapist, and if she had not been raped before.

Women who said they felt angry were more likely than women who did not say they felt angry to have been attacked later in the day (3.16 vs. 3.07), $t(2294) = 2.03$, $p < .05$; to be older (26.86 vs. 25.83), $t(2511) = 2.14$, $p < .05$; to have faced more types of Coercion (1.95 vs. 1.82), $t(2511) = 3.43$,

TABLE 7-1. VARIABLES RELATED TO EMOTIONAL EXPERIENCE[a]

| | Chi-square value and percentage experiencing emotion | | | | | |
| | Fear | | Anger | | Guilt | |
Variable	χ^2	%	χ^2	%	χ^2	%
Verbal strategies	304.57***		10.67**		n.s.	
Used		79		28		
Not used		38		21		
Degrading acts	150.64***		16.70***		7.95**	
Yes		77		29		5
No		52		21		8
Prior relationship	63.47***		21.50***		12.33***	
Yes		60		30		7
No		75		21		4
Raped before	15.64***		7.02**		n.s.	
Yes		59		31		
No		69		25		
Multiple rapists	n.s.		4.91*		n.s.	
Yes				23		
No				28		

[a]The n's for these tests vary from 2,379 to 2,513.
*$p < .05$.
**$p < .01$.
***$p < .001$.

$p < .001$; and to have used more physical resistance (2.26 vs. 1.86), $t(2379) = 11.44$, $p < .001$. With regard to the nominal level variables (see Table 7-1), anger was more likely to have been reported if the victim had used verbal strategies, if she had suffered degrading acts, if she knew the rapist, if she had been raped before, and if there was a single rapist.

To approximate the level of severity of the assault, we created a composite score (Severity) by adding nine aggravating factors (each coded 1 if present and 0 if not): if the rapist was a stranger, if a weapon was used, if there was oral penetration, if there was anal penetration, if other sexual acts had been forced, if there were multiple rapists, if there were degrading acts, if the victim suffered major additional injury, and if the victim had been held for more than three hours. Thus, this composite score could range from 0 to 9.

A two-way analysis of variance on Severity was conducted with victims' reported fear and anger as the grouping variables. There was a significant effect for fear, $F(1, 2509) = 159.49$, $p < .001$, so that women who reported feeling fear had faced more severe assaults ($M = 2.71$) than women who had not reported feeling fear ($M = 1.94$). There was no main effect for anger, $F(1, 2509) = 1.09$, n.s. However, there was a significant interaction between fear and anger, $F(1, 2509) = 22.28$, $p < .001$. Victims who reported feeling only fear had faced the most severe assaults ($M = 2.74$), followed by victims who reported feeling both anger and fear ($M = 2.54$), victims who reported feeling only anger ($M = 2.22$), and victims who did not report feeling anger or fear ($M = 1.78$). All differences between groups were statistically significant.

Women who said they felt guilty, compared to women who did not, were more likely to have known the rapist and not to have suffered degrading acts (see Table 7-1). Guilt was more likely to be reported by victims who said they felt only fear (7%) or who did not say they felt either anger or fear (7%) than by victims who said they felt both anger and fear (1%) or only anger (2%), $\chi^2(3) = 30.43$, $p < .001$. No other variables were significantly related to guilt.

Some caution is needed in interpreting these results concerning emotional reactions. First, as in all correlational studies, the order of events cannot be clearly stated. It may be that particular emotions followed particular acts of the rapist, although it is equally plausible that those same emotions elicited the behaviors. Second, the relatively simple analyses conducted here do not capture the complexity of the emotional experience. In spite of these limitations, these analyses of emotions give us some insight into victims' behavior after the crime was completed.

First Action Taken

The first action 28% of the victims said they took was to call the police. Another 41% of the women said they first spoke to someone else: 11% called their family, 15% called a friend, and 15% spoke to a stranger.[1] Almost 19% of the women said they went home first, and 12% engaged in some other behavior, such as going to work. We combined these six categories into three: calling the police, speaking to someone else, and taking some other action. These three categories were then used in subsequent analyses.

Victims' first action was affected by their age, $F(2, 2378) = 10.26$, $p < .001$; how much Coercion they had faced, $F(2, 2510) = 59.14$, $p < .001$; and how much physical resistance they had used, $F(2, 2378) = 9.47$, $p < .001$. Victims who had called the police were significantly older ($M = 27.5$) than were those who had talked with someone ($M = 26.1$), who, in turn, were older than those who had taken some other action ($M = 25.1$).[2] Also, victims who called the police ($M = 1.96$) or who talked with someone ($M = 2.01$) had experienced more Coercion than victims who took some other action ($M = 1.61$). Finally, victims who called the police ($M = 2.04$) or who talked with someone ($M = 1.99$) had used significantly more resistance than women who took some other action ($M = 1.87$).

The first action a victim was likely to take was significantly related to whether or not she knew the offender, $\chi^2(2) = 93.05$, $p < .001$. If the victim did not know the assailant, she was most likely to talk with someone else first and least likely to take some other action (see Table 7-2). If the victim knew the assailant, she was most likely to take some other action first and least likely to report the crime.

The presence or absence of all three of the emotional reactions we coded were significantly related to the first action victims took (Fear: $\chi^2(2) = 105.79$, $p < .001$; Anger: $\chi^2(2) = 40.44$, $p < .001$; Guilt: $\chi^2(2) = 13.95$, $p < .001$; see Table 7-2). Of those who experienced fear, talking with someone was the most likely first action. Of those who did not experience fear, taking some other action was the most likely first action. Of the women who said they felt angry, talking with someone and reporting to the police were the most likely first responses. Of those who did not say they were angry, talking with someone and taking some other action were the most likely first behaviors. Of those women who said they felt guilty, taking some other action and talking with someone were the most common first responses. Of those women who did not say they felt guilty, talking with someone and taking some other action were the common first actions, but calling the police was also a likely first response.

---

[1] The actual number of victims who talked with at least one other person is probably higher than this figure. Some of the victims who called the police and some who took another action may have talked with friends or relatives after they performed their first behavior.

[2] All *post hoc* tests used the Newman-Keuls procedure ($p < .05$).

TABLE 7-2. VARIABLES SIGNIFICANTLY
RELATED TO THE FIRST ACTION TAKEN BY VICTIMS (PERCENTAGE OF VICTIMS)[a]

	First action taken by victim		
Variable	Reported to police	Talked with someone	Other action
Knew offender	23	33	44
Did not know offender	29	45	25
Experienced fear	28	44	28
Did not experience fear	23	28	49
Experienced anger	35	38	28
Did not experience anger	23	39	38
Experienced guilt	14	40	46
Did not experience guilt	27	39	34

[a]The n's for these tests vary from 2,373 to 2,456. Within a row, percentages may not add to 100 because of rounding.

Reporting to the Police

A total of 89% of the sample reported their victimization to the police. This group included the 656 women who said the first thing they did was to call the police and an additional 1,545 women who called the police later. In the group of victims who did not report the crime immediately, the first action was significantly related to whether or not the police were eventually called, $\chi^2(1) = 85.74, p < .001$. Of this group whose sexual assaults were not immediately reported, 92% of the cases were eventually reported to the police if the victims spoke to someone else first. In contrast, only 77% of the cases were eventually reported if victims did not speak to someone else. There is some support, in other words, for what LaFree (1989) called the "social nature of rape reporting" (p. 63).

Table 7-3 shows that reporting to the police was significantly more likely if a weapon was present, if a threat was used, if the attack occurred outdoors, if degrading acts were inflicted, if the rapist was black, and if there was no prior relationship between the rapist and the victim. Victims who were black, who had not been raped before, who had used verbal strategies during the rape, who did not say they felt guilty, who said they felt angry, and who said they felt afraid were more likely to report than were victims who were not in these categories.

Reporters were more likely to have been attacked later in the day ($M = 3.11$), whereas nonreporters were attacked earlier ($M = 2.97$), $t(2283) = 2.06, p < .05$. Reporters tended to have suffered greater injury ($M = 1.54$) than nonreporters ($M = 1.41$), $t(2424) = 3.48, p < .001$, and to have faced more severe incidents, based on the composite measure ($M = 2.43$) than victims who did not report ($M = 2.00$), $F(1, 2454) = 42.43$, $p < .001$. The decision to report or not was unrelated to the types of sexual acts forced on the victim, whether or not there was an assault, the amount

TABLE 7-3. VARIABLES SIGNIFICANTLY RELATED TO REPORTING[a]

Variable	Chi-square	Percentage reporting by category			
Circumstantial variables					
Rapist's race	49.29***	Black	92	White	80
Prior relation	20.94***	Yes	87	No	93
Location	6.28*	Indoors	88	Outdoors	91
Weapon	11.74***	Yes	92	No	88
Threat	4.37*	Yes	91	No	88
Degrading	7.82**	Yes	91	No	87
Victim variables					
Victim race	20.97***	Black	92	White	86
Raped before	7.90**	Yes	86	No	91
Guilt	48.50***	Yes	72	No	91
Anger	7.71**	Yes	93	No	89
Fear	8.13**	Yes	91	No	87
Verbal strategies	11.77***	Yes	91	No	86

[a]The n's for these tests vary from 2,373 to 2,456.
*$p < .05$.
**$p < .01$.
***$p < .001$.

of time the victim was held, whether or not there were multiple offenders, and the degree to which the victim physically resisted.

Multiple Linear Regression. Because many of the variables are significantly related to one another, as well as to the reporting decision, a multivariate procedure was required to control for the collinearity. Traditionally, researchers have used multiple linear regression to examine the independent effects of variables or groups of variables.

We used this procedure with all of the variables found to be significant in the bivariate analyses. Across all of the victims in the sample, this analysis revealed that factors about the situation (location, weapon, threat, degrading acts, vaginal penetration, oral penetration, degree of injury, rapist's race, prior relationship, and time of day) accounted for an independent 2% of the variance, $F(10, 2174) = 4.99$, $p < .001$; factors about the victim (age, race, and whether raped before) accounted for no independent variance, $F(3, 2174) = 2.44$, $p < .07$; the victim's actions during the rape (verbal strategies and physical resistance) accounted for no independent variance, $F(2, 2174) = 2.54$, $p < .08$; and the victim's emotional reactions after the rape (fear, anger, and guilt) accounted for an independent 2% of the variance, $F(3, 2174) = 16.20$, $p < .001$. Together, all 18 variables accounted for an adjusted 6% of the variance in the reporting decision, $F(18, 2174) = 8.79$, $p < .001$. Thus, situational factors were stronger predictors of reporting than were demographic characteristics of victims, a result that was similar to our findings from the field-laboratory experiments (see Chapter 5).

We conducted a separate multiple linear-regression analysis, using the same predictor variables, of those who did not call the police immediately. This analysis of those who spoke to someone first or who took some other action was designed to determine if social influence significantly affected the reporting decision. In this analysis, whether or not the victim spoke to someone accounted for an independent 3% of the variance, $F(1, 1575) = 53.35$, $p < .001$. As with the bivariate analysis, victims were more likely to report if they spoke with someone first (beta = .18). Together, all 19 variables in the analysis accounted for an adjusted 10% of the variance, $F(19, 1575) = 9.86$, $p < .001$.

Logistic Regression. We used multiple linear regression because it is generally considered a robust statistic. However, it could be argued that linear regression is not appropriate in this instance, because it assumes constant variance of the error term across observations (homoscedasticity). This assumption cannot be satisfied with dichotomous dependent variables like reporting or not reporting to the police. Thus, for the reporting decision we also used logistic regression analysis, which produces equations directly analogous to ordinary least-squares regression.

The coefficients of the logistic regression equation are the natural logarithms of the odds ratios for the independent variables. A significant value of the likelihood ratio statistic ($-2 \times$ log likelihood), which is distributed as chi-square, indicates that for the equation the values of the coefficients are significantly different from zero. There is no generally accepted measure for logistic regression comparable to R^2 in multiple linear regression. However, Aldrich and Nelson (1984, p. 57) proposed a "pseudo-R^2," which we report for our analyses, to give the reader an idea of how well the analyses explain the underlying variation.

For the multiple linear-regression analysis, we analyzed the entire data base and reported statistics on the entire sample. One of the problems with such a procedure is that some of the findings may have been due to chance. Thus, one reason for using logistic regression is to try to replicate the results from the linear regression analysis using a statistical procedure that makes different assumptions about the error terms.

A second way we guarded against the possibility of chance findings was to construct a logistic regression equation on part of the sample and to validate it on the remainder of the sample. To accomplish this task, we created three equal subsamples drawn randomly from the entire sample. We then further divided in half two of these subsamples. Using a computer program written by Richard Linster (1987), we entered 18 predictor variables found in the bivariate analyses to be related to reporting, to who reported, or to both measures.

The program by Linster constructs a model using one subsample, validates it against another subsample, simultaneously constructs a model using the second sample, and validates it against the first. Using an iterative procedure, the program eliminates variables one at a time on the basis of whether such an elimination improves the joint validation. The program stops at the point where eliminating any other variable would lower the combined cross-validation log likelihood.

We ran this program using the two halves of the first third of the sample and then again using the two halves of the second third of the sample. Thus, our procedure to reduce the possibility of chance findings was to regard two thirds of the entire sample as being four independent samples. The output of each of the two runs was a list of significant predictor variables. The common variables from the two lists were then used as predictors of reporting for the combined two thirds of the sample. The variables that were still significant predictors after this final stage of the model construction process were used in the final validation process, which was conducted on the remaining third of the sample.

The logistic equation for the reporting decision constructed on two thirds of the sample is presented in Table 7-4. The coefficients of the equa-

TABLE 7-4. LOGISTIC EQUATIONS PREDICTING REPORTING AND WHO REPORTED[a]

Variable	Reporting (0 = yes 1 = no)		Who reported (0 = victim 1 = other)	
	Coefficient	t	Coefficient	t
Time of day	−.20	2.32*	−.22	3.97***
1 = 600–1200; 2 = 1200–1800;				
3 = 1800–2400; 4 = 000–600				
Rapist's race	.74	3.54***		
1 = black; 2 = white				
Weapon			.37	3.31***
1 = yes; 2 = no				
Degrading acts			.39	3.24**
1 = yes; 2 = no				
Prior relationship	.40	2.15*		
1 = none; 2 = some				
Age of victim			−.02	3.83***
Verbal strategies	.58	2.88**		
1 = yes; 2 = no				
Anger			.68	5.63***
1 = yes; 2 = no				
Guilt	−1.38	5.35***		
1 = yes; 2 = no				
Constant	−1.22	1.64	−1.05	2.70**
Pseudo-R^2	.37		.57	
−2 log likelihood	891.96		1990.13	
Validation χ^2	$\chi^2(9) = 1.92, p = .99$		$\chi^2(13) = 53.88***$	

[a]The construction of the logistic equations involved samples of 1,490 and 1,504, respectively. Validation tests involved samples of 735 and 746, respectively. Sample sizes differed because of missing values.
*$p < .05$.
**$p < .01$.
***$p < .001$.

tion indicate that reporting was more likely if the attack occurred later in the day, if the rapist was black, if the rapist was a stranger, if the victim had used verbal strategies during the attack, and if she did not report feeling guilty. No other factors were significant, including the interaction of the race of the rapist and the race of the victim. The validation test of these coefficients on the remaining third of the sample indicated that they provided an excellent fit for the data, $\chi^2(9) = 1.92$, $p = .99$.

Who Reported

In addition to knowing whether or not the crime had been reported, we were also interested in knowing who had reported the crime. In 55% of the cases, the victim herself notified the police, whereas a family member or friend reported in 25% of the cases, a stranger reported in 12% of the cases, the Rape Crisis Center reported in 3% of the cases, and someone else reported in 5% of the cases.

We first looked at who reported the crime at the bivariate level in combination with each of several other variables. Both victim variables and situational variables were considered, in that both groups of variables may determine who calls the police.

Nominal variables significantly related to who reported are presented in Table 7-5. In terms of factors about the attack (both nominal and continuous), the victim was more likely to report the crime herself if the rapist was black; if he had used a weapon; if he had threatened her; if he had penetrated her vaginally and orally; if he had performed a greater number of sexual acts, $t(2511) = 3.10$, $p < .01$; if he had performed degrading

TABLE 7-5. NOMINAL VARIABLES RELATED TO WHO REPORTED[a]

Variable	Chi-square	Percentage of rapes reported by victims by category			
Circumstantial variables					
Vaginal penetration	42.69***	Yes	49	No	25
Oral penetration	3.99*	Yes	51	No	46
Weapon present	18.44***	Yes	53	No	44
Threat present	17.38***	Yes	50	No	41
Rapist's race	7.80**	Black	50	White	42
Prior relationship	4.73*	Yes	49	No	45
Degrading acts used	21.14***	Yes	52	No	41
Victim variables					
Guilt experienced	18.91***	Yes	29	No	48
Anger experienced	76.10***	Yes	62	No	42
Fear experienced	4.24*	Yes	49	No	44
Verbal strategies used	15.36***	Yes	51	No	41

[a]The n's for these tests vary from 2,386 to 2,513.
*$p < .05$.
**$p < .01$.
***$p < .001$.

acts on her; if she knew him; and if the crime occurred later in the day, $t(2294) = 5.83$, $p < .001$.

In terms of factors about the victim, the victim was more likely to report the crime herself if she had used verbal strategies during the attack, if she did not say she felt guilty, if she said she felt angry, and if she said she was afraid.

Victims who reported the crime themselves were also older, $t(2511) = 3.92$, $p < .001$, and had offered more physical resistance than those for whom someone else had reported, $t(2379) = 2.36$, $p < .05$. Consistent with intuition, women who reported the crime themselves did so sooner than did women for whom someone else reported, $t(2099) = 6.44$, $p < .001$.

The variables found to be significant in the bivariate analyses were used as predictors in a multiple linear-regression analysis of who reported the attack. Nine factors about the attack (rapist's race, whether the rapist knew the victim, weapon, threat, time of day, degrading acts, vaginal penetration, oral penetration, and number of sexual acts) independently accounted for 2% of the variance, $F(9, 2198) = 6.30$, $p < .001$; the victim's age independently explained slightly less than 1% of the variance, $F(1, 2198) = 17.56$, $p < .001$; the victim's actions during the rape (physical resistance and verbal strategies) did not account for any independent variance, $F(2, 2198) = 1.75$, $p > .10$; and the victim's emotional reactions after the rape (fear, anger, and guilt) independently explained more than 2% of the variance, $F(3, 2198) = 19.80$, $p < .001$. Together, all 15 variables accounted for an adjusted 6% of the variance, $F(15, 2198) = 10.64$, $p < .001$.

As with the reporting decision, a logistic regression equation was constructed using two thirds of the sample. The coefficients of the equation, presented in Table 7-4, indicate that the victim was more likely to report the crime herself if the crime had occurred later in the day, if the rapist had used a weapon, if the rapist had performed degrading acts, if the victim was older, and if the victim said that she felt angry. The validation test of this equation against the remaining third of the sample indicated that the fit was not particularly good, $\chi^2(13) = 53.88$, $p < .001$.

Delay in Reporting

The data archive allowed us to investigate not only whether or not the victim reported and who reported but also how quickly the victim reported. Reporting delay is an important dependent variable because police and prosecutors often think they have a stronger case if the crime was reported sooner (Law Enforcement Assistance Administration, 1977b, c). In almost all of the 2,102 victimizations for which information was available (96% of reporters), the police were notified soon after the crime ended: 72% of the reports were within 30 minutes, an additional 8% were within an hour, an additional 7% were within three hours, and an additional 12% were made more than three hours after the crime.

Obviously, victims' first action was significantly related to how quickly the crime was reported, $F(2, 2098) = 445.72$, $p < .001$. Reports of crimes by victims who called immediately ($M = 1.08$) came significantly sooner than did those in which victims talked to someone else first ($M = 1.41$), and reports from both of these groups came significantly sooner than did those in which the victim took some other action first ($M = 2.55$). Delay was also greater if the victim knew the offender ($r = .19$, $p < .001$); if the victim had not employed verbal strategies during the rape ($r = .12$, $p < .001$); if the victim had faced less Coercion during the rape ($r = -.11$, $p < .001$); and if the attack had lasted a longer period of time ($r = .12$, $p < .001$).

A 2×2 analysis of variance was conducted on reporting delay; rapist's race and victim's race were used as the grouping factors. The crime was reported sooner when the rapist was black ($M = 1.58$) than when he was white ($M = 1.82$), $F(1, 2072) = 16.97$, $p < .001$. Attacks on white victims were reported with slightly less delay ($M = 1.61$) than were attacks on black victims ($M = 1.62$), $F(1, 2072) = 4.71$, $p < .05$. The interaction of rapist's race and victim's race was also significant, $F(1, 2072) = 4.19$, $p < .05$. Attacks on black victims were reported with about the same delay whether the rapist was black ($M = 1.62$) or white ($M = 1.63$). In contrast, attacks on white victims were reported sooner when the rapist was black ($M = 1.45$) than when he was white ($M = 1.85$).

Victims' emotional reactions were significantly related to delay in reporting. Attacks on women who said they were afraid were reported sooner ($M = 1.58$) than were attacks on women who did not say they were afraid ($M = 1.71$), $t(2099) = 2.62$, $p < .01$. Similarly, attacks on women who said they were angry were reported sooner ($M = 1.52$) than were attacks on women who did not say they were angry ($M = 1.65$), $t(2099) = 2.39$, $p < .05$. Whether or not the victim expressed guilt was unrelated to delay in reporting.

A multiple-regression analysis was conducted on reporting delay that used as predictors those variables found to be significantly related to the first action victims took, to the reporting decision, or to both. For all cases reported to the police, this analysis revealed that situational variables (location, weapon, threat, degrading acts, oral penetration, vaginal penetration, degree of injury, rapist's race, prior relationship, and time of day) independently explained 5% of the variance, $F(10, 1921) = 10.74$, $p < .001$; victim characteristics (age, race, and whether raped before) independently explained slightly less than 1% of the variance, $F(3, 1921) = 4.72$, $p < .01$; the victim's actions during the rape (verbal strategies and physical resistance) independently explained slightly less than 1% of the variance, $F(2, 1921) = 6.90$, $p < .001$; and the victim's emotional reactions after the rape (fear, anger, and guilt) independently explained no variance, $F(3, 1921) = 1.78$, $p > .10$. All 18 variables together explained an adjusted 7% of the variance in reporting delay, $F(18, 1921) = 8.94$, $p < .001$.

This same multiple-regression analysis was also used in a second analysis involving only those cases that were not reported immediately. This second analysis, which used only those who spoke to someone first or who took some other action, was conducted to determine if social influence had a significant impact on the reporting decision. Among these cases, situational variables independently explained 4% of the variance, $F(10, 1324) = 7.03$, $p < .001$; characteristics of the victim independently explained 1% of the variance, $F(3, 1324) = 4.67$, $p < .01$; the victim's actions during the rape independently explained no variance, $F(2, 1324) = 2.35$, $p < .10$; the victim's emotional reactions after the rape independently explained no variance, $F < 1$; and whether the victim spoke to someone or not independently explained 17% of the variance, $F(1, 1324) = 299.96$, $p < .001$. As was true at the bivariate level, reporting delay was longer if victims did not talk with someone first (beta = .42). Together all 19 variables explained an adjusted 26% of the variance, $F(19, 1324) = 25.33$, $p < .001$.

Subsequent Intentions

In addition to examining the reporting decision, we looked at two indicators of victims' subsequent intentions: the number of individuals they planned to tell about the assault and whether or not they left with the crisis center a phone number where they could be reached. These variables are important because they may be related to victims' recovery from the attack.

Most victims said they would tell someone about the attack: 36% said they would tell one person, 35% said they would tell two persons, 8% said they would tell three persons, and 2% said they would tell four or more persons. Only 19% said they would tell no one of the rape. Victims' first action was significantly related to the number of people they said they would tell, $F(2, 2510) = 59.77$, $p < .001$. Victims who talked with someone else first said they would tell significantly more people ($M = 1.64$) than did victims who either called the police ($M = 1.22$) or took some other action ($M = 1.23$).

The number of people whom victims said they would tell was positively related to the amount of Coercion they faced during the rape, $r = .20$, $p < .001$; to the number of sexual acts suffered, $r = .10$, $p < .001$, and to victims' use of verbal strategies during the rape, $r = .10$, $p < .001$. The number of people whom victims planned to tell was negatively related to age, $r = -.20$, $p < .001$, and to whether there had been vaginal penetration, $r = -.11$, $p < .001$, so that younger victims and victims who had not suffered vaginal intercourse were likely to tell more people.

The number of people victims said they would tell was significantly related to whether victims said they had experienced fear and guilt immediately after the rape. Women who stated they were afraid said they would tell more people ($M = 1.53$) than did women who did not say they were afraid ($M = 1.08$), $t(2511) = 11.47$, $p < .001$. Similarly, victims who expressed guilt said they would tell more people ($M = 1.59$) than did women who did not say they felt guilty ($M = 1.37$), $t(2511) = 2.71$, $p < .01$.

Victims' leaving a phone number with the Rape Crisis Center was significantly related to the first action they took, $\chi^2(2) = 12.27$, $p < .01$. Fewer individuals whose first action was to report left their phone number (78%) than did victims who talked with someone else (85%) or who took some other action (84%). Leaving a phone number was also significantly related to expressed fear, $\chi^2(1) = 28.28$, $p < .001$, and guilt, $\chi^2(1) = 4.28$, $p < .05$. Victims who said they were afraid were more likely to leave a telephone number (86%) than were women who did not say they were afraid (77%). Victims who said they felt guilty were more likely to leave a number (90%) than were women who did not say they felt guilty (83%).

These findings suggest that the experience of fear and guilt is related to talking with others immediately after the sexual assault was completed, with leaving a valid telephone number, and with a prediction of telling more people about the crime. These expressions of affiliative behavior are consistent with Schachter's work (1959), which indicated that anxiety often leads people to want to affiliate with others.

Despite this consistency with prior research, it must be remembered that victims' emotions were assessed after they had taken some action. Thus, the emotional reactions may have followed rather than preceded the behavior. For example, women who reported the crime may, in retrospect, have judged that they must been angry or else they would not have called the police.

GENERAL DISCUSSION OF THE ARCHIVAL RESEARCH

The research reported in this chapter reinforces and extends the findings of the previous chapters concerning the role played by social and emotional factors in victim decision making. Our results show that it is common for victims of spouse abuse and sexual assault to talk with others after the crime. For example, in Study 15, victims were initially more likely to talk with others than they were to notify the police. Among those who did not notify the police immediately, initially talking with others as opposed to first taking some other action produced a higher rate of reporting, and among those who eventually reported, talking with others led to shorter delays in reporting.

It is reasonable to infer from these findings that for a significant number of victims, social influence affected both the decision to report the crime and the delay in reporting. This reasoning is consistent with a normative view of reporting that was presented in the previous chapter. Given our findings in Study 10, showing that there is strong normative support among diverse groups in the United States for reporting crimes of rape (see Tables 6-2 and 6-6), it is highly likely that in their conversations with others, victims were encouraged to report the crime to the police.

Consistent with our experimental findings (see Chapters 3 and 5), emotional factors were found to play an important role in the decision-making process of victims. Results of Study 15 showed that emotional factors figured prominently in the decision to report the crime, who did the reporting (victim or other), and the delay in reporting. Anger and fear, but not guilt, were associated with higher levels of reporting. Victims who described themselves as angry were more likely to report the crime themselves than those who did not report being angry. And among those who reported the crime, feelings of anger or fear were associated with shorter delays in reporting (in the bivariate but not the multiple-regression analysis).

The emotion of fear was also a particularly good predictor of affiliative behavior following the victimization. Victims who were rated as being fearful, as opposed to those who were not, were more likely to (1) initially talk with others; (2) express the intention to tell a greater number of others about the crime; and (3) leave their phone number with the Rape Crisis Center.

Study 15 yielded interesting insights into the antecedents of anger and fear among victims of sexual assault. Certain features of the crime were associated with *both* fear and anger. They included facing more coercion, experiencing degrading acts in addition to the rape, and offering more resistance to the attacker. Two variables that were related differentially to the experience of anger and fear concerned whether or not the victim had been raped before and whether or not the attacker was a stranger or someone previously known by the victim. Anger was associated with having known the rapist and having been raped before, whereas fear was associated with being raped by a stranger and not having been raped before. In the case of anger, being raped by an acquaintance, a person who was presumably trusted, and having been raped before may have made the victim angry because they are likely to produce particularly strong feelings of injustice and a sense of having been wronged.

Victims who had not been raped before may have been fearful because the present victimization destroyed any illusions they had about their invulnerability (Janoff-Bulman, 1985; Perloff, 1983). That the rapist was a stranger may have made them fearful because the randomness of the choice ("Why me?") increased their sense of vulnerability to subsequent harm. Clearly, the victim's emotional state must be incorporated into any model that attempts to account for victim decision making immediately after the crime. Our efforts to develop such a model are detailed in Chapter 9.

The archival approach has increased our understanding of the role played by social and emotional factors in victim decision making, but we must not neglect its limitations. We noted at the outset of this chapter that a major disadvantage of this approach is that the investigator does not exercise control over the information contained in the archive. This lack of control raises the distinct possibility that the archive may contain a non-representative sample of cases. For example, the women who chose to contact the Rape Crisis Center may have constituted a self-selected sample of women who were not representative of rape victims in general or of victims who call the police but do not visit a crisis center. The selectivity of the sample can be seen in the relatively high rate of reporting (89%) compared to the 51% figure obtained in the National Crime Survey (Bureau of Justice Statistics, 1992).

Further, investigators' lack of control means that they are limited to the information collected by the agency to meet its needs rather than those of the investigators. Thus, for example, our concern with the effects of social influence on reporting is addressed only incompletely by the archival data. Although we found a relationship between talking with others and reporting the crime, we do not know if victims received advice from others about what to do and what that advice was. To answer questions such as these requires a methodology that allows for a detailed probing of those specific variables of interest to the investigators.

In order to obtain the information that we were interested in regarding social influence, we needed to talk to victims about their decision-making process and the variables that may have influenced this process. The interview studies we conducted to obtain such information are presented in the next chapter.

8

Self-Reports
SURVEYING CRIME VICTIMS

The five studies presented in this chapter involved the collection of information directly from crime victims by means of questionnaires and interviews. The purpose of these studies was to collect in-depth information about victims' immediate and delayed responses to the crime and the role played by others in mediating such responses. Victims of a variety of crimes, including burglary, theft, robbery, and rape, were asked to provide information about the crime and their subsequent reactions, particularly the factors that may have influenced their decision to call or not to call the police.

There are numerous advantages to using self-reports to investigate decision making by crime victims, the most important of which is that it allows for in-depth questioning of victims about their thoughts, feelings, and behavior upon learning of their victimization. There are, though, certain inherent weaknesses in this approach when it is used to study victim decision making. These weaknesses derive from several unsubstantiated assumptions of this approach, namely, that (1) victims know the reasons for their decisions; (2) victims can accurately recall details about their feelings, thoughts, and behavior when asked to do so on subsequent occasions; and (3) they are willing to disclose this information to an interviewer. As we have documented elsewhere (Greenberg, Ruback, & Westcott, 1982), these assumptions are quite tenuous. There is evidence that victims are often unaware of the reasons for their behavior (Nisbett & Wilson, 1977), that their memory is frequently inaccurate (Loftus, 1979; *Victim Recall Pretest*, 1970), and that they may deliberately withhold information from the interviewer (*San Jose Methods Test*, 1972). Despite these limitations, the self-report approach is probably the most common method of studying victims' reactions to crime because of its convenience and capacity for in-depth probing.

The best known example of this approach may be the National Crime Survey (NCS) conducted jointly by the Department of Justice and the Bureau of the Census (Bureau of Justice Statistics, 1990c). Initiated in 1972, the NCS is a continuing survey involving interviews at six-month intervals with occupants of 50,000 dwellings located throughout the United States. Adult occupants are questioned about their involvement as crime victims during the preceding six months. Information is collected about the details of the crime (e.g., the time, the place, and the nature of the suspect) and the reasons why the police were or were not notified. The NCS includes victims who have *not* notified the police as well as those who have. It is regarded, therefore, as providing a more complete accounting of criminal victimizations than does the FBI's *Uniform Crime Reports*, which reflects only reported crimes.

This chapter reports on five studies that used the self-report approach to collect information on victims' reactions to their victimization. The first (Study 16) consisted of telephone interviews with sexual assault victims who sought assistance from a rape crisis center located in Pittsburgh. In the second study (Study 17), we conducted face-to-face interviews with victims of burglary, theft, and robbery who reported their victimization to the police. The third (Study 18) and fourth (Study 19) involved questionnaire and telephone interviews, respectively, administered to college students who had identified themselves as victims of either a burglary or a theft. Finally, Study 20 was a longitudinal study of rape victims who had contacted a rape crisis center in Atlanta. They were interviewed on three occasions; the first was a face-to-face interview, after which notes were made in archival records, and the remaining two were by telephone.

STUDY 16: SELF-REPORTS OF RAPE VICTIMS

This study was designed to deal with several issues raised by our previous analysis of the data archives kept by the Rape Crisis Center (RCC) of Grady Memorial Hospital in Atlanta (see Study 15). First, we wished to determine whether the same pattern of results would obtain with a different sample of rape victims located in a large northern industrial city (i.e., Pittsburgh). We were particularly interested in ascertaining victims' emotional reactions and behavioral responses immediately after the attack. In addition, we wanted to determine the percentage of the incidents that had been reported to the police, who had actually notified the police, and how much time had elapsed before the police were notified. Second, the interviews allowed us to answer questions that were not answerable from the archival analysis. Namely, after the assault, did anyone offer the victims advice about whether or not to notify the police? Who offered the advice, what was the advice, and did the victims tend to follow the advice?

METHOD

Participants and Procedure

Participants in the interviews were 364 female victims of rape who had sought assistance from Pittsburgh Action Against Rape (PAAR), a rape crisis center serving the greater Pittsburgh area since 1972. The victims tended to be white females (75%) between the ages of 18 and 55. The information was collected as part of a routine intake interview (usually by telephone) conducted with victims when they initially contacted the center (between February 1983 and December 1984). The intake counselors were not guided by a formal interview schedule. Instead, the clients and their needs dictated the content of the interviews. No written notes were taken during the interviews. Immediately after each interview ended, however, counselors completed a questionnaire prepared by the center. The questions allowed them to record as much of the conversation as their memory permitted. The center cooperated with our project by allowing us to append a series of nine questions to the questionnaire. Each question had from three to eight response alternatives. It was not always possible for the counselors to obtain answers to the questions which we appended, owing to their primary concern with responding to the client's needs. For this reason the data set contains a high number of missing cases.

RESULTS

The results obtained from this largely white sample of rape victims in Pittsburgh (PAAR) are remarkably consistent with the results obtained from the predominantly black sample in Atlanta (RCC; Study 15). Among the PAAR respondents, fear was the major emotional response (63%) immediately after the crime, followed by guilt (14%) and anger (11%). These responses parallel the findings in Atlanta, where fear was the predominant response (67%), followed by anger (26%) and guilt (6%). The first thing that victims said they did following the attack was to talk with another person (38%). These others included friends (49%), family (32%), strangers (13%), and the PAAR hotline counselor (6%). Just 18% said that the first thing they did was to call the police. Once again, these findings are consistent with the RCC data from Atlanta, where 41% first talked with others and 28% first notified the police. Victims reported 72% of the incidents to the police, somewhat less than the 89% figure reporting to police in the Atlanta sample. The discrepancy is attributable to differences in how clients are referred to the two centers. Those contacting the center in Atlanta had frequently been referred to the center by the police, whereas those who contacted PAAR typically did so on their own.

In the instances where the police were notified, the person most likely to notify them was the victim (53%), followed by family and/or friends (25%). These figures are almost identical to those obtained in the RCC study, where 55% of the incidents were reported by the victim and 25% by family and friends. Of the PAAR sample, 40% reported the incidents to the police less than an hour after the crime, compared to 80% in the RCC study in Atlanta.

As previously noted, the most common *first* action taken by victims was to talk to some other person (other than the police). The interview approach allowed us to answer a more fundamental question: Did victims consult with others *at any time* prior to their decision to call or not to call the police? Although this information was not contained in the RCC archive, our interviews with the PAAR sample revealed that 78% of the victims consulted with others before making their decision to report the crime. Those most often consulted were family (26%) and friends and acquaintances (24%).

Of those who talked with others, 76% said that the person with whom they talked offered them advice about what to do. Of those who offered advice, 40% tended to be family and 27% to be friends. Strangers and bystanders rarely offered the victim advice (5%). Most victims who received advice were advised to call the police (75%), whereas just 4% were advised not to call the police. An additional 21% were given some other form of advice. In order to determine the effect of the advice on the report decision, we made a comparison of those who were advised to call and those who either were advised not to call or received some other advice. Of those advised to call the police, 93% reported the incident, compared to 60% of those who were advised not to call or who were given some other advice, $\chi^2(1) = 6.87$, $p < .01$. Of those who received advice about calling the police, 84% followed that advice.

DISCUSSION

The results of the interviews with victims of rape in Pittsburgh are remarkably consistent with the analysis of the data archives kept by the Rape Crisis Center of Grady Memorial Hospital in Atlanta. Despite differences in race and locality, the studies are consistent in showing that the most common initial reaction of victims was to talk with someone other than the police. The vast majority of incidents in both studies were reported to the police, the victim being the primary notifier in slightly more than half the cases.

The interview data strongly suggested that social influence is an important factor in the decision to notify the police. Three out of four victims consulted with others before deciding whether or not to report the incident to the police. Of these, 76% said that in these conversations the other person offered advice about what to do, and that they tended to act in a manner consistent with the advice.

These data should not be accepted uncritically. The interviewers did not record victims' responses as they were made. Rather, the questionnaires were completed by the interviewers *after* the interviews were completed. Errors of omission and commission were certainly possible, if not likely. The generalizability of the data is limited by the nature of the sample. Participants represented a self-selected sample of rape victims: those who sought help from a rape crisis center. As we noted in the last chapter, such individuals may be very different from victims of rape who chose not to contact a rape crisis center. Conceivably, victims who contact crisis centers may be more in need of advice and support and are therefore more susceptible to social influence. Interpretations one can make from the data are further limited by the fact that respondents consisted of female victims of a single category of crime. We need to look at the reactions of other types of crime victims and the role played by social influence in their decision making.

STUDY 17: INTERVIEWS WITH
VICTIMS OF BURGLARY, THEFT, AND ROBBERY

In an effort to learn about the reactions of other types of crime victims, we conducted structured in-depth interviews with victims of residential burglary, theft, and robbery who had reported their victimization to the police. Since the sample included only victims who had reported to police, we focused on the determinants of *delay* in reporting rather than on the determinants of reporting. More specifically, we attempted to ascertain the extent to which victims of crimes other than sexual assault are exposed to social influence attempts, as well as the impact of such attempts on delay in reporting the crime. A second purpose of this study was to compare the impact of situational variables (e.g., social influence) and person variables (e.g., the victim's race and education) on delay in reporting to the police.

METHOD

Participants and Instruments

Participants consisted of 61 volunteers who had been victims of residential burglary, theft, or robbery (commercial and noncommercial) between January 1978 and December 1980 in four communities in Pennsylvania and

Georgia. Three of the communities were located in the greater Pittsburgh area (McKeesport, Mount Lebanon, and Swissvale), and the fourth was Atlanta. The police departments in the four municipalities sent letters to recent victims informing them of our project and of our willingness to pay them $10 for a one-hour interview. The letter emphasized that their participation was voluntary and that the project was not connected in any way with the police. The letter provided a phone number where we could be reached. In this way, victims' privacy was respected. That is, we learned the names of only those who chose to contact us. Respondents were required to meet two criteria before an interview was scheduled: (1) they had to have been victims of a residential burglary, theft, or robbery, and (2) they had to be the person who had actually reported the incident. A total of 525 letters were sent out, producing 72 replies (a 14% response rate).

Interviews were conducted with 61 of these respondents, but 3 were excluded from the final analysis: 2 because they provided insufficient information and 1 because it was highly doubtful whether a crime had actually taken place. The 58 remaining participants consisted of 24 victims of burglary, 21 victims of theft, and 13 robbery victims. There were 24 males and 34 females, predominantly white (76%), between the ages of 16 and 76 ($M = 40$), with a median annual family income of $17,000 and a mode of $10,000 to $15,000. At the time of the interview, most were employed (74%) and owned their own homes (62%). The average interval between the victimization and the interview was 12 months.

The interviews were usually conducted in the participant's residence by one of two male graduate students. Two interview schedules were employed: one for victims of burglary and theft, and the other for robbery victims. The 130-item questionnaire administered to burglary and theft victims dealt with the following areas: (1) details about the crime, such as the time and place of occurrence, the property taken, and its value; (2) victims' immediate affective, cognitive, and behavioral reactions to the event; (3) their decision process regarding notification of the police, including the role of social influence; (4) attitudes of victims toward the local police and the criminal justice system in general; and (5) victims' demographic characteristics. The 160-item questionnaire administered to robbery victims included a number of additional items pertaining to their recall of the confrontation with the robber(s).

RESULTS

Ninety percent of participants had been victims of a completed crime (as opposed to one that was attempted). Typically, the person who first discovered the crime was the victim or his or her spouse (84%). The stolen property most often consisted of cash (26%), a bicycle (25%), a wallet or purse (17%), or household goods and jewelry (15%). The estimated dollar value of the losses ranged from $5 to $2,500, with a mean of $332 and a median loss of $125. The value of the losses varied with the type of crime. Burglary victims lost an average amount of $683, robbery victims lost $190, and theft victims lost $135, $F(2, 48) = 6.83$, $p < .01$.

When burglary and theft victims were asked to recall how they had felt when they realized that they were victims of a crime (robbery victims were not asked this question), the most commonly reported feelings were of anger (51%), upset (26%), and surprise (16%). Only 11% described themselves as feeling "scared." Burglary and theft victims also rated the intensity of their feelings on seven-point scales (7 = high and 1 = low). Interestingly, while the monetary losses of burglary victims were greater than those of theft victims, they reported being *less* angered by the event than were theft victims, $F(1, 42) = 4.34$, $p < .05$. However, burglary victims rated themselves as more scared than did theft victims, $F(1, 42) = 3.95$, $p = .05$. The first action taken by burglary and theft victims upon discovering that something was missing was to talk with others (49%), followed by searching the scene (40%) and calling the police (11%). The first action taken by robbery victims after the robber left the scene was the exact reverse; most of them called the police (62%), while fewer searched the scene first (23%) or talked with others (15%).

The results suggest that social influence may have affected the decision to report the crime and the amount of time that victims waited before making the report. Sixty-two percent of the victims (of burglary, theft, and robbery combined) said that before notifying the police they had spoken with at least one other person. One quarter of these indicated that they had talked to two or more others. Moreover, over half of those who talked with others (58%) said that the other(s) had offered them advice about what to do. In all but one instance, victims were advised to notify the police (95%). Since every victim in the study notified the police, it is safe to conclude that victims acted in a manner consistent with the advice given them. However, as we noted earlier, because the study lacked a group of nonreporting victims, the conclusion that the advice influenced reporting is only suggestive. At the very least, the data testify to the high frequency with which victims of burglary, theft, and robbery were exposed to social influence attempts, a finding consistent with our results with victims of rape.

The number of people that victims spoke to varied with the nature of the crime $F(2, 55) = 8.16$, $p < .001$. Planned pairwise comparisons indicated that theft victims talked with more people ($M = 1.86$) than did both burglary victims ($M = .71$), $F(1, 55) = 12.18$, $p < .001$, and robbery victims ($M = .54$), $F(1, 55) = 11.5$, $p < .005$, who did not differ significantly from each other.

We next examined the relationship between social influence attempts and delay in reporting. The delay interval was defined as the victim's estimate of the time elapsing from the time of the discovery of the crime to the time when the police were called. The median delay time across all three types of crime was 15 minutes. More importantly, the results revealed a strong positive relationship ($r = .54$, $p < .001$) between the number of people that victims said they had spoken with and the reported delay in notifying the police. The greater the number of people consulted, the longer was the delay in reporting. This may explain in part why theft victims delayed longer in reporting the crime (Mdn = 59 minutes) than did either burglary (Mdn = 9 minutes) or robbery victims (Mdn = 5 minutes), $F(2, 55) = 4.40$, $p < .02$. Planned pairwise comparisons between theft and burglary, $F(1, 55) = 6.99$, $p < .025$, and between theft and robbery, $F(1, 55) = 5.73$, $p < .025$, were both significant. In conclusion, the data strongly suggest that an important reason why theft victims were slowest to report the crime was that they talked with more people before notifying the police.

In order to test this reasoning further, we performed a hierarchical multiple-regression analysis on the delay measure. Type of crime (as two dummy variables) was entered first, and number of people talked to was entered second. The type of crime accounted for 14% of the variance in the delay score, $F(1, 56) = 8.93$, $p < .005$. However, despite being entered second, the number of people talked to accounted for an additional 17% of the variance in reporting delay, $F(1, 54) = 13.7$, $p < .001$. Although type of crime influenced delay in reporting, the number of people talked to made an independent contribution to delay in reporting even when entered second.

In order to determine the relative strength of situational versus person variables as predictors of delay in reporting, we looked at the bivariate correlations between a number of variables and reporting delay. Results of this analysis (see Table 8-1) support the generalizability of our experimental findings that situational factors are better predictors of delay than are person factors (see Chapter 5). As can be seen in Table 8-1, the best predictor of delay in reporting is a situational variable: the number of people spoken with. Of the 10 best predictors, only 3 were clearly person variables (i.e., race, education, and employment status).

DISCUSSION

The findings from the interviews with victims of burglary, theft, and robbery reinforce and extend the findings from the interviews with victims of sexual assault. Burglary, theft, and robbery victims, like victims of rape, tend to talk with and receive advice from others when deciding whether to notify the police. In addition, victims in both studies tended to act in a manner consistent with the advice received. This finding suggests that victims' decision to call the police, as well as the delay in reporting, may be subject to social influence.

As in the previous study, the results must be interpreted with caution. The sample consisted of an extremely small subset of victims (14% response rate) who chose both to report the crime to the police and to participate in

TABLE 8-1. VARIABLES CORRELATED WITH DELAY IN REPORTING

Variable	Pearson r
Number of people talked with prior to reporting	.54***
Desire to see thief caught as reason for reporting	
(1 = not at all important, 7 = very important)	−.37**
Type of crime (burglary vs. robbery and theft)	−.22
Education of respondent	.21
Desire to get property back as reason for reporting	
(1 = not at all important, 7 = very important)	.17
Type of dwelling (1 = house, 2 = apartment)	−.17
Employment status (1 = employed, 2 = unemployed)	−.16
Race of respondent (1 = black, 2 = white)	−.08
Anything stolen? (1 = yes, 2 = no)	.06
How upset were you? (1 = not at all, 2 = very)	.04

**$p < .01$.
***$p < .001$.

this study. Clearly, the findings from this study cannot be generalized to individuals who chose *not* to report their victimization to the police. We therefore conducted two additional studies in order to learn more about the role of social influence factors in the decisions of nonreporters as well as reporters of property crimes such as burglary and theft.

STUDY 18: SURVEY OF REPORTER AND NONREPORTER VICTIMS OF BURGLARY AND THEFT

Study 17 yielded information about the immediate reactions of burglary, theft, and robbery victims, and about the impact of social influence on the delay in reporting such crimes to the police. Study 18 attempted to extend these findings by examining the effect of social influence on the *decision to report* the crime, as well as on the delay in reporting. Another purpose of this study was to compare the reactions of burglary and theft victims, a goal that was not fully realizable in the previous study because of the small sample size.

METHOD

Participants

Participants consisted of 97 introductory psychology students who had identified themselves as victims of burglary ($n = 32$) or theft ($n = 65$) in the 12 months prior to October 1986. A two-stage recruitment process was employed. First, potential participants answered a series of 10 questions concerning their possible involvement as victims of attempted or completed property crimes in the previous 12 months. Second, those who claimed that they had been victims of such crimes were questioned on the telephone so that we could determine whether or not they fit the protocol; they were then scheduled for a time to complete the written questionnaire. Individuals who passed the second stage of the screening process consisted of 49 males and 48 females with a mean age of 19.2 years. The vast majority of the sample was white (91%); just 7% was black, and 1% was Asian. Most participants were freshmen (63%) or sophomores (26%). In terms of family income, the median was $37,700, and the mode was $40,000 and above.

Instruments

Two questionnaires were constructed, one containing 71 items for those who had reported the crime ($n = 40$) and one containing 63 items for those who had not ($n = 57$). The questionnaire for reporters was slightly longer because they answered additional questions concerning their interactions with the police. In both questionnaires victims were asked to provide information about (1) the nature of the crime (e.g., the value of the stolen property); (2) their feelings, thoughts, and behavior upon learning of the crime; (3) any interactions they had with others immediately after the incident; (4) their attitudes toward the police and the criminal justice system; and (5) their demographic characteristics. A variety of question formats were employed, including open-ended and closed-ended questions. Participants anonymously completed the questionnaires in small groups ranging from two to five members. The questionnaires took about 30 minutes to complete.

RESULTS AND DISCUSSION

First we compared the responses of burglary and theft victims. Unlike the results of Study 17, this analysis yielded no significant differences on any of the variables compared. That is, victims of burglary were no more angered, upset, or scared, nor were they less likely to talk with others, report the crime to the police, or report the crime more quickly, than were victims of theft. Consequently, the results reported below are based on the findings collapsed across type of crime.

The crimes most often took place in the street (44%), in the victim's residence (39%), and at work or school (17%); 84% were completed crimes. Victims reported a wide variety of stolen items, ranging from $2 stolen from the glove compartment of a car to a car valued at $13,000. Other items reported stolen included bicycles, stereo equipment, and wallets or purses containing cash or credit cards. Several unusual items were stolen, including a bikini bathing suit (valued at $35) and two Siberian Husky dogs (described as "priceless"). The mean dollar value of the stolen property was $590. Because the dollar value of some of the stolen items was extremely high (e.g., $4,000 and higher), the mean is not an accurate reflection of the dollar value of the stolen property. A better indicator is the median, which was $60.

Victims' immediate emotional reactions to discovering the crime were similar to the reactions of burglary and theft victims in Study 17. In response to an open-ended question concerning how they had felt when they realized that they were victims of a crime, victims used "angry" (54%) and "upset" (19%) most often to describe such feelings. In comparison, just 10% described themselves as feeling "scared." Similarly, when asked to rate how they felt on a series of seven-point bipolar scales, victims rated "angry" ($M = 6.14$) and "upset" ($M = 5.74$) high and "confused" ($M = 3.63$) and "scared" ($M = 2.85$) relatively low. Perceived seriousness of the crime was correlated with ratings of anger ($r = .27$, $p < .01$), upset ($r = .33$, $p < .001$), and scared ($r = .30$, $p < .01$), and with reporting ($r = .22$, $p < .05$).

In response to the question "What did you *do* when you first learned that something was missing?" respondents most often said that they had either contacted others (34%) or searched the scene (27%). Just 13% said that the first thing they had done was to notify the police. Afterward, victims admitted thinking about or asking themselves: "What can I do to prevent it from happening again?" (93%); "Could I have avoided this?" (87%); "It could have been worse" (79%); and "Why me?" (76%).

Social Influence and the Decision to Report the Crime

As in our previous findings, victims consulted with others when deciding what to do. Seventy-seven percent said that they had talked with one or more others. Of these, 15% had spoken with one other, 34% had spoken with two others, and 51% had spoken with three or more others. The mean number of others spoken with was 2.36. Typically, the first person that they had consulted was someone who was with them when they learned of the crime (56%). The first person to whom they talked tended to be either a friend (49%) or one of their parents (30%). The major reason for contacting others was to obtain information (17%) concerning what had happened and advice (27%) about what to do. Of those who had talked with others, 81% recalled receiving advice about what to do. In most instances the other person had volunteered the advice (69%). Regardless of whether the advice had been volunteered or solicited, victims tended to follow the advice in 90% of the instances.

In order to identify the best predictors of (1) the number of others consulted with, (2) the type of advice received from others, and (3) the decision to notify the police, a series of hierarchical multiple-regression analyses were performed. We first conducted bivariate analyses in order to identify the predictors to be entered in the regression equations. The predictors for the regression analyses were those variables that the bivariate analyses showed were significantly correlated with each dependent variable.

When performing the regression analyses, we used a conservative approach in which the predictor variable of interest was always entered last in the equation. In this way, we were able to determine the amount of variance accounted for by the predictor *after* all other predictors had been entered.

Eight variables (identified by the bivariate analysis) were entered into the regression analysis to predict the number of people talked to. This analysis revealed that the difficulty in deciding what to do independently explained 3% of the variance, $F(1, 79) = 3.24$, $p < .08$. None of the remaining variables even approached significance. (They included how confused, surprised, upset, and scared the victims were, as well as the type of crime, the dollar value of the stolen items, and the perceived seriousness of the crime.) All eight variables together explained an adjusted 10% of the variance in the number of people talked to, $F(8, 79) = 2.22$, $p < .05$.

A similar procedure was used to predict the type of advice received from others. Since most of those who received advice had tended to receive advice from multiple others, a *composite index* of advice was created. A "majority" decision rule was employed. Thus, if two of the three advice givers had favored reporting the crime, then the victim was judged to have been advised to report the incident. When there had been two advice givers and the advice had been contradictory, the advice was categorized as not to report. A multiple-regression analysis on this composite advice score involved four predictors: the seriousness of the crime, the type of crime, the dollar value of the stolen property, and the difficulty in deciding what to do. Two predictors accounted for a marginally significant proportion of the unique variance: the difficulty of the decision accounted for 6% of the unique variance, $F(1, 50) = 3.63$, $p < .07$; and the perceived seriousness of the crime independently accounted for another 6% of the variance, $F(1, 50) = 3.63$, $p < .07$. The less the judged difficulty of the decision and the greater the perceived seriousness of the crime, the greater was the likelihood of victims' being advised to call the police. The four variables together accounted for an adjusted 12% of the variance, $F(4, 50) = 2.89$, $p < .05$.

A third regression analysis was conducted on the reporting decision (report–not report). Six variables identified from the bivariate analysis were entered into the equation (participant's sex, perceived seriousness, difficulty of decision, type of crime, dollar value of stolen property, and composite advice). The best predictor was the composite advice received. It independently explained 42% of the variance in reporting, $F(1, 48) = 60.66$, $p < .001$, more than the remaining five variables combined. Together, the six variables accounted for an adjusted 63% of the variance in reporting, $F(6, 48) = 16.25$, $p < .001$.

Delay in Reporting. We also examined the factors that predicted the delay in reporting. The median delay time for all participants who had reported the crime ($n = 40$) was 15 minutes. We first conducted bivariate correlation analyses in order to identify predictors of delay to be entered into the regression equation. Seven correlates of delay in reporting were identified: the type of crime, the victims' level of confusion, how scared they were, how serious they perceived the crime to be, how difficult it was to decide what to do, the number of people talked with before the crime was reported, and the sex of the victim. A regression analysis involving the seven variables revealed that victims' level of fear (i.e., their self-ratings of how "scared" they were) independently explained 9% of the variance in delay, $F(1, 32) = 5.54$, $p < .03$; type of crime accounted for an additional 8% of the variance, $F(1, 32) = 4.54$, $p < .05$; and perceived seriousness of crime explained an additional 7% of the variance, $F(1, 32) = 4.06$, $p = .05$. Victims delayed longer in reporting the crime when they were less scared, the crime was burglary, and it was perceived as very serious. None of the remaining predictors accounted for a significant proportion of the variance. Together, the seven variables accounted for 34% of the adjusted variance in reporting delay, $F(7, 32) = 3.83$, $p < .01$. Unlike in the previous study, the number of people talked to did not explain a significant amount of the variance in reporting delay (2%, $p > .10$). However, negative findings should be treated with caution owing to the small sample size. In addition, unlike in the previous study, burglary victims delayed *longer* in reporting the crime than did theft victims.

The findings from this study both reinforce and extend the findings from the experimental research and the previous two studies. Social influence proved to be an important factor in the decision to report the crime. Burglary and theft victims tended to talk with others immediately after the crime, to receive advice from these others, and to follow the advice. Moreover, the findings regarding social influence were shown to apply to those who had not reported the crime as well as to those who had.

STUDY 19: TELEPHONE INTERVIEWS WITH VICTIMS OF BURGLARY AND THEFT

A fourth study was conducted using a similar sample of college student-victims of burglary and theft. By conducting additional interviews with victims of burglary and theft we hoped to test the reliability of the findings from the previous study using a different mode of collecting self-reports. Data in this study were collected by means of telephone interviews rather than questionnaires. Telephone interviewing has gained increased popularity in recent years as a method for studying reactions to crime (e.g., Bureau of Justice Statistics, 1989b; Skogan & Maxfield, 1981). Anonymous questionnaires certainly afford the respondent a measure of privacy, but telephone interviews allow respondents to answer potentially embarrassing questions in the privacy of their own homes without the physical presence of the interviewer. In addition to our methodological concerns, we were also interested in exploring in greater depth the role of social influence in victim decision making, and in exploring both the immediate and long-term affective, cognitive, and behavioral consequences of the victimization.

METHOD

Participants

Participants consisted of 98 introductory psychology students (49 males, 48 females)[1] who had identified themselves as victims of burglary ($n = 23$) or theft ($n = 74$)[2] in the 12 months prior to November 1987. As in the previous study, the recruitment process involved two steps. Potential participants responded to a written inquiry concerning their belief that something had been stolen from them in the previous year. Additional telephone screening ascertained the approximate date of the crime, whether or not it had been reported to the police, and, if it had been reported, whether the respondent was the one who had made the report. The 98 participants who passed the second stage of the screening process had a mean age of 18.9, were predominantly white (82%), and were generally either freshmen (67%) or sophomores (21%). The median family income was $34,400, and the mode was between $30,000 and $45,000.

Instruments

As in the previous survey, two questionnaires were employed, one for reporters ($n = 24$) and one for nonreporters ($n = 74$). The reporters' questionnaire contained 67 items, and the nonreporters' questionnaire contained 57 items. Both questionnaires included items dealing with (1) the nature of the crime; (2) the victims' initial feelings, thoughts, and behavior upon discovering the crime; (3) their interactions (if any) with others immediately after the incident; (4) their attitudes toward the police and the criminal justice system; (5) their present feelings, thoughts, and behavior regarding the incident; and (6) their demographic characteristics. The items consisted primarily of bipolar rating scales, with a few open-ended and fill-in items also included. Two females and one male served as the interviewers. At the time of the screening interview, participants were asked to provide a time and date when it would be convenient for the interview to take place. The telephone interviews took between 15 and 35 minutes to complete.

---

[1] One participant failed to provide this information.
[2] One participant failed to provide this information.

RESULTS

A preliminary comparison of the responses of burglary and theft victims yielded no significant differences on any of the items. Consequently, the analyses reported below are based on the results collapsed across type of crime. With regard to the characteristics of the crime, 92% had been completed. The stolen items ranged in value from $5 to $4,000 (auto theft), the median being $100. The stolen items included cash (18%), stereo equipment (17%), wallet or purse (16%), clothing (15%), sporting equipment (11%), jewelry (10%), and miscellaneous items (e.g., books and tools; 12%).

The immediate emotional reactions to the crime closely paralleled the reactions of victims in Studies 17 and 18. In response to an open-ended question about how they had felt when they first realized that they were the victim of a crime, 65% said that they were angry, and 31% said that they were upset. Only 5% reported feeling scared. These findings are supported by responses to the bipolar rating scales. When asked to rate the strength of their feelings on a series of seven-point bipolar scales, victims rated anger ($M = 5.97$) and upset ($M = 5.76$) somewhat (but not significantly) higher than scared ($M = 2.61$). As in the previous study, the perceived seriousness of the crime was correlated with ratings of anger ($r = .32, p < .002$), upset ($r = .37, p < .001$), and scared ($r = .35, p < .001$), and with the decision to report the crime ($r = .21, p < .05$).

In response to four questions dealing with their thoughts after discovering the crime, victims reported thinking about or asking themselves: "Could I have avoided this?" (91%); "What can I do to prevent this from happening again?" (89%); "Why me?" (89%); and "It could have been worse" (72%). Like the first action of the burglary and theft victims in the previous two studies, the first action taken by these victims was to talk with others (45%) or to search the scene (20%). Only 7% said that their first action had been to notify the police.

Social Influence and the Decision to Notify the Police

Reporters and nonreporters rated the importance of various factors in their decision to call (not to call) the police on a seven-point bipolar scale ranging from *very important* (7) to *unimportant* (1). As shown in Table 8-2, the reasons rated most important by reporters were "desire to see the thief punished" and to "prevent it from happening to me again." Of the seven reasons rated, advice from others ranked sixth. Nonreporters rated as most important the beliefs that "The police wouldn't think it was important enough to act," and that the police would be unable to do anything. Victims claimed, therefore, that social influence played only a minor role in their decision making. Advice from others ranked sixth in importance for report-

TABLE 8-2. MEAN RATINGS OF IMPORTANCE OF REASONS FOR CALLING AND NOT CALLING THE POLICE BY REPORTERS AND NONREPORTERS[a]

Reporters' Reasons ($n = 24$)	Mean	Standard deviation
Desire to see the thief punished	5.88	1.73
Prevent it from happening to me again	5.17	1.95
Prevent it from happening to others	4.58	2.23
Likelihood of getting my property back	4.41	2.34
It was my duty, the right thing to do	4.38	2.28
Advice from others	4.25	2.19
Couldn't think of anything better to do	1.92	1.53

Nonreporters' Reasons ($n = 74$)	Mean	Standard deviation
Police wouldn't think it was important	5.20	1.88
Police unable to do anything	5.10	1.96
Preferred other solution	4.80	1.92
Not a matter for the police	4.37	2.05
Too inconvenient and time-consuming	4.07	2.22
Loss was not important enough to me	3.85	1.96
Advice from others	3.11	2.01
Negative attitude toward the police	1.99	1.43
Fear of retaliation	1.81	1.33

[a]Scale read *Very important* (7) to *Unimportant* (1).

ers and seventh for nonreporters. However, additional data collected from participants suggests that just the opposite was true.

Like victims in the earlier studies, these victims tended to consult with others when deciding what to do. Eighty-five percent stated that they had talked with one or more others. For those who had talked with others, the mean number of persons talked with was 2.39; 19% had spoken with just one other, 23% had spoken with two others, and 58% had spoken with three or more others. In most cases (60%) the first person contacted was with the victim when the crime was discovered. The first person consulted tended to be either a friend (49%) or a parent (27%). (The comparable figures for Study 18, which used a similar sample, were 49% and 30%.) The major reasons for talking with someone were "because he or she was there" (26%), to obtain information (23%), or to get advice about what to do (11%). Of those who had talked with others, the percentage who had received advice about what to do was 43%, well below the 81% who had received advice in the previous study. In most instances the advice was volunteered by the other (69%, a figure identical to that obtained in the previous study). Sixty-eight percent of the advice givers remained with the victim while the victim was deciding what to do. In most instances (77%) victims followed the advice given them.

Hierarchical multiple-regression analyses similar to those employed in the previous study were used to identify the best predictors of (1) the number of others consulted with; (2) the type of advice received from others; and (3) the decision to notify the police. On the basis of the bivariate correlation analysis, eight predictors were entered into the regression equation concerning the number of other people consulted. The variables included how confused, angry, and surprised the victims had been, the perceived seriousness of the incident, the dollar value of the stolen property, the extent to which the victims had asked "Why me?", their age, and their race. Three of the predictors independently accounted for a significant proportion of the unique variance: victims' level of anger independently accounted for 5% of the variance, $F(1, 79) = 5.86$, $p < .02$; the dollar value of the stolen items accounted for 4% of unique variance, $F(1, 79) = 4.69$, $p < .05$; and victims' age accounted for an additional 3% of the variance, $F(1, 79) = 3.75$, $p = .05$. Talking with a greater number of others was associated with being very angry, with the stolen items' having a lower dollar value, and with the victim's being younger. The eight variables together accounted for an adjusted 23% of the variance in the number of people talked to, $F(8, 79) = 4.20$, $p < .001$.

A similar multiple-regression analysis was used to identify the best predictors of the type of (composite) advice received from others. Of the three variables that were correlated with the type of advice received (victims' sex, type of crime, and victims' level of surprise), the only significant predictor was victims' sex. It accounted for 12% of unique variance, $F(1, 31) = 4.64$, $p < .05$. Females were more likely than males to be advised not to call the police. The three variables together accounted for an adjusted 11% of the variance, $F(3, 31) = 2.40$, $p < .09$.

A third regression analysis was conducted on the reporting decision (report–not report). Eight variables identified from the bivariate analysis were entered into the equation as predictors: victims' sex, type of crime, dollar value of stolen items, perceived seriousness of incident, initial level of anger, the extent that victims thought that "It could have been worse," the extent to which they could have avoided the incident, and finally, the composite measure of advice received from others. As in the previous study, type of advice was the best predictor of victims' decision to call the police. It independently explained 12% of the variance, $F(1, 23) = 5.42$, $p < .03$. The dollar value of the stolen property accounted for an additional 10% of the variance, $F(1, 23) = 4.38$, $p < .05$. Victims were more likely to call the police when they were advised to do so and when the value of the stolen property was greater. Together, the eight variables accounted for an adjusted 31% of the variance, $F(8, 23) = 2.74$, $p < .03$.

The median delay time for participants who had reported the crime ($n = 24$) was 23 minutes, slightly greater than the 15-minute median delay found in the previous two studies. On the basis of the bivariate analyses, seven variables were entered as predictors in the regression equation on delay. The predictors were type of crime, number of people talked to, victims' desire to retrieve the stolen property, the extent to which they asked themselves if they could have done anything to prevent the incident, their belief that the crime could have been worse, whether they thought of any reasons not to call the police, and their ratings of how important the advice from others had been in their decision to notify the police. Results of this analysis showed that the importance of others' advice independently explained 15% of the variance, $F(1, 16) = 5.52$, $p < .05$, and that thinking of reasons not to call the police independently accounted for 14% of the variance, $F(1, 16) = 5.16$, $p < .05$. Longer delays in reporting were associated with rating others' advice as important and with having thought of reasons why the police should not be called. None of the remaining five predictors accounted for a significant proportion of the variance in reporting delay. Unlike in Study 17, but consistent with Study 18, the number of people talked to did not explain a significant amount of the variance. However, because of the small number of cases in this analysis, negative findings should be treated with caution. Together, the seven variables accounted for 38% of the adjusted variance in reporting delay, $F(7, 16) = 3.05$, $p < .05$.

Longer-Term Consequences of the Victimization

Since the mean interval between the occurrence of the crime and the interview was 5.3 months, we were able to learn about the longer term impact of the victimization by questioning respondents about their *present* beliefs, feelings, and behavior. The results showed that many victims had been profoundly affected by the experience, and that five months later, such effects remained. While 53% rated the incident as being "not as bad" as other unhappy experiences they had had, and just 25% rated it as "worse," many victims said that as a result of the crime they tended to view life as less predictable (43%), to view themselves as less trusting of others (48%), and to estimate the chances of being revictimized as highly or somewhat likely (36%).

When asked, "How often do you find yourself thinking about the incident?" 39% said, "Hardly ever"; 41% said, "Sometimes"; 19% said, "Quite frequently"; and 1% said, "Almost always." Sixty percent admitted fantasizing about what they would do if they caught the suspect. Males were more likely to have fantasized than females (74% vs. 47%), $\chi^2(1) = 6.13$, $p < .02$. The most common fantasies were of physically harming the suspect (62%) and retrieving the stolen property (20%). Males were more likely to have violent fantasies than were females (74% vs. 40%), $\chi^2(1) = 4.97$, $p < .05$.

The extreme violence of many of these fantasies cannot be overstated. Victims fantasized about "breaking all four of his limbs," "shooting him," "killing him," and "beating the shit out of him." Typically, the fantasized response far exceeded the visible harm done to the victim. For example, a 21-year-old male who had had plastic side panels from his motorcycle stolen described the following fantasy:

> I fantasize staying up all night at the window with a gun—thief comes to bike—
> sign on bike reads, "Look up at window." They turn toward window and I
> blast them!

Fantasies such as these no doubt reflect the extreme anger that remained toward the offender.

Support for this reasoning can be found in victims' responses to questions abut their present feelings. When asked whether they were still bothered by the incident, 19% said, "No"; 40% said, "Slightly"; 25% said, "Moderately"; and 16% said, "Very much." Thus, five months on the average after the incident, 81% of the respondents said they were still bothered by the incident. Fantasizing about the incident was correlated with how bothered victims reported themselves to be ($r = .25$, $p < .02$). When asked to describe in what way they were bothered, victims mentioned angry (37%), upset (24%), and violated (19%) most frequently. These data suggest that the feelings of anger and of being upset that had characterized victims' initial emotional response to the incident remained with them five months later. Moreover, it was these feelings of anger and upset that appeared to fuel victims' fantasies about the incident. Consistent with this reasoning, the data show that the greater the initial level of anger the more likely victims were to fantasize about the incident ($r = .35$, $p < .001$).

In order to identify the best predictors of how bothered victims would claim they now were (roughly five months after the incident), bivariate analyses were performed. Seven variables were significantly correlated with how bothered victims said they now were: level of income; perceived seriousness of incident; how initially surprised, scared, and confused victims were; how this incident compared with other unhappy incidents; and the extent to which victims initially asked themselves, "Why me?" When these seven variables were entered as predictors in a regression analysis on how bothered the victims stated they now were, two predictors accounted for a significant proportion of the variance: how the incident compared with other unhappy incidents independently explained 8% of the variance, $F(1, 85) = 10.87$, $p < .002$; and the victim's income accounted for an additional 6% of the variance, $F(1, 85) = 7.87$, $p < .01$. Victims said they were more bothered by the incident when it was perceived as worse than most unhappy experiences that they had had, and when their level of income was higher. Together, the seven predictors accounted for an adjusted 32% of the variance, $F(7, 85) = 7.30$, $p < .001$.

DISCUSSION

The results of Study 19 both reinforce and extend the findings of the first three studies presented in this chapter. No differences were found between the reactions of burglary and theft victims. Like those of the previous studies, the results confirmed the importance of social influence in burglary and theft victims' decision to call the police. With regard to the first action taken after the crime, victims were almost six times as likely to consult with others (40%) as they were to call the police (7%). Moreover, the study yielded the highest rate of consulting with others (85%) of the four studies. However, it also yielded the lowest percentage of those who had received advice from others (43%). As in the previous study, the regression analysis showed that the type of advice received from others was the best predictor of the decision to notify the police. Victims' rating of the *importance* of the advice was the best predictor of delay in reporting.

The thoughts that victims had immediately after the crime focused on issues concerning causality ("Why me?" "Could I have avoided this?"), the magnitude of the potential harm ("It could have been worse"), and their vulnerability to subsequent harm ("What can I do to prevent this from happening again?"). Consistent with the findings from Studies 17 and 18, victims used the terms *angry* and *upset* most often to describe their immediate emotional reaction to the crime. These emotional reactions persisted for some time after the event. At the time of the interview (about five months, on the average, after the incident), four out of five victims said that they were still bothered by the event, with feelings of anger and upset again being mentioned most often. Further evidence of the long-term emotional impact of the event comes from the finding that 60% had fantasies about what they would do if they caught the suspect. The fantasies were typically of an extremely violent nature. In addition to influencing their long-term emotional reactions, the victimization experience had altered their assumptions about their safety and security. Five months, on the average, after the incident, many said that as a result of the incident they had become less trusting of others, tended to view life as less predictable, and believed that their chances of becoming a victim in the future had increased.

Decision making by victims does not end with the decision to call the police. Once the police have been notified, victims must decide whether and to what extent they wish to cooperate with the authorities in pursuing the case. Given the fact that the victim is often the key witness in the prosecution's case, this decision by the victim frequently determines whether or not the case will be prosecuted (McCleod, 1983). For example, Hall (1975) found that, particularly with misdemeanors and minor felonies, a victim who does not want the case prosecuted can often have the case against the offender dropped, since the prosecutor will be unlikely to invest resources in a case in which the victim is reluctant to testify.

What is the impact of social influence on victims' decisions after the crime is reported? To what extent are victims subjected to influence attempts by others to cooperate with the authorities or to drop the case? Under what conditions do victims seek out and receive support from others, and what is the impact of these contacts on victims' willingness to assist in the prosecution of the case? Study 20 was concerned with investigating these questions, specifically the degree of support victims receive from others and the extent of the pressure exerted on them to drop charges or to continue prosecution.

STUDY 20: A LONGITUDINAL STUDY OF RAPE VICTIMS

METHOD

Design and Participants

A three-stage panel design was employed. Participants were interviewed when they first appeared at the Rape Crisis Center (RCC) at Grady Memorial Hospital in Atlanta, Georgia; they were interviewed again by telephone two months later and six to nine months following the last interview.

Potential participants were women aged 18 and older who had visited the RCC during the months December 1984 through May 1985. During the six-month period, 327 women visited the RCC. Of the 327 women who were potential participants, 111 did not leave a working local telephone number and could not be reached, 47 could not be reached after at least two telephone calls, and 17 had such severe emotional problems that either they were not called or, if called, they were not asked to participate. Of the 152 women who were initially reached by telephone, only 2 refused to participate. Thus, interviews were obtained from 150 women (46% of the total; 99% of those who had been reached by telephone).

The women ranged in age from 18 to 75 ($M = 28$; Mdn = 26). Less than 14% were married and living with their spouse; the remainder were single (56%), separated (12%), widowed (5%), or divorced (14%). Most of the women were black (78%); the rest were white (22%). This sample had a higher percentage of blacks and of women who had called the police than did our study of every adult victim who had visited the RCC during the three years immediately preceding this study (Ruback & Ivie, 1987a). In other respects, however, the two samples appeared comparable.

Procedure

Initial Intake Interview. Initial data collection came through the standard record-keeping procedure of the RCC (see the procedure section of Study 15). As part of this procedure, a trained volunteer stayed with each client while she received treatment at Grady Hospital. Immediately after the client left the emergency room, the volunteer completed a six-page form, in use at the RCC since 1974, with information related to her by the client. This information was subsequently coded by one of the authors. A prior test (Ruback & Ivie, in press) had shown coding reliability to be greater than 97%. The information coded concerned four general categories (the victim, the rapist, the circumstances of the rape, and the victim's actions subsequent to the attack), all of which were described more fully in Chapter 7.

Second Interview. Approximately two months after the clients visited the RCC, the interviewer (a female trained in counseling) attempted to call them. When the interviewer reached them, she briefly described the study, assured the women of confidentiality, and then asked for permission to conduct an interview. During this interview, which lasted 20 minutes, the interviewer asked the women if they had received advice to call the police, and, if so, whether it had been solicited or volunteered, from whom it had come, and how heavily they had weighed the advice. They were also asked if the decision to call the police had been a difficult one.

They were then questioned about whether the rapist had threatened them, how seriously they had taken the threat, and whether or not they had called the police. The interviewer also inquired about who they had talked with concerning the rape (up to five different persons) and how these people had reacted to them (i.e., believed them or not, made them feel responsible or not, supported them or not). In addition, for each participant we counted the number of persons who had reacted positively to them and the number who had reacted negatively to them. Finally, participants were asked to evaluate their treatment by the police, such as the degree of courtesy and concern shown to them by the police and whether they had had any contact with the police since they had come to the RCC.

Third Interview. At 6–9 months after the second interview (8–11 months after they had been attacked), the women were called again and asked questions about their treatment by the criminal justice system, the reactions of other people to them, and their subsequent behavior regarding preventing future assaults. In particular, the interviewer inquired whether they had had any further contacts with the criminal justice system and whether they felt anyone in the system had pressured them to drop their case. Participants were then asked if they would be willing to report again.

Next, participants were questioned about the reactions of other people to them. Specifically, they were asked if anyone had pressured or attempted to intimidate them not to pursue their case, how people had reacted to them (supportive, not supportive, mixed), and whether anyone had given them any advice since the prior interview.

They were then asked if they had taken any actions to try to prevent a future victimization and, if so, to describe them. The actions mentioned included moving their residence, living with another person, adding home security devices, changing their patterns of going outside, obtaining a weapon, and changing their interactions with males (e.g., not dating). Participants were questioned about any help that they had sought from others (e.g., from family, friends, the RCC, mental health professionals, and clergy) and whether they had told additional people about the crime.

Next, the interviewer inquired about how they felt the crime had affected their lives. Answers to this question were coded as positive (e.g., made them stronger), neutral (no effect), or negative (e.g., greater fear, forced changes in lifestyle, and flashbacks). In addition to this coding, we counted the number of negative effects (up to four) the women had mentioned. Finally, participants were questioned about the extent to which their case had been processed by the criminal justice system (no further action, arrest, grand jury, or trial) and whether they had decided not to pursue the case.

RESULTS

Initial Intake Interview

Data collected during the initial interview indicated that most of the rapists had been black (89%) and about half had been known in some way by the victim (52%). Multiple rapists had been involved in 16% of the cases. Slightly over half of the rapists (54%) had had a weapon, 52% had physically assaulted the victims, and 63% had used some type of threat. Virtually all of the women (95%) had suffered vaginal penetration. Lower percentages had been penetrated orally (28%) or anally (13%).

Almost all of the victimizations (96%) had been reported to the police, with 61% of the women reporting it themselves. Most of the reports (70%) had been made within 30 minutes. An additional 7% had been made within an hour, an additional 9% had been made within three hours, and an additional 14% had been made over 3 hours later. The first thing half of the women (51%) had done was to talk to someone. Only 22% had called the police immediately, and 27% had taken some other action (e.g., going home). The number of people participants said they would tell about the crime ranged from 0 to 4 ($M = 1.68$; $Mdn = 2$).

A multiple linear-regression analysis of the reporting decision involving 15 predictors was significant, $F(15, 105) = 1.77$, $p < .05$ (Adjusted $R^2 = .09$). Neither the subset of three variables relating to victims' characteristics (age, race, and whether or not raped before) nor the subset of variables relating to victims' reactions during the attack (verbal strategies and physical resistance) was significant (both p's > .15). The subset of 10 situational variables and rapist characteristics (location, time of day, use of weapon, use of a threat, degrading acts, vaginal penetration, oral penetration, degree of injury, rapist's race, prior relationship between rapist and victim) was marginally significant, $F(10, 105) = 1.85$, $p = .06$.

A multiple linear-regression analysis of victims' delay in reporting, using the same 15 predictors as the prior analysis, was significant, $F(15, 87) = 2.02$, $p < .05$ (Adjusted $R^2 = .13$). Although none of the three subsets of variables was significant, all three were marginally significant predictors: victim characteristics, $F(3, 87) = 2.56$, $p < .06$; victim reactions, $F(2, 87) = 2.49$, $p < .09$; and situational factors, $F(10, 87) = 1.77$, $p < .08$).

Second Interview

Within two months after visiting the RCC, all 150 women were called by a volunteer and asked several questions about their initial reporting decision and their subsequent decisions. Of the 150 women, 55 (37%) said they had received advice about reporting: 51 had been advised to report, and 4 had been advised not to report. Of the 55 women who said they had received advice, 12 (22%) said they had asked for advice, and 43 (78%) said the advice had been volunteered to them. When asked how much weight they had given this advice, 46 (87%) said very much, 2 (4%) said some, and only 5 (9%) said none (2 women did not answer this question). Of the entire group, 40 (73%) said the reporting decision had been difficult for them.

The number of people the women actually talked to about the crime ranged from 0 to 5 ($M = 2.55$; Mdn = 2.00) and was significantly correlated with the number of people they said they would talk to at the time of their initial visit to the hospital ($r = .48$, $p < .001$). Most of the women felt they had been believed and supported by others. Of the 382 people these women had talked to, 363 (95%) were said to have believed them very much, 13 (3%) were described as believing them somewhat, and 6 (2%) were judged not to have believed them at all. The women said 28 (8%) of these people had made them feel responsible for the crime's occurrence. The number of people whom participants perceived as reacting negatively to them ranged from 0 to 4 ($M = .22$). In comparison, the number of people whom participants perceived as acting positively to them ranged from 0 to 5 ($M = 2.22$).

Consistent with the results of earlier studies (e.g., Burgess & Holmstrom, 1975), the women felt they had been treated positively by the police. On a three-point scale, with the anchors being 1 (*not at all*) and 3 (*very much*), the women rated the police as being very courteous ($M = 2.76$) and very concerned ($M = 2.72$).

Third Interview

Six to nine months after the second interview 79 of the 150 participants were contacted by telephone, and 77 (51% of the sample; 97% of those contacted) agreed to be reinterviewed. Those who were contacted for the third interview tended to be older ($M = 29.9$) than those who were not reached ($M = 26.6$), $t(129) = 2.17$, $p < .05$. In addition, they were more likely to have been attacked later in the day ($M = 3.29$) than those who were not reached ($M = 2.92$), $t(129) = 2.17$, $p < .05$; and they were more likely to have been attacked by multiple rapists than were those who were not reached, $t(147) = 2.92$, $p < .01$. On all other measures, there was no significant difference between those who were reached and those who were not. Of the 77 respondents, 46 (60%) had had contact with criminal justice systems agents after their initial report to the police, and 31 (40%) had not. Only 5 (11%) of those who had had contact said they had been pressured by the police or assistant district attorney to drop charges.

Given the often-found relationship between anxiety and affiliation in the social psychological literature (Schachter, 1959), we examined the relationship between the number of negative long-term effects reported by victims and their affiliative behavior. The number of long-term negative effects that participants reported ranged from 0 to 4 ($M = 1.57$) and was positively related to the number of people that participants stated they would tell about the crime when they first visited the RCC ($r = .37$, $p < .001$), the number of people they actually talked to ($r = .28$, $p < .05$), the number of people they sought help from ($r = .52$, $p < .001$) and the number of people who advised them not to notify the police ($r = .25$, $p < .05$). In other words, reporting more negative effects was linked with talking with more people. This result may be a methodological artifact in that women who talked to more others may also have been more candid in disclosing negative effects to the interviewer.

The number of preventive changes in behavior the women reported ranged from 0 to 4 ($M = 1.70$). This number was significantly related to the number of people the women had said they would talk to ($r = .38$, $p < .001$), the number of people they actually talked to ($r = .37$, $p < .001$), the number of people they had talked to about reporting the incident ($r = .23$, $p < .05$), the number of people they had sought help from ($r = .48$, $p < .001$), and the number of negative long-term effects they reported ($r = .45$, $p < .001$). That is, more changes in behavior were related to talking to more people and to reporting more negative effects. The number of changes in behavior was not related to fear, anger, or guilt reported by the women when they had initially visited the RCC.

Seventeen of the women said they had decided not to pursue their cases. This decision was positively related to the number of people the women said they had talked to about the reporting decision ($r = .27$, $p < .05$) and was negatively related to the number of people who had advised them to report ($r = -.26$, $p < .05$). The greater the number of people who had advised them to report, the less likely the women were to drop the case. The number of individuals who had advised them not to report was not related to the decision to drop the case.

We learned about the subsequent outcome of 78 of the cases by questioning the victims or their relatives and by consulting the RCC and police records. Of these cases, there was no legal action in 47 (60%), arrest only in 5 (6%), an indictment in 9 (12%), a finding of not guilty in 5 (6%), and a plea or finding of guilt in 12 (15%). This roughly ordinal sequence (no action, arrest, indictment, finding of not guilty, finding of guilt) was significantly correlated with three variables: the number of positive responses partici- pants had reported receiving from others at the second interview ($r = -.22$, $p < .05$), perceived pressure from others to .drop the case ($r = -.29$, $p < .05$), and the presence of sperm ($r = -.28$, $p < .05$). The case was likely to have gone farther in the sequence if more people had reacted positively to the victims within two months after the attack, if others had not pressured them to drop the charges, and if the test for sperm had been positive.

DISCUSSION

The findings from this study support the idea that crime victims are influenced by others both before and after the decision to notify the police. Consistent with the other studies reported in this chapter, we found that victims' most common first response had been to talk with others rather than to call the police, and that a significant minority of victims (37%) said they had received specific advice about calling the police before or while deciding what to do. The 37% figure is probably a conservative estimate. Whereas in Studies 16–19, the percentage receiving advice was based on the subset of those who said they had talked with others when deciding what to do, the 37% figure in Study 20 is based on the total sample. The total sample was used as the base because we neglected to ask participants in Study 20 to indicate whether they had talked with others *before* deciding what to do. Therefore, the 37% figure probably underestimates the percent- age of victims who received advice. At the very least, the figure suggests that a sizable minority of crime victims are subject to social influence before they decide to call or not to call the police.

The results of this study further suggest that social influence remains an important determinant of victim decision making *after* the decision to report the crime has been made. It appears that others' supportive behav- ior (i.e., advice to call the police, positive reactions to the victim, and the ab- sence of pressure to drop the case) may be related to victims' willingness to pursue a case through the criminal justice system as well as to the likelihood of the case's proceeding farther along in the system. In essence, others act not only as gatekeepers to the system but as *ushers* through the process.

In addition, social influence seems to be related to changes victims make in their lifestyles to prevent future victimizations. The greater the number of people victims had talked to, both before and after the reporting decision, the more changes they said they had made to prevent future attacks. However, the data do not permit us to specify the causal mecha- nism. Conceivably, talking to others elicits advice, and victims simply act on this advice. Another possibility is that the act of talking about the assault is beneficial because victims receive social support, which tends to increase their self-worth and lower their level of arousal. This explanation seems reasonable, as women with more negative symptoms were also likely to have talked to more people. A third possibility is that talking to others about a negative event like a criminal victimization in itself has positive mental health consequences (see, e.g., Pennebaker, 1989).

SUMMARY AND CONCLUSIONS

The five studies presented in this chapter paint a detailed picture of victims' immediate and longer term reactions to crime and the important role played by others in influencing these reactions. Table 8-3 shows that on most variables the studies yielded highly consistent results. The immediate emotional reactions of burglary, theft, and robbery victims were very similar; anger and upset were the predominant reactions, while few expressed being fearful. In contrast, victims of rape tended to react with fear rather than anger. Rather than calling the police as their first reaction to the crime, victims of burglary, theft, and rape preferred to talk with others first. Burglary and theft victims may have sought out others for purposes of information about what had happened and advice about what to do, whereas rape victims may have sought the company of others to obtain protection and emotional support. In contrast, the first response of robbery victims was to call the police rather than to contact others. Robbery victims, unlike burglary and theft victims, may have found little value in contacting others since there was no ambiguity about what had happened and less uncertainty about the need to call the police. Moreover, robbery victims may not have experienced the same degree of emotional trauma experienced by rape victims and therefore did not have as strong a need for social support.

The impact of social influence can be seen in the consistent findings that victims frequently spoke with others when deciding what to do. In Studies 16–19, the percentage of victims who consulted with others was, respectively, 78%, 62%, 77%, and 85%. Typically, the person(s) talked to were friends and family. Of those who talked with others, the percentage that received advice about what to do ranged from 37% to 81%. The percentage of victims who acted in accordance with the advice ranged from 77% to 95%. In Studies 18 and 19, no consistent predictors emerged in regression analyses that were performed to identify the best predictors of the number of others talked to and the type of advice received. However, the regression analyses performed on the reporting decision in these studies supported the role of social influence. In both studies, the best predictor of the reporting decision was the type of advice received from others.

Regression analyses on delay in reporting in Studies 17 and 19 suggested that social influence was an important predictor of delay. In Study 17 the number of people talked to was associated with longer delays, and in

TABLE 8-3. SUMMARY OF MAJOR FINDINGS FROM STUDIES 16–20[a]

Variable	Study 16	Study 17	Study 18	Study 19	Study 20
Sample size	364	58	97	98	150
Median dollar value of stolen property	—	$125	$60	$100	—
Immediate emotional response (%)					
Fear	63	11 (burg/theft)	10	5	—
Anger	11	51 (burg/theft)	54	65	—
Upset	—	26 (burg/theft)	19	31	—
First action taken (%)					
Called police	18	11 (burg/theft) 62 (robbery)	13	7	22
Talked with others	38	49 (burg/theft) 15 (robbery)	34	45	51
Searched the scene	—	40 (burg/theft) 23 (robbery)	27	20	—
Percentage who talked with others	78	62	77	85	—
Predictors of number talked to	—	—	Difficulty of decision	Anger, $ value, age	—
Percentage who received advice	76	58	81	43	37
Percentage who followed advice	84	95	90	77	—
Predictors of advice received	—	—	Difficulty of decision, seriousness	Victim's sex	—
Percentage who reported to police	72	100	41	25	96
Predictors of report decision	—	—	Advice	Advice, $ value	—
Median delay in reporting	1–3 hr	15 min	15 min	23 min	< 30 min
Predictors of reporting delay	—	Number talked to, type of crime	Scared, type of crime, seriousness	Importance of advice, thought of reasons not to call	—

[a]Spaces are blank (—) where information was not obtained for this variable.

Study 19, victims' rating the advice of others as important in their decision to call the police was associated with longer delays in reporting.

Finally, the results of Study 20 demonstrate that social influence was related not only to victims' decision to report the crime, but also to their subsequent willingness to cooperate in the prosecution of the case. The greater the number of people who had advised them to notify the police, the less likely the victims were to drop the case.

Concluding this chapter, we should remember that data obtained via self-reports are susceptible to specific types of error. Memory and motivational factors may conspire to distort the accuracy of self-reports. Moreover, the absence of experimental control raises the possibility of alternative interpretations of the data. For example, the relationship of reporting and being influenced by advice may be the reverse: respondents' knowledge of their decision to report the incident may have biased their recall of the advice received.

Having presented the findings from 20 empirical studies, we attempt to achieve a broader integration of the findings in the following two chapters. In Chapter 9 we present a theoretical model designed to (1) provide an integrative framework for interpreting the findings and (2) relate our findings to the work of others in the field. In Chapter 10 we discuss the implications of the findings for public policy research and for theoretical issues in social psychology.

9

A Model of Crime-Victim Decision Making

Having presented the findings from 20 studies involving a variety of methodologies, we now introduce a theoretical framework that gives conceptual coherence to these findings. The proposed model, which emerged from our own empirical work and the work of others, offers several advantages. It provides an explanatory tool for comparing the decisions of various types of victims. In addition, it allows for the integration of the present findings with the existing literature on victim decision making. Further, the model suggests directions for future research, while at the same time laying the foundation for public policy decisions (see Chapter 10).

In this chapter, we present an overview of the model of victim decision making along with a discussion of the model's assumptions—both implicit and explicit. Then we offer a detailed presentation of the model and relevant empirical research.

The proposed model is based on several assumptions. First, it is postulated that for many victims the decision to report an incident to the police is the product of several prior decisions. The victim must first label the event a crime, decide that it is sufficiently serious to involve the police, and decide that reporting the crime is more advantageous than other available options. The second assumption of the model is that the decision to call the police represents only one of several modes of coping with the stress of the victimization. Third, the model holds that there are multiple sources of distress for crime victims and that identifying these sources is essential for understanding the decision-making process. Fourth, the model postulates that cognitive and affective factors are involved in the decision process as both causes and consequences. Fifth, the model proposes that the decision to notify the police must be viewed in the context of other options that victims perceive to be available. Sixth, the model postulates that the decision is based in part on stored information that victims have acquired via direct and indirect experience. Finally, the model assumes that the intensity of the stress and affect immediately following the crime produces decisions that fall short of perfectly rational decision making.

Figure 9-1 represents a three-stage decision process culminating in a decision concerning what to do in response to a criminal event. Each stage is influenced by a distinctive set of variables. First, victims label a suspicious event a crime; second, they determine its seriousness; and third, they decide what to do. In order for a suspicious event to be labeled a crime, it must first be discovered. As indicated in Figure 9-1, the mere discovery of a suspicious event (e.g., discovering the contents of one's apartment in disarray upon returning home) is likely to trigger arousal and distress. Whether or not a suspicious event is labeled a crime depends on the individual's personal definition of what constitutes a crime (which may or may not agree with the legal definition) and the degree to which the event fits or matches that definition. The failure to label the event a crime will produce little incentive to notify the police. If, however, victims label the event as a crime, the level of distress is likely to increase, and they will move to the second stage of the model: determining the seriousness of the victimization. The more serious the event is perceived to be, the greater the ensuing level of arousal and distress. However, as shown in Figure 9-1, the model allows for the reverse possibility: the level of arousal and distress may influence how serious the crime is considered (see Schachter, 1964). Victims make this judgment of seriousness based on how "wronged" or unfairly treated they perceive themselves to be and how vulnerable they feel they are to subsequent victimization. The sense of being wronged and feeling vulnerable is a function of (1) the *unexpectedness* of the crime; (2) the perceived magnitude of *actual* harm (i.e., physical, material, and psychological); and (3) the perceived magnitude of *potential* or possible harm in the situation.

Having evaluated the seriousness of the crime, victims move to the third stage of the model: deciding what should be done. The response alternatives available to victims include (1) seeking a private solution; (2) cognitively reevaluating the situation; (3) notifying the police; and (4) doing nothing. Presumably, victims tend to choose the option or combination of options toward which they have the most favorable attitude. Their attitudes toward

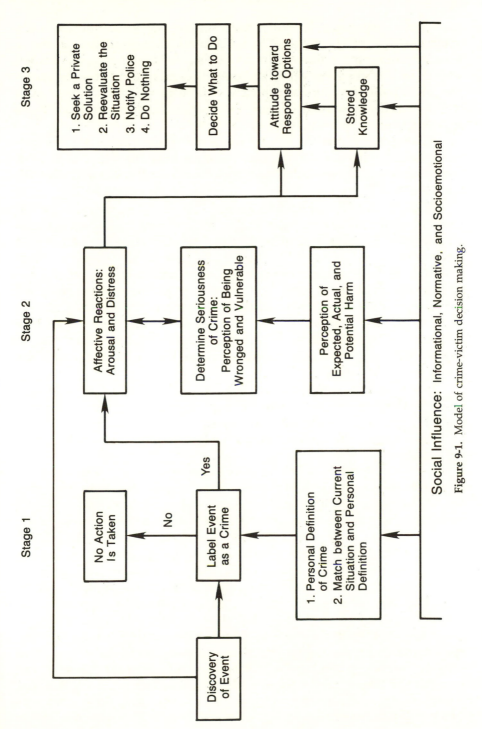

Social Influence: Informational, Normative, and Socioemotional

Figure 9-1. Model of crime-victim decision making.

the various response options are based on the subjective utility of each option (i.e., perceived net benefits as indicated by rewards minus costs). When choosing among these options, victims examine their "stored" knowledge about these options, which has been acquired directly from past experience and indirectly from the experience of others. Owing to victims' state of heightened arousal and distress, the examination process tends to be superficial and incomplete.

As noted in Figure 9-1, at each successive stage victims are susceptible to social influence. Others can influence how the event is labeled, how seriously it is viewed by the victim, and how the victim deals with the event.

At this point a caveat must be entered. The model may not be applicable to all victims in all circumstances. For some victims the decision process may involve minimal mediating cognitive activity above the activity of labeling the event a crime. Their decisions may be more reflexive than reflective, because of the combined effects of prior socialization and the stress of the situation. In such cases, no effort would be made to assess the seriousness of the crime or the utility of the various alternatives. Once the incident has been labeled, the decision would be automatic (Shiffrin & Schneider, 1977) or governed by simple heuristics (Chaiken, Liberman, & Eagly, 1989) (e.g., when a crime occurs, regardless of its seriousness, the police should be called).

That victims may respond automatically or with very little thought in some instances suggests that the stages need not occur in the predicted sequence. In some cases a suspicious event will be reported to the police *before* it is labeled a crime. Only after making the call might the victim consider labeling it or reflect on its seriousness. In such instances the proposed model is probably inappropriate. However, research on decision making has shown that complex reasoning strategies are likely to be employed in situations typically confronted by victims, namely, when personal involvement is high and when one anticipates having to justify one's actions to others (Harkness, DeBono, & Borgida, 1985; Tetlock, 1983). Consistent with these findings, our results suggest that for many victims of crime the decision to call the police is not an easy one. Considerable time is spent labeling the event, evaluating its seriousness, weighing the pros and cons of alternative responses, and considering the opinions of family, friends, and others who happen to be on the scene. For these reasons, we believe that the proposed model is a reasonable framework for explaining the decisions of victims in most circumstances, though subsequent research may suggest modifications and extensions. If the proposed framework stimulates empirical research that enhances our understanding of crime-victim decision making, then our efforts will have succeeded.

STAGE 1: LABELING THE EVENT A CRIME

In order for individuals to label themselves as victims of a crime, they must perceive that they are or have been the target of a criminal action. Two elements are involved in the labeling process: the individual's personal definition of a crime and a belief that the present situation matches or fits that definition. A crime is legally defined as a "violation of the criminal law" (Rush, 1977, p. 92), but individuals in their roles as victims, witnesses, and jurors have personal definitions, which may not match the legal definition (Block, 1974; Kalven & Zeisel, 1966; Quinney, 1970). For example, victims of attempted crimes, such as attempted robbery or burglary, may not regard themselves as having been victimized, even though such acts are legally defined as criminal. Similarly, while child and spouse abuse are criminal offenses, victims of domestic violence may not define the violence as crimes.

Despite the obvious importance of personal definitions of crime, this is a relatively neglected area of study. What little we know comes from the literature on rape, which tells us that victims are most likely to perceive themselves as having been raped when the assailant is a stranger, when the attack involves a considerable degree of force (Koss, Dinerio, & Seibel, 1988; Oros, Leonard, & Koss, 1980; Skelton & Burkhart, 1980; Williams, 1984), and when phallic sex is involved (Scheppele & Bart, 1983). For example, interviews with female victims of sexual assault led Scheppele and Bart (1983) to conclude:

> When women experience phallic sex they consider themselves raped while experiencing non-phallic sex acts leads them to consider themselves avoiders. The cue is not just any sexual activity, but sexual activity of a particular sort. Rape, therefore, is what is done with a penis, not what is done to a vagina. (p. 75)

Research by Remer and Witten (1988) suggests that distinguishing between rape and "making love" is facilitated by prior rape experience. Those who have had direct experience as victims of rape or who have had a close family member victimized by rape have less difficulty distinguishing between rape and lovemaking than do those with no prior experience.

That an individual has personal definitions of crime does not guarantee that such definitions will be easily applied. Cognitive and motivational factors can affect the availability or accessibility of these criminal labels. For example, situational cues such as a dimly lit street and an approaching stranger can activate or "prime" crime labels (Fiske & Taylor, 1984; Higgins & King, 1981). Alternatively, when the situation is one in which a crime is not expected to occur, criminal labels are unlikely to be primed and are therefore more likely to remain unavailable. For example, LeJeune and Alex (1973) found that victims of street muggings in New York City typically did not expect to be victims of a crime and were usually slow to label the event a crime. They concluded from their interviews with mugging victims that when the victims were initially confronted by the suspect, they were reluctant or unwilling to define the physical invasion of their private space as a physical threat, preferring instead to define it in more acceptable and less threatening terms. In addition, Scheppele and Bart (1983) noted that rape victims, before the attack, noticed that "something was wrong" but dismissed their feelings as overly paranoid or sensitive. Similarly, Maguire (1980, 1982) found that burglary victims were slow to label the event as a burglary. According to Maguire (1980), "Their first instinct seems to have been to find a more 'normal' explanation of what had occurred" (p. 262).

These results suggest that suspected criminal events are often initially shrouded in *ambiguity*, particularly when the event is unexpected. For personal victimizations in which the victim is present during the commission of the crime, such as assault and robbery, the ambiguity is resolved as the event unfolds. However, when a discovery crime such as a burglary or a theft is discovered after it occurs, labeling the event is more difficult. Typically, in such instances victims engage in information-gathering activities resulting in longer delays in reporting (Spelman & Brown, 1981; Van Kirk, 1978).

The reluctance to label a suspicious event a crime may reflect more than cognitive uncertainty. People often harbor illusions of invulnerability (Perloff, 1983) because of the need to maintain a feeling of control over their lives, which permits them to go about their daily activities without the immobilizing feelings of anxiety and fear. Research has documented the tendency of people to view themselves as less vulnerable than others to a variety of victimizations, including crime (Perloff, 1982; Weinstein, 1989), disease (Harris & Guten, 1979), and serious automobile accidents (Robertson, 1975). The "need" to view themselves as uniquely invulnerable (Perloff, 1987) may cause people to perceive events as nonthreatening, producing longer latencies in labeling the event a crime or resulting in denial that a crime actually has occurred. Labeling the incident a noncrime typically terminates the decision process, as there is little incentive to notify the authorities.

The research presented in this volume did not focus on the labeling stage. When we employed archival and self-report methodologies to study victim decision making, we studied a population of individuals who had already labeled themselves as crime victims. However, labeling the event a crime was a key element in the construction of our experimental paradigm. In order for participants to label themselves as victims of a crime, participants had to be made aware that their poor performance was a result of a theft of their work from their outbox. An abundance of clues were provided them to facilitate the labeling process. Such clues included the suspect's hasty departure from the scene and the subsequent discovery of four of their completed worksheets among the suspect's completed work. These clues, in combination with others provided in the work situation (i.e., the slower work pace of the suspect and his easy access to the participant's outbox), enabled the vast majority of participants to view themselves as victims of a theft. However, a small minority failed to label the incident as criminal. Instead, they labeled the incident as a case of "cheating" and were reluctant to notify the police. When they were questioned afterward about their reason for not calling the police, the reason most frequently offered was that it was a "private matter."

STAGE 2: DETERMINING THE SERIOUSNESS OF THE CRIME

Even the labeling of an event as a crime does not in itself ensure that victims will notify the police or take any overt action. The form and content of victims' responses depend, in part, on the perceived seriousness of the crime. The more serious the crime as perceived by victims, the greater the level of stress and, consequently, the stronger the motivation to take corrective action. As shown in Figure 9-1, how serious victims judge their victimization to be depends on two variables: (1) the extent to which they believe that they were "wronged," in which feelings of injustice and inequity figure prominently, and (2) the extent to which they view themselves as vulnerable to being victimized again. Each variable represents a violation of a different meaning of the term *expectations*. The sense of being wronged represents a violation of expectations concerning what "ought" to be (Heider, 1958). It represents a violation of the moral order, with concomitant affective consequences, of which feelings of anger and vengeance are quite prominent (Averill, 1982; Shaver, Schwartz, Kirson, & O'Connor, 1987). In contrast, the belief that one is vulnerable to subsequent victimization represents a violation of expectations in the *probabilistic* sense. Representing a violation of the predictive order, the event therefore produces feelings of fear and uncertainty about the future.

The stronger the perceptions of being wronged and of being vulnerable to subsequent victimization, the more serious the victimization is viewed as being, and, consequently, the greater will be the ensuing arousal and distress. The resultant arousal and distress are presumed to be a weighted function of *both* sources of distress, with each being weighted according to its salience or vividness (i.e., the degree to which each source stands out or is prominent at the time). As shown in Figure 9-1, how wronged and vulnerable victims perceive themselves to be is a function of the perceived magnitude of the *unexpectedness* of the harm, the perceived amount of *actual* harm experienced (physical, material, and psychological), and the perceived magnitude of *potential* harm (i.e., that could have occurred during the commission of the crime).

STRESS RESULTING FROM PERCEPTION OF BEING WRONGED

Psychologists have documented people's need to believe in a just and orderly world and their reactions to violations of this belief (Adams, 1965; Homans, 1961; Lerner *et al.*, 1976; Walster, Walster, & Berscheid, 1978). When individuals perceive that they have been treated unfairly, they experience a feeling of inequity and respond with disappointment and anger. This appears to be particularly true of victims of crime. Numerous studies have documented crime victims' sense of being wronged and ensuing anger (e.g., Baril, 1984; Becker, Skinner, Abel, Howell, & Bruce, 1982; Fischer, 1977; LeJeune & Alex, 1973; Maguire, 1980, 1982; Maguire & Corbett, 1987; Manzanera, 1984). Our own data tend to support these findings. Anger was the dominant immediate affective response reported by theft victims in our laboratory experiments (Chapters 2 and 3) and also among burglary and theft victims interviewed in Studies 17, 18, and 19. Moreover, the reason most often given for reporting the crime in Studies 3 and 4 was "The principle of the thing—it wasn't right." These data testify to the strong beliefs among certain types of crime victims about being wronged and the anger that results from such beliefs. We will now examine some of the proposed determinants of this sense of being wrongly treated.

Unexpectedness of the Victimization

The model predicts that the greater the unexpectedness of the crime, the stronger the sense of being wronged. The rationale for this prediction derives from the hypothesized tendency of people to integrate what they expect to occur in a predictive sense with what they believe "ought" to occur in a moral or normative sense: What *is* becomes what *ought* to be (Heider, 1958; Waller & Hill, 1951). Violations of the predictive order thus become violations of the moral order and are perceived not merely as unexpected, but as wrong and unfair as well. Correspondingly, crimes having a higher expectancy ought to produce less of a feeling of injustice because they represent less of a violation of the moral order. Moreover, when people knowingly place themselves at risk of criminal victimization, that knowledge may cause them to perceive themselves as more deserving of their fate and, therefore, less unjustly treated.

This reasoning suggests that crimes occurring in situations where victims believe they are safe, such as those committed by trusted others at an unexpected time and place, ought to elicit stronger feelings of unfairness and anger. In support of this proposition, Maguire and Corbett's analysis of data (1987) from the British Crime Survey found that across a wide variety of crimes, those committed by acquaintances produced greater emotional upset than those committed by complete strangers. Findings from our analysis of the Rape Crisis Center archives in Atlanta (Study 15) provided additional support for this proposition. Victims of rape were significantly more angered by the attack when they had previously been acquainted with the rapist.

Perceived Amount of Actual Harm

According to our model, the greater the perceived amount of *actual* harm suffered by the victim, the stronger the sense of having been wronged and treated unfairly. Laboratory research on the effects of inequity provide supportive evidence (Adams & Freedman, 1976; Walster *et al.*, 1973). This literature, however, has not dealt with inequitable events that are considered *criminal*. Research on crime victims provides mixed support for the hypothesis linking amount of actual harm and feelings of being wronged and treated unfairly. Waller and Okihiro (1978) found that among burglary victims, retributive feelings were not related to the dollar value of the loss or damage. Similar negative findings concerning dollar value were reported by Maguire (1980). Our own interview data with burglary and theft victims (Chapter 8) also showed a weak relationship between dollar value and felt anger. The correlations between the two in Studies 18 and 19 were, respectively, .14 and .17 (neither was statistically significant). Moreover, in Study 17, burglary victims suffered greater monetary losses than theft victims, yet they were *less* angered by the crime. These results are not surprising, because other sources of perceived value (such as the sentimental value of the objects) may be a more important determinant of perceived actual harm than dollar value. Thus, when perceived harm is measured by criteria other than dollar value, the results look different. For example, Waller and Okihiro (1978) found that burglary victims expressed stronger retributive feelings when their belongings had been extensively disarranged than when there had been little or no disarrangement. In addition, our analysis of the Rape Crisis Center data archives in Atlanta (Study 15) found that victims expressed greater anger when they had suffered more degrading acts and when they had faced more types of coercion during the attack.

Magnitude of Potential Harm

The third determinant of how wronged victims perceive themselves to be is the degree of potential harm that could have resulted from the crime. Recent research and theorizing by cognitive psychologists suggest that people evaluate an outcome in part by comparing it to imagined alternative outcomes. The easier it is to imagine an alternative outcome, the greater the likelihood that it will serve as a comparison standard (Kahneman & Miller, 1986; Kahneman & Tversky, 1982) For example, victims of minor assault who can easily imagine having suffered even worse injuries in the assault would consider themselves fortunate. Alternatively, if they imagine having taken a different route home and thus avoiding the assault altogether, they would consider themselves unfortunate. This construction of alternatives to factual events is known as *counterfactual processing*. In a provocative paper, Kahneman and Miller (1986) contended that the easier it is to construct or imagine positive counterfactual alternatives for some bad event, the more unusual and unjust the event will appear, and the stronger will be the emotional reaction to it. For example, a victim of a burglary who is victimized because he uncharacteristically left his door unlocked will feel more wronged by the event than another victim who routinely left his door unlocked. In the former instance, the victim can more easily imagine locking the door and thus avoiding the crime than in the latter instance. Data consistent with this reasoning have been provided in studies by Folger (1987), Johnson (1986), Kahneman and Miller (1986), Kahneman and Tversky (1982), Miller and McFarland (1986), and Miller, Turnbull, and McFarland (1990).

On the basis of the above reasoning, we would predict that victims who can easily imagine avoiding the victimization will experience intensely negative emotional feelings stemming from their perception of being more wrongfully treated. In contrast, victims who can easily imagine suffering potentially worse outcomes will feel relatively fortunate to have avoided the more dire outcomes and will thus feel less negative about the event. Indeed, this tendency to contemplate potentially worse outcomes appears to be quite common among burglary victims (Maguire, 1980, 1982; Waller & Okihiro, 1978). We have observed similar tendencies in our interviews with burglary and theft victims. For example, a significant percentage of victims in Studies 18 and 19 admitted thinking "It could have been worse" (79% in Study 18, and 72% in Study 19). In summary, these data suggest that the reactions of crime victims depend not only on what happened to them, but also on their perceptions of what *could* have happened to them.

STRESS RESULTING FROM PERCEIVED VULNERABILITY

Criminal victimization experiences can create in victims the belief that the world is neither predictable nor controllable and, therefore, not safe. Victims may reason that if it happened today, it could happen tomorrow or the next day, a conclusion that is likely to enhance their feelings of vulnerability and fear. Numerous studies have noted that recently victimized individuals tend to experience such feelings (Burgess & Holmstrom, 1974; Davis & Friedman, 1985; Knudten, Meade, Knudten, & Doerner, 1976; Krupnick, 1980; LeJeune & Alex, 1973; Maguire, 1980; Maguire & Corbett, 1987; Manzanera, 1984; Reppetto, 1974; Waller & Okihiro, 1978). Fear appears to be a particularly common reaction to personal crimes of violence, such as robbery and assault (Maguire & Corbett, 1987), as well as burglary (Lurigio, 1987; Reppetto, 1974; Maguire, 1980). Our own research is partially consistent with these findings. The archival analysis of the Rape Crisis Center (RCC) records in Atlanta (Study 15) and interviews with victims of rape in Pittsburgh (Study 16) indicated that fear was the predominant reaction among such victims. In Studies 18 and 19, however, few burglary and theft victims recalled being fearful in the moments following discovery of the crime.

We propose that, as with the belief that one has been wronged, feelings of vulnerability and fear subsequent to a criminal victimization are primarily a function of the unexpectedness of the crime and the perceived amount of actual and potential harm. In the following paragraphs we present the rationale for our predictions and a review of the available empirical evidence.

Unexpectedness of the Victimization

We propose that feelings of vulnerability and fear following a criminal victimization are a positive function of the unexpectedness of the crime. Unexpected victimizations, such as those that occur in safe circumstances (e.g., in one's home or by trusted others), shatter basic assumptions about prediction and control of one's outcomes, and thus about one's safety (Janoff-Bulman, 1985). As Perloff (1983) noted, "In general, unexpected, unforeseen, or unpredictable events are more difficult to cope with than expected, foreseen, or predictable ones" (p. 49). This reasoning was supported by Scheppele and Bart (1983); in their study of the reactions of female victims of sexual assault, they found that women who had believed that the attack situation was safe became more fearful of future victimization than did women who had suspected that the attack situation was dangerous. In addition, anecdotal evidence suggests that the feelings of fear and vulnerability experienced by burglary and purse-snatching victims are attributable, in part, to the unexpectedness of these crimes (Rause, 1981). Victims of purse snatching become aware that such crimes can occur in broad daylight and in public settings in which they have previously felt safe and secure. As one victim of purse snatching stated, "It was an awareness of my own vulnerability. If those 15-year olds could look me in the eyes and still steal my wallet, would my life be next?" (Barkas, 1978, p. 149).

Perceived Amount of Actual Harm

According to the model, feelings of vulnerability and fear tend to vary as a function of the perceived amount of actual harm experienced; the greater the harm, the greater the fear of revictimization (Cook, Smith, & Harrell, 1987; Scheppele & Bart, 1983; Smale, 1984). Accordingly, we predict that crimes involving severe injury to the victim, such as rape and aggravated assault, will produce stronger feelings of fear and vulnerability than will crimes such as theft and vandalism. Existing evidence demonstrates that victims of rape are more fearful of subsequent victimization than are those who were sexually assaulted but perceived that they had avoided being raped (Scheppele & Bart, 1983). Moreover, interviews conducted in the Netherlands by Smale (1984) indicate that the fear of recurrence was greater for victims of violent crimes than for victims of property crimes. Among the latter, fear of recurrence varied with the amount of the damage and the extent to which the victim was "attached" to the property. Our own data tend to support these findings. Analysis of the RCC archives in Atlanta (Study 15) show that the magnitude of fear expressed by victims was greater if the victim had suffered greater physical injury, had been forced to perform more degrading sexual acts, or had been held captive for a longer period of time.

Magnitude of Potential Harm

Victims' fear of subsequent victimization depends in part on the ease with which they can imagine potentially more harmful outcomes occurring. According to Kahneman and Tversky (1982) and Kahneman and Miller (1986), thoughts about what might have happened during the victimization not only serve as a standard against which actual outcomes are compared but also influence victims' estimation of the *likelihood* of future occurrences of such events. Thus, the more easily a victim can imagine the occurrence of more dire consequences of the crime, the higher the victim's estimate of the probability of such consequences. Victims who reason this way tend to feel more vulnerable and fearful of subsequent victimization. In support of this reasoning, Dukes and Mattley (1977) found that the amount of fear manifested by rape victims immediately after the attack was a function of the perceived *willingness* and *ability* of the rapist to hurt them physically. Willingness was operationalized as the number of times the rapist threatened to hurt the victim, whereas ability was operationalized in terms of the presence of a gun. A multiple correlation coefficient of .61 was obtained between willingness and ability and the victim's level of fear.

The perception of potential harm in the situation helps tie together several disparate findings concerning victims' fear of revictimization. It accounts for Waller and Okihiro's finding (1978) that burglary victims were more fearful in those instances where the burglars appeared to be "mucking about" and where victims discovered their possessions in extreme disarray. Such victims may have found it easier to imagine that if they had been home they would have been attacked and perhaps seriously injured. Similarly, the consideration of potential harm may account for the finding by Kilpatrick, Best, Veronen, Amick, Villeponteaux, and Ruff (1985) that, compared to completed crimes, *attempted* molestation and attempted robbery generated more negative mental health consequences. Victims of attempted attacks, because of their greater uncertainty about what could have happened, may have found it easier to imagine being killed or seriously injured than did victims of completed attacks.

Victims' consideration of potential harm may also help to explain why it is that across a variety of crimes, female victims evidence greater fear than do male victims (Cook *et al.*, 1987; Davis & Friedman, 1985; Maguire, 1980; Maguire & Corbett, 1987; Reppetto, 1974; Studies 18 and 19 in this volume). It may be easier for female than male victims to envision experiencing worse hypothetical outcomes, such as physical harm. Similar reasoning accounts for our findings that the amount of fear shown by rape victims in Atlanta (Study 15) was related to the magnitude of coercion employed by the assailant. In addition, in that study we found, as did Dukes and Mattley (1977), that victims who were confronted with a weapon or threats of physical assault were more fearful afterward than were those not exposed to a high level of coercion. The tendency for victims to more easily imagine more serious negative outcomes when a weapon is employed may account for the higher reporting rates for crimes involving a weapon (e.g., Block, 1974; Bureau of Justice Statistics, 1990b; Hindelang, 1976). Hindelang (1976), for example, found that in robberies involving no injury to the victim, the robber's use of a weapon resulted in a higher rate of reporting (57%) than did no use of a weapon (40%).

In this section we have attempted to show that victims' perceptions of the seriousness of their victimization depend on the combined effects of two sources: their sense of being wronged by the attack and their concern about being vulnerable to subsequent victimization. A cluster of emotional reaction is associated with each source. Allied to the sense of being wronged and treated unfairly are feelings of anger, resentment, and revenge. Associated with perceptions of vulnerability are feelings of fear and anxiety. In brief, we are proposing that victims feel angry and vengeful in response to the perceived wrong that *was* done to them, and fearful and anxious about their perceived vulnerability to subsequent harm.

In summary, the extent to which victims perceive themselves as wronged and/or vulnerable depends on three features of the crime: its perceived expectedness, the magnitude of the perceived harm suffered by the victim, and perceptions of potential harm in the situation. The sense of being wronged is greatest when the crime is unexpected, the perceived harm is severe, and the potential harm in the situation is low. Perceptions of vulnerability are enhanced when the crime is unexpected and when there is a high degree of perceived and potential harm. The model specifies a positive relationship between the level of anger and fear and the perceived seriousness of the crime. Our interview data supported this reasoning. Perceived seriousness was significantly correlated with both anger and fear ("scared") in Studies 18 and 19. In Study 18 the correlations between seriousness and anger and between seriousness and fear were, respectively, .27 ($df = 95$,

$p < .01$) and .30 ($df = 95$, $p < .01$). In Study 19,the corresponding figures were .32 ($df = 96$, $p < .01$) and .35 ($df = 96$, $p < .001$).

There is also extensive evidence supporting the proposed relationship between the magnitude of the perceived amount of actual harm and the perceived seriousness of the crime. As previously noted in the discussion of perceived seriousness in Chapter 6, personal crimes of violence (such as homicide, rape, robbery, and assault) in which the victim is physically harmed or threatened with harm tend to be evaluated, by victims and non-victims alike, as more serious than are property crimes such as burglary and larceny (Greenberg, Wilson, Carretta, & DeMay, 1979; Hoffman & Hardyman, 1986; Wolfgang et al., 1985). Our own investigation of normative support for notifying the police (see Chapter 6) also supports the proposed linkage between perceived harm and perceived seriousness, as well as the relationship between potential harm and perceived seriousness. Our data gathered from four countries located on three continents showed that the best predictors of perceived seriousness were the presence of physical injury to the victim and the assailant's possession of a gun.

The model further postulates that the arousal and distress derived from evaluating the seriousness of the crime affect both the strength of the victim's *motivation* to decide what to do and the *process* involved in reaching that decision. With regard to the strength of the victim's motivation, the greater the arousal and distress, the stronger is the victim's motivation to find a solution to the situation. The specific mode of response depends on its perceived efficacy in reducing the salient source(s) of distress. In other words, the strength of the victim's motivation to notify the police depends in part on the magnitude of the victim's distress and the belief that reporting the crime will eliminate the sources of this distress. The impact of stress on the decision-making process is discussed in the following section, where we examine the third stage of the decision process.

STAGE 3: DECIDING WHAT TO DO

Having labeled the incident a crime and determined its seriousness, victims are next faced with the decision about what action to take. As shown in the last column of Figure 9-1, the multitude of options open to victims can be grouped under four broad headings. Victims can call the police, deal with the situation privately, cognitively reevaluate the situation, or simply do nothing. Whether or not a particular option or combination of options is chosen depends on the victim's attitude toward the option(s). Presumably, the option chosen is the one toward which the victim has the most favorable attitude. The attitude, in turn, is a joint product of the victim's beliefs that certain consequences will result from choosing that option and of the victim's evaluation of those consequences (Fishbein & Ajzen, 1975). One can calculate victims' attitudes toward a particular response option by first obtaining their subjective probability that certain consequences will occur and then multiplying this figure by their evaluation of each consequence. The victim's attitude represents the sum of these products. Thus, victims will be favorably disposed toward an option that they believe is highly likely to produce desired consequences, and they will be unfavorably disposed toward an option that they believe is highly likely to yield undesired consequences.

Once having chosen an option for examination, victims conduct their examination by employing mental simulations (Taylor & Schneider, 1989). That is, they imagine or play through an option in order to predict what the likely consequences would be (Nuttin, 1984). The simulations are often guided by and informed by knowledge structures such as a script (i.e., a stereotyped sequence of events). That is, when victims reach into their chest of information for guidance, what they tend to withdraw are not isolated beads of information but "necklaces" of information linked together by knowledge structures such as scripts (Abelson, 1981; Schank & Abelson, 1977). The examination of scripts, such as those relating to "calling the police" or "talking with the suspect," allows people to anticipate what to expect when electing a particular response option. A study by Greenberg, Ruback, and Westcott (1982) illustrated this reasoning. With the use of procedures borrowed from Bower, Black, and Turner (1979), college students were asked to list in chronological order the typical events that would occur when reporting either a $5 or $300 theft to the police. There was considerable overlap in the two scripts, but those completing the $300 script believed that the police were more likely to come to the victim's home, to ask the victim questions about the theft, to fill out a report, and to investigate the incident. When scripts are conceptualized in this manner, as bundles of expectations, it is easy to see how scripts help victims assess the consequences of different options.

Decision Making under Stress

Our analysis of the third stage of the decision process closely resembles Fishbein and Ajzen's expectancy-value model (1975). The major difference is that theirs is a model of "reasoned action," while ours is a model of "semireasoned action." The decision process is not always perfectly rational because of the stressful conditions under which crime victims often have to operate. Under ideal conditions, the perfectly rational decision maker would conduct an extensive examination of all of the known options and their presumed consequences, choosing the one that appears to offer the best outcomes (i.e., a maximizing decision strategy). Even under the best of conditions, however, individuals are not completely rational decision makers (Nisbett & Ross, 1980). The fact that crime victims often must make their decision under very stressful conditions further precludes a careful search and appraisal of the benefits and costs of each option. Easterbrook (1959) showed that attention becomes narrowed under high levels of arousal. Other research suggests that high stress impairs the assimilation of information (Wright & Weitz, 1977), causes decision makers to scan their alternatives in a nonsystematic fashion, and leads them to choose solutions before all available alternatives have been considered (Janis & Mann, 1977; Keinan, 1987).

These data suggest that crime victims may lack the ability and the patience to consider *all* the available response options. Instead, their attention may be focused on finding an option that seems *sufficient* rather than *optimal*. The use of this "satisficing" strategy (Simon, 1976) probably varies as a function of the level of arousal and distress: the greater the stress, the stronger the intention to seek an adequate rather than a best solution (Janis & Mann, 1977). The option victims choose to examine first probably depends on the option's momentary salience or availability, which is, in turn, a function of characteristics of the victim (e.g., previous experience and self-concept) and of the situation (e.g., access to a telephone and identification of suspect). The examination of the option itself is likely to be cursory, with the final choice often appearing to the victim as "automatic" or "reflexive" (Baril, 1984; Maguire, 1980).

VICTIMS' OPTIONS

In this section we review the four response options typically available to crime victims and the relevant empirical research regarding choices from among these options. That victims elect a particular option does not mean that no others can or will be chosen. Indeed, victims are likely to avail themselves of several options, but they do so sequentially. Thus, after failing to locate the suspect (a private option), the victim may decide to report the crime to the police. To the extent that an option proves successful in ameliorating their distress, victims will feel less need to employ additional options. Consequently, in order to obtain a better accounting of why the police are notified, we must first examine how competing options can diminish victims' distress.

Private Solutions for Reducing Feelings of Being Wronged

Victims may prefer to seek a private solution to their distress. Private efforts to deal with the sense of being wronged can take various forms. The victim can attempt to retaliate if the offender's identity is known. As the experimental literature on responses to inequity has shown (e.g., Walster *et al.*, 1978), making the harm-doer pay for the misdeed is an effective mode of restoring equity. In order to employ this mode, however, victims must first identify and then locate the suspect. These tasks are not easily accomplished, and retaliation poses both physical and legal risks to the victim. The victim risks more severe harm from the assailant by initiating a cycle of escalating attacks and counterattacks. In addition, by retaliating, victims convert their status from victim to victimizer and thus incur the risk of being criminally prosecuted. The victim's retaliation sometimes exceeds the original harm and may result in serious injury, even homicide (Blitman & Green, 1975; Browne, 1987; Wolfgang, 1958).

If victims can identify and locate the suspect, they can seek compensation from the suspect by demanding or coercing the return of the stolen property or its financial equivalent. These demands can be supported by threats of retaliation or by threats to notify the suspect's family or employer or the police. Alternatively, victims can use positive reinforcers to achieve the same end. The personal columns of newspapers frequently contain advertisements offering monetary rewards for the return of "missing" property with "no questions asked." Victims can also attempt to obtain compensation from state-financed compensation schemes or by filing a civil suit against the suspect. Civil suits are easier to win than criminal cases because of a less demanding standard of proof (proof by the preponderance of the evidence rather than proof beyond a reasonable doubt). Victims infrequently choose the civil route, however, partly because of the length of time it takes to process such cases, but primarily because suspects rarely have sufficient resources to compensate the victim (Barkas, 1978; Rottenberg, 1980).

In recent years victims have sought compensation from third parties rather than from the actual harm-doer. For example, victims may seek payment of damages from delivery companies for not properly screening employees, or from motel chains for not providing proper security devices such as dead-bolt locks. Finally, rather than obtaining compensation from a third party via legal channels, victims may attempt to recover their losses and thus reduce their sense of unfairness by stealing from others. A number of recent studies conducted in the United States and in Europe show that among certain subpopulations, prior victimization is associated with subsequent victimization of others (Singer, 1981, 1986; Sparks et al., 1977; Van Dijk & Steinmetz, 1979; Wolfgang & Ferracuti, 1967).

Private Solutions for Reducing Vulnerability

Three categories of private options for reducing vulnerability to subsequent victimization can be identified. Victims can move *away, toward,* or *against* the perpetrator. We define moving "away" as any effort by victims to erect barriers between themselves and potential harm-doers. Actions designed to prevent burglary, known as "hardening the target" (Conklin, 1975), can include the purchase of an alarm system, a guard dog, dead-bolt locks, window bars, and outdoor lighting. Additional precautions when one will be away from home may include canceling delivery of newspapers and mail and installing an automatic timer to control indoor lighting. Perceived efficacy appears to be the major determinant of whether or not a precaution will be employed (Lavrakas, 1981). Other options that have proved effective in reducing fear of crime in and outside the home include purchasing a gun (*Figgie Report*, 1980), participation in a self-defense training course (Cohn, Kidder, & Harvey, 1978; Ozer & Bandura, 1990), participation in neighborhood watch programs (Cohn, 1978), and changing one's residence from a high- to a low-crime area (Skogan & Maxfield, 1981).

These cautionary behaviors appear to reduce fears of victimization. But are crime victims any more likely to avail themselves of these options than nonvictims? Weinstein's review of 17 studies (1989) revealed mixed findings. He noted that a number of studies report no significant differences in the precautions taken by victims and nonvictims, but that "in-depth" studies (e.g., Friedman *et al.*, 1982; Maguire, 1980) report substantial changes in cautionary behavior following criminal victimization. As Weinstein noted, however, such studies often lack appropriate nonvictim control groups.

For victims of crime involved in a continuing relationship with the perpetrator, such as victims of domestic violence, moving "away" from the perpetrator is often not a viable option. Economic and psychological barriers may prevent one from fleeing the situation. These victims may make use of the second private mode of reducing vulnerability: moving *toward* the victimizer. Efforts to move toward the perpetrator include actions designed to ingratiate oneself with the harm-doer. Whereas victims who move away from the harm-doer attempt to reduce the harm-doer's *ability* to harm them, victims who move toward the harm-doer hope to reduce the harm-doer's *motivation* to harm them. For example, victim of domestic abuse attempt to avoid triggering subsequent attacks by pleasing the harm-doer and complying with her or his wishes (Ferraro, 1983). Employment of this tactic is not unlike that used by a 10-year-old to deal with a schoolyard bully. In order to avoid having his or her lunch stolen and to appease the bully's appetite, the child may bring extra candies and goodies to share with the bully. The adult counterpart is the small-shop owner who pays "protection" money to avoid having his or her store broken into. In each of the above examples, the victim provides the perpetrator with benefits in order to avoid more serious harm.

Finally, rather than moving away or toward the perpetrator, victims may attempt to discourage future attempts at harm by acting *against* the perpetrator. Retaliation in the form of physical and/or verbal attacks may cause potential harm-doers to think twice about attacking the victim in the future, thereby weakening the perpetrator's motivation to repeat the crime. Victims may have another purpose in mind when they choose to retaliate. Severe physical retaliation may incapacitate perpetrators, depriving them of not only the motivation but the *ability* to render harm to the victim (Browne, 1987; Wolfgang, 1958). In recent years some courts have accepted a broader definition of imminent danger and therefore have lent a sympathetic ear to battered women who have retaliated against their perpetrators (Walker, 1989). Little is known about the extent to which private acts of vengeance occur, because attention is drawn only to those cases where the police are notified.

Cognitive Reevaluation of the Situation

Another way that victims can reduce their distress is to reassess one or more of the decisions that produced the distress. In many cases such reassessment may distort reality. Taylor and Brown (1988) provided a well-documented case for the argument that "the mentally healthy person appears to have the enviable capacity to distort reality in a direction that enhances self-esteem, maintains beliefs in personal efficacy, and promotes an optimistic view of the future" (p. 204). Presumably, cognitions most susceptible to reevaluation are those that are least subject to disconfirmation by objective and/or social reality (i.e., the opinions of others). The reevaluation process may begin with victims' reconsidering their decision to label the event a crime. For example, it is not uncommon for female victims of domestic assault to question the criminality of the incident because of their role in precipitating the attack (Ferraro, 1983; Frieze, 1979). After examining the match between the updated evaluation of the incident and their personal definition of a criminal assault, they may conclude that while they were undeniably victims of an assault, they were not victims of a *criminal* assault.

If they are not able to deny the criminality of the event, they can perhaps reevaluate its seriousness. This can be done by directly reexamining their feeling of being wronged and of being vulnerable to subsequent victimization, or it can be done by reevaluating the antecedents of these two sources of distress. Research on hindsight reveals a well-documented tendency for people to distort and misrecall their expectations so as to conform with what actually happened (Fischoff, 1975; Hawkins & Hastie, 1990; Ross & McFarland, 1988). Thus, victims can decide that upon further reflection the crime was to be expected.

The seriousness of the crime can also be reduced by cognitive activity that reassesses the severity of the harm. Victims can accomplish this by minimizing the perceived severity of their injuries (Ferraro, 1983) or the perceived value of the stolen property, or by deciding that the stolen items can be easily replaced. They can also minimize the perceived magnitude of harm by discovering compensating benefits from the victimization experience. For example, victims sometimes experience the discovery of personal insights and self-growth following criminal attacks (e.g., Barkas, 1978; Maguire & Corbett, 1987; Taylor et al., 1983).

In addition, cognitive activity may be directed at reassessing the amount of potential harm in the situation. Victims' sense of being wronged by the criminal attack can be assuaged by imagining worse outcomes that could have occurred (Fischer, 1977; Taylor et al., 1983). The frequency with which victims engage in such thinking was suggested by results from Studies 18 and 19. When asked whether they "thought about the fact that it [the crime] could have been worse," 79% of participants in Study 18 and 72% in Study 19 responded affirmatively. As we have noted previously, such cognitive activity may reduce victims' anger, but it may also enhance their fear by reminding them of their vulnerability to subsequent victimization. Our reasoning would suggest that victims can reduce their sense of vulnerability by imagining the occurrence of potentially better, rather than worse, outcomes in the situation. By constructing scenarios in which the negative outcomes were avoided, victims can view the victimization as "abnormal" or unusual and therefore unlikely to recur (Kahneman & Miller, 1986). Furthermore, by employing logic from the "gambler's fallacy," they may reassure themselves that the chances of a second victimization are quite remote (Slovic, Kunreuther, & White, 1974).

Perhaps the best documented form of cognitive reassessment is the tendency for victims to blame themselves, at least in part, for the crime. In our interviews with burglary and theft victims (Studies 18 and 19), we found that victims were very concerned about ascertaining responsibility for the crime. Of those in Study 18, 76%, and of those in Study 19, 89% admitted asking themselves, "Why me?" They appeared particularly concerned about determining the extent of their *own* responsibility for the crime, as evidenced by the finding that 87% of victims in Study 18 and 91% in Study 19 recalled asking themselves, "Could I have avoided this?"

Other researchers also have noted the tendency of victims to blame themselves. It has been observed among victims of rape (Burgess & Holmstrom, 1975; Janoff-Bulman, 1979; Medea & Thompson, 1974), victims of domestic assault (Ferraro, 1983; Frieze, 1979), and to a lesser extent, victims of burglary and robbery (Friedman et al., 1982; Maguire & Corbett, 1987; Miransky & Langer, 1978). Attributing blame to oneself can reduce feelings of anger and fear by its effect on perceptions of injustice and vulnerability. Blaming the victimization on their behavior may allow victims to view themselves as deserving of their fate, thereby causing them to perceive the situation as less unjust or unfair. Moreover, by blaming the victimization on their behavior (a controllable source) rather than on their character (a less controllable source), victims can reassure themselves that they will not repeat their mistake; this makes it easier for them to view future victimization as unlikely (Janoff-Bulman, 1979). According to data gathered from rape crisis counselors, rape victims who made "characterological" attributions tended to view their rape as more deserved than those who did not (Janoff-Bulman, 1979).

Consistent with this reasoning, Janoff-Bulman (1982) found that behavioral self-blame was associated with high self-esteem and the perception of avoidability of subsequent victimization. Similarly, Davis and Lurigio (1989) reported that victims who engaged in behavioral self-blame were less likely to suffer from distressing thoughts and dreams. In a recent statement paralleling theoretical distinctions made in this chapter, Janoff-Bulman (1985) insightfully noted, "While the behavioral self-blamer is concerned with the future and the avoidability of misfortune, the characterological self-blamer focuses on the past and the question of deservedness rather than avoidability" (p. 29). The ease with which victims are able to blame themselves depends, of course, on the circumstances of the crime. In less ambiguous circumstances (for example, when the violence is more severe), rape victims as well as battered women are less likely to blame themselves for the attack (Baker & Peterson, 1977; Frieze, 1979; Miller & Porter, 1983).

Cognitive distortions may reduce victims' distress, but their use is not without risk. Victims of rape who blame themselves for the attack tend to be evaluated more negatively by others (Coates, Wortman, & Abbey, 1979; Thornton, Ryckman, Kirchner, Jacobs, Kaczor, & Kuehnel, 1988; Yee, Beach, Greenberg, & Marsh, 1991). Moreover, with the exception of behavioral self-blame, when victims' efforts to deal cognitively with feelings of vulnerability are more successful, they are likely to be less motivated to take precautionary actions such as locking doors, maintaining surveillance over their property, and walking in safe areas. Further, such cognitive efforts may provide victims with unrealistic expectations about their safety, which could produce profound feelings of vulnerability should they be victimized again. Ironically, by cognitively reducing their sense of vulnerability, victims may ultimately enhance their chances of being revictimized, and further victimization would, in turn, increase the magnitude of their distress.

Notifying the Police

According to our model, the incentive for reporting crimes to the police varies as a joint function of victims' level of distress and the belief that notification will ameliorate the distress. Our studies and the research of others tend to support this reasoning. Findings from the British Crime Survey show that victims who notified the police were more affected emotionally by the crime than were nonreporters (Maguire & Corbett, 1987). Other data show that the best predictor of reporting is the perceived seriousness of the crime (e.g., Fishman, 1979; Schneider et al., 1976; Skogan, 1984; Sparks et al., 1977; Waller & Okihiro, 1978; Webb & Marshall, 1989). Similarly, our interviews with burglary and theft victims (Studies 18 and 19) yielded a significant correlation between perceived seriousness and reporting ($r = .22$ and .21 for the two studies, respectively).

Other research shows that factors related to the seriousness of the victimization are also related to reporting. Victims are more likely to report when the crime has been completed rather than attempted (Bureau of Justice Statistics, 1990b; Hindelang, 1976), when the perceived value of the property is great rather than small (Bureau of Justice Statistics, 1990b; Schneider *et al.*, 1976; Schwind, 1984; Waller & Okihiro, 1978), and when the crime has resulted in more serious injury to the victim (Block, 1974, 1989; Bureau of Justice Statistics, 1985). Similarly, in our study of rape victims in Atlanta (Study 15), we found that the victims who had suffered the greater injury were more likely to report the incident. That victims consider the perceived magnitude of *potential* as well as actual harm is supported by the finding of higher rates of reporting for crimes that involved a weapon, particularly a gun (Block, 1974; Bureau of Justice Statistics, 1985; Hindelang, 1976; Webb & Marshall, 1989), and of crimes where threats were employed (Study 15).

Consistent with the proposed model, reporting the crime is also related to feeling wronged or angered. In our experimental studies we tended to find a statistically significant relationship between self-reported anger and willingness to call the police. (The relationship was significant in Studies 2–5, but not in Study 6). Moreover, the reason offered most often by reporters in Studies 3 and 4 was "The principle of the thing—it wasn't right." Across all six experiments, reporters were more angered, expressed a greater desire to see the thief punished, and felt a greater moral obligation to report than nonreporters (see Chapter 5). Additional evidence linking anger and reporting was obtained in the archival analysis of rape victims in Atlanta (Study 15). However, Waller and Okihiro's study of burglary victims (1978) found no relationship between anger and reporting. Their failure to find a relationship may have been due in part to the long time interval between the burglary and the interview, up to three years in some cases.

Evidence supporting the facilitating effect of fear and vulnerability on reporting was obtained by Dukes and Mattley (1977), who found that rape reporters, as opposed to nonreporters, were more fearful of reprisal and were more strongly motivated to prevent a recurrence of the attack. Examination of the reasons offered for reporting crimes lends additional weight to feelings of vulnerability and fear as sources of decisions to notify the police. Indeed, a major reason offered by victims is to prevent the crime from happening again (Bureau of Justice Statistics, 1990b; Waller & Okihiro, 1978; Study 19 in this book).

The model proposes that it is not only the magnitude of the victim's distress that motivates reporting the crime, but also the belief that reporting is likely to reduce the distress. Support for this proposition comes from a study by Dukes and Mattley (1977), who found that rape victims were most likely to report the crime when they were fearful *and* anticipated a positive response from the police. Similarly, Schneider *et al.* (1976) found that beliefs in police effectiveness were related to the reporting of serious but not minor property crimes. Additional support for the importance of expecting assistance as a motive for calling the police can be found in the reasons offered by victims for *not* notifying the police. Results from the National Crime Panel indicate that some of the most frequently given reasons for not summoning the police are that "Nothing could be done" and that "The police would not want to be bothered" (Law Enforcement Assistance Administration, 1982), a finding that is bolstered by other studies as well (Waller & Okihiro, 1978; Study 19 in this book).

What, exactly, do victims hope to gain when they call the police? According to our model, they are motivated to reduce the feeling of being wronged and of being vulnerable to subsequent victimization. How might these aims be achieved? If we look first at the sense of being wronged, victims may be mobilized to report the crime because they believe that the police will be able to apprehend the offender and, in the case of property crimes, recover the stolen property. Justice would also be achieved if the offender were convicted and punished and/or forced to make restitution to the victim. The latter goal has become increasingly more feasible in recent years as a result of the judiciary's more favorable attitudes toward restitution (Chesney, Hudson, & McLagen, 1978).

Even if victims believe it is unlikely that the suspect will be brought to justice (which recent Federal Bureau of Investigation figures indicate is the case, at least in cases of property crimes), they may still anticipate positive consequences from reporting the crime. For example, the crime must be reported to the police if the victim is to receive compensation from third parties such as insurance companies and state-sponsored victim compensation programs (Cain & Kravitz, 1978).

Notifying the police can also reduce victims' fear of future victimization. If the suspect is arrested and subsequently imprisoned, then he or she no longer poses a threat to the victim. Moreover, victims may believe that such punishment will deter other would-be offenders. Even when victims see little likelihood of the offender's being apprehended, informing the police can lead to more intensive police patrolling, which can reduce victims' fear of subsequent victimization.

While victims may anticipate numerous positive consequences from calling the police, the fact that a little more than a third of victimizations are reported (Bureau of Justice Statistics, 1990c) suggests that many victims are pessimistic about these outcomes or that they expect additional costs from their involvement with the police and other elements of the criminal justice system. Research documents a number of potentially negative consequences of victim involvement with the police and the criminal justice system, including costs of transportation and parking, lost time from work or school, and costs of child care (Knudten *et al.*, 1976). Questioning by the police and opposing attorneys can also exact their toll on victims. Victims of rape, in particular, often feel embarrassed and frustrated as a result of their encounters with the police and courts and sometimes conclude that they are the ones on trial (Amir, 1971; Binder, 1981). In addition, fear of retaliation by the suspect, although infrequently cited in victimization surveys, may nevertheless be an important cost for certain classes of victims. In one survey, 75% of racial minority victims of completed rapes gave fear of reprisal as their reason for not notifying the police (Hindelang & Davis, 1977).

What these studies suggest is that for many victims of crime the anticipated benefits of calling the police are outweighed by the anticipated negative consequences. Indeed, one of the reasons frequently cited by victims for not reporting is that "The crime was not important enough" (Bureau of Justice Statistics, 1990b; Law Enforcement Assistance Administration, 1982). For such victims, the adage "Crime doesn't pay" has become "Reporting the crime doesn't pay." When victims perceive that none of the three options is likely to yield satisfactory consequences, they may simply decide to do nothing about the crime.

Doing Nothing about the Crime

After appraising the available options, victims may conclude that any attempt to "right" the wrong or reduce their feelings of vulnerability is an exercise in futility. Having no effective means of alleviating their distress and forced to confront their helplessness, these victims may become dejected, apathetic, and depressed (Seligman, 1975). As we have stated elsewhere (Greenberg et al., 1983), "Perceiving no visible solution to their distress, these victims have no recourse but to live with the injustice and wait in fear for the inevitable occurrence of the next victimization" (p. 98).

SOCIAL INFLUENCE AND VICTIM DECISION MAKING

Social influence plays an important role in our three-stage model of victim decision making. As Bard and Sangrey (1979) noted:

> A crime victim's entire structure of defenses becomes weakened under the stress of violation, leaving him or her unusually accessible to the influence of others. This characteristic response makes the behavior of other people unusually powerful in the period right after the crime. (pp. 37–38)

This tendency is well documented in the work of others (Burgess & Holmstrom, 1975; Spelman & Brown, 1981; Van Kirk, 1978) and in the preceding chapters of this book. The data further indicate that the interactions that victims have with others immediately following the criminal event have a substantial impact on their decision making. In this final section we spell out in greater detail the nature of the social influence process.

As shown in Figure 9-1, we propose that social influence may exist at each stage of the decision process: labeling the event, determining its seriousness, and deciding what to do. The influence exerted by others may take one or more of the following three forms: (1) providing *information;* (2) applying *normative pressure;* and (3) providing *socioemotional support* or *nonsupport.*

PROVIDING INFORMATION

Others may influence the victim by providing information that aids the victim in labeling the incident, assessing its seriousness, and deciding what to do. The information may merely "prime" or make available some consideration that the victim has forgotten or not thought about. For example, a victim of an attempted burglary may view herself as a crime victim only after being reminded that an attempted burglary is a crime. Similarly, when deciding what to do, a victim who fails to consider a particular option may be reminded by others that "This may be a matter for the police," or "You may want to think about installing a burglar alarm."

Others may provide the victim with *new* information that affects decisions at each of the three stages. For example, a person whose lawn mower is missing may be informed by a neighbor that he saw someone steal it. Others may also provide information that affects how seriously the victimization is viewed by the victim. This may be done by introducing information that intensifies or reduces the victim's sense of being wronged or feelings of vulnerability. In addition, others may influence the victim's attitude toward an option by supplying information that affects (1) the perceived likelihood of certain consequences and/or (2) the desirability of such consequences.

When others actively try to persuade victims, the information conveyed may consist of *advice* and/or *arguments. Advice,* as the term is used here, represents a recommendation or conclusion about some particular course of action (e.g., "I think you should call the police"). *Arguments* are statements or premises concerning why the advice should be followed (e.g., "The police are likely to apprehend him"). That victims are receptive to information, and to advice in particular, is supported by results from experimental Studies 2–6 and from interview Studies 18 and 19. In the two interview studies, the major reasons victims offered for contacting others were to obtain information and to obtain advice about what to do. Moreover, the five interview studies showed that among those who talked with others after the crime, the percentage receiving advice ranged from 37% to 81%.

RECEPTIVITY TO INFORMATION FROM OTHERS

Social psychological research suggests that individuals are most receptive to information from others when they are faced with a difficult judgment, especially one involving a high degree of uncertainty and ambiguity

(Festinger, 1954; Sherif, 1935). Victims of crime clearly fit this definition, in that they may have difficulty labeling the event, determining its seriousness, and deciding what action should be taken. The difficulty or uncertainty may derive from a number of sources: a lack of sufficient information, a choice between equally attractive (or unattractive) alternatives, or diminished reasoning ability occasioned by the stress of the victimization. Results from several of our studies support this reasoning. The degree of difficulty experienced by burglary and theft victims in deciding what to do was the best predictor of the number of others spoken with (Study 18). Similarly, in Study 19 the number of others victims talked to varied with factors related to decision difficulty: lower dollar value of stolen property, higher emotionality (anger), and younger age of victim. Moreover, in the laboratory Studies 3–5, where theft victims proved highly susceptible to social influence, *angry* and *confused* were the two words used most often by victims to describe their psychological state following the crime.

Our theorizing suggests that seeking information from others is likely to vary with the type of crime. Crimes that ought to produce the greatest reliance on others for information are those that are difficult to label or that involve thought-disruptive emotional sequelae. In the first category are crimes that are discovered after their occurrence (discovery crimes), such as theft and burglary. The labeling of such crimes often requires a preliminary search for information from others who may have witnessed the incident. In contrast, ongoing criminal events in which the victim is crucially involved (i.e., involvement crimes, such as robbery and assault) are less ambiguous and ought to require less information from others. Two studies of victims' delay in reporting yielded data consistent with this reasoning. In the first, Van Kirk (1978) found that there were longer delays in reporting discovery crimes than in reporting involvement crimes. A follow-up study by Spelman and Brown (1981) found that discovery crimes produced a higher percentage of citizens who engaged in information-gathering activities, such as investigating the crime scene and talking to someone else, than did involvement crimes. Finally, our interviews with burglary, theft, and robbery victims (Study 17) showed that theft victims spoke with more people than either burglary or robbery victims. Conceivably, victims of theft were more in need of information from others because this crime is the most ambiguous of the three. In addition, owing to the minimal dollar value of the loss, theft probably produced the greatest uncertainty about the advisability of calling the police.

Serious crimes, such as rape, ought to involve a high degree of thought-disruptive emotional sequelae and should produce informational dependence on others (Burgess & Holmstrom, 1975; Medea & Thompson, 1974). Rape victims sometimes need information from others in order to help them label the event and help them decide among the available response options, but they often seek the assistance of others because the emotional trauma interferes with their decision-making ability. Rape victims' tendency to seek assistance from others immediately after the crime is reflected in our archival and interview findings, which revealed that the first action taken most often by victims following the attack was to contact others (see Studies 15, 16, and 20). More importantly, the interviews with rape victims in Study 16 indicated that 78% talked with others when deciding what to do. Evidence of others' involvement was also reflected in the findings from the three studies showing that in those cases reported to the police, someone other than the victim did the reporting in almost half the instances (45% in Study 15, 47% in Study 16, and 39% in Study 20).

The foregoing discussion suggests that the motive for seeking information from others varies with the type of crime. The heightened stress experienced by victims of serious involvement crimes, such as rape, is likely to impair their ability to process arguments for and against a particular course of action. Under such conditions, victims may both seek and be more receptive to information that is simple and direct, such as advice about what to do. This reasoning is supported by our interview findings showing that 76% of rape victims in Study 16 who talked with others received advice about what to do. A somewhat lower figure (37%) was obtained in Study 20. As we indicated in our earlier discussion of the interview studies, the 37% figure probably underestimates the actual percentage who received advice. With regard to discovery crimes, particularly less serious ones, the need for information derives less from the stress of the victimization (as it does in the involvement crimes) than from the uncertainty and confusion about how to label the incident and what to do about it. For example, such victims may be unsure about whether or not it is worthwhile to call the police and therefore may turn to others for both arguments (e.g., "They can recover the stolen property") *and* advice (e.g., "call the police").

The importance of advice from others in crime-victim decision making is clearly supported by much of the evidence presented in this book. Advice from others is by far the best predictor of victims' decision to call the police. Under what conditions is this advice most likely to have a persuasive impact on victims? Results from our laboratory experiments (Chapters 2 and 3) allow us to advance some tentative hypotheses. It would appear that victims' perception of the advice-giver as *sincere* and *understanding* are critical elements in the success of the influence attempt. These two qualities were most often cited by the participant-victims in Studies 5 and 6 who said that they had been influenced by the bystander's advice. The presence of these qualities may also explain why the covictim exerted more influence than the bystander in Study 6. Victims probably viewed the covictim as sharing their perspective more than did the bystander, therefore attributing greater understanding to the covictim. Moreover, the covictim demonstrated greater sincerity by not merely advising the victim, as the bystander did, but by stating her intention or willingness to call (not to call) the police. The possession of these twin attributes, sincerity and understanding, may also explain the results of Study 4. It may be recalled that victims were most likely to follow the bystander's advice to report the theft when the bystander offered to support the victim and remained present, actions that could be seen as gestures of sincerity and understanding on the part of the bystander. Further, as we noted in Chapter 3, if the bystander's advice is to be followed, it must be comprehended and must be sufficiently precise and specific.

In addition to providing victims with information in the form of arguments and advice, others may inform victims about the seriousness of their victimization by serving as sources of social comparison (Festinger, 1954; Suls & Miller, 1977; Suls & Wills, 1991). Victims may assess the appropriateness of their anger and fear by comparing themselves with those who have suffered similar harm. As recent research indicates, however, victims' choices concerning whom to compare themselves with are often dictated by the need to minimize feelings of being wronged and being vulnerable to subsequent harm (Perloff, 1987; Taylor et al., 1983; Wills, 1981, 1987, 1991). As these studies have shown, victims often prefer to compare themselves with those who have suffered more negative outcomes than they themselves have experienced. Such "downward" comparisons allow victims to minimize the perceived amount of harm they have suffered and thereby to reduce their feelings of injustice and inequity. Similarly, by comparing themselves with others who are more at risk of being harmed, victims' feelings of vulnerability may also be reduced.

While downward comparisons with those who have suffered more severe outcomes often diminish negative feelings, they may also have unanticipated consequences whereby such negative feelings are enhanced. Learning about more serious negative consequences suffered by others increases the ease of imagining suffering such consequences oneself (Tversky & Kahneman, 1973), thereby increasing feelings of vulnerability and fear. As a victim of robbery told Maguire and Corbett (1987), "I avoided telling people who would not be sympathetic, but some made me more frightened by telling me about what happened to them" (p. 72).

It is important to be able to predict when downward comparisons will increase rather than reduce negative emotional reactions to criminal victimization. On the basis of reasoning discussed more fully in Chapter 10, we hypothesize that victims are likely to feel more vulnerable and fearful when those who have suffered more severe outcomes are perceived as being equally or less vulnerable than the victim. Persons falling in this category may include people living in the victim's neighborhood and those living in relatively safe, low-crime neighborhoods. Consistent with this hypothesis, research by Tyler (1980) and by Skogan and Maxfield (1981) shows that learning about the victimization of friends and neighbors is associated with higher levels of fear and vulnerability. The more similar these others are to the victim in personal characteristics and place of residence, the greater the amount of fear generated by such knowledge (Shotland, Hayward, Young, Signorella, Mindingall, Kennedy, Rovine, & Danowitz, 1979). Studies by Heath (1984) and Liska and Baccaglini (1990) found that newspaper reports of local crimes increased fear whereas reporting of nonlocal crimes decreased fear. These studies suggest that negative events occurring close to home tend to be threatening, whereas those occurring in distant places tend to be comforting or reassuring.

On the basis of the above reasoning we would expect that victims whose distress derives primarily from their perceived vulnerability to future victimization to avoid downward comparisons with similar others and to prefer to make upward comparisons (i.e., between themselves and non-victims or victims of less serious crimes). Such comparisons are likely to inform victims of the rarity of serious victimization, thereby reassuring them of their safety and invulnerability to future harm. This is not to say that downward comparisons with similar others always increase feelings of vulnerability. As we discuss in the next chapter, beliefs in *controllability* may be an important moderator of such feelings.

APPLYING NORMATIVE PRESSURE

As we noted in Chapter 6, norms represent generally agreed-upon rules of conduct and can be found in all groups, both large and small. They specify actions that should or should not be taken, and failure to comply with such rules results in rejection, ridicule, and loss of status (Forsyth, 1983). Friends, relatives, and bystanders may attempt to influence victim decision making through the application of normative pressures. Others may bring normative pressures to bear through their continued surveillance of the victim or by verbal reminders, such as "Friends and neighbors expect you to view this as a crime. It's a serious matter. They're going to wonder why you failed to act." As this example suggests, normative pressure may be applied at one or more of the three decision stages: labeling the event, evaluating its seriousness, and deciding what to do.

As previously noted in Chapter 6, there is considerable empirical support for the existence of norms that define the seriousness of crimes (e.g., Rossi *et al.*, 1974; Wolfgang *et al.*, 1985). Yet there is much less evidence for the existence of norms that define the appropriateness of various responses to criminal victimization. One such study (Baril, 1984) noted the presence of strong social pressure on shopkeepers who were robbery victims to report their victimization to the police. Sparks *et al.* (1977) found normative support for a violent response to various forms of victimization. In the latter instance, normative support for a violent response was higher when an intruder had been found in the house at night than when one had been found outside the house. Biderman (1981) provided a personal account of normative pressures on theft victims in military groups to take private action, such as stealing from others. In his words, "Only in special and extreme cases was mobilization of the official system sanctioned by peers" (p. 223).

Evidence of the presence of normative expectations concerning notification of the police can be found in Studies 10–12 discussed in Chapter 6. Approval of reporting tended to vary with the characteristics of the crime and with the population studied. Despite vast cultural differences among participants, the single best predictor of approval for calling the police was the perceived seriousness of the crime. Such crimes represent gross violations of community standards and therefore are probably seen as meriting formal intervention. Thus, victims who report crimes that the culture defines as serious can anticipate receiving approval and support from others. The presence of such normative support creates a sympathetic moral climate that provides victims with a sense of "doing the right thing." On the other hand, victims who contemplate reporting less serious crimes to the police may hesitate to do so because of the anticipated disapproval of others. In such instances they may prefer to deal with the matter privately or to do nothing at all. The relationship between the offender and the victim was also found to influence normative expectations for reporting. With the exception of participants in the United States, less approval was expressed for reporting crimes where the offender and the victim were relatives than when they were strangers. Less approval of reporting incidents involving relatives may reflect the failure to label such incidents as crimes, or it may reflect the belief that such incidents are best dealt with privately.

Normative pressure to comply with advice is greatest when the influence agent maintains surveillance over the target individual (Deutsch & Gerard, 1955). Conceivably, normative influence contributed to some of our experimental findings. It may be recalled that in Study 4 victims were most inclined to follow the bystander's advice to call the police when the bystander offered to support them in their dealings with the police and when the bystander remained at their side. The continued presence of the bystander may have produced normative pressure on victims to comply with the advice. The cogency of this argument, however, is called into question by results from Study 5 showing that neither surveillance by bystanders nor their motives for maintaining it affected compliance with their advice. Finally, it may be recalled that in Study 6, 15% of the participants who said that they had been influenced by the covictim cited normative pressure as the reason for being influenced. Clearly, we need to know more about the role of normative influence pressures in victim decision making.

PROVIDING SOCIOEMOTIONAL SUPPORT OR NONSUPPORT

As we noted earlier, the intense stress often experienced by victims of crime may affect their information-processing ability, thereby leading to less effective decisions. In some cases the emotional upset may be so intense as to immobilize victims and prevent them from even a minimal consideration of the response options. Family, friends, and bystanders, through their words and deeds, can help ameliorate this distress and create a better climate for victim decision making. As Bard and Sangrey (1986) noted, "Minutes of skillful support by any sensitive person immediately after the crime can be worth more than hours of professional counseling later" (p. 41). Elsewhere (Ruback, Greenberg, & Westcott, 1984) we described the benefits of social support in the following way:

> Support from others can help victims reestablish ties and bonds with others, and thus reduce their sense of isolation and distrust. Such support can also help reduce their sense of helplessness and powerlessness, and thus remobilize and remotivate them to find a constructive solution to their plight. (p. 66)

Many victims seem to be the recipients of precisely this kind of support. Maguire and Corbett (1987) found that 70% said that they had received "an attentive and very sympathetic 'listening ear' from their friends or family" (p. 72) that had helped reduce the emotional impact of the offense. Leymann and Lindell (1990) reported similar findings in their interviews with Swedish bank employees who had been holdup victims. Our own findings (Study 20) provide additional corroborative evidence. Victims of rape reported that almost everyone whom they had talked to (95%) tended to believe them and that many more people had responded positively than negatively to them. Study 20 also revealed a longer term effect of social support. Cases were likely to advance further in the criminal justice sequence if more people had reacted positively to victims within two months after the attack. Longer term benefits of social support were also observed by Friedman *et al.* (1982), who noted that those receiving support from three or more others reported significantly less fear of crime in a four-month follow-up interview than did those with two or fewer supporters.

In addition to reducing victims' level of distress, providing socioemotional support may increase the supporter's ability to influence the victim. This influence can be achieved in at least two ways. First, as a result of receiving support, victims may feel indebted to the supporter and therefore feel obligated to reciprocate by following the supporter's advice (Greenberg, 1980; Greenberg & Westcott, 1983). Second, by providing socioemotional support, supporters may be viewed by victims as more "sincere" and "understanding," qualities that appear to enhance their ability to persuade victims. These explanations may help account for the inclination of participants in Study 4 to follow the advice of a bystander who offered them support and remained at their side.

Rather than providing a basis for changing victims' decisions, social support may simply reinforce or sustain such decisions before they have been acted upon, a function that was observed in Study 6. Participants who said that they had been influenced by the covictim most often stated that the covictim had increased their confidence and resolve, for example, "Her position was the same as mine, which gave me more confidence."

Of course, not all victims receive socioemotional support from others (Leymann & Lindell, 1990; Maguire & Corbett, 1987). The reasons for this lack of support are many and varied. Sometimes relatives, friends, and bystanders are incapable of empathy and understanding. Alternatively, lack of support may reflect a motivation to blame the victim (Ryan, 1971). This tendency has been well documented and is explained by a need to believe in a just world (Lerner *et al.*, 1976). When one is faced with another's victimization, the world suddenly seems dangerous and unpredictable. Relatives, friends, and bystanders who come in contact with victims can reduce such feelings by blaming victims for their misfortune. The failure to receive sympathy and support from others is likely to increase victims' level of arousal and to interfere with their decision-making capability.

SUMMARY

In this chapter we have described a model of crime-victim decision making that integrates past findings and suggests directions for future research. The model details how the discovery of a suspicious event initiates a chain of cognitive-affective activity that culminates in a decision to call the police or to take some other action. Decision making by victims involves three interrelated stages: Victims must label the event a crime, determine its seriousness, and decide what to do. The decision at each stage is affected by a particular set of antecedent variables. Social influence factors, which may take any of three forms, play a pivotal role at each stage of the decision process. According to the proposed model, failure to notify the police may result from one or more factors: labeling the event as something other than a crime, perceiving the crime as minor and not serious, and deciding to deal with the crime by means other than notification of the police. The scope of the model provides a conceptual tool for examining the dynamics of decision making for a wide array of victimizations, ranging from petty theft to sexual assault.

Demographic variables (e.g., age, sex, race, and socioeconomic status) as well as individual difference variables (e.g., those relating to self-concept, coping styles, and attitudes toward the police) are not explicitly described by the model, but their omission does not mean that they have no role in the model. Such variables may influence the decision process (although supporting empirical evidence is weak), but they do so only via their impact on the antecedent variables at each stage of the model. For example, whether or not one has been criminally victimized in the past may affect one's personal definition of a crime and how it matches with the current situation. Previous experience as a crime victim may also influence how seriously the present crime is viewed by its impact on perceptions of expected, actual, and potential harm. Finally, previous victimization experience may influence a person's stored knowledge and attitudes regarding the various response options.

In the next chapter, we use the model to identify areas where empirical data are lacking and suggest directions for future research. The proposed model of victim decision making also has important implications for matters relating to public policy. These also are discussed in the next chapter.

10

Summary and Implications
of the Research

In Chapter 1, we described research since the early 1970s that is relevant to understanding decision making by crime victims. There we argued that prior research on crime-victim decision making suggested that (1) individual difference variables are not significant predictors of the decision to report; (2) social influence is an important factor in the decision making of bystanders; and (3) crime seriousness is an important predictor of reporting. Beginning with Chapter 2, we presented in some detail our own multi-method research program. Our studies focused on factors affecting victims' decision to call the police, but we also investigated victims' long-term reactions to the crime and their ability to recall details of the event and to recognize the individual suspected of committing the crime. In this final chapter, we summarize the consistent results across studies and then turn to the research and policy implications of our investigations.

SUMMARY OF THE RESEARCH

Our findings replicate and extend the conclusions with which we began our investigations. We focus this summary on victims' reporting decision and their capacity to testify accurately about people and events.

THE REPORTING DECISION

Consistent with prior research, such as the National Crime Survey (Bureau of Justice Statistics, 1990c), our research showed wide variation in the percentage of crimes reported to the police. At the low end were spouse abuse (24%; Study 13) and theft (37%; Studies 17–19). At the high end was rape (72%–96%; Studies 15, 16, and 20). Of course, these figures are very much dependent on their source. For example, our use of police records in Study 14 ensures that all crimes in that study were reported to the police.

We found fairly consistent evidence that victims themselves were most likely to report the crimes to the police. All of our studies that examined this question suggested that a majority of reporters were victims. This general finding across studies, which is consistent with prior research (e.g., Van Kirk, 1978), indicated that it is important to examine decision making by crime victims.

This and other findings are presented in Table 10-1, which summarizes our research in terms of type of criminal victimization. The columns of the table represent the four types of crimes we investigated (theft, burglary, assault, and rape) and, within each type of crime, the individual study or studies that investigated victims of that particular type of crime. For those studies that examined more than one type of criminal victimization, we separated the victims by type of crime and recomputed the appropriate statistics. Robbery victims (from Study 17) were not included in the table, because there were so few of them ($n = 13$). The rows of the table contain descriptive information about the studies, as well as substantive information from the studies. Our discussion of consistencies across studies focuses on the rows of the table.

Our program of research on the reporting decision obtained three consistent findings across studies and, more importantly, across methods: (1) in general, crime and situational variables are better predictors of the reporting decision than are individual difference variables; (2) even when the type of crime and other situational variables are held constant, social influence is an important determinant of reporting; and (3) in response to a victimization, crime victims have two common emotional reactions, fear and anger, both of which seem to affect short-term behavior and long-term responses to the crime.

Situational versus Individual-Difference Variables

We were able to compare the relative importance of situational and individual-difference variables for all four types of crimes that we investi-

TABLE 10-1. SUMMARY OF STUDIES INVESTIGATING DECISION MAKING BY CRIME VICTIMS[a]

Type of study	Theft victims			Burglary victims		Assault victims	Rape victims		
	Field-laboratory experiments	Archival police records	Interviews	Archival police records	Interviews	Archive of Council on Battered Women	Archive of Rape Crisis Center	Rape center interviews	Long-term interviews of rape victims
Study numbers	1-6	14	17-19	14	17-19	13	15	16	20
Sample size Total N = 5,439	768	597	160	392	79	413	2,526	364	150
% of cases reported to the police	41	100	37	100	63	24	89	72	96
Of cases reported, % reported by the victim	100	89	100	80	98	77	55	—	61
Individual difference variables related to reporting	Small effects for age, income, and gender	None	None	None	None	—	None	—	—
Role of anger	Reporters were angrier; angry victims were more accurate witnesses	—	64% angry	—	51% angry	—	26% angry; angrier if attacker known; raped before	11% angry	19% angry

Table continues on next page

TABLE 10-1. (CONTINUED)

	Theft victims			Burglary victims		Assault victims	Rape victims		
	Field-laboratory experiments	Archival police records	Interviews	Archival police records	Interviews	Archive of Council on Battered Women	Archive of Rape Crisis Center	Rape center interviews	Long-term interviews of rape victims
Role of fear	—	—	5% afraid	—	14% afraid	—	67% afraid; more if attacker unknown; first time raped	63% afraid	48% afraid
% of victims who talked with someone immediately	—	—	53	—	35	—	41	38	51
% of victims who talked with someone at some time before contacting police	—	—	82	—	71	At least 76	—	78	—
Of those who talked with someone, % of victims receiving advice	78	—	62	—	59	—	—	76	37[b]
Of those who received advice, % of victims following advice	58	—	88	—	85	—	—	90	91

[a]Spaces are blank (—) where information was not obtained for this variable in the study.
[b]Because the total number of victims who talked with others was not known, this number represents the percentage of all victims.

gated (theft, burglary, assault, and rape). Consistent with prior research, we found that situational variables generally were better predictors of reporting than were individual difference variables. In our examination of theft victims (Studies 1–6), we found that advice alone accounted for 4% of the variance in the reporting decision and for about 3% of the variance in the delay before reporting, whereas all individual-difference variables together accounted for 5% of the variance in reporting and for about 3% of the variance in delay. One reason why situational variables in the field-experimental studies did not explain more of the variance in the reporting decision may be that there was relatively little variance in these situational variables. That is, the amount of money taken was small in all of the studies and varied in only one of the six studies. Similarly, other factors in the experiment remained essentially unchanged across studies. As a consequence, the only real situational variable that did vary was the type of advice the bystander gave, and it explained almost as much variance as all individual-difference variables combined.

The interview studies of theft and burglary victims (Studies 18 and 19) indicated that the only significant predictors of victims' reporting decision was the type of advice they received. Finally, the archival study of rape victims (Study 15) indicated that individual-difference variables independently explained nothing about the reporting decision and less than 1% of the variance in the delay in reporting, whereas situational variables (e.g., presence of a weapon and amount of injury) explained independently 2% of the variance in reporting and 5% of the variance in delay in reporting. That these crime-related variables are good predictors of reporting (good at least relative to other variables) is consistent with the fact that people's judgments about whether crimes should be reported are related to many of these same variables (see Chapter 6). In fact, these situational variables are, in most cases, determinants of the perceived seriousness of the crime. Although seriousness is an important predictor of reporting, its effects may be moderated by other variables, including advice from others.

Social Influence

Our strongest and most consistent findings concern the effect of social influence variables on victims' decision to report or not to report the crime to the police. First, our results indicate that real crime victims often talk with others before making a decision about calling the police. For the adult sexual assault victims in Study 15 (the archival study of rape victims in Atlanta), 41% of the individuals said the first action they had taken after the crime was completed was to talk with someone. In the interview study of rape victims in Pittsburgh (Study 16), 38% said they had talked with someone immediately after the crime was completed. Similarly, in the other interview studies, high percentages of victims said they had spoken with someone immediately after the discovery of the crime (e.g., 53% of theft victims and 35% of burglary victims). Even higher percentages of the victims said they had spoken about the crime with someone at some time prior to calling the police (82% of theft victims, 71% of burglary victims, and 78% of rape victims).

Second, our results suggest that many of the individuals with whom victims consulted had provided advice about what the victims should do. The interview studies of burglary and theft victims (Studies 17–19) found that 61% of victims who had talked with others received advice about what they should do. Concerning rape victims, research in Pittsburgh (Study 16; 76%) and Atlanta (Study 20; 37%) also indicated that a sizable percentage had received advice about whether or not they should report the crime to the police.

Third, our results indicate that victims often follow the advice they receive from others. In the field-laboratory experimental studies, 58% of the victims followed the advice to report or not to report the crime that they were given, although the percentage was higher for nonreporters (77%) than for reporters (50%). These numbers are particularly high when one recognizes that the bystander who gave the advice was a complete stranger who had no past ties to the victims, offered little likelihood of future interaction with them, and had no way to compel them to comply with the advice.

Compared to the results from the field-laboratory experiments, the percentages of victims who followed the advice they had been given were even higher when we interviewed theft victims (88%), burglary victims (85%), and rape victims (90%). These percentages may be somewhat inflated by memory distortion and victims' desire to show that their actions had been consistent with what they had been advised to do; but they are certainly consistent with the idea that victims consider and often act on the advice others give them.

It is not surprising that victims follow the advice they are offered, especially in situations where they are uncertain about what to do. This reliance on the advice of others affects not only the reporting decision, but also victims' delay in reporting. Across studies we found that, consistent with intuition, reporters who consulted with more individuals prior to reporting the crime to the police took longer to report the crime. Moreover, in the multiple-interview study of rape victims (Study 20), we found some support for the idea that initial advice to report the crime affects not only victims' short-term reporting decision but also their long-term willingness to remain active participants in the criminal justice process.

One of the reasons that victims are so likely to follow the advice they receive is that the individuals who give them this advice are transmitting information about the criminal justice system as well as information about what they believe to be appropriate behavior in this particular instance. It was because of this underlying, and sometimes overt, normative pressure that we investigated differences in normative beliefs about the appropriateness of invoking the criminal justice process in different types of crimes. We found some consistency across four countries concerning normative beliefs (Study 10), but we also found that the appropriateness of calling the police depended on the country, the type of crime, and the type of victim. Even within one community in the United States (Study 12), different ethnic groups had significantly different normative beliefs about the appropriateness of reporting more than half of the crimes rated.

Emotional Responses

Across studies we found that anger and fear were common emotional responses to criminal victimizations and that these emotions were related to subsequent behavior and coping. In general, it appeared that anger was a common response to property crimes (theft and burglary) and that very angry victims were more likely to report the crime than were less angry victims. This difference was apparent in both the field-laboratory experiments and in the interviews of theft and burglary victims. There was also some support for this effect of anger in the archival study of rape victims (Study 15). There we found that anger, although a less common reaction than fear, was very strongly related to reporting by the victim rather than by some other person.

As would be expected, fear was a common emotional reaction to sexual assault in all three of our studies. Type of crime and sex of victim were confounded, however, so it is unclear how much this reaction is due to the nature of the crime (i.e., a violent involvement crime) and how much is due to gender differences in emotional reactions. In the interview studies of theft and burglary victims, we found that females were more fearful than males. This result might reflect either gender differences in perceived vulnerability (Burt & Katz, 1985; Skogan & Maxfield, 1981) or gender differences in acknowledging fear (Sommers & Kosmitzki, 1988).

RECALL AND RECOGNITION

In addition to our research regarding reporting, we also obtained findings consistent with those of others regarding recall and recognition. Our research on eyewitness identification suggested that crime victims are subject to the same problems as are bystander eyewitnesses. In particular, our results indicated that (1) same-race identifications are more accurate than cross-race identifications, especially for white theft victims, and (2) confidence and accuracy are not significantly related. These two conclusions are consistent with what most researchers in the area of eyewitness identification believe to be the current state of knowledge regarding bystander witnesses (Kassin, Ellsworth, & Smith, 1989). We also found that the accuracy of eyewitness identifications in lineups decreases over time, especially by 15 months after the event. We did not find, however, that the accuracy of participants' descriptions of the thief decreased from just after the event to 2 months later. Those items that participants accurately described initially (e.g., hair color and presence or absence of facial hair) were accurately described 2 months later.

Of particular importance to the criminal justice system is the finding that, two months after the crime, participants who had reported the theft tended to be more accurate and more confident than were nonreporters. In addition, there was a small but significant effect for anger, so that victims who recalled being more angry at the time of the theft were more accurate and more confident of the correctness of their choice.

In the field-laboratory experimental studies, we also investigated victims' recall of information about the theft. We found that participants who had reported the theft were significantly more accurate than were nonreporters in remembering the number of papers that the thief had taken and in recalling the bystander's name and the thief's name. This difference in accuracy was consistent with our finding that reporters tended to give more accurate lineup identifications than did nonreporters.

IMPLICATIONS OF THE RESEARCH

The findings from our research program are interesting in their own right, but they also have implications for the development of theory in social psychology and for future research directly relevant to the formulation of policy. Moreover, our multimethod research program illustrates how we think applied social research should be conducted. We begin our discussion of the implications of our research with an examination of the strengths and ramifications of a multimethod approach to investigating an applied social issue (Cook, 1985).

MULTIMETHOD RESEARCH

Our major strategy in conducting this research was to use multiple methods to understand crime-victim decision making. Reliance solely on one method can lead to erroneous conclusions, because results from one method or data source confound true findings with method variance. As an illustration of this problem, consider what Pointing and Maguire (1988) called the danger of creating an "orthodox" view of victimization. They argued that knowledge about crime victims in Great Britain is biased by the fact that the way the government learns about crimes (police records, victim services, and the national crime survey) results in the overrepresentation of some types of crimes (discrete rather than continuing crimes, criminal acts by strangers rather than by friends or relatives, and crimes against stake-holding rather than marginal members of society). This bias toward some types of victimizations because of the research methods used means that any theoretical or policy judgments based on the data will also reflect the inherent bias of the methods used to obtain them.

There have been numerous calls for multimethod approaches (e.g., Mark & Shotland, 1987), but researchers have rarely used them (see Ebbesen & Konecni, 1982, for one of the few exceptions). Our approach in this project was to establish a finding through experimental means (the importance of social influence on theft victims) and then to extend it (1) by investigating actual crime victims to obtain a measure of the generalizability of the findings, and (2) by looking at theoretically important implications of that finding. Another approach would have been to use correlational analyses of real-world data to discover a relationship between variables and then to confirm this relationship by using experimental methods. Thus, as we see it, the two alternative approaches are to conduct experiments first and then do correlational studies or to do correlational studies first and then conduct experiments.

These two approaches appear to be similar, but in practice they are likely to be different, because the development of research depends in great part on what has been found in prior studies and what strikes the researchers as important and interesting at the time. As external societal conditions (e.g., the economy, the political party in power, and the funding priorities of federal agencies) and researchers' interests change over time, there is a high probability that the way in which research is conducted is somewhat unsystematic, a point that Kidder and Fine (1987) also raised regarding triangulation with qualitative and quantitative methods.

We think that this lack of completely systematic research is inherent in the conduct of social research. One might even argue that very highly structured research projects inhibit investigators from taking advantage of new, interesting, and surprising findings. The inherent problems in such an *ad hoc*, hit-or-miss approach, however, suggest that a better way should be sought. We agree with Mark and Shotland (1985) that a more conscious planning of multimethod research, a "theory" of multiplism that guides the choice of methods in particular orders and in particular settings, is more likely to produce comprehensive findings. The need for such a theory is particularly compelling when one recognizes that multiple methods cannot always investigate exactly the same questions and that different methods may share the same direction of bias (Shotland & Mark, 1987).

In addition to the various dimensions of multiplism that Mark and Shotland (1985) discussed (e.g., multiple subject populations, multiple sites, multiple dependent measures, and multiple statistical analyses), it would be helpful if theories of multiplism considered multiplistic dimensional analysis. This idea refers to a consideration of the same set of results along different theoretical and empirical dimensions. For example, we found it helpful to analyze the data for each study separately and to combine the data from several studies by using the same methodology (e.g., interviews) so that we could analyze the data in terms of types of crime (see Table 10-1).

A true multimethod approach uses a number of different procedures, with more methods generally producing greater confidence in results. In general, we believe that the best results are attained by the use of as many methods as possible. We also believe, however, that if decisions have to be made between ecological validity (i.e., a high degree of resemblance between the procedure involved in a research study and what happens in natural settings) and generalizability (i.e., a high degree of applicability of the results to other settings and populations), the correct judgment is almost always to go with generalizability (Banaji & Crowder, 1989).

In most cases, generalizability comes only with experimental control. One's initial tendency might be to use nonexperimental methods with complex phenomena like victims' decisions to report or not to report crimes to the police. We agree with Banaji and Crowder (1989), however, that the more complex the phenomenon, the greater the necessity to study it with experimental methods. Thus, for an issue like crime-victim decision making, we believe that at least some of the research must be experimental.

The basic reason for taking a multiplist research approach (Cook, 1985) is to have greater confidence in the findings, confidence that comes as a result of the replicated results and the elimination of alternative explanations arising from method or sample. Only if researchers are confident that their findings are valid can they then go on to suggest theoretical and policy implications of their research. Even if there is not true triangulation of results on a single answer, there may be "bracketing" (Reichardt & Gollob, 1987), so that researchers can offer a range of estimates that is very likely to include the correct answer (Mark & Shotland, 1987).

THEORY-RELATED RESEARCH

In addition to implications regarding the use of multiple methods in applied social research, our research program has implications for research related specifically to the development of psychological theory. Our research calls attention to gaps in the theoretical literature on reactions to negative life events. In this section we examine the relationship between reactions to victimization and theory regarding (1) affective and emotional processes; (2) cognitive modes of coping with negative life events; and (3) social comparison processes.

The Role of Affect and Emotion

One finding that appeared in several studies was that victims often made decisions while experiencing strong emotional feelings of fear and anger. Clearly, more needs to be known about the determinants of these emotions and their consequences in victim decision making.

Determinants of Fear and Anger. As we discussed in Chapter 9, evidence shows that among crime victims, fear and anger have cognitive precursors, namely, the beliefs that one is vulnerable to subsequent victimization and that one has been wrongly or unfairly treated. Further, we showed how such beliefs and emotions are related to features of the crime, in particular, the degree to which the crime was unexpected, the perceived magnitude of harm, and the potential harm in the situation. Because expectations of being victimized are so critical, more research is needed on the determinants of these expectations. For example, it would be helpful to understand the role that schemata play in influencing expectations, especially people's crime scripts (Abelson, 1981), prototypes of criminals, and self-schemata (Markus, 1977).

For some, these expectations derive from previous experience as a victim. Research and theorizing by Fazio and Zanna (1981) suggest that knowledge structures formed on the basis of direct experience are more vivid and accessible than are those derived from indirect experience (e.g., learning about the victimization of others). If so, we would expect that the disconfirmation of expectations derived from previous (direct) experience produces more intense emotional reactions than the disconfirmation of expectations derived from indirect experience.

Research on attributional processes may further contribute to our understanding of the emotional reactions of crime victims. Fear and anger are what Weiner, Russell, and Lerman (1978) called outcome-independent–attribution-dependent. They contended that the attribution of the event, rather than the outcome, determines which emotion is experienced. In contrast, some emotions, like grief, are a function only of the outcome (i.e., outcome-dependent–attribution-independent). This formulation suggests an interesting question concerning the factors that determine such attributions. In the context of achievement-related outcomes, Weiner *et al.* suggested that, following failure, an attribution to the amount of effort exerted leads to fear, whereas an attribution to the effort of another leads to anger. It would be helpful to know if this same pattern holds true in crime victims.

Schachter and Singer (1962) offered yet another theoretical perspective for understanding the emotional reactions of crime victims. They theorized that when people label their emotional states they make use of environmental cues, such as the reactions of others in the situation. This theorizing was the basis for our Study 2, in which the bystander modeled one of three levels of anger. Our failure to confirm Schachter and Singer's prediction suggests that the role played by others in helping people label their emotional states is conditional. As we noted, participants may have been very clear about what their emotions were and therefore did not need to rely on situational cues. In addition, other situational cues may have weakened the impact of the bystander's behavior on participants' labeling of their emotional state.

One possible explanation of the diminished influence of the bystander is that the victim viewed the bystander as dissimilar. If the model had shared the victim's fate (i.e., was a covictim), perhaps the model's behavior would have had a greater impact on how angry the victim labeled himself or herself. It is also possible that other dimensions of similarity (e.g., the bystander's sex, age, and socioeconomic status) influenced the labeling process. Overall, our results call attention to the need for empirical research and theorizing on the labeling of emotional states and the role played by others in this process.

Consequences of Decision Making. As Easterbrook (1959) and others (e.g., Janis & Mann, 1977; Wright & Weitz, 1977) have shown, high levels of arousal and stress impair the decision-making process. Under such conditions, thought processes are disrupted, and individuals opt for a "satisficing" rather than a maximizing decision strategy (Simon, 1976). A question of both theoretical and practical importance is whether the effect of stress on decision making is simply a function of the magnitude of the stress, or whether it is a function of the *type* of emotion underlying the stress (e.g., fear or anger). Stated somewhat differently, are anger and fear equally disruptive of thought? We know of no research that has addressed this question. In addition, anger and fear may have different implications in victims' choice of decision strategies. For example, anger may induce risk-taking strategies (e.g., retaliation), while fear may induce risk-avoidant strategies (e.g., staying indoors). Our understanding of victim decision making would be enhanced by empirical and conceptual work that further delineates the cognitive and behavioral consequences of anger and fear.

Consequences of Affiliative Behavior. Social psychologists have long recognized the role played by emotion as an impetus for affiliative behavior. Schachter (1959) theorized that the need to clarify emotional states increases affiliative tendencies. Tests of this proposition, however, have focused on the emotional states of anxiety and fear (Sarnoff & Zimbardo, 1961; Schachter, 1959). We know of no comparable efforts to study the effect of anger on affiliative tendencies. It would be interesting to learn whether angry victims are as desirous of contacting others as are fearful victims. Our own research has not yielded consistent findings (see Chapters 7 and 8).

There is an alternative to framing the question in terms of whether fear and anger differentially motivate affiliative behavior among crime victims. It might be better to ask whether we can identify the motivational goals served by contacting others under conditions of fear and anger. Greater understanding of the motivational consequences of these two emotional states may help us understand why victims choose to contact one person rather than another. Anxious and fearful individuals may feel uncertain about their present and future safety and may therefore seek out others who can reduce their uncertainty and provide them with socioemotional support and protection. In comparison, anger may motivate victims to seek out very different individuals. Victims who are angry may prefer to contact people to whom they can ventilate their feelings (Silver & Wortman, 1980). In addition, because such victims may be particularly desirous of revenge, they may prefer contact with others who will aid them in this endeavor.

In summary, our research suggests that an understanding of victims' reactions will be enhanced by research and theory that focus on the causes and consequences of fear and anger.

Cognitive Modes of Coping with Negative Life Events

Theoretical attempts to understand how people cope with negative life events such as disease, accidents, and crime have focused increasingly on cognitive rather than behavioral efforts (Janoff-Bulman, 1989; Lazarus & Folkman, 1984; Taylor, 1983; Taylor & Brown, 1988). Taylor and Schneider (1989) proposed a particularly compelling cognitive theory of coping that centers on the mental simulation of past, future, and hypothetical events. Their theorizing illuminates some of our findings and suggests hypotheses for future research. They contended that victims often cope by *simulating* events, by which they meant that victims cognitively construct hypothetical scenarios or reconstruct real scenarios. Such simulations may include:

> (1) rehearsals of likely future events, such as what will happen at a meeting later in the day; (2) reconstruction of past events, such as going back over an argument one recently had with one's spouse; (3) fantasies, such as imagining oneself as the head of a hot new consulting firm; and (4) mixtures of real and hypothetical events, such as the reconstruction of a past event (e.g., a rape) with a new ending [e.g., successfully fighting off the attacker]. Taylor & Schneider, 1989, p. 175

Such simulations facilitate problem solving and emotional regulation (Lazarus & Folkman, 1984) by helping victims "make sense" of the event, altering their emotional states, and enabling them to test out strategies for avoiding future victimization.

In our own work we have observed several instances of victims' use of simulations. For example, in Studies 18 and 19 a high proportion of victims acknowledged thinking about the fact that the victimization "could have been worse" (79% in Study 18 and 72% in Study 19). Apparently, such thinking involved the reconstruction of the victimization with new endings. As we noted in the previous chapter, victims may have used these hypothetical (i.e., counterfactual) endings as standards for comparing what actually happened to them. Compared to what could have happened, victims may have felt fortunate that their fate had not been worse. It is reasonable to believe that when asking themselves, "Could I have avoided this?" and "What can I do to prevent it from happening again?" victims employed simulations to answer these questions.

Direct evidence of simulation activity was obtained in Study 19. Sixty percent of the victims admitted fantasizing about what they would do if they caught the suspect. The vast majority of such thoughts were retaliatory and particularly violent. For the significant minority of victims who admitted engaging in such fantasies "quite frequently" (19%) or "almost always" (1%), the activity may well have represented ruminative thought (Horowitz, 1976; Martin & Tesser, 1989).

The functions of such thoughts are discussed in a theory of rumination proposed by Martin and Tesser (1989). Following "goal blockage" (e.g., a victimization experience), individuals are likely to engage in a relatively specific sequence of behaviors or thoughts in which "problem solving" and "end-state thinking" are central. Problem solving involves the search for instrumental means of attaining one's goals. Thus, victims may ruminate about the event in order to find some clues to the identity of the perpetrator. When victims are frustrated by their problem-solving efforts, they may abandon such efforts and engage in end-state thinking, that is, thinking about the goal object and the pleasant feelings associated with its attainment. Much as a hungry person ruminates about food, crime victims in Study 19 ruminated about what they would do if they caught the perpetrator. Victims probably found the feelings associated with harming the perpetrator to be pleasant and satisfying. Thus, emotional regulation was a likely function of such ruminative thought.

Simulations not only contribute to regulating emotions and planning future actions but also motivate a person to take action (Taylor & Schneider, 1989). The simulation of a particular action may convince the victim that the action is likely to yield positive consequences; this conviction may, in turn, increase the victim's motivation to perform the action. Further, the emotional states produced by the simulation may provide further impetus for the action. That is, the anticipatory feeling of satisfaction that accompanies a simulated positive outcome (e.g., capture of the suspect) further enhances the motivation to perform the action. Some interesting implications follow from this reasoning, in that it provides another explanation of why victims tend to replay negative life events. Repeated reruns of the crime may serve to sustain the victim's arousal and motivation to take action. This may be particularly true of victimizations that produce anger (Novaco, 1975).

Perhaps anger is an emotion that certain victims (particularly males) are reluctant to relinquish (Frodi, 1978). It *empowers* victims in a way that fear does not (Novaco, 1975; Shaver, Schwartz, Kirson, & O'Connor, 1987). Anger is mobilizing, whereas fear, at least in its extreme form, is immobilizing. Moreover, anger both inspires and justifies an aggressive posture toward the perpetrator and thus may have positive implications for self-esteem and public self-presentation. For these reasons, it is reasonable to speculate about the possibility of victims' alternating the focus of their simulations in order both to *maintain* and to *regulate* their emotional state. That is, victims may replay the victimization in order to heighten their anger, which subsequently fuels arousal-reducing aggressive end-state simulations, a sequence that victims find temporarily satisfying.

Thus, contrary to the reasoning in our model of victim decision making (see Chapter 9), anger may not always be aversive; it may be instrumental in attaining goals (Averill, 1982; Novaco, 1975) and therefore may be maintained by thoughts and selective contact with others. Stage models of recovery from victimization (e.g., Bard & Sangrey, 1986; Shontz, 1975) suggest that anger sustained over a long period of time is a sign of failure to come to grips with the victimization and is therefore evidence of maladjustment. In our opinion, however, it may reflect an effort on the part of victims to maintain a positive view of themselves. By maintaining their anger, victims may be proclaiming that they are still in control and have not given up or been beaten (Averill, 1982). In this sense, anger and its display sustain a positive view of the self and constitute a self-presentational strategy designed to win approval from some audiences.

An additional question about the use of cognitive simulations by crime victims is the timing of such strategies: when they are most likely to be employed. Taylor and Schneider (1989) hypothesized that simulations are frequently used in situations where people experience unexpected and very important negative life events. These situations probably constitute major violations of one's assumptions about the world and thus require a more intense search for meaning and understanding (Janoff-Bulman, 1985; Perloff, 1983).

Nevertheless, mental simulation of events may, under some circumstances, be dysfunctional. We can hypothesize several situations where simulations may increase rather than reduce victims' stress. For example, while end-state simulations may be relatively satisfying, they represent a diversion and are likely to provide only temporary relief. Ultimately, it would seem that such thoughts are probably nonadaptive (Martin & Tesser, 1989). Moreover, the simulations may produce unhappy endings (e.g., after being caught, the perpetrator overpowers the victim and escapes) and thus negative affect. Research is needed to discover the factors that determine the ease with which victims can imagine different types of endings (for some interesting suggestions, see Kahneman & Miller, 1986). We need to learn much more about cognitive simulation as a coping mechanism, particularly, its relationship to problem solving and emotional regulation.

Social Comparison Processes

Our research has shown a strong tendency among crime victims to consult with others in the moments immediately following the crime. Recent research and conceptualization with regard to social comparison processes provide useful insights into and hypotheses about the kinds of persons contacted and the motives underlying these contacts.

As originally conceived by Festinger (1954) and later extended by Schachter (1959), the need for self-evaluation motivates people to compare their attitudes, abilities, and emotions with those of people who are *similar* in these dimensions. Presumably, comparison with similar others yields more valid information than does comparison with dissimilar others. While this hypothesis has received much support, it is reasonable to speculate that comparison activities under stress may be less discriminating. The results of Study 6 support this hypothesis. Victims were more attentive to and influenced by the reactions of a similar other (i.e., a covictim) than by those of a dissimilar other (a bystander), but they were unresponsive to the magnitude of the covictim's losses. Indeed, we found that victims were no more likely to follow the actions of a covictim who had lost the same amount as they had (i.e., a similar other) than they were to follow the actions of a covictim who had lost more or less than they had (i.e., a dissimilar other), although it should be noted that the range of losses in Study 6 was relatively restricted. It may be that, under the stress of victimization, victims are content to make only gross distinctions in terms of similarity. This reasoning is consistent with recent theorizing by Taylor, Buunk, and Aspinwall (1990), who contended that "similarity may be defined, *not* as how close another individual is to the self on a dimension of evaluation, but as whether or not another person has undergone the same victimizing event or has been confronted with the same stressor" (p. 81).

Recent research on social comparison processes suggests that they can be driven by motives other than self-evaluation, such as "self-enhancement" and "self-improvement" (Wood, 1989). An accumulating body of evidence shows that these motives prompt individuals to compare or associate themselves with *dissimilar* others, such as those who are inferior on the dimension under evaluation (a "downward comparison"; Wills, 1981, 1987, 1991), or those who are superior (an "upward contact"; Taylor & Lobel, 1989). Comparison with less fortunate others appears to serve victims' needs for self-enhancement, whereas upward contacts with more fortunate others serves victims' needs for self-improvement.

Downward Comparisons. Wills (1981, 1987, 1991) has reviewed a large body of evidence demonstrating that under conditions of threat, individuals often make downward comparisons. Moreover, when less fortunate others are not readily available, individuals seem quite capable of constructing hypothetical others who satisfy this requirement (Taylor *et al.*, 1983). Much of the empirical support for downward comparison preferences among victims comes from the work of Taylor and her associates on cancer patients (e.g., Collins, Dakof, & Taylor, 1988; Wood, Taylor, & Lichtman, 1985).

However, it is reasonable to question whether research findings on comparison processes among cancer patients are generalizable to crime victims. After all, being a victim of a crime differs in a number of ways from being a victim of an illness. Crimes often differ from illnesses in their cause, the intentionality of the causal agent, the severity of the harm, and the type of onset. Crimes are person-caused, intentional, typically sudden, and only sometimes serious. For the further development of social comparison theory, we would need to know whether and how these dimensions affect the comparison process.

Are such downward comparison tendencies evident in victims of crime? Unfortunately, our own data are uninformative on this point. Results from our archival and interview studies show that victims tended to consult most often with friends and family. Since we did not collect background information on the previous victimization status of those contacted, it is difficult to know if the comparisons were downward, upward, or with similar others. Conceivably, victims contacted some people because they had suffered more serious victimization in the past. However, it is equally plausible that victims chose particular others because they had experienced *similar* victimizations in the past, or because they had successfully avoided victimization. Another explanation of victims' choice is that they sought out those who were similar on "related" or "surrounding" dimensions (e.g., age, attitudes toward reporting, and vulnerability to victimization) rather than on the dimension under evaluation, victimization status (Goethals & Darley, 1977; Wood, 1989). Social comparison theory clearly suggests that future research needs to look more carefully at the background characteristics of those with whom victims consult.

Our discussion of victims' choice of comparison others may exaggerate the extent to which victims *choose* to contact or compare themselves with specific others. Wood (1989), in her review of social comparison research, made the point that the environment often imposes comparisons on the individual. Consistent with this reasoning, we found in Studies 18 and 19 that 73% and 60% of the first persons contacted were already present when the victim discovered the crime. Similarly, it may also be the case that victims obtain social comparison information from individuals originally contacted for some other reason, such as for socioemotional support.

Recent theorizing on social comparison processes has called attention to some of the risks and dangers of downward comparisons (Major, Testa, & Bylsma, 1991). While serving self-enhancement needs, such comparisons may heighten victims' awareness of worse outcomes that could befall them, which in turn could elevate concerns about their safety and vulnerability to future harm (see discussion in previous chapter; Taylor & Lobel, 1989). Thus, a fundamental task for social comparison theory is to identify the conditions under which victims are likely to ignore these dangers and make downward comparisons. Efforts need to be directed at identifying variables that determine *when* downward comparisons increase rather than reduce victims' distress (Major *et al.*, 1991).

Building on theorizing by Major *et al.* (1991), we propose two moderators of reactions to downward comparisons. First, we suggest that such reactions are a function of the comparison other's *degree* and *direction* of dissimilarity on dimensions related to or predictive of the dimension under evaluation. For example, assume that future victimization is the dimension being evaluated and that vulnerability is the related dimension used as the basis for the prediction. Downward comparisons with others similar to the victim in terms of vulnerability (the related dimension) are likely to raise the victim's concerns about suffering worse victimization in the future (the dimension under evaluation), the implied reasoning being, "If it happened to them, it could happen to me." This notion may explain why Collins *et al.* (1988) found that most cancer patients disliked doctors' waiting rooms because they found the presence of more seriously ill patients upsetting. This finding suggests that support groups for crime victims may be detrimental for victims who have coped well if, at the group meeting, they come into contact with individuals who have not coped well. Similarly, separate waiting rooms for victims at courthouses, a laudable step to get victims away from defendants, may have some harmful effects if these other victims have suffered visibly.

In addition to finding downward comparisons with similar others threatening, victims may find downward comparisons with certain types of *dissimilar* others particularly threatening. This would occur when victims make downward comparisons with others who are *less* vulnerable than they are. Victims may reason that if the other was victimized despite being less vulnerable, then they are in even greater danger of being seriously victimized in the future. The following reaction reported by Davis and Friedman (1985) illustrates this reasoning: "The mother of a victim said that she 'never had thought about being robbed' before her daughter's apartment had been burglarized. She added that because her daughter lived in a better area than she did, 'it makes me think more' " (p. 108). We would expect victims, therefore, to avoid downward comparisons with those who are equally or less vulnerable. Most preferred would be downward comparisons with others perceived to be *more* vulnerable, since such comparisons would satisfy victims' self-enhancement needs while minimizing their concerns about future safety. For example, we would predict that a burglary victim would prefer comparing himself to a more seriously victimized other who lived in a high-crime neighborhood than to one who lived in the same neighborhood or a neighborhood with a lower crime rate. One implication of this reasoning is that when circumstances force victims into contact with a more seriously harmed other, victims will be motivated to perceive the other as having been more vulnerable than they (e.g., the other lives in a high-crime neighborhood) in order to minimize threats to their own safety.

In addition to the degree and direction of the comparison other's dissimilarity on related dimensions, we propose that reactions to downward comparisons are moderated by the perceived *controllability* of one's standing on the dimension under evaluation (Major *et al.*, 1991). Such control-related expectancies may influence the degree to which individuals believe that they can ward off the threat imposed by the downward comparison. Individuals who feel that they have or will have the power to control or alter the threatening elements will perceive the aversive consequences as more avoidable and therefore less threatening. In contrast, those who have lower control expectancies are likely to perceive the aversive consequences as less avoidable and therefore more threatening. Feelings of depression and helplessness are likely consequences of such expectancies (Abramson, Seligman, & Teasdale, 1978).

Perceived uncontrollability may be another reason why cancer patients are uncomfortable being in waiting rooms with other cancer patients. Exposure to others who are worse off may make them feel particularly vulnerable because of their uncertainty about being able to control the progression of their illness.

The concept of controllability generates a number of interesting predictions about victims' comparing themselves with those suffering more serious harm. For example, burglary victims may be more inclined to compare themselves with worse-off victims when they believe that they can or will be able to control their future victimization status (e.g., by installing an elaborate alarm system). Similarly, this reasoning suggests that rape victims who gain a sense of controllability by blaming the victimization on their behavior are less threatened by downward comparisons than victims who blame their character.

Finally, the concept of controllability suggests that future research should examine the role of individual differences in control expectancies. We would anticipate finding higher control expectancies among individuals who are high in self-esteem and self-confidence and who have an internal locus of control (Major *et al.*, 1991; Taylor, Buunk, & Aspinwall, 1990). We would also expect these individuals to be more willing to make downward comparisons than those low on these dimensions.

Upward Comparisons. Research by Taylor and her colleagues (Taylor & Lobel, 1989; Taylor *et al.*, 1990) suggests that upward contacts meet important informational and problem-solving needs of victims. Individuals can learn from and be inspired by those who have superior accomplishments (Brickman & Bulman, 1977; Taylor & Lobel, 1989; Wood, 1989). In support of this reasoning, Taylor and Lobel (1989) reported that cancer patients show a distinct preference for interacting with patients who are perceived as better off or who are coping better. We would expect that crime victims have particularly strong needs for self-improvement with regard to practical matters (e.g., repairing locks) and with regard to avoiding future victimization (Friedman *et al.*, 1982; Maguire & Corbett, 1987). Further, we would expect that these needs might be best served by contacts with nonvictims and with those less seriously victimized.

While victims stand to gain from upward contacts, such contacts may also have aversive consequences. Comparisons with more fortunate others may produce feelings of relative deprivation (Crosby, 1976) and injustice (Walster *et al.*, 1978) and may be threatening to one's self-esteem (Tesser, 1988, 1991). The extent to which upward comparisons produce positive or negative consequences for crime victims depends, we suggest, on the two moderators previously discussed (degree and direction of the comparison other's dissimilarity on related dimensions) and on perceived controllability.

The degree and direction of the comparison other's dissimilarity appear to enhance both positive and negative reactions to the contact. For example, consider a situation where vulnerability to victimization constitutes the related dimension. In this situation, a victim's contact with one who is perceived as having been equally or more vulnerable, but who has avoided victimization (i.e., an upward contact) is likely to increase the intensity of both positive *and* negative reactions. Upward contacts may be inspiring and informative about prospects for self-improvement, but they may also be threatening to one's self-esteem and one's sense of justice.

Victims who perceive that they have experienced more serious negative outcomes than a comparison other who was equally or more vulnerable are likely to have negative feelings of inequity and relative deprivation. They may also feel a loss in self-esteem. When such victims ask "Why me?" they may really be asking, "Why was I victimized when others who were equally or more vulnerable were not?" (Miller & Porter, 1983).

Victims may also react positively to the success of another who has succeeded despite being equally or more vulnerable, because they derive inspiration from the knowledge that the comparison other has succeeded in the face of adversity. This inspiration derives from the reasoning that if the comparison other has been able to avoid or escape serious victimization despite his or her equal or greater vulnerability, then certainly the victim can, too. Of course, it is also possible that upward contacts with others who are judged to have been *less* vulnerable are a source of self-improvement. Victims may learn from such persons what they need to do to make themselves less vulnerable to future victimization (e.g., purchase an alarm system or install dead-bolt locks).

It would appear, then, that upward contacts with more vulnerable others serve primarily to *inspire* self-improvement, whereas upward contacts with less vulnerable others provide information about *how* to attain this goal. Whether or not this information regarding self-improvement is reacted to positively or negatively depends on the second moderator of reactions to social comparisons: perceived controllability.

Victims' perceptions of controllability may moderate their perceptions of threats to self-esteem and of feelings of inequity, as well as their beliefs about their prospects for self-improvement. Victims are likely to view upward contacts as threatening to their self-esteem when they attribute their victimization to personally controllable factors. Their feelings of failure to prevent the victimization are likely to be magnified when they are in contact with others who have avoided victimization. In contrast, feelings of inequity and relative deprivation occasioned by upward contacts are likely to be heightened when the victimization is attributed to factors beyond the victim's control.

Perceptions of controllability may also moderate positive reactions to upward contacts. Whether an upward contact represents an opportunity for self-improvement depends on victims' beliefs that they have the capability of changing their victimization status. Upward contacts are likely to be useful and satisfying when victims perceive that the information and insights gained from such contacts can be translated into action. When a burglary victim learns from an upward contact that future burglaries can be prevented by installing better locks and an alarm system, the victim's belief that she has the financial resources to install such devices is likely to satisfy her needs for self-improvement. However, learning from upward contacts that the conditions for preventing future victimization are beyond her control will make such contacts frustrating and aversive.

As we noted earlier in this chapter, our research did not yield sufficient data to test our theorizing about victims' choice of comparison others. More specifically, in the archival and interview studies we failed to collect information about victims' perceptions of the victimization status of the person(s) with whom they had spoken shortly after the crime. We were unable, therefore, to determine whether such contacts were upward, downward, or with similar others. In addition, we did not measure victims' perceptions of others' similarity on related dimensions (i.e., those predictive of victimization such as the extent to which they had taken self-protective measures). Nor did we assess victims' beliefs about the controllability of past and future outcomes.

One of the experimental studies (Study 6), however, provided limited information relevant to social comparison. It may be recalled that in this experiment victims paid more attention to the words from the covictim than to those from the bystander. This finding is consistent with the hypothesis that victims preferred to compare themselves with similar as opposed to dissimilar others. Study 6 provided one additional test of the role of social comparison processes. Participants were paired with a covictim who had lost more than, less than, or the same amount as they had. This allowed us to evaluate the effects of three types of comparisons: downward in the case of a covictim with greater losses ($20), upward in the case of a covictim with smaller losses ($3), and similar in the case of a covictim with equal losses ($11). Our theorizing suggests that an upward comparison generates the strongest feelings of inequity and deprivation and therefore produces the greatest anger, whereas a downward comparison generates the weakest of such feelings and therefore produces the least anger. However, no differences were found among the three groups with regard to self-reported anger or willingness to report the theft. The failure to confirm our predictions may reflect the weak manipulation of relative loss. As previously noted, very few dollars separated the relative losses of the three groups. Moreover, this variable had no significant impact on any of the other dependent variables in this study. The validity of our theorizing awaits further testing.

From the above discussion it is clear that social comparison theory has the potential to provide useful insights into the persons with whom victims choose to contact and compare themselves. The discussion suggests that future research on victims' choice of other should focus on three variables: (1) the victim's motivation for comparison; (2) the other's degree and direction of dissimilarity on dimensions related to the dimension under evaluation; and (3) perceptions of controllability of past and future outcomes. Our discussion also suggests that when studying the impact of related dimensions on choice of comparison other, future research should examine not only the *degree* of dissimilarity but the *direction* as well. This strategy would require designs that include three levels of similarity (i.e., dissimilar in one direction, similar, and dissimilar in the other direction) instead of the two levels (similar-dissimilar) typically employed.

Policy Implications

Thus far we have discussed the implications of our work in terms of multimethod approaches to applied social research and in terms of theory. We turn now to the policy implications of our research, which we discuss in two ways. First, we describe how our research can help us understand some legal issues regarding criminal procedure, evidence, and torts. Second, we suggest how our findings can be used to investigate policy-relevant questions.

Legal Issues

Some of our research on crime-victim decision making has general implications for criminal procedures and evidence used in criminal trials. In particular, our research may contribute to a better understanding of the issues involved in the use of an "outcry witness" defense and the spontaneous-declaration exception to the hearsay rule. In addition, reporting to third parties rather than to the police has implications for suits regarding negligence in failure to prevent crime.

The Outcry Witness. It is not uncommon for defense attorneys to use the behavior or absence of behavior of an alleged victim or witness in support of their argument that a crime did not occur. For example, defense attorneys sometimes argue that if there had been a crime, the witness or victim would have given an outcry of some sort and would have reported the crime immediately (e.g., *State v. Saldana*, 1982). The failure to give an outcry is thus perceived as evidence that a crime must not have occurred. Basically, then, the defense attorneys are appealing to the fact finder's intuition about what would be the natural response of individuals if a crime had occurred.

Our research suggests that the failure to give an outcry soon after a crime may occur more frequently than does an immediate outcry to the police. What we have found is that rather than report the crime right away (the outcry), crime victims are more likely to consult someone else first. Thus, far from being evidence that a crime did not occur, talking with someone before calling the police is both natural and consistent with the way people in many traumatic situations behave.

This absence of an initial outcry to the police often raises questions in cases attracting large-scale media attention, especially those involving celebrities. For example, in 1991 and 1992 three prominent individuals, William Kennedy Smith, Mike Tyson, and Clarence Thomas, were accused of rape or sexual harassment. In all three cases, the accusers waited before bringing the crime to the attention of authorities. Patricia Bowman, (Smith's accuser) waited a few hours, Desiree Washington (Tyson's accuser) waited a day before reporting and three and a half days before filing charges, and Anita Hill (Thomas's accuser) waited nine years before making her victimization public.

Common to all three cases, however, is the fact that they talked to friends or relatives soon after the crimes occurred. Patricia Bowman called a friend who came and picked her up at the Kennedy compound (Williams, 1991). Desiree Washington told other contestants in the Miss Black America pageant that she had been raped by Tyson (Stinson, 1992), and it was her mother who finally convinced her to call the police ("Q & A on the news," 1992). Likewise, Anita Hill told several of her friends of Thomas's behavior, although she did not report the crime ("Backers say Hill told of sexual advances years ago," 1991).

Our research suggests that the delay present in these three cases is very common. Victims are likely to need information, advice, and support, and they are likely to talk with others in order to receive them, thereby causing the delay in reporting. Thus, our research suggests that the failure of a victim to make an immediate outcry to the police is not sufficient evidence to believe that the subsequent report is false.

Spontaneous Declarations. As we and others have found, crime victims may not talk to the police for minutes, hours, or even days after the crime has occurred. However, they are likely to have talked with someone about the crime. A legal question arises concerning whether what they have told this person can be admitted as evidence at trial (Rothstein, 1981). For example, the victim may have discussed with someone what occurred during the crime or described to him or her what the criminal looked like. At trial the prosecutor may want this testimony admitted to bolster the evidence against the criminal, particularly if the victim is reluctant to testify. Should it be admissible?

The traditional answer from the law of evidence would be no, because such a statement would be hearsay. Hearsay is a statement made outside of the courtroom that is offered as evidence in court to prove the truth of the matter asserted in the statement (Cleary, 1984). In this example, the statement is hearsay because the prosecutor would want to use the out-of-court statement to prove that the crime occurred in a particular way or that a particular person committed the crime. Hearsay evidence is generally not admissible because it relies on the credibility of a person who made the statement outside of the courtroom, without the safeguards of oath and confrontation (Cleary, 1984).

There are exceptions to the general rule barring hearsay testimony, on the assumption that under some conditions nonsworn statements made outside of court are likely to be reliable. One exception is what is known as a *spontaneous declaration*. Some spontaneous statements are assumed to be trustworthy, even though the law recognizes that there is a possibility that the person said something because it was self-serving. One type of spontaneous declaration assumed to be particularly trustworthy is the "excited utterance." If a person makes a spontaneous statement in reaction to an event so startling that it makes normal reflective thought impossible, the law is likely to presume that the statement is true (Cleary, 1984).

In recent years, courts in some states have allowed testimony from individuals to whom alleged victims spoke as evidence that the person was victimized. Moreover, in rape cases and sex offenses the trend across jurisdictions is to allow in evidence details about the crime as communicated to this other person under the excited-utterance exception to the rule against hearsay (Cleary, 1984).

Our research suggests that spontaneous declarations by victims to others are fairly common. The question we need to address is whether these declarations should be believed. Unfortunately, there is not much research on this question. What is needed is a comparison of what these consultants say the victim told them with what victims told the police, what victims told others, and what other witnesses said occurred.

Another exception to the hearsay rule that may also be relevant to victims' statements to others concerns victims' declarations about then-existing mental, emotional, or physical condition, as long as the declaration is not used to prove the fact remembered or believed (Federal Rules of

Evidence, Rule 803(3), 1975). The issues, however, are complex, and different courts can reasonably come to different conclusions.

For example, consider two cases from Texas (Addison, 1991). In one case the appeals court held that it was erroneous for a trial court to permit testimony from three persons to whom a girl had complained of sexual abuse by her stepfather (*Ochs v. Martinez*, 1990). The appeals court held that the girl's statements were not admissible, in that they were not spontaneous remarks made while she was experiencing the sensation or physical condition.

In a different case (*Posner v. Dallas County Child Welfare Unit*, 1990), a suit to end parental rights, a different appeals court held that the daughter's statement "[g]ive me your doll, and I will show you with mine how daddies sex their little girls" (p. 587) was admissible. The court reasoned that the statement was offered to show the girl made the statement, which would be evidence of her then-existing mental and emotional condition, and was not offered to prove the truth of the girl's statement (i.e., that "daddies sex their little girls" in the manner she described).

Clearly, the issues of evidence law are complicated. This brief discussion is intended merely to suggest that victims' comments to others may have important implications for decisions in both the criminal and civil justice systems.

Suits for Negligence. Another implication of our research concerns the person or organization to whom victims should report crimes. In this book, we have assumed that crimes will be reported to the police. There are some cases, however, in which victims will report a crime to someone but not to the police. Some third parties (e.g., businesses, hotels, and shopping malls) would prefer to handle the crime themselves, either by looking for the offender themselves or by not taking any action at all. If they do not involve the police, these third parties can prevent any bad publicity that might accompany a report of the crime. Moreover, if there is no report of a crime to the police there may be no record that these companies knew about the crime. Proof of such knowledge would be important for a victim who contended that the third party knew or should have known of a danger and failed to take reasonable precautions to prevent it. Thus, there are legal implications about why it is important to understand victims' decision to tell third parties about a crime.

Beginning in 1970 and particularly since the early 1980s, victims have successfully sued third parties in tort for failing to exercise reasonable care to prevent criminal victimization (Hanson & Thomas, 1988). For the most part, these suits have been aimed at residential landlords (e.g., apartment owners) and other commercial real estate owners (e.g., of shopping malls and office buildings) for criminal acts such as rape and aggravated assault that occurred on the premises. For such suits to be successful, victim-plaintiffs must show that the defendants knew or should have known of the risks of victimization. One way the owners would have known, of course, is if prior victims had told them about their victimizations. Presumably, owners who know of a prior criminal victimization have a duty to future users to take reasonable steps to reduce that risk, or they face the possibility of monetary loss in a civil suit. If victims report a crime to the police, there will be documentation that the owners knew of the risk. Thus, from a crime control perspective, it would be important for crime victims to report every crime to the police, not to third parties.

In summary, our multimethod research program suggested that victims are likely to talk with others before reporting the crime to the police. This finding has implications for the legal system in terms of whether the witness is believed, whether these others can relate at trial what the victim told them, and whether the third parties to whom victims reported a crime are liable for injury to subsequent victims.

Policy-Relevant Research

Much of our motivation for conducting research on victim decision making was to provide information that could be useful to decision makers in the criminal justice system. That is, we wanted practitioners as well as academic researchers to know about our findings. However, even though we think our research has some policy implications, we have reservations about making specific policy recommendations based solely on our research findings. First, we are concerned that our research does not have direct relevance to policy, in that we did not experimentally manipulate variables that policymakers can change (see Ruback & Innes, 1988). Thus, rather than make explicit recommendations, we can only suggest research that would have direct relevance to policy decisions.

Even if we could make specific policy recommendations, however, we would feel uncomfortable doing so because of our second reservation: our concern that social scientists should not make policy. Policy recommendations embody implicit value judgments, whether acknowledged or not. We believe, as Hammond and Adelman (1976) argued, that social scientists should limit themselves to providing and interpreting data, whereas policymakers should make judgments concerning values. In particular, we think that the proper role for social scientists is to inform policymakers of the likely results of specific policies.

What is unclear is exactly what goals regarding crime victims policymakers are trying to further. Is it controlling crime? If so, perhaps government should encourage victims to report every crime. Is it making victims feel better? If so, perhaps government should focus on providing tangible and socioemotional support (Office of Justice Programs, 1986). Is it making the criminal justice system work more efficiently? If so, perhaps government should encourage only victims of serious crimes to report their victimizations (Mayhew, 1985). As is apparent, the three goals of crime control, victim welfare, and system efficiency may not be compatible, particularly for less serious crimes. Until the goals are made clear, we think that the most productive advice we can give is to suggest a research study, based on our findings, that would have policy implications.

One of the implications of our research is that an important, and generally neglected, decision maker in the criminal justice system is the individual with whom a victim consults before deciding to call or not to call the police. Our research suggests that victims are often highly aroused during this decision-making period, which is one reason why they seem so susceptible to the influence of others. For several reasons, we believe that policy-related research should focus on these consultants (Ruback et al., 1984) for the following reasons: (1) because they are likely to be experiencing less stress than are victims, their thinking is likely to be more rational, and their advice is likely to be particularly helpful; (2) their presence is likely to provide emotional support, which may reduce victims' distress; (3) they are likely to provide the victim with the appropriate normative standards for the victim's group; and (4) since the consultants tend to be relatives and friends of the victim, their satisfaction is likely to affect, directly or indirectly, how happy the victim will be with his or her reporting decision.

Because of the importance of consultants in the decision-making process of victims, we think it is imperative that the criminal justice system provide information to potential advisers (i.e., virtually everyone) about their importance to the system and about how their actions and advice can affect whether or not the victim reports the crime, whether or not victims suffer short-term mental distress, and whether or not victims cope well over the long run with the crime and its aftermath. Consultants also should be advised about sources of victims' distress and how their words can ameliorate or exacerbate such distress.

We believe that there should be information campaigns directed at educating those who can influence victims, because our research suggests that victims' strong emotionality can impair their ability to think rationally after a crime. These information campaigns, similar to those aimed at preventing drunk driving, would be targeted at making consultants more aware of the impact of their actions. For example, our experimental research suggests that if a consultant wanted a victim to report a crime, the consultant should give specific advice to report, should remain with the victim while the reporting decision is made, and should offer to be of continuing help in the future.

These information campaigns directed at consultants may further sensitize them to suspicious events so that they can better help victims label ambiguous events as crimes. We might also give advisers a more realistic assessment of what the police can and cannot do, because many victims complain that they are totally confused by the workings of the criminal justice system (Sales, Rich, & Reich, 1987). By alerting these potential consultants to how the police operate (e.g., how quickly they are likely to arrive after being called) and what outcomes are likely (e.g., low rates of success for many property crimes), these consultants may be able to prevent the second injury victims often feel from being inadequately informed and sometimes rudely treated by the criminal justice system. Further, these information campaigns need to address the changes in laws and policies in some jurisdictions that are intended to increase reporting by minimizing the costs (e.g., rape shield laws; see, e.g., Borgida, 1981) or by maximizing benefits (e.g., arresting abusing spouses; see, e.g., Sherman & Berk, 1984).

We call this "policy-related" research, because we would want to see an experimental demonstration of its effectiveness before we advocated its adoption. A simple study might be to provide different types of information to different neighborhood-watch groups around the city. Dependent measures for such a study would include not only reporting rates, which are unlikely to change with such an intervention, but also crime victims' satisfaction with the system and the community's awareness of what the police can and cannot do.

In addition to looking at how consultants can better affect victims' decision making, research should also explore the decision process of the consultants. Because consultants' advice is such a powerful variable, it is important that we know the factors that explain the kind of advice they offer (Greenberg, 1991). Preliminary research suggests they are influenced by the same factor that affects victims, namely, the seriousness of the crime (Beach & Greenberg, 1991). However, we currently know very little about how the reactions of the victim during and immediately after the crime influence the type of advice and quality of support offered by consultants. For example, how are the intervention strategies of consultants affected by the amount of resistance offered by a victim during a robbery (Marsh & Greenberg, 1991) and by the victim's level of anger and fear during the interaction with the consultant? To what extent are such intervention strategies influenced by the victim's initial coping responses (e.g., denial or self-blame)?

As part of this projected research, it would also be important to investigate the biases of consultants because the advice they offer may not necessarily be in the victim's interest. For example, they may blame the victim in order to reduce their own sense of vulnerability. Further, they may give advice that is in their own interest rather than in the victim's. For example, bystanders may hesitate to advise calling the police because of their reluctance to get involved with the system themselves. Finally, we may also want to examine the costs to the consultant (e.g., higher levels of fear) of giving advice and comfort to the victim.

SUMMARY

In this chapter we summarized our results concerning victims' decision making after the crime. In general, there were consistent findings concerning the relative importance of situational over individual factors in predicting the reporting decision. More importantly, the results across studies indicated that social influence is often the key factor in determining victims' final reporting decision. This finding has an important implication for how one views the activation of the criminal justice process. Traditionally, the police have been viewed as the "gatekeepers" of the system. With the advent of the victimization surveys in the 1970s, we came to recognize that it is not the police but the victim who is the true gatekeeper of the system. In light of our consistent findings demonstrating the strong influence exerted by others on victims' reporting decision, we must now conclude that the *real* gatekeepers are those people with whom victims consult in the moments immediately after the crime. If one wants to know whether or not a victim will activate the system, the best predictor is likely to be the type of advice received from others.

In this chapter we also presented some of the general implications of our research for the conduct of multimethod applied research and for the development of theory related to victim decision making. Particularly promising for understanding victims' reactions to crime is theory development relating to (1) affective and emotional processes; (2) cognitive modes of coping with victimization; and (3) social comparison processes.

We also discussed the policy implications of the research. First, we described the relevance of our findings to understanding legal issues regarding criminal procedure, evidence, and torts. Then we suggested how our findings can be used to investigate a policy-related question concerning the advisability of conducting information campaigns directed at consultants rather than at victims.

In making policy recommendations, one must first know what goals society is trying to achieve. Should priority be given to controlling crime, facilitating the recovery of victims, or increasing the efficiency of the criminal justice system? As we discussed, in cases of less serious crimes these goals may not always be compatible. In addition to stimulating research on decision making by crime victims, we hope this book will encourage policymakers and citizens to discuss what those goals should be.

Appendix
A LAWSUIT AGAINST THE RESEARCHERS

In Chapters 2 and 3 we described the procedures and results of the field-laboratory experiments we conducted to investigate the effects of social influence on victims' decision to report or not to report a theft to the police. In this chapter we discuss in some detail one of the costs of conducting experimental research with a wide range of participants: a lawsuit. Our goal in describing this incident is to inform social scientists about the legal issues that may be raised by research participants. In an increasingly litigious society, investigators should know what negligence entails. Moreover, researchers should be aware of the negative practical effects of being a defendant in a lawsuit: the emotional toll that it takes, the disruption of research, and the sheer amount of time involved in fighting the suit, even one that is groundless.

Before we began the experimental research, we were mindful of the ethical questions involved as well as areas of potential legal liability (see Ruback & Greenberg, 1986). We took many precautions to protect participants against harm as a result of taking part in the experimental studies. These efforts included an initial screening at the time of the first telephone contact, a second screening when participants were scheduled for an appointment, and a third screening at the beginning of the experiment (see Chapter 2). In addition to these safeguards, we had incorporated several other features at the suggestion of outside reviewers and a clinical psychologist. In spite of our best efforts, however, one woman became upset during an experimental session. Later she sued us and the University of Pittsburgh for damages she alleged resulted from her experience in our laboratory.

DESCRIPTION OF THE INCIDENT

The precipitating incident for the lawsuit occurred on April 13, 1977, during the second experiment, in which we manipulated the kind of advice participants received (advised action, advised no action, or no advice) and the level of the bystander's anger (none, low, or high). In response to the initial screening questions, the participant, a 52-year-old homemaker, said she had no physical problems, including high blood pressure, or any other problem that would keep her from participating. Moreover, the supervisor and research assistants noted no obvious physical or mental problems or obvious signs of anxiety when she appeared at the laboratory.

The woman behaved normally throughout the first part of the experiment. The supervisor and the two confederates noticed nothing strange or unusual about the woman's behavior during the initial description of the study, the alphabetizing task, and the bookkeeping task.

The problems began when the woman learned, over the intercom system, that she had scored below the norms for her age group. She and the two confederates then walked to the secretary's office from the room where the clerical tasks had been performed. In the office, the woman gave the $11 she had lost to the thief, began filling out the final reactions forms, and listened when the secretary told her and the two confederates that there appeared to be a problem with some of the papers.

After the theft was discovered and the secretary left to look for her supervisor, the bystander began delivering her prepared communication concerning her anger and the need to do something. For this particular participant, the bystander described her high level of anger and advised the participant to report the crime to the police.

At this point, the participant, in the words of her lawsuit, "decided that something was amiss and that it was time for her to leave" (*Wessell v. University of Pittsburgh*, 1979, Complaint p. 4). She left the secretary's office, exited through the outer office, and started descending the stairs. Immediately upon learning of this, the secretary rushed to the back room to tell the supervisor of the participant's hasty departure.

The supervisor, upon receiving this information, went out into the hallway. Meanwhile, the secretary had gone out to the hallway through the back office and was calling after the participant to come back, as there was something that the organization had not told her. The woman proceeded down the steps, followed by the supervisor, who was hurrying to catch up with her in order to tell her about the deception. By the time the woman had reached the front doors, the experimenter was at the landing on the staircase, a distance of about 20 feet. By the time the supervisor reached the sidewalk in front of the building, the woman had run off to the right.

Realizing that the woman would not listen to him, the supervisor returned to the office to get another staff member to talk to the participant. The supervisor then described the woman's actions to another supervisor who happened to be there that day. They both went out into the street and saw the woman standing next to a middle-aged male who appeared to be protecting her. (We later learned that he was a friend who had just happened by as she emerged from the building.) The two supervisors attempted to talk to the woman, trying to tell her more about the study and the fact that she was entitled to some additional money. However, the man with her told the two supervisors that she was not interested in the money or in hearing any more about the study.

The two supervisors then returned to the office and telephoned the project director (Martin Greenberg) about what had happened. In addition, they called the two consultants to the research project (a clinical psychologist and a burglary detective with the Pittsburgh Police Department) and the in-house legal counsel for the University of Pittsburgh. About half an hour after the participant had left, two officers from the Pittsburgh Police Department, accompanied by the participant and her husband, came to the office suite. The participant, we learned later, had called her husband, and he had taken her to the nearest police station (yet more evidence that reporting to the police is often the product of social influence).

The police officers asked for an explanation of what had occurred. For the next 15 minutes or so, one of the supervisors explained exactly what the study was about, the deceptions involved, and the need for these deceptions. Understandably, the husband of the participant was very upset that his wife had become distraught. In contrast to the two officers and the participant, he did not appear to be satisfied with the explanations offered. He was quite irate and stated that if the police had not been there, he would have beaten the supervisor with a tire iron.

The police report defined what had happened as a "miscellaneous incident." The final verbatim report was as follows:

> Comp[lainant] involved in a research project with U. of Pgh. had a misunderstanding with project assistant Chauncey Wilson. Both parties satisfied. No action to be taken by comp[lainant].

Within an hour after the police left, the clinical psychologist who served as a consultant to the project came to the office suite to learn what had happened. Two issues were important to him. First, he had to learn if the woman had suffered any harm. Second, he had to establish whether the clinical debriefing, which he had earlier approved as meeting ethical requirements, needed to be changed.

After discussing the incident with the staff members, he concluded that the basic screening procedures of the study were satisfactory. However, it was also decided that in the future, if a participant left the building, the staff were not to follow. The psychologist also took the participant's name and telephone number. When he attempted to talk to the participant that evening and again the next evening, he was told that she did not want to talk to him.

The staff were made anxious by the incident, but we all assumed that the incident was over. We were mistaken.

THE LAWSUIT

Pennsylvania has a two-year statute of limitations for civil actions in torts. That is, a person must file a lawsuit for damages within two years of the event causing the alleged harm (or, when the harm is hidden, within two years of the discovery of the harm), or the person is forever barred from bringing a suit on the basis of the event. On March 14, 1979, one year, 11 months, and one day after she had participated in the experiment, the participant and her husband filed suit against us.

CAUSES OF ACTION

In the suit, the woman and her husband (the plaintiffs) filed a civil action naming the University of Pittsburgh and the researchers as defendants. Their suit set forth two legal causes of action: negligence and the infliction of emotional distress. These two actions fall under the broad category of tort law.

Torts are civil, not criminal, actions and include all civil wrongs "other than breach of contract, for which the court will provide a remedy in the form of an action for damages" (Keeton, Dobbs, Keeton, & Owen, 1984, p. 2). All civil actions, including those in tort, must be set forth in a document or pleading referred to as a *complaint*. The complaint must state sufficient allegations of fact to give the person against whom it is filed (the defendant) notice of the incident giving rise to the civil action. In addition to giving the defendant notice, the filed pleadings must contain allegations that constitute a legal wrong, generally referred to as a *cause of action*.

The first cause of action the plaintiffs alleged was negligence. Negligence is the failure to take reasonable care to guard against foreseeable risks of injury. In general terms, the tort of negligence is regarded as having four necessary elements: (1) the existence of a legal duty to protect another person from an unreasonable risk; (2) the violation (breach) of that duty; (3) proximate causation between the breach of duty and the injury to the person; and (4) damages resulting from the breach of duty. In civil litigation, the burden of proof is on the plaintiffs, so that they must show the existence of each of the four necessary elements of negligence.

The first element, duty, is based on the notion that under particular circumstances citizens must assume a duty to act according to a certain standard of care. For example, motorists have a duty to drive within the speed limit. The speed limit is a legislatively imposed standard of care. Generally, the standard of care is determined by a fictitious notion of how a reasonable person would act under the specific circumstances in question.

In our case, the plaintiffs had to prove that the law imposed on us as researchers a duty to act according to a standard of care, that of a "reasonable social scientist." The proof of the existence of this duty often comes through testimony by a witness for the plaintiffs who is similarly situated to the defendant. In our case, the plaintiffs would have needed to present one or more social scientists who would state that the average experimenter would have acted with a greater degree of care under the same or similar circumstances.

Even if the plaintiffs could have established that we, the defendant researchers, were under a duty to act according to a higher standard of care, they would also have to prove the element of breach. That is, they would have to show that we failed to act according to that standard of care.

The third and fourth elements of the plaintiffs' case of negligence are closely related. The plaintiff must show that the breach of the standard of care caused harm or damage. The third element is termed *causation* and the fourth element *damages*. Even if there is a standard of care that the defendant breached and even if the plaintiff suffered damages, there must be a sufficiently close link between the actions of the defendant and the alleged damage suffered by the plaintiffs for the court to impose liability on the defendants. This link is termed *proximate causation*.

For example, assume a speeding motorist has a passenger in his car. While the motorist is speeding, the passenger suffers a heart attack. In this example, there is a breach of duty to act according to an established standard of care, because the motorist was driving faster than the speed limit. In addition, there were damages, because the passenger suffered a heart attack. The question, however, is whether the speeding caused the heart attack or whether the heart attack was caused by independent forces. Unless the passenger-plaintiff can prove that the defendant-driver's speeding caused the heart attack, the plaintiff will not prevail.

Negligence is probably most often used in connection with traffic accidents resulting from a driver's failing to exercise reasonable care (e.g., by not looking at the road). Car drivers have a legal duty to engage in reasonable behavior, and such actions as not looking at the road are violations of that duty. In most traffic accidents, the connection between the violation of duty and the injury to the person is quite clear. For example, consider a driver who, had he not been reading his map while driving, would not have hit and killed a child in a crosswalk. In legal terms, "but for" the defendant's negligence, the death would not have occurred.

The link between the breach of duty and the harm (referred to as *causation*) is generally not difficult to establish. In the example above, the cause of the child's death, the negligently driven car, would be fairly easy to prove. Problems of proof become more difficult, however, if the link between the breach of duty and the injury to the person is attenuated. Consider the following variation in the example. The child's mother is standing in her front yard and witnesses the car strike and kill her child. Almost two years later she sues the driver, claiming that ever since the incident she has suffered severe emotional distress. She claims that the driver's negligence was the cause of her injuries. Does she have a valid claim to recover damages?

One way in which such issues are resolved is a determination of foreseeability: Was it foreseeable that the event, the injury to the specific plaintiff, would occur (Keeton *et al.*, 1984)? The law generally extends liability only to those who should have foreseen the risk of harm.

In their lawsuit, the plaintiffs alleged that the defendants were negligent in the following ways:

a) in failing to follow accepted psychological research techniques during the course of gathering data;
b) in conducting research in such a negligent and reckless manner as to cause harm to the subject without her permission;
c) in employing scare tactics within their psychological research;
d) in employing anxiety producing techniques without regard to the psychological makeup of each subject;
e) in failing to take any measure as to determine whether the Plaintiff, La Verne Wessell, was a proper subject for psychological research;
f) in completely failing to obtain any type of consent from the Plaintiff, La Verne Wessell, prior to or during the experimentation done upon her;
g) in generally failing to exercise that degree of care and caution required under the circumstances;
h) in conspiring to illegally subject the Plaintiff, La Verne Wessell, to psychological tests without her consent. (*Wessell v. University of Pittsburgh*, pp. 5–6)

In addition to negligence, the plaintiffs alleged a second cause of action, the infliction of emotional distress. Historically, the law has required that the harm to the plaintiff must be observable and measurable, in terms of either monetary damage to property or physical harm to his or her person. In recent years, however, the supreme courts of several states have ruled that emotional distress by itself, without preceding or subsequent physical harm, may constitute an actionable legal wrong (Keeton *et al.*, 1984).

The danger of allowing recovery for emotional distress, however, is that it is not observable and therefore presents the possibility of fraudulent allegations. To reduce the possibility of such misrepresentation, the courts have required that the tort of intentional infliction of emotional distress involve extreme and outrageous conduct and the intention to cause severe emotional distress (American Law Institute, 1965).

At the time of the lawsuit, Pennsylvania (and a few other states) had allowed recovery for the negligent infliction of emotional distress. Recovery was limited to very circumscribed conditions, however, because of the possibility of fraudulent allegations. It was not clear from the pleadings whether the plaintiffs were alleging the intentional or negligent infliction of emotional distress.

DAMAGES

The plaintiff and her husband claimed damages in excess of $10,000, which in Pennsylvania was the minimum amount necessary to ensure that the case would be heard in the court of general jurisdiction, the Court of Common Pleas. At that time, in Pittsburgh, cases claiming lower amounts of damages were heard in a form of arbitration, the decisions of which were appealable to the Court of Common Pleas for a new trial.

The plaintiff alleged she had suffered the following injuries:

insomnia, traumatic neurosis, paranoid ideas of reference, depression, recurrent neurotic anxiety, personality transformation, and a severe shock to the nervous system, resulting in digestive disturbances, insomnia, irritability, headaches and a complete and permanent change in personality.

Her husband alleged that he had "been deprived of the assistance, help and comfort of his wife for a long period of time" and had "suffered the loss of his wife's care, comfort and society."

The attorney for the plaintiffs took the case on contingency. If the plaintiffs won their lawsuit, he would be entitled to a set amount (which is generally somewhere between a third and a half of the recovered damages). If the plaintiffs lost their lawsuit, however, he would not receive any payment for the time he had devoted to the case. The purpose of the contingency fee arrangement is to enable individuals who would otherwise not be able to afford the expenses of a lawsuit to go to court to seek redress for legal wrongs.

THE IMMEDIATE AFTERMATH OF THE FILING

On March 15, 1979, the day after the lawsuit had been filed, articles appeared in both of the Pittsburgh daily newspapers, which had a common owner and shared reporters (see Figure 11-1). The headlines were sufficient to catch people's attention: "Test Caused Trauma, Woman Says in Suit" (Donalson, 1979) and "Testing Trickery Charged in Suit" (Christensen, 1979). Essentially, both articles restated the allegations of the lawsuit and included some information about the researchers. With all the attendant publicity, we decided to discontinue the experimental research. The validity of any subsequent research using this methodology would be suspect, because future participants would be likely to know of the deceptions.

Six days later, on March 21, 1979, there was a front-page story entitled "Is Lying Justified in Psychological Research?" (Pierce, 1979a). The author of the article was the science reporter for one of the local newspapers. About a year before the suit was filed, he had contacted Greenberg after reading a preliminary report of our findings that was presented at a professional meeting. He was very interested in writing an article about the research for the Pittsburgh audience. When I (Greenberg) explained my reluctance to

Figure 11-1. Local media's response to filing of lawsuit against researchers.

publicize the research because of its potential for jeopardizing the validity of the findings from future participants, he relented. I explained to him that when the project was completed, I would be happy to provide him with all the information that he needed to write his article. When he learned about the lawsuit, he insisted on interviewing me. When I explained to him that I did not want to give the issue any more publicity than it had already received, he said that he would interview the plaintiff and write his article regardless of any input from me. Under such circumstances, there was no option but to consent to the interview. It took place the next day in our laboratory. The article that resulted took our case as the starting point for a general discussion of deception research. The reporter also quoted from his interview with me:

> "I'm not a moral absolutist," Greenberg asserted. "That is, I'm opposed to deception in principle, but very few people would say that one should never employ deception in his life—that if you see someone running with a knife, and he said, 'Which way did Bill go?' and you told him, 'Bill went that way,' I doubt very much whether that would be ethical behavior. One would probably say, 'I don't know where Bill went.' "

Three days later this same reporter wrote an article in the other newspaper (Pierce, 1979b) condemning the use of deception generally, because it reduces the level of trust in society.

Also in the March 21, 1979, issue of the paper was an article by a clerk at the newspaper who, more than a year earlier, had participated in the research study (Patton, 1979). The headline of the article (" 'I Felt Like a Fool,' Woman Who Took the Test Says") did not capture her mixed feelings about having participated in the study:

> I felt as if Alan Funt and the whole Candid Camera crew were behind the mirror getting a good laugh. At my expense.
>
> The monitor led me through an elaborate questionnaire to see what reaction I had to the test. He took great care to answer my questions and was sensitive to any discomfort the test caused me.
>
> He assured me that all my reactions, the embarrassment and paranoia, were normal. His thorough explanation of what the test hoped to accomplish made me feel as if it was all very timely and necessary.
>
> My paranoia and the sense that my rights had been violated stayed with me for the rest of the day. But I also felt that the research this group was doing was valuable.

On March 27, 1979, an editorial appeared in the Pittsburgh *Post-Gazette* ("Research Is Called to Court," 1979). The editorial described the research and focused on the generalizability of the results: "Those thoroughly convoluted circumstances seem like an unreliable basis upon which to hypothesize the reactions of real victims of crime." The ethical question of the deception involved seemed not to bother the authors of the editorial.

In that same issue of the *Post-Gazette* and again the next day, there appeared two letters from other participants who wrote that they had been pleased to participate in the research. One woman even wrote that "This ridiculous suit should be thrown out of court so that serious academic work may proceed for the benefit of all of us."

PRETRIAL DISCOVERY

The law of civil procedure allows for what is know as *pretrial discovery*, in order to help both sides of a lawsuit to prepare their cases adequately. This process allows both parties to know basically what evidence the other side will present at the trial. Thus, pretrial discovery is generally seen as a way to reduce unfair surprises at trial (i.e., to prevent what is sometimes called *trial by ambush*). More importantly, it often serves as an incentive for the parties to settle the case instead of going to trial, because they know the strengths and weaknesses of their own and their opponent's case. Discovery may be through written questions, called *interrogatories*, which are filed with the court and also sent by registered mail to the person being questioned or, in the case of a party to the lawsuit, to his or her attorney. The person has 20 days in which to respond to the interrogatories.

We received interrogatories in early September, 1981. Among the 51 questions included in the interrogatories were questions about the identity of those who had personal knowledge of the events, the purpose of the research, the precautions taken by the researchers, the ethical standards governing the research and the standards of review used, the nature of the University of Pittsburgh's insurance coverage, and whether any disciplinary action had been instituted against the defendant researchers.

In addition to interrogatories, pretrial discovery may include oral depositions. A deposition is testimony taken under oath, usually before a court reporter, who records what is said. In recent years, depositions have been taken on audiotape and videotape. The testimony from the deposition can be used at trial, particularly if the witness says something different on the stand from what he or she said earlier during the deposition. In addition, a deposition preserves a witness's testimony, should the witness be unavailable during the trial (e.g., by being out of the court's jurisdiction or being deceased).

Attorneys generally prefer oral depositions because, unlike written interrogatories, depositions give them a chance to ask follow-up questions. Moreover, oral depositions allow the attorneys to get a sense of how good a witness the person (called a *deponent*) would be at the trial.

On October 1, 1981, oral depositions were taken by the plaintiffs' attorney in his office. We were accompanied by two attorneys, with whom we had met beforehand to go over possible questions. The attorneys had been hired by the insurance company that insured the University of Pittsburgh.

On the next day, October 2, 1981, the plaintiffs' attorney wrote a letter to our attorney requesting documents relevant to the plaintiffs' case. These documents included the following: written reports based on the study in which the plaintiff had participated, funding applications made to the National Institute of Mental Health, reports made to the National Institute of Mental Health, the written format used for screening prospective subjects, the application for and approval of the College of Arts and Sciences Human Studies Committee, the consent form used in the study, a list of the names and addresses of the participants in the study in which the plaintiff had participated, and a list of names and addresses of all participants in the five other studies in the series.

In response to the last request, we informed the judge that we had promised all participants in the six studies that the information that they had provided, including their names, was confidential. The judge responded to our concern by ordering that only the reactions of those who had participated in the same study as the plaintiff were relevant to the case. Further, in recognition of our pledge of confidentiality, he did not order us to reveal the names of these participants to the plaintiffs' attorney. Instead, he ordered us to forward requests for information from the plaintiff directly to the participants. Thus, in December, 1981, under the court's order, we sent a letter written by the plaintiffs' counsel to each of the 120 participants in the second study. This letter described the lawsuit and asked the participants to contact the plaintiffs' attorney if they were willing to talk about their experience in the experiment.

To prevent surprise at the trial, both sides of the case, if asked, are required to list the witnesses they may call to testify and the exhibits they may introduce. These statements are filed with the court and sent by registered mail to the attorney for the other side. In our case, both sides filed these statements and obtained the requested information.

In order to encourage parties in civil suits to try to settle their case without going to trial, Pennsylvania law authorized the court to require a pretrial conference (Pennsylvania Rules of Civil Procedure, 1975). At this meeting, held on January 8, 1982, the plaintiffs' lowest demand was $12,000. Consistent with the stand of the University's insurance carrier, our attorney refused to accept this offer for settlement.

THE TRIAL

The case came to trial on September 14, 1982, about 3½ years after the suit had been filed and more than 5½ years after the alleged harmful incident had occurred. The case, which was tried before a judge as factfinder rather than before a jury, lasted a day and a half. Apparently, the plaintiff's attorney had made a mistake and had failed to request a jury trial.

The Plaintiff's Case

Initial statements were made by the two attorneys, and the plaintiff's attorney began introducing testimony. The plaintiff put five witnesses on the stand, four on the first day and one on the second day. The first witness was the plaintiff. She described how she had responded to the advertisement in the newspaper, how she had come to the experimental situation thinking it was a job interview, how the situation seemed suspicious, and how she had run out of the laboratory. She then went on to describe the mental problems she had suffered since the incident. For example, she claimed that because of the incident she had felt uncomfortable changing clothes in public dressing rooms because of the belief that people might be watching her through the mirrors.

On cross-examination, our attorney first asked the plaintiff about her understanding of what she had volunteered for. Even after he showed her the newspaper advertisement and read aloud the standardized instructions that the secretaries had read to her before scheduling her appointment, she still insisted that she had thought it was an interview for a job rather than participation in a research project.

During the cross-examination, the plaintiff made an admission that was very damaging to her case. This admission concerned her use of medications at the time of the incident. When she said she was using a medication at the time, our attorney asked her if she was aware that this medication caused hallucinations. She said she did not know that, at which point the attorney read the appropriate section directly from the *Physician's Desk Reference*. As his question had implied, this section indicated that hallucinations are a possible side effect of the drug.

The second witness was the plaintiff's husband, who described the events after his wife had phoned him. He had not been present during the experiment, so his testimony added little about the procedure itself. He also testified about the harms he and his wife had suffered since the incident.

A third witness for the plaintiff was a psychiatrist on the staff of the University of Pittsburgh School of Medicine. He was unable to testify in person, so his testimony under direct examination and cross-examination had been given under oath on videotape. He stated that the plaintiff who had participated in the experiment was suffering from several problems, but he could not state that these problems had been caused by the experiment rather than existing prior to it. Indeed, his characterization of her condition as chronic suggested that the condition was preexisting.

Moreover, on cross-examination he stated that at the suggestion of the plaintiff's attorney, he had seen the plaintiff on several occasions in his office subsequent to her participation in the experiment. This statement was true, no doubt, but it had the effect of undermining the plaintiff's case. It suggested that the plaintiff had visited the psychiatrist not because she was suffering from particular problems, but because her attorney was trying to establish a medical record from the time of the incident to the time of the trial. A psychiatrist more experienced in testifying in court might not have been so candid about his reasons for seeing the patient.

The last two witnesses the plaintiff presented were questioned to make a point about the unreasonableness of the procedure. In response to the letter sent to all individuals who had participated in the same study as had the plaintiff, a few individuals had contacted the plaintiffs' attorney. Before the trial, our attorney had requested a list of all individuals whom the plaintiffs' attorney had said he might call, and this list included these individuals. With this information, we were able to examine the participants' files (participants' names were connected to participant identification numbers in one file, so that we were able to look at the data under that particular identification number kept in another file) to see how they had reacted at the time of the experiment and subsequently. One of these persons did testify at the trial, as did the clerk at the newspaper who had written the article in one of the Pittsburgh papers six days after the lawsuit had been filed. This clerk had been a participant in a different study.

Both women testified that they had been upset by the experiment. Their credibility was undermined during cross-examination, however, when our attorney showed them postexperimental questionnaire forms that they had completed and signed indicating that their reaction to the experiment had been quite positive. The second woman's testimony ended on the morning of the second day of the trial.

MOTION FOR A DIRECTED VERDICT

At the completion of the plaintiff's case, our attorney moved for a directed verdict against the plaintiff. For a directed verdict to be granted, the judge must rule that the plaintiff has failed to present enough evidence (even without any counterevidence by the defendant) to establish a cause of action. It is routinely requested by all defendants in civil actions, but it is infrequently granted, because it means that the plaintiff has failed to establish a *prima facie* case.

There was a short recess of about 15 minutes, during which the judge considered our motion for a directed verdict. The judge also considered the trial briefs given to him by the two attorneys. Our trial memorandum argued that although Pennsylvania law allowed recovery for the intentional infliction of emotional distress, certain items had to be proved. To recover on this basis, the plaintiff had to show that the harm had been caused by conduct that was so outrageous in character as to be beyond all possible bounds of decency and intolerable in civilized society and extreme in degree (*Banyas v. Lower Bucks Hospital*, 1981; *Jones v. Nissenbaum, Rudolph, & Seidner*,

1976). Our attorney argued that no such outrageous behavior was present in this case.

In addition to rejecting a claim on the basis of the intentional infliction of emotional distress, our memorandum also argued that the negligent infliction of emotional distress is limited in Pennsylvania to situations in which an individual personally observes physical injury that was negligently inflicted on another individual by a third person. In the case that set this precedent (*Sinn v. Burd*, 1979), a mother who had seen a car strike and kill her daughter was able to recover for her emotional distress, even though she herself could not have been hurt in the accident and the driver of the car had not intended to cause the damage.

Finally, our trial memorandum included a discussion of factors that might limit recovery of damages for the negligent infliction of emotional distress. In general, when persons commit a tort against someone, they are said to "take their victim as they find him or her." For example, assume that without provocation Person A punches Person B in the jaw. Assume further that a person with a jaw of normal sensitivity would feel some pain but would suffer no permanent damage. Assume finally that Person B has unusually brittle bones and, as a result, suffers broken bones on the entire side of his face. Under general tort law, Person A would be liable not only for the pain that any normal person would have suffered, but also for the additional damages that Person B has suffered because of his unusually high sensitivity to injury. This notion is sometimes called the *thin skull rule* (*Watson v. Rinderknecht*, 1901).

The situation is different, however, when the damage is mental rather than physical harm (American Law Institute, 1965). According to Pennsylvania law, when there is a negligent infliction of emotional distress, the standard is whether the behavior in question would cause harm in a person of average sensibilities. Because there is a danger of claiming emotional harm when there is none, the Supreme Court of Pennsylvania held that "it would be unreasonable to hold the defendant responsible for the mental distress that may be experienced by the most timid or sensitive members of the community" (*Sinn v. Burd*, 1979).

THE VERDICT

After the recess the judge granted the motion for the directed verdict (also called a *compulsory nonsuit*). In his statement, the judge said that the plaintiffs should have called other witnesses, including the police officers who had investigated the incident when it occurred in 1977. Their testimony might not have ensured that there would be no directed verdict, but in the absence of testimony meeting the requirements of the law, the judge said he had no choice but to dismiss the lawsuit.

With regard to the claim of the intentional infliction of emotional distress, the judge did not believe the researchers had engaged in outrageous conduct. Even when the researchers had followed the plaintiff out onto the street to try to debrief her about the study, their behavior could not be called outrageous.

Further, the judge said the facts did not support a finding of negligent infliction of emotional distress. It appeared to him that the researchers had acted reasonably. Moreover, given that the standard for negligent infliction of emotional distress is a person of average sensibilities, it was clear that the plaintiff did not have average sensibilities. Her psychiatrist had testified that she suffered from chronic depression, and the judge inferred that she was more susceptible to a negative reaction, even if reasonable researchers could not have detected her preexisting condition. Finally, the two witnesses who had testified that they had been upset by the experiment appeared to the judge to be persons of average sensibilities, and they had not suffered the severe consequences the plaintiff alleged she had suffered.

In sum, although the judge did say that perhaps the researchers could have been more considerate of her feelings, he indicated that there was simply no evidence that a legal harm had been done.

POSTTRIAL ACTIVITIES

The plaintiffs had the right to appeal the judgment against them, because the judge's ruling was a question of law and not of fact. They did not appeal, however, because the chances of a successful appeal were virtually nil.

The local newspapers never published an article saying that the case had been thrown out. By contrast, the initial filing of the suit, with the attendant possibility that unethical behavior had occurred, had been noteworthy and had merited news articles, commentary, and an editorial. The fact that the accusations had been groundless was apparently not of interest to the local news media. Years later, in a chance meeting with one of the researchers, a senior editor of one of the local newspapers expressed regret that his paper had failed to print the final outcome of the case.

THE DEFENDANTS' CASE

We were glad to have won the case and to have been vindicated without even having to present any evidence. Yet it was somewhat frustrating not to have had our side heard. In the interest of completeness, we present the information here. At the trial, our attorney was going to present evidence showing that our actions had been reasonable, from the design of the research to the way it had been carried out. In addition, we would have shown that the plaintiff was an overly sensitive woman with preexisting problems that could not be detected by reasonable screening methods.

REASONABLENESS OF THE PROCEDURES

We had taken extreme care initially to establish an ethical procedure, and the defense attorney would have had little difficulty showing that all of the experimental procedures were reasonable. First, the procedures were reasonable because of the multiple steps we took to minimize the risks to participants. Participants were screened on three separate occasions. Although the experimental procedure involved deception, we used only the amount that was necessary for the experimental manipulation of the independent variables. On arrival at the experiment, participants were paid the money promised them in the newspaper ad, and they had the opportunity at that point to leave without any further obligation. In other words, participation was completely voluntary and not contingent on the advertised money.

As noted in Chapter 2, the experimental procedure involved an extensive debriefing of all participants that included the reasons for the research, the factors being studied, and the reasons for the deception. At the end of this debriefing, all participants were asked to sign a consent form giving us permission to use the anonymous information they had provided. If they did not give consent (a few did not), their data were destroyed.

Finally, we attempted to minimize risk to participants by employing a licensed clinical psychologist who served as a consultant to the project. He advised us on the experimental procedure, helped us develop the debriefing, and was on call to speak with any participant who, at the end of the debriefing, still felt uncomfortable about participating in the study.

Second, the procedures were reasonable because we sought and obtained approval from peers in psychology and from an institutional review board (IRB) at the University of Pittsburgh. Moreover, the review panel of the Criminal and Violent Behavior Research Review Committee of the National Institute of Mental Health (NIMH), which funded the research, also approved the experimental methods. Both the IRB and the NIMH review panel contained individuals from disciplines other than psychology. In addition, the IRB included members from the community. Prior to seeking approval from these groups, we sought the advice of individuals from different backgrounds, including a philosopher of ethics, an attorney, and a police detective. In other words, we behaved as reasonable social scientists who acted at least to the standard of care of similarly situated researchers.

Third, the fact that virtually all research participants reacted positively to the study further supported our assertion that the procedures were reasonable. In anonymous questionnaires, participants in the initial research during which the procedures were established responded very positively to the experiment. The responses of participants in the actual experiments indicated that they were virtually unanimous in their belief that they had been treated with respect, had learned something, and were glad to have participated.

SENSITIVITY OF THE PARTICIPANT

In addition to the reasonableness of the procedure, we were prepared to argue that the participant-plaintiff was particularly sensitive, and that this sensitivity could not have been detected by a reasonable person. There was evidence that she had long-standing symptoms of depression and was on medication at the time of the incident. Moreover, there was strong evidence that her behavior was aberrant compared to the rest of the participants in the research during more than three years of experiments. The woman's reaction was qualitatively different from that of the hundreds of other participants in the research.

As part of their training, the secretaries who spoke with the participants calling in response to the newspaper advertisement had been instructed not to schedule any person who had physical health difficulties or who seemed to have any mental problems. In addition, when a participant arrived at the experimental setting, the confederates (the thief and the bystander), the secretary, and the supervisor all had the opportunity to observe him or her and to discontinue the study if the participant appeared to have any physical or mental health problems. In a few cases, this was done. The fact that none of our staff detected a problem, especially in light of their prior experience in the study, is strongly suggestive that the participant's preexisting mental problems could not be detected by average individuals without expertise in psychiatry or clinical psychology. In other words, it would be unreasonable to expect the staff to discover the woman's preexisting problems.

CONSEQUENCES OF THE LAWSUIT

To be the object of a highly publicized lawsuit ranks with other negative life experiences such as root-canal work and poison ivy. While not fatal, such experiences are to be avoided, if possible. When word of the suit reached the local press, it elicited accusing stares from tenants in the building where the research was conducted. The discomfort experienced by Greenberg was assuaged by the strong support of family and friends. Most colleagues studiously avoided bringing up the topic in Greenberg's presence. Those who did were sympathetic and supportive. They included the department chair and colleagues in the Social/Personality Program. Offers of reassurance and support were received from officials at the agency that funded the research, the National Institute of Mental Health's Center for Studies of Crime and Delinquency (now known as the Violence and Trau- matic Stress Research Branch).

Ruback's experience was slightly different from Greenberg's. When word of the lawsuit reached the local press, he was fortunate enough to be interviewing for a job many miles away in Atlanta, Georgia. Ruback's return to Pittsburgh after the interview could not have been much worse: his flight was several hours late, his luggage had been lost, a window in his apart- ment had been broken, and late that night he received a call from Greenberg informing him about the lawsuit and the termination of the experimental research program. When he subsequently received a job offer, he told the faculty at the university about the lawsuit, since they had the right to know about any bad publicity from the case that they might be attracting with their new hireling. They, however, were supportive and dismissed any possible negative repercussions.

But not everyone responded positively. The termination of the experi- mental work following the publicity given the lawsuit necessitated our moving to the next phase of the research: testing the generalizability of the findings. A logical way to do this was to interview actual victims of prop- erty crime. Efforts to enlist the cooperation of the Pittsburgh Bureau of Police in identifying such victims proved unsuccessful when the chief of police learned of the lawsuit. However, police chiefs in three suburban communities showed no such reluctance, and their assistance allowed us to collect data for Study 16. Moreover, one of these chiefs of police made his department's files available for detailed analysis (Study 14).

In retrospect, the lawsuit had some positive consequences. It caused us to move more quickly into the next phase of the research and to employ a variety of alternative methods to test the generalizability of the findings and to explore issues that could not be tested by an experimental paradigm. The lawsuit taught us something else.

LESSONS TO BE LEARNED

Our experience with the lawsuit taught us about the kind of problems that confront social science researchers who venture beyond the comfortable and relatively safe confines of the university laboratory. The decision to do so requires trade-offs between the control that researchers can exercise in the laboratory with a relatively homogeneous sample of college students, and the generalizability that one can obtain best through studies conducted in the field with a broader range of participants. Our reason for stepping outside the laboratory was to maximize generalizability. By trying to obtain a wide variety of subjects, however, we left ourselves vulnerable to a person with preexisting mental problems.

Should the Study Have Been Conducted?

Deciding whether or not a study should have been conducted can be a difficult decision, especially after an event such as we encountered. We cannot be expected to be totally disinterested parties, of course, as we were the ones who were sued. Nevertheless, because of the claimed harm, we have examined the research and believe our behavior was ethical and the study was worth doing.

The standard we have used is the utilitarian one, advocated by the guidelines of the American Psychological Association (Committee for the Protection of Human Participants in Research, 1982), which requires balancing the potential benefits against the potential costs of the research. We believed that society—and in particular, future victims—would benefit from increased understanding of victim decision making in the moments immediately following the crime. Such understanding and its dissemination, we believed, could increase the ability of potential aid givers to render assistance to victims. We believed that the potential knowledge to be gained could be used in information campaigns directed at family and friends of victims to help them provide wiser counsel.

The findings could also lead to more effective intervention by the police. By sensitizing the arriving officers to victims' likely emotional state and expectations and the factors that victims were likely to have weighed when deciding to report the crime, the police might be more responsive to victims' needs. In turn, victims might be more motivated to cooperate with the police, which could benefit society in the form of increased crime control. We also believed that the findings could help mental health personnel provide more effective service for crime victims. The insights derived from the research could help develop more informed intervention strategies that better meet victims' needs. Further, we thought our research would be useful for the discipline of psychology, in that the results of our studies have implications for theory and for the conduct of applied research (see Chapter 10).

The potential harms of the field-laboratory studies were primarily to the participants in the studies. Some may have felt uncomfortable at being deceived and at being placed in the role of a victim. This discomfort may have translated into anxiety and lowered self-esteem and possibly into physical symptoms. At a more global level, our deception research could have resulted in negative publicity for our University, for social psychology as a field, for the American Psychological Association, and for the National Institute of Mental Health. Negative perceptions about this kind of research might mean that fewer researchers will conduct similar studies in the future and fewer agencies and organizations will support it. After carefully weighing these benefits and costs and after obtaining the opinions of others within and outside our discipline, we decided that the research was worth doing.

We recognize that reasonable people can disagree about the value of research and that we, as the researchers, may have overestimated the potential worth of our studies. We are also aware that the utilitarian approach we took has special problems in instances like ours, where the potential benefits are more distant and abstract and the potential harms are often more immediate and concrete. Finally, we recognize that reasonable people can take the Kantian position that it is never correct to treat human individuals as a means to an end (Murray, 1982). Under this position, it would never be right to deceive individuals, regardless of the potential value of the research and the minimal amount of intrusion on the research participants.

COULD THIS RESEARCH BE CONDUCTED TODAY?

Even if there had not been a lawsuit, we suspect that the experimental portion of our research would not be approved or funded in today's legal climate. Funding agencies have become more conservative and fearful of lawsuits, and IRBs are reluctant to approve research that has the potential for causing damaging publicity.

This reluctance to approve and fund applied field research involving deception is not necessarily bad, if society considers the rights of research participants more important than any other goal. If, however, society places value on potentially useful research, then, in the long run, the failure to approve and fund such research will be harmful to us all.

References

Abel, E. M., & Suh, E. K. (1987). Use of police services by battered women. *Social Work, 32,* 526–528.

Abelson, R. P. (1981). Psychological status of the script concept. *American Psychologist, 36,* 715–729.

Abramson, L. Y., Seligman, M. E., & Teasdale, J. D. (1978). Learned helplessness in humans: Critique and reformulation. *Journal of Abnormal Psychology, 87,* 49–74.

Adams, J. S. (1963). Toward an understanding of inequity. *Journal of Abnormal and Social Psychology, 67,* 422–436.

Adams, J. S. (1965). Inequity in social exchange. In L. Berkowitz (Ed.), *Advances in experimental social psychology* (Vol. 2, pp. 267–299). New York: Academic Press.

Adams, J. S., & Freedman, S. (1976). Equity theory revisited: Comments and annotated bibliography. In L. Berkowitz (Ed.), *Advances in experimental social psychology* (Vol. 9, pp. 43–90). New York: Academic Press.

Addison, L. L. (1991, October). Admitting statements of then-existing mental, emotional, or physical condition under Rule 803(3). *Texas Bar Journal,* 1006.

Adorno, T. W., Frenkel-Brunswik, E., Levinson, D. J., & Sanford, R. N. (1950). *The authoritarian personality.* New York: Harper.

Akman, D. D., & Normandeau, A. (1967). The measurement of crime and delinquency in Canada. *British Journal of Criminology, 7,* 125–128.

Aldrich, J. H., & Nelson, F. D. (1984). *Linear probability, logit, and probit models.* Beverly Hills, CA: Sage.

American Law Institute. (1965). *Restatement of the law (Second): Torts 2d.* St. Paul: American Law Institute.

American Psychiatric Association. (1980). *Diagnostic and statistical manual of mental disorders* (3rd ed.). Washington, DC: Author.

Amir, M. (1971). *Patterns in forcible rape.* Chicago: University of Chicago Press.

Anthony, T., Copper, C., & Mullen, B. (1991, April). *Cross-racial facial identification: An integration*. Paper presented at the meeting of the Eastern Psychological Association, New York.

Archer, D., & Gartner, R. (1984). *Violence and crime in cross-national perspective*. New Haven: Yale University Press.

Aronson, E., & Carlsmith, J. M. (1968). Experimentation in social psychology. In G. Lindzey & E. Aronson (Eds.), *The handbook of social psychology* (2nd ed., Vol. 2, pp. 1–79). Reading, MA: Addison-Wesley.

Asch, S. E. (1952). *Social psychology*. Englewood Cliffs, NJ: Prentice-Hall.

Averill, J. R. (1982). *Anger and aggression: An essay on emotion*. New York: Springer-Verlag.

Backers say Hill told of sexual advances years ago. (1991, October 14). *The Atlanta Constitution*, p. A6.

Baker, A. L., & Peterson, C. (1977). Self-blame by rape victims as a function of the rape's consequences: An attributional analysis. *Crisis Intervention, 8*(3), 92–104.

Banaji, M. R., & Crowder, R. G. (1989). The bankruptcy of everyday memory. *American Psychologist, 44*, 1185–1193.

Bard, M., & Sangrey, D. (1979). *The crime victim's book*. New York: Basic Books.

Bard, M., & Sangrey, D. (1980, Special Issue). Things fall apart: Victims in crisis. *Evaluation and Change*, 28–35.

Bard, M., & Sangrey, D. (1986). *The crime victim's book* (2nd ed.). New York: Brunner/Mazel.

Baril, M. (1984). The victims' perceptions of crime and the criminal justice system: A pilot study of small shopkeepers in Montreal. In R. Block (Ed.), *Victimization and fear of crime: World perspectives* (pp. 75–86). Washington, DC: U.S. Government Printing Office.

Barkas, J. L. (1978). *Victims*. New York: Scribner's.

Bates, F. L. (1956). Position, role, and status: A reformulation of concepts. *Social Forces, 34*, 313–321.

Beach, S. R., & Greenberg, M. S. (1991, April). *Effects of objective loss and victim emotion on reactions to crime victims*. Paper presented at the meeting of the Eastern Psychological Association, New York.

Becker, J. V., Skinner, L. J., Abel, G. G., Howell, J., & Bruce, K. (1982). The effects of sexual assault on rape and attempted rape victims. *Victimology: An International Journal, 7*, 106–113.

Bem, D. J. (1972). Self-perception theory. In L. Berkowitz (Ed.), *Advances in experimental social psychology* (Vol. 6, pp. 1–62). New York: Academic Press.

Berger, S. M. (1977). Social comparison, modeling, and perseverance. In J. M. Suls & R. L. Miller (Eds.), *Social comparison processes: Theoretical and empirical perspectives* (pp. 209–234). Washington, D.C.: Hemisphere.

Bickman, L. (1976). Attitude toward an authority and the reporting of a crime. *Sociometry, 39*, 76–82.

Bickman, L., & Green, S. K. (1975). Is revenge sweet? The effect of attitude toward a thief on crime reporting. *Criminal Justice and Behavior, 2*, 101–112.

Bickman, L., & Green, S. K. (1977). Situational cues and crime reporting: Do signs make a difference? *Journal of Applied Social Psychology, 7*, 1–18.

Bickman, L., & Rosenbaum, D. P. (1977). Crime reporting as a function of bystander encouragement, surveillance, and credibility. *Journal of Personality and Social Psychology, 35*, 577–586.

Biderman, A. D. (1981). Sources of data for victimology. In *Victims of crime: A review of research issues and methods* (pp. 207–239). Washington, DC: National Institute of Justice.

Billings, A. G., & Moos, R. H. (1985). Life stressors and social resources affect posttreatment outcomes among depressed patients. *Journal of Abnormal Psychology, 94*, 140–153.

Binder, R. L. (1981). Why women don't report sexual assault. *Journal of Clinical Psychiatry, 42*, 437–438.

Blitman, N., & Green, R. (1975, May). Inez Garcia on trial. *Ms. Magazine*, pp. 49–54, 84–88.

Block, R. (1974). Why notify the police: The victim's decision to notify the police of an assault. *Criminology, 11*, 555–569.

Block, R. (Ed.). (1984). *Victimization and fear of crime: World perspectives*. Washington DC: U.S. Government Printing Office.

Block, R. (1989). Victim-offender dynamics in stranger to stranger violence: Robbery and rape. In E. A. Fattah (Ed.), *The plight of crime victims in modern society* (pp. 231–251). London: Macmillan.

Borgida, E. (1981). Legal reform of rape laws. In L. Bickman (Ed.), *Applied social psychology annual* (Vol. 2, pp. 211–241). Beverly Hills, CA: Sage.

Bower, G., Black, J., & Turner, T. (1979). Scripts in text comprehension and memory. *Cognitive Psychology, 11*, 177–220.

Bowker, L. (1982). Police services to battered women: Bad or not so bad? *Criminal Justice and Behavior, 9*, 476–494.

Boyle, R. H., & Jackson, R. (1982, August 9). Bringing down the curtain. *Sports Illustrated, 63–66*, 70, 72–76, 79.

Brickman, P., & Bulman, R. J. (1977). Pleasure and pain in social comparison. In J. M. Suls & R. L. Miller (Eds.), *Social comparison processes: Theoretical and empirical perspectives* (pp. 149–186). Washington, DC: Hemisphere.

Brigham, J. C., & Barkowitz, P. (1978). Do "they all look alike"? The effect of race, sex, experience, and attitudes on the ability to recognize faces. *Journal of Applied Psychology, 8*, 306–318.

Brigham, J. C., Maass, A., Snyder, L. D., & Spaulding, K. (1982). Accuracy of eyewitness identification in a field setting. *Journal of Personality and Social Psychology, 42*, 673–681.

Browne, A. (1987). *When battered women kill*. New York: Free Press.

Buckhout, R., Figueroa, D., & Hoff, E. (1975). Effects of suggestion and bias in identification. *Bulletin of the Psychonomic Society, 6*, 71–74.

Bureau of Justice Statistics. (1985). *Reporting crimes to the police*. Washington, DC: U.S. Department of Justice.

Bureau of Justice Statistics. (1987a). *Lifetime likelihood of victimization*. Washington, DC: U.S. Department of Justice.

Bureau of Justice Statistics. (1988). *Criminal victimization in the United States*. Washington, DC: U.S. Department of Justice.

Bureau of Justice Statistics. (1989b). *Redesign of the national crime survey*. Washington, DC: U.S. Department of Justice.

Bureau of Justice Statistics. (1990a). *Crime and the nation's households, 1989*. Washington, DC: U.S. Department of Justice.

Bureau of Justice Statistics. (1990b). *Criminal victimization in the United States, 1988*. Washington, DC: U.S. Department of Justice.

Bureau of Justice Statistics. (1992). *Criminal victimization in the United States, 1990*. Washington, D.C.: U.S. Department of Justice.

Bureau of the Census. (1982). *1980 Census of population. Vol. 1: Characteristics of the population Chap. B, General population characteristics, Part 40 Pennsylvania*. Washington, DC: U.S. Department of Commerce.

Burgess, A. W., & Holmstrom, L. L. (1975). Rape: The victim and the criminal justice system. In I. Drapkin & E. Viano (Eds.), *Victimology: A new focus. Vol. 3: Crimes, victims, and justice* (pp. 21–30). Lexington, MA: Heath.

Burt, M. R., & Katz, B. L. (1985). Rape, robbery, and burglary: Responses to actual and feared victimization, with special focus on women and the elderly. *Victimology: An International Journal, 10*, 325–358.

Byrne, D. (1971). *The attraction paradigm*. New York: Academic Press.

Cain, A. A., & Kravitz, M. (1978). *Victim/witness assistance: A selected bibliography*. Washington, DC: U.S. Government Printing Office.

Campbell, D. T. (1957). Factors relevant to the value of experiments in social settings. *Psychological Bulletin, 54*, 297–312.

Campbell, D. T., & Stanley, J. C. (1966). *Experimental and quasi-experimental designs for research.* Skokie, IL: Rand McNally.

Carlson, B. (1977). Battered women and their assailants. *Social Work, 22,* 455–460.

Chaiken, S., Liberman, A., & Eagly, A. H. (1989). Heuristic and systematic information processing within and beyond the persuasion context. In J. S. Uleman & J. A. Bargh (Eds.), *Unintended thought* (pp. 212–252). New York: Guilford Press.

Chance, J., & Goldstein, A. (1976). Recognition of faces and verbal labels. *Bulletin of the Psychonomic Society, 7,* 384–387.

Chesney, S., Hudson, J., & McLagen, J. (1978). New look at restitution: Recent legislation, programs, and research. *Judicature, 61,* 348–357.

Christensen, H. (1979, March 15). Testing trickery charged in suit. *Pittsburgh Post-Gazette,* p. 16.

Cialdini, R. B., Reno, R. R., & Kallgren, C. A. (1990). A focus theory of normative conduct: Recycling the concept of norms to reduce littering in public places. *Journal of Personality and Social Psychology, 58,* 1015–1026.

Cleary, E. W. (1984). *McCormick on evidence* (3rd ed.). St. Paul: West Publishing Company.

Coates, D., Wortman, C. B., & Abbey, A. (1979). Reactions to victims. In I. H. Frieze, D. Bar-Tal, & J. S. Carroll (Eds.), *New approaches to social problems: Applications of attribution theory* (pp. 21–52). San Francisco: Jossey-Bass.

Cohen, S., & Wills, T. A. (1985). Stress, social support, and the buffering hypothesis. *Psychological Bulletin, 98,* 310–357.

Cohn, E. S. (1978). *Fear of crime and feelings of control: Reactions to crime in an urban community.* Unpublished doctoral dissertation, Temple University.

Cohn, E. S., Kidder, L., & Harvey, J. (1978). Crime prevention vs. victimization prevention: The psychology of two different reactions. *Victimology: An International Journal, 3,* 285–296.

Collins, R. E., Dakof, G., & Taylor, S. E. (1988). *Social comparison and adjustment to a threatening event.* Unpublished manuscript. Cited in Taylor, S. E., & Lobel, M. (1989). Social comparison activity under threat: Downward evaluation and upward contacts. *Psychological Review, 96,* 569–575.

Committee for the Protection of Human Participants in Research (CPHPR). (1982). *Ethical principles in the conduct of research with human participants.* Washington, DC: American Psychological Association.

Conklin, J. E. (1975). *The impact of crime.* New York: Macmillan.

Conklin, J. E., & Bittner, E. (1973). Burglary in a suburb. *Criminology, 11,* 206–232.

Cook, T. D. (1985). Postpositivist critical multiplism. In R. L. Shotland and M. M. Mark (Eds.), *Social science and social policy* (pp. 21–62). Beverly Hills, CA: Sage.

Cook, R. F., Smith, B. E., & Harrell, A. V. (1987). *Helping crime victims: Levels of trauma and effectiveness of services.* Washington, DC: National Institute of Justice.

Craik, F. I. M., & Lockhart, R. S. (1972). Levels of processing: A framework for memory research. *Journal of Verbal Learning and Verbal Behavior, 11,* 671–684.

Crosby, F. (1976). A model of egoistical relative deprivation. *Psychological Review, 83,* 85–113.

Cross, J. F., Cross, J., & Daly, J. (1971). Sex, race, age and beauty as factors in recognition of faces. *Perception and Psychophysics, 10,* 393–396.

Crowne, D. P., & Marlowe, D. (1964). *The approval motive.* New York: Wiley.

Dalal, A. K., Singh, A. K., Sinha, A., & Sah, U. (1988). The *sati* of Deorala: An attributional study of social reactions. *Indian Journal of Social Work, 49,* 349–358.

Darley, J. M., & Latané, B. (1970). Norms and normative behavior: Field studies of social interdependence. In J. Macaulay & L. Berkowitz (Eds.), *Altruism and helping behavior: Social psychological studies of some antecendents and consequences* (pp. 83–101). New York: Academic Press.

Das, V. (1988, February 28). Strange response. *The Illustrated Weekly of India,* pp. 30–32.

Davis, R. C., & Friedman, L. N. (1985). The emotional aftermath of crime and violence. In C. R.

Figley (Ed.), *Trauma and its wake: The study and treatment of post-traumatic stress disorder* (pp. 90–112). New York: Brunner/Mazel.

Davis, R. C., & Henley, M. (1990). Victim service programs. In A. J. Lurigio, W. G. Skogan, & R. C. Davis (Eds.), *Victims of crime: Problems, policies, and programs* (pp. 157–171). Newbury, CA: Sage.

Davis, R. C., & Lurigio, A. J. (1989). *Adjusting to criminal victimization: The correlates of post-crime distress.* Manuscript submitted for publication.

Deutsch, M., & Gerard, H. B. (1955). A study of normative and informational social influences upon individual judgment. *Journal of Abnormal and Social Psychology, 51,* 629–636.

Donalson, A. (1979, March 15). Test caused trauma, woman says in suit. *Pittsburgh Press,* p. A2.

Dukes, R. L., & Mattley, C. L. (1977). Predicting rape victim reportage. *Sociology and Social Research, 62,* 63–84.

Dunkel-Schetter, C., & Bennett, T. L. (1990). Differentiating the cognitive and behavioral aspects of social support. In B. R. Sarason, I. G. Sarason, & G. R. Pierce (Eds.), *Social support: An interactional view* (pp. 267–296). New York: Wiley.

Eagly, A. H. (1983). Gender and social influence: A social psychological analysis. *American Psychologist, 38,* 971–981.

Eagly, A. H., & Carli, L. L. (1981). Sex researchers and sex-typed communications as determinants of sex differences in influenceability: A meta-analysis of social influence studies. *Psychological Bulletin, 90,* 1–20.

Eagly, A. H., Wood, W., & Fishbaugh, L. (1981). Sex differences in conformity: Surveillance by the group as determinant of male nonconformity. *Journal of Personality and Social Psychology, 40,* 384–394.

Easterbrook, J. A. (1959). The effect of emotion on cue utilization and the organization of behavior. *Psychological Review, 66,* 183–201.

Ebbesen, E. B., & Konečni, V. J. (1982). An analysis of the bail system. In V. J. Konečni & E. B. Ebbesen (Eds.), *The criminal justice system: A social-psychological analysis* (pp. 191–229). San Francisco: W. H. Freeman.

Egan, D., Pittner, M., & Goldstein, A. G. (1977). Eyewitness identification: Photographs vs. live models. *Law and Human Behavior, 1,* 199–206.

Elias, R. (1990). Which victim movement?: The politics of victim policy. In A. J. Lurigio, W. G. Skogan, & R. C. Davis (Eds.), *Victims of crime: Problems, policies, and programs* (pp. 226–250). Newbury Park, CA: Sage.

Ellis, E., Atkeson, B., & Calhoun, K. (1981). An assessment of long-term reaction to rape. *Journal of Abnormal Psychology, 90,* 263–266.

Ennis, P. H. (1967). *Criminal victimization in the United States: A report of a national survey.* Field Surveys II, President's Commission on Law Enforcement and Administration of Justice. Washington, DC: U.S. Government Printing Office.

Evans, S. E., & Scott, J. E. (1984a). Effects of item order on the perceived seriousness of crime: A reexamination. *Journal of Research in Crime and Delinquency, 21,* 139–151.

Evans, S. E., & Scott, J. E. (1984b). The seriousness of crime cross-culturally. *Criminology, 22,* 39–59.

Fazio, R. H. (1979). Motives for social comparison: The construction-validation distinction. *Journal of Personality and Social Psychology, 37,* 1683–1698.

Fazio, R. H., & Zanna, M. P. (1981). Direct experience and attitude-behavior consistency. In L. Berkowitz (Ed.), *Advances in experimental social psychology* (Vol. 14, pp. 161–202). New York: Academic Press.

Federal Rules of Evidence, 28 U.S.C. Rule 803 (1975).

Feldman-Summers, S., & Ashworth, C. D. (1981). Factors related to intentions to report a rape. *Journal of Social Issues, 37*(4), 53–70.

Feldman-Summers, S., & Lindner, K. (1976). Perceptions of victims and defendants in criminal assault cases. *Criminal Justice and Behavior, 3,* 135–149.

Ferraro, K. J. (1983). Rationalizing violence: How battered women stay. *Victimology: An International Journal, 8,* 203–212.

Festinger, L. (1954). A theory of social comparison processes. *Human Relations, 7,* 117–140.

The Figgie report on fear of crime: America afraid (Part 1). (1980). Willoughby, OH: A-T-O, Inc.

Figley, C. R. (Ed.). (1985). *Trauma and its wake: The study and treatment of post-traumatic stress disorder.* New York: Brunner/Mazel.

Fischer, C. T. (1977). *Being criminally victimized: A qualitative account.* Unpublished manuscript, Duquesne University.

Fischoff, B. (1975). Hindsight ≠ foresight: The effect of outcome knowledge on judgment under uncertainty. *Journal of Experimental Psychology: Human Perception and Performance, 1,* 288–299.

Fishbein, M., & Ajzen, I. (1975). *Belief, attitude, intention, and behavior: An introduction to theory and research.* Reading, MA: Addison-Wesley.

Fishman, G. (1979). Patterns of victimization and notification. *British Journal of Criminology, 19,* 146–157.

Fiske, S. T., & Taylor, S. E. (1984). *Social cognition.* Reading, MA: Addison-Wesley.

Fleet, M. L., Brigham, J. C., & Bothwell, R. K. (1987). The confidence-accuracy relationship: The effects of confidence assessment and choosing. *Journal of Applied Social Psychology, 17,* 171–187.

Folger, R. (1987). Reformulating the preconditions of resentment: A referent cognitions model. In J. C. Masters & W. P. Smith (Eds.), *Social comparison, social justice, and relative deprivation* (pp. 183–215). Hillsdale, NJ: Erlbaum.

Forst, B. E., & Hernon, J. C. (1985). *The criminal justice response to victim harm.* Washington, DC: National Institute of Justice.

Forsyth, D. R. (1983). *An introduction to group dynamics.* Monterey, CA: Brooks/Cole.

Friedman, L. N., & Shulman, M. (1990). Domestic violence: The criminal justice response. In A. J. Lurigio, W. G. Skogan, & R. C. Davis (Eds.), *Victims of crime: Problems, policies, and programs* (pp. 87–103). Newbury Park, CA: Sage.

Friedman, K., Bischoff, H., Davis, R., & Person, A. (1982). *Victims and helpers: Reactions to crime.* Summary of grant report for National Institute of Justice Grant No. 79-NI-AX-0059. New York: Victim Services Agency.

Frieze, I. H. (1979). Perceptions of battered wives. In I. H. Frieze, D. Bar-Tal, & J. S. Carroll (Eds.), *New approaches to social problems: Applications of attribution theory* (pp. 79–108). San Francisco: Jossey-Bass.

Frieze, I. H., Hymer, S., & Greenberg, M. S. (1987). Describing the victims of crime: Psychological reactions to victimization. *Professional Psychology: Research and Practice, 18,* 299–315.

Frodi, A. (1978). Experiential and physiological responses associated with anger and aggression. *Journal of Research in Personality, 12,* 335–349.

Goethals, G. & Darley, J. M. (1977). Social comparison theory: An attributional approach. In J. M. Suls & R. L. Miller (Eds.), *Social comparison processes: Theoretical and empirical perspectives* (pp. 259–278). Washington, DC: Hemisphere.

Gondolf, E. W., & McFerron, J. R. (1989). Handling battering men: Police action in wife abuse cases. *Criminal Justice and Behavior, 16,* 429–439.

Gottlieb, B. H. (1983). Social support as a focus for integrative research in psychology. *American Psychologist, 38,* 278–287.

Greenberg, M. S. (1980). A theory of indebtedness. In K. J. Gergen, M. S. Greenberg, & R. H. Willis (Eds.), *Social exchange: Advances in theory and research* (pp. 3–26). New York: Plenum Press.

Greenberg, M. S. (1991). *Victims of residential burglary: Coping and recovery.* Unpublished manuscript.

Greenberg, M. S., & Ruback, R. B. (1982). *Social psychology of the criminal justice system.* Monterey, CA: Brooks/Cole.

Greenberg, M. S., & Westcott, D. R. (1983). Indebtedness as a mediator of reactions to aid. In J. D. Fisher, A. Nadler, & B. M. DePaulo (Eds.), *New directions in helping: Recipient reactions to aid* (Vol. 1, pp. 85–112). New York: Academic Press.

Greenberg, M. S., Wilson, C. E., Carretta, T., & DeMay, A. (1979). Historical trends in perceived seriousness of crimes. *Replications in Social Psychology, 1,* 136–138.

Greenberg, M. S., Wilson, C. E., Ruback, R. B., & Mills, M. K. (1979). Social and emotional determinants of victim crime reporting. *Social Psychology Quarterly, 42,* 364–372.

Greenberg, M. S., Ruback, R. B., & Westcott, D. R. (1982). Decision making by crime victims: A multimethod approach. *Law and Society Review, 17,* 47–84.

Greenberg, M. S., Wilson, C. E., & Mills, M. K. (1982). Victim decision making: An experimental approach. In V. J. Konečni & E. B. Ebbesen (Eds.), *The criminal justice system: A social-psychological analysis* (pp. 73–94). San Francisco: Freeman.

Greenberg, M. S., Ruback, R. B., & Westcott, D. R. (1983). Seeking help from the police: The victim's perspective. In A. Nadler, B. M. DePaulo, & J. D. Fisher (Eds.), *New directions in helping: Applied perspectives on help seeking and receiving* (Vol. 3, pp. 71–103). New York: Academic Press.

Hall, D. F., Loftus, E. F., & Tousignant, J. P. (1984). Postevent information and changes in recollection for a natural event. In G. L. Wells & E. F. Loftus (Eds.), *Eyewitness testimony: psychological perspectives* (pp. 124–141). New York: Cambridge University Press.

Hall, D. J. (1975). Role of the victim in the prosecution and disposition of a criminal case. *Vanderbilt Law Review, 28,* 931–985.

Hammond, K., & Adelman, L. (1976). Science, values, and human judgment: Integration of facts and values requires the scientific study of human judgment. *Science, 194,* 389–396.

Hanson, L. S. C., & Thomas, C. W. (1988). Third party tort remedies for crime victims: Searching for the "deep pocket" and a risk free society. *Stetson Law Review, 18,* 1–33.

Harkness, A., DeBono, K., & Borgida, E. (1985). Personal involvement and strategies for making contingency judgments: A stake in the dating game makes a difference. *Journal of Personality and Social Psychology, 49,* 22–32.

Harris, D. M., & Guten, S. (1979). Health-protective behavior: An exploratory study. *Journal of Health and Social Behavior, 20,* 17–29.

Hawkins, R. O. (1973). Who called the cops?: Decisions to report criminal victimization. *Law and Society Review, 7,* 427–444.

Hawkins, S. A., & Hastie, R. (1990). Hindsight: Biased judgments of past events after the outcomes are known. *Psychological Bulletin, 107,* 311–327.

Heath, L. (1984). Impact of newspaper crime reports on fear of crime: Multimethodological investigation. *Journal of Personality and Social Psychology, 47,* 263–276.

Heider, F. (1958). *The psychology of interpersonal relations.* New York: Wiley.

Hembroff, L. A. (1987). The seriousness of acts and social contexts: A test of Black's theory of the behavior of law. *American Journal of Sociology, 93,* 322–347.

Higgins, E. T., & King, G. (1981). Accessibility of social constructs: Information-processing consequences of individual and contextual variability. In N. Cantor & J. F. Kihlstrom (Eds.), *Personality, cognition, and social interaction* (pp. 69–121). Hillsdale, NJ: Erlbaum.

Hindelang, M. J. (1976). *Criminal victimization in eight American cities: A descriptive analysis of common theft and assault.* Cambridge, MA: Ballinger.

Hindelang, M. J., & Davis, B. J. (1977). Forcible rape in the United States: A statistical profile. In D. Chappell, R. Geis, & G. Geis (Eds.), *Forcible rape: The crime, the victim, and the offender* (pp. 87–114). New York: Columbia University Press.

Hindelang, M. J., & Gottfredson, M. (1976). The victim's decision not to invoke the criminal justice process. In W. F. McDonald (Ed.), *Criminal justice and the victim* (pp. 57–78). Beverly Hills, CA: Sage.

Hoffman, P. B., & Hardyman, P. L. (1986). Crime seriousness scales: Public perception and feedback to criminal justice policymakers. *Journal of Criminal Justice, 14,* 413–431.

Homans, G. C. (1961). *Social behavior: Its elementary forms.* New York: Harcourt, Brace & World.

Horowitz, I. A. (1976). Effects of experimentally manipulated levels of moral development and potential helper's identifiability on volunteering to help. *Journal of Personality, 44,* 243–259.

Hosch, H. M., & Bothwell, R. K. (1990). Arousal, description and identification accuracy of victims and bystanders. *Journal of Social Behavior and Personality, 5,* 481–488.

Hosch, H. M., & Cooper, D. S. (1982). Victimization as a determinant of eyewitness accuracy. *Journal of Applied Psychology, 67,* 649–652.

Hsu, M. (1973). Cultural and sexual differences on the judgment of criminal offenses: A replication study of measurement of delinquency. *Journal of Criminal Law and Criminology, 64,* 348–353.

Janis, I. L., & Mann, L. (1977). *Decision making: A psychological analysis of conflict, choice, and commitment.* New York: Free Press.

Janoff-Bulman, R. (1979). Characterological versus behavioral self-blame: Inquiries into depression and rape. *Journal of Personality and Social Psychology, 37,* 1798–1809.

Janoff-Bulman, R. (1982). Esteem and control bases of blame: "Adaptive" strategies for victims versus observers. *Journal of Personality, 50,* 180–192.

Janoff-Bulman, R. (1985). The aftermath of victimization: Rebuilding shattered assumptions. In C. R. Figley (Ed.), *Trauma and its wake: The study and treatment of posttraumatic stress disorder* (pp. 15–35). New York: Brunner/Mazel.

Janoff-Bulman, R. (1989). The benefits of illusions, the threat of disillusionment, and the limitations of accuracy. *Journal of Social and Clinical Psychology, 8,* 158–175.

Janoff-Bulman, R., & Frieze, I. H. (1983). A theoretical perspective for understanding reactions to victimization. *Journal of Social Issues, 39*(2), 1–17.

Johnson, C., & Scott, B. (1976, September). *Eyewitness testimony and suspect identification as a function of arousal, sex of witness, and scheduling of interrogation.* Paper presented at the meeting of the American Psychological Association, Washington, DC.

Johnson, J. T. (1986). The knowledge of what might have been: Affective and attributional consequences of near outcomes. *Personality and Social Psychology Bulletin, 12,* 51–62.

Joseph, A. A. (1977). Victims of household property crimes in Ilorin, Kwara State. Unpublished bachelor dissertation, Ahmadu Bello University.

Kahneman, D., & Miller, D. (1986). Norm theory: Comparing reality to its alternatives. *Psychological Review, 93,* 136–153.

Kahneman, D., & Tversky, A. (1982). Availability and the simulation heuristic. In D. Kahneman, P. Slovic, & A. Tversky (Eds.), *Judgment under uncertainty: Heuristics and biases* (pp. 201–208). New York: Oxford University Press.

Kalven, H., Jr., & Zeisel, H. (1966). *The American jury.* Boston: Little, Brown.

Karlins, M., Coffman, T. L., & Walters, G. W. (1969). On the fading of social stereotypes: Studies in three generations of college students. *Journal of Personality and Social Psychology, 13,* 1–16.

Kassin, S. M. (1984). Eyewitness identification: Victims versus bystanders. *Journal of Applied Social Psychology, 14,* 519–529.

Kassin, S. M., Ellsworth, P. C., & Smith, V. L. (1989). The "general acceptance" of psychological resarch on eyewitness testimony. *American Psychologist, 44,* 1089–1098.

Keeton, W. P., Dobbs, D. B., Keeton, R. E., & Owen, D. G. (1984). *Prosser and Keeton on torts* (5th ed.). St. Paul: West.

Keinan, G. (1987). Decision making under stress: Scanning of alternatives under controllable and uncontrollable threats. *Journal of Personality and Social Psychology, 52,* 639–644.

Kelley, H. H. (1967). Attribution theory in social psychology. In D. Levine (Ed.), *Nebraska Symposium on Motivation* (Vol. 15, pp. 192–238). Lincoln: University of Nebraska Press.

Kelly, D. (1990). Victim participation in the criminal justice system. In A. J. Lurigio, W. G. Skogan, & R. C. Davis (Eds.), *Victims of crime: Problems, policies, and programs* (pp. 172–187). Newbury Park, CA: Sage.

Kidder, L. H., & Fine, M. (1987). Qualitative and quantitative methods: When stories converge.

In M. M. Mark & R. L. Shotland (Eds.), *Multiple methods in program evaluation* (pp. 57–75). San Francisco: Jossey-Bass.

Kilpatrick, D. G., Best, C. L., Veronen, L. J., Amick, A. E., Villeponteaux, L. A., & Ruff, G. A. (1985). Mental health correlates of criminal victimization: A random community survey. *Journal of Consulting and Clinical Psychology, 53,* 866–873.

Kirk, R. E. (1968). *Experimental design: Procedures for the behavioral sciences.* Belmont, CA: Brooks/Cole.

Klecka, W. R. (1980). *Discriminant analysis.* Beverly Hills, CA: Sage.

Knudten, R. D., Meade, A., Knudten, M., & Doerner, W. (1976). The victim in the administration of criminal justice: Problems and perceptions. In W. F. McDonald (Ed.), *Criminal justice and the victim* (pp. 115–146). Beverly Hills, CA: Sage.

Koss, M. P., Dinerio, T. E., & Seibel, C. A. (1988). Stranger and acquaintance rape: Are there differences in the victim's experience? *Psychology of Women Quarterly, 12,* 1–12.

Krupnick, J. (1980). Brief psychotherapy with victims of violent crime. *Victimology: An International Journal, 5,* 347–354.

Kuehn, L. L. (1974). Looking down a gun barrel: Person perception and violent crime. *Perceptual and Motor Skills, 39,* 1159–1164.

Kunreuther, H. (1978). *Disaster insurance protection: Public policy lessons.* New York: Wiley.

Kurian, G. T. (1984). *The new book of world rankings.* New York: Facts on File.

LaFree, G. D. (1989). *Rape and criminal justice: The social construction of sexual assault.* Belmont, CA: Wadsworth.

Latané, B., & Darley, J. M. (1970). *The unresponsive bystander: Why doesn't he help?* New York: Appleton-Century-Crofts.

Latané, B., & Nida, S. A. (1981). Ten years of research on group size and helping. *Psychological Bulletin, 89,* 308–324.

Lavrakas, P. J. (1981). On households. In D. A. Lewis (Ed.), *Reactions to crime* (pp. 67–85). Beverly Hills, CA: Sage.

Law Enforcement Assistance Administration (1977a). *Criminal victimization in the United States: A comparison of 1975 and 1976 findings.* Washington, DC: Department of Justice.

Law Enforcement Assistance Administration (1977b). *Forcible rape: A national survey of the response by police* (Vol. 1). Washington, DC: U.S. Government Printing Office.

Law Enforcement Assistance Administration (1977c). *Forcible rape: A national survey of the response by prosecutors* (Vol. 1). Washington, DC: U.S. Government Printing Office.

Law Enforcement Assistance Administration (1982). *Criminal victimization in the United States, 1980.* Washington, DC: U.S. Government Printing Office.

Lazarus, R. S., & Folkman, S. (1984). *Stress, appraisal and coping.* New York: Springer.

Lehman, D. R., Ellard, J. H., & Wortman, C. B. (1986). Social support for the bereaved: Recipients' and providers' perspectives on what is helpful. *Journal of Consulting and Clinical Psychology, 54,* 438–446.

Leippe, M. R., Wells, G. L., & Ostrom, T. M. (1978). Crime seriousness as a determinant of accuracy in eyewitness identification. *Journal of Applied Psychology, 63,* 345–351.

LeJeune, R., & Alex, N. (1973). On being mugged: The event and its aftermath. *Urban Life and Culture, 2,* 259–287.

Lerner, M. J., Miller, D. T., & Holmes, J. G. (1976). Deserving and the emergence of forms of justice. In L. Berkowitz (Ed.), *Advances in experimental social psychology* (Vol. 9, pp. 133–162). New York: Academic Press.

Leymann, H., & Lindell, J. (1990). Social support after armed robbery in the workplace. In E. C. Viano (Ed.), *The victimology handbook: Research findings, treatment, and public policy* (pp. 285–304). New York: Garland.

Linster, R. (1987). *Modeling recidivism: NIJ discussion paper.* Washington, DC: National Institute of Justice.

Liska, A. E., & Baccaglini, W. (1990). Feeling safe by comparison: Crime in the newspapers. *Social Problems, 37,* 360–374.

Lloyd-Bostock, S. M., & Clifford, B. R. (1983). *Evaluating witness evidence: Recent psychological research and new perspectives.* Chichester, NY: Wiley.

Loftus, E. F. (1976). Unconscious transference in eyewitness identification. *Law and Psychology Review, 2,* 93–98.

Loftus, E. F. (1979). *Eyewitness testimony.* Cambridge: Harvard University Press.

Lurigio, A. J. (1987). Are victims all alike? The adverse, generalized, and differential impact of crime. *Crime and Delinquency, 33,* 452–467.

Maguire, M. (1980). The impact of burglary upon victims. *British Journal of Criminology, 20,* 261–275.

Maguire, M. (1982). *Burglary in a dwelling.* London: Heinemann.

Maguire, M., & Corbett, C. (1987). *The effects of crime and the work of victims support schemes.* Aldershot: Gower.

Major, B., Testa, M., & Bylsma, W. H. (1991). Responses to upward and downward social comparisons: The impact of esteem-relevance and perceived control. In J. Suls & T. A. Wills (Eds.), *Social comparison: Contemporary theory and research* (pp. 237–260). Hillsdale, NJ: Erlbaum.

Malpass, R. S., & Devine, P. G. (1980). Realism and eyewitness identification research. *Law and Human Behavior, 4,* 347–358.

Malpass, R. S., & Devine, P. G. (1981). Guided memory in eyewitness identification. *Journal of Applied Psychology, 66,* 343–350.

Manzanera, L. R. (1984). Victimization in a Mexican city. In R. Block (Ed.), *Victimization and fear of crime: World perspectives* (pp. 51–56). Washington, DC: U.S. Government Printing Office.

Mark, M. M., & Shotland, R. L. (1985). Toward more useful social science. In R. L. Shotland & M. M. Mark (Eds.), *Social science and social policy* (pp. 335–370). Beverly Hills, CA: Sage.

Mark, M. M., & Shotland, R. L. (Eds.). (1987). *Multiple methods in program evaluation.* San Francisco: Jossey-Bass.

Markus, H. (1977). Self-schemata and processing information about the self. *Journal of Personality and Social Psychology, 35,* 63–78.

Marsh, D., & Greenberg, M. S. (1991). *Attitudes toward victim resistance during a robbery attempt.* Unpublished manuscript, University of Pittsburgh.

Martin, L. L., & Tesser, A. (1989). Toward a motivational and structural theory of ruminative thought. In J. S. Uleman & J. A. Bargh (Eds.), *Unintended thought* (pp. 306–326). New York: Guilford Press.

Mayhew, P. (1985). The effects of crime: Victims, the public and fear. In *Research on Victimisation: Reports presented to the Sixteenth Criminological Research Conference (1984)* (Vol. 23, pp. 67–103). Strasbourg: Council of Europe.

McCleod, M. (1983). Victim noncooperation in the prosecution of domestic assault. *Criminology, 21,* 395–416.

McMullen, P. A., & Gross, A. E. (1983). Sex differences, sex roles, and health-related help-seeking. In B. M. DePaulo, A. Nadler, & J. D. Fisher (Eds.), *New directions in helping: Vol. 2. Help seeking* (pp. 233–263). New York: Academic Press.

Medea, A., & Thompson, K. (1974). *Against rape.* New York: Farrar, Straus & Giroux.

Mendelsohn, B. (1963). The origin of the doctrine of victimology. *Excerpta Criminologica, 3,* 239–244.

Miethe, T. D. (1984). Types of consensus in public evaluations of crime: An illustration of strategies for measuring "consensus." *Journal of Criminal Law and Criminology, 75,* 459–473.

Miller, D. T., & McFarland, C. (1986). Counterfactual thinking and victims compensation: A test of norm theory. *Personality and Social Psychology Bulletin, 12,* 513–519.

Miller, D. T., & Porter, C. A. (1983). Self-blame in victims of violence. *Journal of Social Issues, 39*(2), 139–152.

Miller, D. T., Turnbull, W., & McFarland, C. (1990). Counterfactual thinking and social perception: Thinking about what might have been. In M. P. Zanna (Ed.), *Advances in experimental social psychology* (Vol. 23, pp. 305–331). New York: Academic Press.

Mintz, P. M., & Mills, J. (1971). Effects of arousal and information about its source upon attitude change. *Journal of Experimental Social Psychology, 7*, 561–570.

Miransky, J., & Langer, E. J. (1978). Burglary (non)prevention: An instance of relinquishing control. *Personality and Social Psychology Bulletin, 4*, 399–405.

Moore, M. H., & Trojanowicz, R. C. (1988). *Policing and the fear of crime.* Washington, DC: National Institute of Justice.

Moriarty, T. (1975). Crime, commitment, and the responsive bystander: Two field experiments. *Journal of Personality and Social Psychology, 31*, 370–376.

Murray, D. M., & Wells, G. L. (1982). Does knowledge that a crime was staged affect eyewitness accuracy? *Journal of Applied Social Psychology, 12*, 42–53.

Murray, T. H. (1982). Ethics, power and applied social psychology. In L. Bickman (Ed.), *Applied social psychology annual* (Vol. 3, pp. 75–95). Beverly Hills, CA: Sage.

Nadler, A., & Fisher, J. D. (1986). The role of threat to self-esteem and perceived control in recipient reactions to help: Theory development and empirical validation. In L. Berkowitz (Ed.), *Advances in experimental social psychology* (Vol. 19, pp. 81–122). New York: Academic Press.

National Organization for Victim Assistance (NOVA). (1985). *Victim rights and services: A legislative directory.* Washington, DC: U.S. Department of Justice.

National Organization for Victim Assistance (NOVA). (1990). *Victim rights and services: A legislative directory 1988/1989.* Washington, DC: U.S. Department of Justice.

Newman, G. R. (1976). *Comparative deviance: Perception and law in six cultures.* New York: Elsevier.

Nisbett, R. E., & Ross, L. (1980). *Human inference: Strategies and shortcomings of social judgment.* Englewood Cliffs, NJ: Prentice-Hall.

Nisbett, R. E., & Wilson, T. D. (1977). Telling more than we know: Verbal reports on mental processes. *Psychological Review, 84*, 231–259.

Novaco, R. W. (1975). *Anger control.* Lexington, MA: D. C. Heath.

Nuttin, J. R. (1984). *Motivation, planning, and action: A relational theory of behavioral dynamics.* Hillsdale, NJ: Erlbaum.

Odenkunle, F. (1979). Victims of property crime in Nigeria: A preliminary investigation in Zaria. *Victimology: An International Journal, 4*, 236–246.

Office of Justice Programs. (1986). *Four years later: A report on The President's Task Force on Victims of Crime.* Washington, DC: U.S. Department of Justice.

Olowu, E. U. (1978). *The victims of crime and the police: A case study of Ugbokolo-Edumoga, Benue State.* Unpublished bachelor dissertation. Ahmadu Bello University.

Omer, M., Leanard, A., & Taylor, P. (1985). Personal relationships: Help and hindrance. In N. Johnson (Ed.), *Sociological Review Monograph (Marital Violence)* (Vol. 31, pp. 93–108). Boston: Routledge & Kegan Paul.

Oros, C. J., Leonard, K., & Koss, M. D. (1980, August). *Factors related to self-attribution of rape by victims.* Paper presented at the meeting of the American Psychological Association, Montreal, Canada.

Ozer, E., & Bandura, A. (1990). Mechanisms governing empowerment effects: A self-efficacy analysis. *Journal of Personality and Social Psychology, 58*, 472–486.

Patton, C. (1979, March 21). "I felt like a fool," woman who took the test says. *Pittsburgh Post-Gazette,* p. 6.

Pennebaker, J. W. (1989). Confession, inhibition, and disease. In L. Berkowitz (Ed.), *Advances in experimental social psychology* (Vol. 22, pp. 211–244). New York: Academic Press.

Pennsylvania Rules of Civil Procedure, 42 *Pennsylvania Consolidated Statutes Annotated* Rule 212 (1975).

Perloff, L. S. (1982). *Nonvictims' judgments of unique and universal vulnerability to future misfortune.* Unpublished doctoral dissertation, Northwestern University.

Perloff, L. S. (1983). Perceptions of vulnerability to victimization. *Journal of Social Issues, 39*(2), 41–61.

Perloff, L. S. (1987). Social comparison and illusions of invulnerability to negative life events. In C. R. Snyder & C. E. Ford (Eds.), *Coping with negative life events: Clinical and social psychological perspectives* (pp. 217–242). New York: Plenum Press.

Pierce, H. (1979a, March 21). Is lying justified in psychological research? *Pittsburgh Post-Gazette,* pp. 1, 6.

Pierce, H. (1979b, March 24). The whole truth, nothing but the truth. *Pittsburgh Post-Gazette,* p. 15.

Pigott, M., & Brigham, J. C. (1985). Relationship between accuracy of prior description and facial recognition. *Journal of Applied Psychology, 70,* 547–555.

Platz, S. J., & Hosch, H. M. (1988). Cross-racial/ethnic eyewitness identification: A field study. *Journal of Applied Social Psychology, 18,* 972–984.

Pointing, J., & Maguire, M. (1988). Introduction: The rediscovery of the crime victim. In M. Maguire & J. Pointing (Eds.), *Victims of crime: A new deal?* (pp. 1–13). Milton Keynes: Open University Press.

President's Commission on Law Enforcement and Administration of Justice. (1967). *The challenge of crime in a free society.* Washington, DC: U.S. Government Printing Office.

Q & A on the news. (1992, February 20). *The Atlanta Constitution,* p. A2.

Quinney, R. (1970). *The social reality of crime.* Boston: Little, Brown.

Rapoport, L. (1965). The state of crisis: Some theoretical considerations. In H. J. Parad (Ed.), *Crisis intervention: Selected readings* (pp. 22–31). New York: Family Service.

Rause, V. (1981, July). Burglary. *Pittsburgh Magazine,* pp. 26–31.

Reichardt, C. S., & Gollob, H. F. (1987). Taking uncertainty into account when estimating effects. In M. M. Mark & R. L. Shotland (Eds.), *Multiple methods in program evaluation* (pp. 7–22). San Francisco: Jossey-Bass.

Rengert, G., & Wasilchick, J. (1985). *Suburban burglary: A time and a place for everything.* Springfield, IL: Thomas.

Reppetto, T. A. (1974). *Residential crime.* Cambridge, MA: Ballinger.

"Research is called to court." (1979, March 27). *Pittsburgh Post-Gazette,* p. 4.

Resick, P. A. (1990). Victims of sexual assault. In A. J. Lurigio, W. G. Skogan, & R. C. Davis (Eds.), *Victims of crime: Problems, policies, and programs* (pp. 69–86). Newbury Park, CA: Sage.

Riggs, D. S., & Kilpatrick, D. G. (1990). Families and friends: Indirect victimization by crime. In A. J. Lurigio, W. G. Skogan, & R. C. Davis (Eds.), *Victims of crime: Problems, policies, and programs* (pp. 120–138). Newbury Park, CA: Sage.

Robertson, L. S. (1975). Factors associated with safety belts use in 1974 starter-interlock equipped cars. *Journal of Health and Social Behavior, 16,* 173–177.

Ross, M., & McFarland, C. (1988). Constructing the past: Biases in personal memories. In D. Bar-Tal & A. W. Kruglanski (Eds.), *The social psychology of knowledge* (pp. 299–314). New York: Cambridge University Press.

Rossi, P. H., Waite, E., Bose, C. E., & Berk, R. E. (1974). The seriousness of crimes: Normative structure and individual differences. *American Sociological Review, 39,* 224–237.

Rothstein, P. F. (1981). *Evidence: State and federal rules.* St. Paul: West.

Rottenberg, D. (1980, March 16). Crime victims fighting back. *Parade,* pp. 21, 23.

Ruback, R. B., & Greenberg, M. S. (1985). Crime victims as witnesses: Their accuracy and credibility. *Victimology: An International Journal, 10,* 410–424.

Ruback, R. B., & Greenberg, M. S. (1986). Legal and ethical aspects of applied social psychological research in field settings. In M. J. Saks & L. Saxe (Eds.), *Advances in applied social psychology* (Vol. 3, pp. 207–229). Hillsdale, NJ: Erlbaum.

Ruback, R. B., & Innes, C. A. (1988). The relevance and irrelevance of psychological research: The example of prison crowding. *American Psychologist, 43,* 683–693.

Ruback, R. B., & Ivie, D. L. (1987a, March). *Post-reporting social influence on victims.* Paper presented at the annual meeting of the Academy of Criminal Justice Sciences, St. Louis.

Ruback, R. B., & Ivie, D. L. (1987b). Prior relationship, resistance, and injury in rapes: An analysis of crisis center records. *Violence and Victims, 3,* 99–111.

Ruback, R. B., & Ivie, D. L. (in press). Social influence and the reporting of rape: Analysis of crisis center records. *Victimology: An International Journal.*

Ruback, R. B., Lutz, J. R., & Smith, J. D. (1983, July). *Report to the Atlanta Council on Battered Women: Summary of calls received from January–April 1983.* Georgia State Universiy, Atlanta, Georgia.

Ruback, R. B., Greenberg, M. S., & Westcott, D. R. (1981). An archival analysis of victim reporting. *Victimology: An International Journal, 6,* 318–327.

Ruback, R. B., Greenberg, M. S., & Westcott, D. R. (1984). Social influence and crime victim decision making. *Journal of Social Issues, 40*(1), 51–76.

Ruback, R. B., Gupta, D., & Kohli, N. (in press). Normative standards for crime victims: Implications for research and policy. In R. C. Tripathi (Ed.), *Psychology and social policy.* New Delhi: Sage.

Ryan, W. (1971). *Blaming the victim.* New York: Vintage Books.

Sales, B. D., Rich, R. F., & Reich, J. (1987). Victimization policy research. *Professional Psychology: Research and Practice, 18,* 326–337.

Sales, E., Baum, M., & Shore, B. (1984). Victim readjustment following assault. *Journal of Social Issues, 40*(1), 117–136.

Sanders, G. S., & Warnick, D. H. (1981). Truth and consequences: The effect of responsibility on eyewitness behavior. *Basic and Applied Social Psychology, 2,* 67–79.

San Jose methods test of known crime victims. (1972). Statistics technical report #1. Washington, DC: Law Enforcement Assistance Administration.

Sarason, B. R., Sarason, I. G., & Pierce, G. R. (Eds.) (1990). *Social support: An interactional view.* New York: Wiley.

Sarnoff, I. R., & Zimbardo, P. G. (1961). Anxiety, fear, and social affiliation. *Journal of Abnormal and Social Psychology, 62,* 356–363.

Schachter, S. (1959). *The psychology of affiliation.* Palo Alto, CA: Stanford University Press.

Schachter, S. (1964). The interaction of cognitive and physiological determinants of emotional state. In L. Berkowitz (Ed.), *Advances in experimental social psychology* (Vol. 1, pp. 49–80). New York: Academic Press.

Schachter, S., & Singer, J. (1962). Cognitive, social, and physiological determinants of emotional state. *Psychological Review, 69,* 379–399.

Schank, R. C., & Abelson, R. P. (1977). *Scripts, plans, goals, and understanding.* Hillsdale, NJ: Erlbaum.

Scheppele, K. L., & Bart, P. B. (1983). Through women's eyes: Defining danger in the wake of sexual assault. *Journal of Social Issues, 39*(2), 63–80.

Schneider, A. L., Burcart, J. M., & Wilson, L. A., II. (1976). The role of attitudes in the decision to report crimes to the police. In W. F. McDonald (Ed.), *Criminal justice and the victim* (pp. 89–113). Beverly Hills, CA: Sage.

Schwartz, L., Jennings, K., Petrillo, J., & Kidd, R. F. (1980). Role of commitments in the decision to stop a theft. *Journal of Social Psychology, 110,* 183–192.

Schwind, H. D. (1984). Investigations of nonreported offenses: Distribution of criminal offenses not known to authorities. In R. Block (Ed.), *Victimization and fear of crime: World perspectives* (pp. 65–74). Washington, DC: U.S. Government Printing Office.

Seligman, M. E. P. (1975). *Helplessness.* San Francisco: Freeman.

Sessar, K., & Kerner, H. J. (Eds.). (1991). *Developments in crime and crime control research: German studies on victims, offenders, and the public.* New York: Springer-Verlag.

Shaver, P., Schwartz, J., Kirson, D., & O'Connor, C. (1987). Emotion knowledge: Further exploration of a prototype approach. *Journal of Personality and Social Psychology, 52,* 1061–1086.

Shepard, R. N. (1967). Recognition memory for words, sentences and pictures. *Journal of Verbal Learning and Verbal Behavior, 6,* 156–173.

Sherif, M. A. (1935). A study of some social factors in perception. *Archives of Psychology, 27*(187), 1–60.

Sherman, L. W., & Berk, R. A. (1984). The specific deterrent effects of arrest for domestic assaults. *American Sociological Review, 50,* 261–272.

Shiffrin, R. M., & Schneider, W. (1977). Controlled and automatic human information processing: II. Perceptual learning, automatic attending, and a general theory. *Psychological Review, 84,* 127–190.

Shontz, F. C. (1975). *The psychological aspects of physical illness and disability.* New York: Macmillan.

Shotland, R. L., & Goodstein, L. (1983). Just because she doesn't want to doesn't mean it's rape: An experimentally based causal model of the perception of rape in a dating situation. *Social Psychology Quarterly, 46,* 220–232.

Shotland, R. L., & Goodstein, L. I. (1984). The role of bystanders in crime control. *Journal of Social Issues, 40*(1), 9–26.

Shotland, R. L., & Mark, M. M. (1987). Improving inferences from multiple methods. In M. M. Mark & R. L. Shotland (Eds.), *Multiple methods in program evaluation* (pp. 77–94). San Franciso: Jossey-Bass.

Shotland, R. L., Hayward, S. C., Young, C., Signorella, M. L., Mindingall, K., Kennedy, J. K., Rovine, M. J., & Danowitz, E. F. (1979). Fear of crime in residential communities. *Criminology, 17,* 34–45.

Shumaker, S. A., & Brownell, A. (1984). Toward a theory of social support: Closing conceptual gaps. *Journal of Social Issues, 40*(4), 11–36.

Silver, R. L., & Wortman, C. B. (1980). Coping with undesirable life events. In J. Garber & M. E. P. Seligman (Eds.), *Human helplessness: Theory and applications* (pp. 279–340). New York: Academic Press.

Silver, R. C., Wortman, C. B., & Crofton, C. (1990). The role of coping in support provision: The self-presentational dilemma of victims of life crises. In B. R. Sarason, I. G. Sarason, & G. R. Pierce (Eds.), *Social support: An interactional view* (pp. 397–426). New York: Wiley.

Simon, H. A. (1976). *Administrative behavior: A study of decision-making processes in administrative organization* (3rd. ed.). New York: Free Press.

Singer, S. I. (1981). Homogeneous victim-offender populations: A review and some research implications. In *Victims of crime: A review of research issues and methods* (pp. 75–86). Washington, DC: National Institute of Justice.

Singer, S. I. (1986). Victims of serious violence and their criminal behavior: Subcultural theory and beyond. *Victims and Violence, 1,* 61–70.

Sinha, D. (1988). The family scenario in a developing country and its implications for mental health: The case of India. In P. R. Darsen, J. W. Berry, & N. Sartorious (Eds.), *Health and cross-cultural psychology: Towards applications* (pp. 48–70). Newbury Park, CA: Sage.

Skelton, C. A., & Burkhart, B. R. (1980). Sexual assault: Determinants of victim disclosure. *Criminal Justice and Behavior, 7,* 229–236.

Skogan, W. G. (1984). Reporting crimes to the police: The status of world research. *Journal of Research in Crime and Delinquency, 21,* 113–137.

Skogan, W. G., & Maxfield, M. G. (1981). *Coping with crime: Individual and neighborhood reactions.* Beverly Hills, CA: Sage.

Slovic, P., Kunreuther, H., & White, G. F. (1974). Decision processes, rationality, and adjustment to natural hazards. In G. F. White (Ed.), *Natural hazards: Local, national, global* (pp. 187–205). New York: Oxford.

Smale, G. J. A. (1984). Psychological effects and behavioral changes in the case of victims of serious crimes. In R. Block (Ed.), *Victimization and fear of crime: World perspectives* (pp. 87–92). Washington, DC: U.S. Government Printing Office.

Smith, A. E., & Maness, D., Jr. (1976). The decision to call the police: Reactions to burglary. In W. F. McDonald (Ed.), *Criminal justice and the victim* (pp. 79–87). Beverly Hills, CA: Sage.

Sommers, S., & Kosmitzki, C. (1988). Emotion and social context: An American-German comparison. Special issue: The social context of emotion. *British Journal of Social Psychology, 27,* 35–49.

Sparks, R. F., Genn, H. G., & Dodd, D. J. (1977). *Surveying victims: Measurement of criminal victimization, perceptions of crime, and attitudes to criminal justice.* London: Wiley.

Spelman, W., & Brown, D. K. (1981). *Calling the police: Citizen reporting of serious crime.* Washington, DC: Police Executive Research Forum.

Stinson, T. (1992, February 4). Tyson's accuser's mood shifted, friends say. *The Atlanta Constitution,* pp. E1, E5.

Straus, M. A., & Winkelmann, D. (1969). Social class, fertility, and authority in nuclear and joint households in Bombay. *Journal of Asian and African Studies, 4,* 61–74.

Suls, J. M., & Miller, R. L. (Eds.). (1977). *Social comparison processes: Theoretical and empirical perspectives.* Washington, DC: Hemisphere.

Suls, J., & Wills, T. A. (1991). *Social comparison: Contemporary theory and research.* Hillsdale, NJ: Erlbaum.

Symonds, M. (1980, Special Issue). The "second injury" to victims. *Evaluation and Change,* 36–38.

Taylor, S. E. (1983). Adjustment to threatening events: A theory of cognitive adaptation. *American Psychologist, 38,* 1161–1173.

Taylor, S. E., & Brown, J. D. (1988). Illusion and well-being: A social psychological perspective on mental health. *Psychological Bulletin, 103,* 193–210.

Taylor, S. E., & Lobel M. (1989). Social comparison activity under threat: Downward evaluation and upward contacts. *Psychological Review, 96,* 569–575.

Taylor, S. E., & Schneider, S. K. (1989). Coping and the simulation of events. Special issue: Stress, coping, and social cognition. *Social Cognition, 7,* 174–194.

Taylor, S. E., Wood, J. V., & Lichtman, R. R. (1983). It could be worse: Selective evaluation as a response to victimization. *Journal of Social Issues, 39*(2), 19–40.

Taylor, S. E., Buunk, B. P., & Aspinwall, L. G. (1990). Social comparison, stress, and coping. Special issue: Illustrating the value of basic research. *Personality and Social Psychology Bulletin, 16,* 74–89.

Tesser, A. (1988). Toward a self-evaulation maintenance model of social behavior. In L. Berkowitz (Ed.), *Advances in experimental social psychology* (Vol. 21, pp. 181–227). New York: Academic Press.

Tesser, A. (1991). Emotion in social comparison and reflection processes. In J. Suls & T. A. Wills (Eds.), *Social comparison: Contemporary theory and research* (pp. 115–145). Hillsdale, NJ: Erlbaum.

Tetlock, P. (1983). Accountability and complexity of thought. *Journal of Personality and Social Psychology, 45,* 74–83.

Thornton, B., Ryckman, R. M., Kirchner, G., Jacobs, J., Kaczor, D., & Keuchnel, R. H. (1988). Reactions to self-attributed victim responsibility: A comparative analysis of rape crisis counselors and lay observers. *Journal of Applied Social Psychology, 18,* 409–422.

Travis, L. F., Cullen, F. I., Link, B. G., & Wozniak, J. F. (1986). The impact of instructions on seriousness ratings. *Journal of Criminal Justice, 14,* 433–440.

Triandis, H. C. (1989). The self and social behavior in differing cultural contexts. *Psychological Review, 96,* 506–520.

Tyler, T. R. (1980). Impact of directly and indirectly experienced events: The origin of crime-related judgments and behaviors. *Journal of Personality and Social Psychology, 39,* 13–28.

Van Dijk, J. J. M. (1988). Ideological trends within the victims movement: An international perspective. In M. Maguire & J. Pointing (Eds.), *Victims of crime: A new deal?* (pp. 115–126). Milton Keynes: Open University Press.

Van Dijk, J. J. M., & Steinmetz, C. H. D. (1979). *The RDC Victim Surveys 1974–1979.* The Hague: Research and Documentation Centre, Ministry of Justice.

Van Kirk, M. (1978). *Response time analysis: Executive summary.* Washington, DC: Law Enforcement Assistance Administration.

Velez-Diaz, A., & Megargee, E. I. (1970). An investigation of differences in value judgements between youthful offenders and nonoffenders in Puerto Rico. *Journal of Criminal Law, Criminology and Police Science, 61,* 549–553.

Veroff, J., Douvan, E., & Kulka, R. A. (1981). *The inner American: A self-portrait from 1957–1976.* New York: Basic Books.

Walker, L. E. (1989). When the battered woman becomes the defendant. In E. C. Viano (Ed.), *Crime and its victims: International research and public policy issues* (pp. 57–69). New York: Hemisphere.

Walker-Smith, G. J. (1978). The effects of delay and exposure duration in a face recognition task. *Perception and Psychophysics, 24,* 63–70.

Waller, I., & Okihiro, N. (1978). *Burglary—The victim and the public.* Toronto: University of Toronto Press.

Waller, W. W., & Hill, R. (1951). *The family, a dynamic interpretation.* New York: Dryden Press.

Walster, E., Berscheid, E., & Walster, G. W. (1973). New directions in equity research. *Journal of Personality and Social Psychology, 25,* 151–176.

Walster, E., Walster, G. W., & Berscheid, E. (1978). *Equity: Theory and research.* Boston: Allyn & Bacon.

Warr, M. (1989). What is the perceived seriousness of crimes? *Criminology, 27,* 795–821.

Webb, E. J., Campbell, D. T., Schwartz, R. D., Sechrest, L. & Grove, J. B. (1981). *Nonreactive measures in the social sciences.* Boston: Houghton Mifflin.

Webb, V. J., & Marshall, I. H. (1989). Response to criminal victimization by older Americans. *Criminal Justice and Behavior, 16,* 239–259.

Weiner, B., Russell, D., & Lerman, D. (1978). Affective consequences of causal ascriptions. In J. H. Harvey, W. J. Ickes, & R. F. Kidd (Eds.), *New directions in attribution research* (Vol. 2, pp. 59–90). Hillsdale, NJ: Erlbaum.

Weinstein, N. D. (1989). Effects of personal experience on self-protective behavior. *Psychological Bulletin, 105,* 31–50.

Wells, G. L. (1978). Applied eyewitness-testimony research: System variables and estimator variables. *Journal of Personality and Social Psychology, 36,* 1546–1557.

Wells, G. L., & Murray, D. M. (1983). What can psychology say about the *Neil v. Biggers* criteria for judging eyewitness accuracy? *Journal of Applied Psychology, 68,* 347–362.

Wells, G. L, Lindsay, C. L., & Ferguson, T. J. (1979). Accuracy, confidence, and juror perceptions in eyewitness identification. *Journal of Applied Psychology, 64,* 440–448.

Wells, G. L., Ferguson, T. J., & Lindsay, R. C. L. (1981). The tractability of eyewitness confidence and its implications for triers of fact. *Journal of Applied Psychology, 66,* 688–696.

Wikstrom, P. H. (1991). *Urban crime, criminals, and victims: The Swedish experience in an Anglo-American Comparative Perspective.* New York: Springer-Verlag.

Williams, L. S. (1984). The classic rape: When do victims report? *Social Problems, 31,* 459–467.

Williams, M. (1991, December 5). Smith's accuser testifies, says she feared for her life. *The Atlanta Constitution,* pp. A1, A24.

Wills, T. A. (1981). Downward comparison principles in social psychology. *Psychological Bulletin, 90,* 245–271.

Wills, T. A. (1987). Downward comparison as a coping mechanism. In C. R. Snyder & C. E. Ford (Eds.), *Coping with negative life events: Clinical and social psychological perspectives* (pp. 243–268). New York: Plenum Press.

Wills, T. A. (1991). Social support and interpersonal relationships. In M. S. Clark (Ed.), *Prosocial behavior* (pp. 265–289). Newbury Park, CA: Sage.

Wilson, C. E., & Greenberg, M. S. (1976, September). *Victim reactions to a crime: A laboratory-experimental approach.* Paper presented at the meeting of the American Psychological Association, Washington, DC.

Wolfgang, M. E. (1958). *Patterns in criminal homicide.* Philadelphia: University of Philadelphia Press.

Wolfgang, M. E., & Ferracuti, F. (1967). *The subculture of violence.* London: Tavistock.

Wolfgang, M. E., Figlio, R. M., Tracy, P. E., & Singer, S. I. (1985). *The national survey of crime severity.* Washington, DC: Bureau of Justice Statistics.

Wood, J. V. (1989). Theory and research concerning social comparisons of personal attributes. *Psychological Bulletin, 106,* 231–248.

Wood, J. V., Taylor, S. E., & Lichtman, R. R. (1985). Social comparison in adjustment to breast cancer. *Journal of Personality and Social Psychology, 49,* 1169–1183.

Wortman, C. B., & Dunkel-Schetter, C. (1979). Interpersonal relationships and cancer: A theoretical analysis. *Journal of Social Issues, 35*(1), 120–155.

Wortman, C. B., & Dunkel-Schetter, C. (1987). Conceptual and methodological issues in the study of social support. In A. Baum & J. E. Singer (Eds.), *Handbook of psychology and health: Vol. 5. Stress* (pp. 63–108). Hillsdale, NJ: Erlbaum.

Wright, P., & Weitz, B. (1977). Time horizon effects on product evaluation strategies. *Journal of Marketing Research, 14,* 429–443.

Yarmey, A. D. (1979). *The psychology of eyewitness testimony.* New York: Free Press.

Yee, J., Beach, S. R., Greenberg, M. S., & Marsh, D. (1991, April). *Attitudes towards various modes of coping with criminal victimization.* Paper presented at the meeting of the Eastern Psychological Association, New York.

Zawitz, M. W. (Ed.). (1988). *Report to nation on crime and justice.* Washington, DC: U.S. Department of Justice.

Table of Cases

Banyas v. Lower Bucks Hospital, 437 A.2d 1236 (Pa. Super. 1981), page 257.

Jones v. Nisserbaum, Rudolph, & Seidner, 368 A.2d 770 (Pa. Super. 1976), page 257.

Miranda v. Arizona, 384 U.S. 436 (1966), page 4.

Ochs v. Martinez, 789 S.W.2d 949 (Tex. App.—San Antonio 1990, writ denied), page 239.

Posner v. Dallas County Child Welfare Unit, 784 S.W.2d 585 (Tex. App.—Eastland 1990, writ denied), page 239.

Sinn v. Burd, 404 A.2d 672 (Pa. 1979), page 258.

State v. Saldana, 324 N.W.2nd 227 (Minn. 1982), page 237.

Watson v. Rinderknecht, 82 Minn. 235, 84 N.W. 798 (1901), page 258.

Wessell v. University of Pittsburgh et al., No. G. D. 79-6651, Court of Common Pleas of Allegheny County, Civil Division, 1979, pages 246, 250.

Index

Acquaintances, rape committed by, 140, 143, 145, 146, 149, 188–189
Affective factors, in crime-victim decision making, 182
Affiliative behavior
  consequences of, 226–227
  fear and, 136, 147–148, 226–227
  of rape victims, 136, 147–148, 149
African-Americans, crime reporting norms of, 121–126
Age factors
  in crime reporting, 86
    by rape victims, 145, 148–149
  in crime reporting delays, 90
  in eyewitness identification, 76
  in victims' anger level, 42
American Psychiatric Association, 5
American Psychological Association, 5
Anger, of crime victims, 38, 91, 187, 188, 202, 221
  affiliative behavior and, 226–227
  age factors, 42
  attributional processes and, 225
  of burglary victims, 189
  bystanders' advice and, 41, 42, 44, 49
  cognitive reevaluation and, 228–229

Anger, of crime victims (*Cont.*)
  determinants of, 225–226
  empowering effects of, 228
  eyewitness identification effects, 76
  perceived seriousness of crime and, 187, 188, 193–194
  of rape victims, 136, 137–138, 139, 189
    affiliative behavior and, 147–148
    rape reporting correlation, 140, 141, 143, 144, 145, 146, 149
  recall of crime and, 92–93
  risk-taking strategies and, 226
  self-esteem and, 228–229
  self-reported levels, 42–43, 44–45
  sex factors, 43–44
  socioeconomic factors, 42
Apathy, of crime victims, 204
Archival analyses, of crime victims' decision making, 129–150
  battered women agency's records, 130–131
  police records, 131–134, 217, 218
  rape crisis center records, 134–150
  reliability of, 129, 149–150
Arousal, effect on crime victims' decision making, 184
  cognitive reevaluation and, 229

Arousal, effect on crime victims' decision
    making (*Cont.*)
  crime seriousness and, 182
Assault
  incidence, 2
  negligence suits regarding, 239–240
  reporting of, 8
    cross-cultural attitudes toward, 109, 110,
      111, 113, 114, 115
    ethnic norms regarding, 122, 123, 124,
      125
Assault victims
  fear of, 190
  perception of harm suffered, 189–190
Atlanta Council on Battered Women, 130–131

Battered women. *See also* Domestic assault
    victims; Spouse abuse
  retaliation against perpetrators by, 199
Battered women agency, calls for assistance
    to, 130–131, 217, 218
Battery, cross-cultural norms regarding re-
    porting of, 109, 110, 111, 112, 113, 114
Bias, in crime reporting, 222–223
Bombings, 103
Bowman, Patricia, 237
Burglary
  economic costs of, 2
  incidence, 2
  police records of, 131–134
  prevention methods, 197–198
  protection money and, 198
  reporting of, 8
    cross-cultural norms regarding, 109, 110
Burglary victims
  anger of, 189
  archival police records study of, 131–134,
      217, 218
  crime labeling by, 185, 186
  delay in crime reporting by, 163
    median delay time, 162
    social influence effects, 177–178
  emotional reactions of, long-term,
      168–169, 170
  fear of, 191, 192
  first reactions to theft, 161, 177
  lack of sense of victimization, 185
  recovery following burglary, 3
  self-blame by, 200
  self-reports of, 155–159
  social influence on, 165–168, 170, 206
  telephone interviews of, 163–171, 217, 218

Bystanders. *See also* Social influence
  eyewitness identification of thief by, 66,
      77, 78
  influence on victim decision making,
      10–11, 62
    emotional arousal factor, 38
    sex factors, 53, 54, 56, 57, 62

Cancer patients, social comparisons by,
      230–231, 232, 233
Civil suits, 197
Cognitive factors, in crime-victim decision
    making, 182
Cognitive reevaluation, by crime victims,
    199–201, 227–229
Compensation, of crime victims, 4
  federally-funded, 5
  from perpetrator, 197
  from third parties, 197
Comprehensive Crime Control Act of 1984, 5
Controllability, in social comparisons,
    232–233, 234, 235, 236
Coping strategies
  of crime victims, 9, 181–182
  for negative life events, 227–229
Counterfactual processing, 189–190
Covictim comparisons, 89, 208–209, 226
  fate similarity factor, 57–62
  as social comparison process, 229–236
    downward comparisons, 230–233,
      235–236
    upward comparisons, 233–236
Crime
  definitions, 182, 185
  emotional effect on victims, 2, 8–9
  impact of, 2–3
Crime labeling, 182, 183, 185–187
  as cognitive reevaluation, 199
Crime prevention, 3
  as crime reporting motivation, 202
  by crime victims, 197–198
Crime rate, 105
Crime reporting, bias in, 222–223
Crime reporting, decision making regarding,
    7–13
  attitudes toward police and, 202–203
  consequences of, 7, 8
  crime seriousness correlation, 8, 201–202,
      210
  anger and, 187, 188, 193–194
  arousal and, 182
  cognitive reevaluation factor, 199–200
  cross-cultural studies, 103–116

Crime reporting, decision making regarding (*Cont.*)
crime seriousness correlation (*Cont.*)
ethnic factors, 121–125, 126, 127
sex of victim factor, 116–121
stress and, 182
type of offender factor, 116–121
victims' determination of, 182–183, 185–187
delays in, 159
age factors, 90
crime labeling correlation, 186
educational factors, 90
median delay time, 162, 167
outcry witness defense and, 236, 237
race factors, 90
sex factors, 90
social influence effects, 177–178, 220
socioeconomic factors, 90
types of advice factor, 90
model, 181–213
advice, 205
arguments, 205
assumptions of, 181–182
covictim comparison, 208–209
nonsupport, 212
normative pressure, 209–210
provision of information, 205–209
reasons for nonreporting, 32–34
social influences, 204–212
socioeconomic support, 211–212
stage 1 (labeling event as crime), 182, 183, 185–187
stage 2 (determining seriousness of crime), 182, 183, 187–194
stage 3 (deciding what to do), 182–183, 184, 194–204
victims' receptivity to information, 205–209
as moral obligation, 91, 92, 93
multimethod research approach, 222–224
policy implications, 236–243
criminal justice system issues, 240–243
legal issues, 236–240
research programs, 11–13
sex factors, 90, 112, 113, 114
social influence factor, 12, 204–212
social psychology of, 8–11
social support and, 11
theory-related research, 224–236
affect and emotion, 224–227
cognitive coping modes, 227–229

Crime reporting, decision making regarding (*Cont.*)
theory-related research (*Cont.*)
social comparison processes, 229–236
victims' options in, 196–204
cognitive reevaluation, 199–201
doing nothing, 204
notification of police, 201–204
private solutions, 196–199
Crime reporting rate, 7–8
Crime seriousness, crime reporting correlation, 8, 210
anger and, 187, 188, 193–194
arousal and, 182
cognitive reevaluation factor, 199–200
cross-cultural studies, 103–116
ethnic factors, 121–125, 126, 127
sex of victim factor, 116–121
stress and, 182
type of offender factor, 116–121
victim's determination of, 182, 183, 185–187
Crime victims. *See also* Burglary victims; Robbery victims; Rape victims
apathy of, 204
attributional processing by, 225
compensation for, 4
federally-funded, 5
by perpetrator, 197
by third party, 197
counterfactual processing by, 189–190
criminal justice gatekeeper role, 7
decision making by. *See* Crime reporting, decision making regarding
perception of harm suffered, 188–190
as prosecution witnesses, 170
recovery following crime, 3
self-blame by, 200–201
self-growth of, 199
sex of, 112, 113, 114
Criminal prosecution, decision-making regarding, 170, 175–176
Crisis theory, 6
Cross-cultural analyses, of crime reporting attitudes, 102–121
crime seriousness correlation, 103–116
sex of victim factor, 116–121
type of offender factor, 116–121
toward violent crime, 103, 109–111, 113, 114, 115–116

Decision making, by crime victims. *See* Crime reporting, decision making regarding

Domestic violence victims
    cognitive reevaluation by, 199
    ingratiation with perpetrators, 198
    lack of concern for, 4
    self-blame by, 200, 201

Educational factors, in crime reporting de-
    lays, 90
Emotional factors, in crime victim's decision-
    making, 38. *See also* Anger; Fear; Guilt
    attributional processes and, 225
Equity theory, 6
Ethnic factors, in crime reporting, 121–125,
    126, 127
Excited-utterance declaration, 238
Expectancy-value model, of crime-victim de-
    cision making, 195
Eyewitness identification, of perpetrators
    by bystanders, 66, 77, 78
    by theft victims, 65–79
        age factors, 76
        anger factors, 76
        descriptive accuracy, 71–72, 73–74, 79
        long-term accuracy, 69–74, 77, 92, 93–94,
            221–222
        prior lineup effects, 66–69, 79
        race factors, 74–76, 77, 92, 93–94, 221–222
        sex factors, 76, 77
        type of identification task effects, 69–74

Family members, as crime victims, 111, 112,
    113, 114, 115
Fantasy, as victimization response, 168–169,
    170, 228
Fate similarity, of covictims, 57–62
Fear, of crime victims, 3, 224–227
    affiliative behavior and, 136, 147–148,
        226–227
    of assault victims, 190
    attributional processes and, 225
    of burglary victims, 191, 192
    as crime reporting motivation, 202, 226
    determinants of, 225–226
    perceived seriousness of crime correlation,
        193–194
    of rape victims, 139
        affiliative behavior and, 136, 147–148
        coercion factor, 137
        perceived potential harm factor, 192
        rape reporting effects, 140, 141, 144,
            145, 146
        severity of assault factor, 138
        subsequent rape-related, 191–192

Fear, of crime victims (*Cont.*)
    risk-avoidant strategies and, 226
    of robbery victims, 190
    sex factors, 193, 221
    of sexual assault victims, 191, 192, 221
    of theft victims, 163
Feminist movement, 4

"Gambler's fallacy," 200
Generalizability, of field-laboratory theft
    studies, 84–86
Genovese, Kitty, 10
Guilt, of rape victims, 137, 138, 139
    affiliative behavior and, 147–148
    rape reporting effects, 141, 143, 144, 145,
        146, 149
Gunshot attacks, cross-cultural attitudes to-
    ward reporting of, 109, 110

Hearsay rule, spontaneous-declaration excep-
    tion to, 236, 237–239
Hill, Anita, 237
Homicide, of spouse, 103
Hooky-playing, 103

India
    crime rate, 105
    crime reporting/crime seriousness correla-
        tion study, 104–121
        sex of victim factor, 116–121
        type of offender factor, 116–121
        widows' ritual suicide in, 120
Industrial Research Associates of Pittsburgh,
    18
Injustice, victims' sense of, 188–190
    as crime reporting motivation, 202
    victims' responses to, 196–197

Just-world model, 6

Korean-Americans, crime reporting norms
    of, 121–126

Larceny, 8. *See also* Robbery; Theft
    nonreporting of, 95–96
    reasons for reporting, 97
Latino-Americans, crime reporting norms
    of, 121–126
Learned helplessness, 6
Legislation, crime victimization-related, 5

Mendelsohn, Benjamin, 6
Mental simulation, as coping strategy, 9. *See
    also* Cognitive reevaluation; Fantasy

Mothers Against Drunk Driving, 4
Motor vehicle theft, 8
Mugging victims, 185–186

National Association of Victim Support
  Schemes, 4
National Crime Survey, 6, 103, 152
National Institute of Justice, 6
National Institute of Mental Health, Vio-
  lence and Traumatic Stress Research
  Branch, 6
National Organization for Assistance to Vic-
  tims and for Mediation, 4–5
National Organization for Victim Assistance, 4
National Science Foundation, Law and So-
  cial Sciences Program, 6
National Survey of Crime Severity, 103
Negative life events, coping strategies,
  227–229
Negligence suits, 236, 239–240
Neighborhood-watch groups, 242
Nigeria, crime seriousness/crime reporting
  correlation study, 104–116
911 number, 4
Norm, definition, 101
Normative influence. *See also* Social influence
  in crime reporting, 101–128, 209–210
    crime seriousness correlation, 103–116
    cross-cultural comparisons, 102–121
    ethnic factors, 121–126, 127
  explicit, 101–102
  implicit, 101–102

Ochs v. Martinez, 239
Office of Victim Assistance, 5
Outcry witness, 236, 237

Parents, assaults on, 111, 124
Parents of Murdered Children, 4
Perpetrator
  crime victims' description of, 71–72,
    73–74, 79
  reprisal by, 204
  victims' actions against, 196–197, 198–199
  victims' distancing from, 197–198
  victims' ingratiation with, 198
Physical abuse, of women, 130. *See also* Battered women
Pickpocketing, 110, 111
Police
  crimes against, 103
  victims' attitudes toward, 91
    negative, 165, 166, 203

Police (*Cont.*)
  victims' attitudes toward (*Cont.*)
    positive, 202–203
  victims' expectations of, 203
  victims' notification of. *See* Crime report-
    ing, decision making regarding
Police records, of theft and, burglary,
  131–134
Posner v. Dallas County Child Welfare Unit,
  239
Posttraumatic stress disorder, 6
President's Task Force on Victims of Crime, 5
Property crime. *See also* Burglary; Robbery;
  Trespassing
  reporting of, 202–203
  seriousness of, 113, 114
  victims' fear of recurrence, 192
Prosecution witness, crime victim as, 170
"Protection" money, 198
Psychological abuse, of women, 130
Purse-snatching, cross-cultural attitudes
  toward reporting of, 111
Purse-snatching victims, 191

Race factors
  in crime reporting, 88–89, 121–125, 126,
    127
    by rape victims, 140, 141, 143, 144, 146
  in crime reporting delays, 90
  in crime seriousness rating, 103
  in eyewitness identification, 74–76, 77, 92,
    93–94, 221–222
Rape
  by acquaintances, 140, 143, 145, 146, 149,
    188–189
  incidence, 2
  negligence suits regarding, 239–240
  reporting of, 8. *See also* Rape victims, rape
    reporting by
    cross-cultural attitudes toward, 109
    ethnic norms regarding, 122
  victim's perception of, 185
Rape crisis center(s), 5
Rape Crisis Center, archival analysis of,
  134–150, 171, 217, 218
Rape trials
  excited-utterance declaration, 238
  of Mike Tyson, 237
Rape victims
  affiliative behavior of, 147–148, 149, 17⁵
  anger of, 136, 137–138, 139, 189
    affiliative behavior and, 147–148

Rape victims (*Cont.*)
  anger of (*Cont.*)
    rape reporting effects, 140, 141, 143,
      144, 145, 146, 149
  failure to report rape, 147
  fear of, 137–138, 139, 191
    affiliative behavior and, 136, 147–148
    coercion factor, 137
    perceived potential harm factor, 192
    rape reporting effects, 140, 141, 144,
      145, 146
    reprisal by perpetrator-related, 204
    severity of assault factor, 138
    subsequent rape-related, 191–192
  first action following rape, 138–140
  guilt of, 137, 138, 139
    affiliative behavior and, 147–148
    rape reporting effects, 141, 143, 144,
      145, 146, 149
  interviews of, 217, 218
  lack of concern for, 4
  longitudinal study of, 171–177
  police interaction with, 203–204
  pre-rape perceptions of, 186
  preventive behavior following rape, 175,
    176
  rape reporting by, 138, 139, 140–147, 216
    age factors, 145, 148–149
    delay in reporting, 145–147
    emotional factors, 139–149
    harm suffered factor, 202
    normative influence, 102
    race factors, 140, 141, 143, 144, 146
    situational factors, 140, 141, 143–144
    social influence, 139, 140, 142, 146,
      147–148, 176
  rapists' threats toward, 140, 141, 144, 145,
    146
  reporting rate, 216
  self-blame by, 200, 201
  self-reports of, 152–155
  social influence on, 206–207
  subsequent intentions of, 147–148
Rapist
  prosecution of, 175–176
  threats made by, 140, 141, 144, 145, 146
Relatives, as crime perpetrators, 116–121,
  126–127
Retaliation, by crime victims, 187, 196–197
  fantasies about, 168–169, 170, 228
  normative pressure for, 209–210
Risk-avoidant strategies, fear and, 226

Risk-taking strategies, anger and, 226
Robbery
  armed, 109, 110
  attempted, 192–193
  economic costs of, 2
  incidence, 2
  reporting of, 8
Robbery victims
  fear of, 190
  lack of sense of victimization of, 185
  perceived seriousness of crime by, 104–105
  self-blame by, 200
  self-reports of, 155–159
Ruminative thought, 228

Sati, 120
Security systems, 3, 197–198
Self-blame, by crime victims, 200–201
Self-esteem, of crime victims, 228–229,
  234–325
Self-growth, of crime victims, 199
Self-improvement, of crime victims, 230,
  231, 233–235
Self-perception theory, 45
Self-reports, by crime victims, 151–179
  by burglary victims, 155–159
  by rape victims, 152–155
  by robbery victims, 155–159
  by theft victims, 155–159
Sex, of crime victims, effect on crime reporting norms, 112, 113, 114, 116–121
Sex factors
  in crime reporting, 112, 113, 114
  in crime reporting delays, 90
  in crime victims' fear, 193
  in eyewitness identification, 76, 77
  social influence correlation, 53, 54, 56,
    57, 62
Sexual assault, 130. *See also* Rape
  attempted, 192–193
  by celebrities, 237
  cross-cultural attitudes toward reporting
    of, 110, 111, 113, 114
Sexual assault trials, 237–239
Sexual assault victims. *See also* Rape victims
  fear of future assaults, 191, 192
  first reactions to assault, 219
  recovery following assault, 3
  services for, 5
Sexual harrassment, Thomas–Hill incident,
  237
Shopkeepers, as robbery victims, 209
Sinn v. Burd, 258

Situational factors. *See also* Social influence
  in crime reporting, 88, 216, 219
  in crime victims' emotional responses,
    225–226
Smith, William Kennedy, 237
Social comparison processes, 57, 229–236
  downward comparisons, 230–233, 235–236
  upward comparisons, 233–236
Social influence, on crime reporting, 45–64,
    204–212, 221
  age factors, 52
  anger and, 40, 42–44, 49, 52
  arguments offered, 45–50, 53–57
  bystanders' proximity and, 50–53
  covictim comparison effects, 57–62, 63,
    208–209
  delay in crime reporting effects, 177–178,
    220
  policy implications of, 240–242
  rape reporting effects, 139, 140, 142, 146,
    147–148
  types of influence
    advice, 205
    arguments, 205
    covictim comparisons, 208–209
    nonsupport, 212
    normative pressure, 209–210
    provision of information, 205–209
    socioemotional support, 211–212
    victims' receptivity to information and,
      205–209
Social psychology, victimization research ap-
    plications, 8–11
Social support
  for battered women, 130–131
  crime reporting and, 11
  inadequate, 9–10
Society's League Against Molestation, 4
Socioeconomic factors
  in crime reporting, 86
  in crime reporting delays, 90
Spouse, murder of, 103
Spouse abuse
  reporting of, 110, 115, 116
    cross-cultural norms, 110, 115, 116
    ethnic norms, 123, 127
  reporting rate, 216
Stabbings, cross-cultural attitudes toward re-
    porting of, 109, 110
Strangers
  crimes against, 103

Strangers (*Cont.*)
  crimes committed by, 2, 116–121
    rape, 140, 149, 188–189
Stress
  coping strategies, 181–182
  victimization-related, 188–190
    crime reporting effects, 184, 195–196, 226
    crime seriousness correlation, 182, 187
    potential harm-suffered factor, 189–190
    unexpectedness of crime factor, 188–189
  vulnerability response, 190–194
Suicide, ritual, 120
Support systems. *See* Social support

Thailand, crime seriousness/crime reporting
    correlation study, 104–116
Theft, field-laboratory studies, 19–36, 217,
    218
  analysis across studies, 81–100
    delay-in-reporting variables, 89–91
    external validity, 82, 84–86
    internal validity, 82–84
    participants' characteristics, 84, 89
    participants' recall-related variables,
      91–94
    reporting-related variables, 86–89,
      94–95, 97–99
  bystanders' influence factor, 27–28, 30,
    32–34, 36
  delay in reporting variables, 89–91
  economic costs of, 2
  experimental paradigm, 17–36
  eyewitness identification of thief by,
    65–79, 92, 93–94
    age factors, 76
    anger factor, 76
    descriptive accuracy, 71–72, 73–74, 79
    long-term accuracy, 69–74, 77
    prior lineup effects, 66–69, 79
    race factors, 74–76, 77
    sex factors, 76, 77
    type of identification task effects, 69–74
  lawsuit related to, 245–264
    causes of action, 248–251
    consequences of, 261–262
    damages, 251
    defendants' case, 259–261
    posttrial activities, 259
    pretrial discovery, 254–255
    trial, 255–259
    verdict, 258–259
  magnitude of crime factor, 21–22, 30–31, 35
  participants' characteristics, 84–85, 86–89

Theft, field-laboratory studies (*Cont.*)
participants' recall of theft, 92–99
anger factor, 92–93
bystanders' influence factor, 92, 93
during debriefing, 92, 93, 95, 96, 97, 98
long-term accuracy, 92–94, 95, 96–97, 98
moral obligation factor, 92, 93
police records regarding, 131–134
reasons for nonreporting, 95–97
reporting rate, 216
reporting-related variables, 86–89
age factor, 86
bystanders' advice, 88–89
covictim comparison factor, 89
individual characteristics, 86–89
race factors, 88–89
situational factors, 88
socioeconomic factors, 86
sex factors, 21, 31, 36
thief's proximity factor, 21–22, 30–31, 35
Theft victims
crime reporting by
archival police record analysis, 131–134,
217, 218
race factors, 133
sex factors, 132, 133
stolen property value factor, 133, 134
delay in crime reporting, 132–134
fear level factor, 163
median delay time, 162, 167
perceived seriousness of crime factor,
163
social influence effects, 163, 165–168, 170
types of crime factor, 163
emotional reactions of, 165, 167
long-term, 168–169, 170
first response to theft, 161, 177
long-term victimization responses, 168–
169, 170
nonreporting reasons, 165–166
normative pressures on, 210
perceived seriousness of crime by, 167
self-reports of, 155–159
social influence on, 161, 163, 165–168, 170,
206, 219
telephone interviews of, 163–171, 217, 218,
219
theft by, 210
Thief, theft victim's identification of, 65–79,
92, 93–94
age factors, 76

Thief, theft victim's identification of (*Cont.*)
anger factor, 76
descriptive accuracy, 71–72, 73–74, 79
long-term accuracy, 69–74, 77
prior lineup effects, 66–69, 79
racial factors, 74–76, 77
sex factors, 76, 77
type of identification task effects, 69–74
Thomas, Clarence, 237
Threats
cross-cultural attitudes toward reporting
of, 110, 111, 113
to rape victims, 140, 141, 144, 145, 146
victims' fear response, 193
to women, 130
Trespassing, 112, 125
Trials
outcry witness defense, 236, 237
spontaneous declarations, 236, 237–239
Tyson, Mike, 237

Uniform Crime Reports, 152
United States Department of Justice, Office
of Victim Assistance, 5
United States Supreme Court decisions, fa-
voring criminals, 3–4

Validity, of field-laboratory studies
external, 82, 84–86
internal, 82–84
Victimization
fantasy response, 168–169, 170, 228
incidence, 2
long-term effects, 12
orthodox view of, 222–223
positive aspects, 199
prevention of subsequent, 234, 235
as social problem, 2–3
as stress cause, 188–190
potential harm suffered factor, 189–190
unexpectedness of crime factor, 188–189
Victimization research, methodology, 6–7
Victimization survey, 6
Victimology, 6
Victims' movement, 3–5
Victim service organizations, 4–5
Victims of Crime Act, 5
Violent crime
impact on victim, 2–3
relative seriousness of, 103
victims' fear of recurrence, 192

Vulnerability, victimization-related, 183, 187,
190–194
  cognitive reevaluation response, 200
  as crime reporting motivation, 202
  perceived harm factor, 191–192
  potential magnitude of harm factor, 192–
  194
  reduction of, 234
  unexpectedness of crime factor, 191
  victims' responses to, 197–199

Washington, Desiree, 237
Watson v. Rinderknecht, 258
Weapons-related crime
  reporting of
    cross-cultural norms, 109, 110, 111, 112,
    113, 114
    ethnic norms, 122, 123, 124, 125, 126
    reporting rate, 193
    victims' fear response 193
Widows, ritual suicide by, 120